VILLAS
medios
Yaguajay
acetas
Mayajigua
mento
Escambray
CAMAGÜEY
Camagüey
Gúaimaro
CENTRAL
HIGHWAY
Holguín
ORIÉNTE
Sagua
de Tanamo
Central
America
Mayarí Arriba
Bayamo
La Maya
Guisa
Maffo
Guantánamo
Palma Soriano
Santiago
de Cuba
Guantánamo
Naval Base

Caribbean Sea

THE WINDS OF DECEMBER

The Winds of December

John Dorschner
and
Roberto Fabricio

Coward, McCann & Geoghegan
New York

Library of Congress Cataloging in Publication Data

Dorschner, John.
  The winds of December.

  Includes index.
  1. Cuba—history—1933–1959. 2. Cuba—History—
Revolution, 1959. I. Fabricio, Roberto, joint author.
II. Title.
F1787.5D67   1980   972.91'063   79-12550
ISBN 0-698-10993-7

To Our Parents

Contents

THE WINDS OF DECEMBER

INTRODUCTION

At the time, it all seemed vaguely romantic and not particularly significant. As the regime of Cuban dictator Fulgencio Batista crumbled during those last weeks of 1958, most Americans knew there were a few idealistic rebels fighting in the hills. They knew there was a right-wing strong man in the Presidential Palace. They knew that Cuba was a land of sugar and tobacco, that Havana had an international reputation as a city thriving on mob-run casinos and tawdry sex markets. That was about all.

The Cuban revolution was not the main story on America's front pages. Often, it wasn't on the front pages at all. The major concern then was the Soviet Union's threat to blockade Berlin. The "space race" was heating up. Columnists agonized about American students' inability to compete in mathematics and science with their Russian counterparts. On the feature pages, writers wondered whether Ricky Nelson would replace Elvis Presley as the latest teenage heartthrob.

In retrospect, of course, it can be seen that something was happening in Cuba that was going to have serious consequences for the entire world over the next twenty years. In April 1961, the Bay of Pigs became a national embarrassment for the United States. In October 1962, the Americans and Russians stood "eyeball to eyeball" during the missile crisis, and people everywhere feared nuclear war was imminent. In the 1970s, the presence of Cuban troops in Africa had global repercussions.

What follows is a story of people—rebels, Batista supporters, American officials and ordinary citizens—who lived through those dramatic weeks of December 1958. Some fell in love because of the revolution, some saw their children reduced to mental cases because of the terrorism, some persecuted men saw their careers soar in a single instant and some lost everything they had. Their tales are occasionally closer to Gothic novels, or Woody Allen comedy, or existentialist absurdity than they are to political theory, but they help put in perspective the causes of the Cuban revolution, the downfall of Batista and the inextricable role of the United States in those events.

Work on this book has taken almost four years. We are particularly grateful for the efforts of our editor, Joseph Kanon, who offered thoughtful suggestions that greatly improved the manuscript, and of our agent, Timothy Seldes, who encouraged us to initiate the project.

We began by going through countless newspaper articles, magazine stories and books (the most valuable of which we have listed in a selected bibliography). The excellent Cuban collection at the University of Miami has been especially helpful, and the Library of Congress, which continued to exchange books and periodicals with Cuba after all other U.S. agencies had stopped contact, has some significant publications unavailable elsewhere in the United States.

To investigate the American involvement, we used the Freedom of Information Act to obtain more than eight hundred pages of classified documents from the State Department. These cables, dispatches and memorandums have been invaluable in revealing new information about the much-debated U.S. role in Batista's downfall.

But the bulk of the research, and the heart of the book, centered around interviews with almost 250 persons in seven U.S. states, Puerto Rico, the Dominican Republic and Cuba. Eulogio Cantillo, the army general facing the largest rebel force and the man most closely connected with Batista's final flight, was especially helpful. Though he had never talked to journalists before about his crucial role, he was patient and cooperative through six lengthy interview sessions and helped shed new light on the last crucial days.

Near the end of the research, we made a one-month trip to Cuba, where we visited Havana, Santiago and the most important battle sites in the outlying provinces. We talked with rebel leaders and townspeople who saw their homes become battlegrounds. On the last day of the trip,

Fidel Castro granted us an interview which lasted five and a half hours and provided important details about his own actions and attitudes.

The Cuban government complied with all our major requests on places to see and people to talk to, with the understanding that one or two staff members of the Central Committee of the Cuban Communist Party would accompany us to all interviews. Such a situation usually inhibits solid journalism, but in this case, because of the vast amount of materials and people outside of Cuba available for corroboration, it did not seriously affect the sessions.

With each interview, whether in the United States or Cuba, the subject was asked only about what he personally saw or did. In all cases, this information was compared with written sources and other interviews. For example, to reconstruct a crucial meeting between army and rebel leaders held at a dilapidated sugar mill in Oriente Province, we talked to six of the eight persons there—three now in Cuba, three outside the country.

To portray the mood of the times, we have used dialogue when interview subjects related the material in that form, though it may be properly argued that no one can perfectly remember conversations held years before. We feel the quotations, when supported by other evidence, give the reader a tone of reality that is missing from conversations only indirectly summarized.

As an informal guide to who told us what, we occasionally have used the style of "Character X saw, or heard, or thought . . ." That indicates the person provided us with that information. At the end of the book, we have listed all major sources, by chapter.

Some minor discrepancies, inevitable when persons try to remember fast-moving events which happened twenty years ago, have been smoothed over. A few major uncertainties have been footnoted. One seriously arguable question, Castro's position on Communism in 1958, is discussed in an appendix.

With these exceptions, people's memories have proved to be remarkably accurate. Perhaps that is understandable because, for all those involved, the events are etched indelibly in their minds, much the way Americans remember exactly what they were doing when they heard John Kennedy had been shot. But for the people of this story, the outcome was far more personal and pervasive. Almost all saw their lives directly and inalterably changed, for better or for worse. It was a time, as one Cuban said, "when the hours seemed like minutes, and the minutes seemed like hours."

PROLOGUE: OLD HAVANA AT TWILIGHT

It was not easy to doze. Around him, in the lobby of the Sevilla-Biltmore Hotel, people were walking over the polished tile floor, their footsteps *click-clicking* in sharp little echoes as they moved through the plate-glass door, shining now in the late-afternoon sun. It had been a muggy day, unusually so for November, and the back of Ted Scott's *guayabera* shirt was pasted against the brown leather chair.

He was resting, his eyes closed, trying to recuperate from an afternoon spent drinking Myer's rum and smoking cigars at the American Club. In his upper-left shirt pocket, he still had a number of his favorite smokes: H. Upmann No. 4s. He was saving them for later, when it became dark and he would climb into his De Soto V-8 for his nightly rounds of the city's casinos and nightclubs, to gather information for his column in the English-language *Havana Post.*

Chin nodding against his chest, he tried to blot out the noise from the nearby street: the street vendors offering ice creams and tropical fruits from their pushcarts, boys hawking newspapers, taxi drivers pushing pornographic postcards on the tourists, sometimes a beggar pleading for coins.

Scott was almost asleep when he heard men laughing. The *click-clicks* increased their speed on the tile floor. Opening his eyes with effort, he saw men hurrying toward the door. Outside, a crowd was gathering.

"*¿Que pasa?*" he mumbled to a passerby.

"A roundup," the man answered.

Scott grunted and lifted himself from his chair. Following the others outside, he found three blue squad cars parked by the curb. Uniformed policemen, nightsticks in hand, were scampering out. A short distance away, a prisoners' van was arriving.

But it was only the periodic roundup of prostitutes. "The Catholic ladies have done it again," Scott mumbled, thinking they had once again pressured the police into the raid.

As the officers fanned out, Scott spotted a statuesque woman with *café con leche* skin. She was standing a few yards away, perplexed, her bright green dress tight against her hips.

The other observers saw her too. "Run," one of them shouted. "Get going."

She looked at the man for a moment, then moved into the street, forced to waddle in her tight skirt and high-heeled shoes.

"No, no," the men yelled, laughing. "Take off the shoes."

A policeman grinned at the ad hoc advisers and jogged halfheartedly after the girl who, shoes in hand, was disappearing into the crowd on the other side of the street.

Scott shrugged and turned back to the lobby. In Old Havana, at least, it was still business as usual.

High above Havana, a red-and-white Cessna floated above the winding shoreline where the city met the blue-green Gulf of Mexico. Rolando Amador, a thirty-one-year-old lawyer, was at the controls. Beside him sat his fiancée Carmen, a dark-haired beauty with creamy white skin. It had become a ritual for them to go on a late-afternoon spin above the city in his single-engine airplane.

Below, they could see the mouth of Havana harbor, guarded by the sixteenth-century gray-stone tower of Morro Castle. Then came Old Havana, with its aged buildings and narrow streets, bordered by covered sidewalks with their endless stretch of archways. Even from several hundred feet up, Amador saw cars battling for the right-of-way with what looked like ants—the vendors with pushcarts.

Soon they were over the Vedado area and its concrete-and-glass high-rises, the condominiums and apartments of the city's middle class. The most spectacular buildings faced the six-lane Malecón Boulevard, separated from the Gulf by only a low stone seawall. The water was calm now, but beginning soon, as it did every December, the turbulent winds would sweep down from the north, *Los Nortes* Cubans called them, churning the Gulf waters and hurling huge waves against the seawall, sending salt spray up to forty feet in the air as the water splashed across the broad boulevard, flooding basements and forcing cars to use inland streets.

This was where Amador lived, and as they passed by, both he and Carmen pressed their foreheads against the side windows trying to see his apartment building on Calle Linea, near the hundred-year-old Vedado Parish church. He lived in a low, modern structure, hard to make out from the air, but it, like his plane, was a symbol that Amador was a lawyer on the way up. He had been a classmate and friend of Fidel Castro in law school, but Amador had chosen the traditional route. He belonged to the law firm of Castro's former brother-in-law, a pro-Batista senator, and the firm did an enormous amount of business with both the government and American companies that wanted a lubricating "in" with the power structure. Amador considered himself apolitical, but his interest was in supporting the status quo, which had been so good to him. He had almost become a confirmed bachelor, with a pleasant life taking girls to the city's spectacular nightclubs, followed by *medianoche* sandwiches at El Carmelo Restaurant, where the social set gathered. But then he had fallen in love with Carmen, and everything changed. They had planned to be married in early January, until his law firm told him he had to go to Paris for several weeks, starting in late December, to help close a business deal. Amador suggested they postpone the wedding, but Carmen insisted they be married before he left, even if it meant just a one-night honeymoon. He had agreed.

With the sinking sun glaring on the Cessna's windshield as they headed west, they crossed the Almendares River and flew over the luxurious suburbs of Miramar, Biltmore and El Country Club, where the gardeners were finishing their day tending the broad lawns and hedges of the city's upper class. Beyond, he could see the lower-class *barrios*, dense, crazy-quilt masses of lanes and structures called *casas de vecindad*, where people were so crowded that each family had only a single room and shared a kitchen-bathroom with other tenants. Beyond that were the makeshift huts, the lowest form of dwelling, with walls of scavenged plywood or even cardboard, and roofs of sheet metal that twinkled in the fading sunlight.

Off to the left was the massive Camp Columbia, its light-yellow concrete wall protecting a sprawling area at the southwestern edge of the city; inside it, around a two-block parade ground, were enough barracks to house five thousand soldiers, plus tank garages, army headquarters, the huge air force landing field, and the offices of the secret military intelligence corps. Now it looked peaceful, even picturesque in the golden light.

Amador's landing was perfectly smooth. A smile of satisfaction crept over his face as he taxied to his parking spot and turned off the engine.

Walking to the other side to help Carmen out, he felt content. The smell of the grass, the coolness that was coming with darkness, the prospect of having a drink with his fiancée—the world at that moment seemed flawless.

Then he happened to notice a dent the size of a quarter in the left wheel cover. A bullet had hit it a few days before, when he was returning from Oriente Province and had flown over a rebel ambush. He had tried to tell his friends how serious the situation was in Oriente, but no one seemed to believe him. He could understand why. In peaceful Havana, the civil war seemed very far away.

In November 1958, the lives of most Havana residents went on, more or less as usual, though the warning signs of the strife to come were inescapable. Near the harbor, the Presidential Palace was protected as if it were a besieged fortress, with guards waving submachine guns at any tourist who dared approach. At almost any street corner could be seen members of the eight-thousand-man police force, which had five antisubversive units ready to crush any dissent. In the Vedado section, the huge campus of the University of Havana was grim and empty, closed for two years to stop student protest. The statue of the alma mater, a woman in a Roman toga, stood at the top of a block-long staircase, her arms spread, palms up, beckoning to students who could not come.

Occasionally, the city's calm was disrupted by rebel supporters who sprinkled heavy industrial nails on the streets or threw pieces of chain over power lines, knocking out electricity for hours. In early autumn, the urban underground had unleashed "The Night of 100 Bombs," most of which were small and exploded harmlessly on street corners, sending off a *pop-pop* firecracker sound throughout the city, but wounding no civilians. Later, a student group attacked a police substation in the suburb of Marianao, killing five and wounding seven.

So it had gone for the past several years: sporadic assassinations of government officials, police machine-gunning clandestine workers in their hideouts, bombs in movie theaters, explosives in dance halls. Now a car's backfire or an oddly wrapped parcel next to a doorway could send everyone scattering for cover. A veneer of tension had taken over, an unmistakable fear that the city could become engulfed in sudden violence.

The press was heavily censored, but residents had little difficulty guessing that something major was happening in the eastern provinces. Signs at the railroad station and the bus terminals showed that no traffic was moving beyond the middle of the island. It was impossible to telephone or to telegraph to Oriente, 500 miles away, and most knew that rebels had even reached the central hills, the Escambray, only 250 miles from Havana.

Would the rebels be able to reach the city? For Cuban adults, that question stirred memories of something that had happened twenty-five years before, in 1933, the last time a Cuban dictator had been overthrown by violence. It was then that frenzied, embittered crowds moved through the streets, burning, ransacking the houses of the dictator's henchmen and killing as many of them as they could find. About a thousand had died, shot in their homes, hung from lampposts or dragged through the streets until they were dead.

The thought of that occurring again seemed almost beyond comprehension, and on the surface, at least, people went about their daily routines as if nothing unusual were happening.

Movie theaters were thriving, and as always they were quick to get the latest American releases, with Spanish subtitles. For those seeking something slightly naughty, there was Brigitte Bardot in *La Parisienne*, but the longest lines were for *Bridge Over the River Kwai*.

Nightlife abounded. The Tropicana had a lavish open-air patio where sequined girls on trapezes descended from palm trees bathed in colored lights. On Sundays, guests could play the Bingo of Fortune; grand prize was a 1958 Chevrolet Impala. The Sans Souci, reached by a majestic driveway lined with erect royal palms, offered elaborate dinners "under the stars." The Copa Room of the Hotel Riviera featured an Israeli singer, Hanna-Haaroni, singing "Cuba-lypso songs." The Carib Room at the Hilton had a special Canadian theme, and the Capri Hotel boasted a French dance troupe. Old Havana held the more rustic nightspots: the Floridita Bar, where Ernest Hemingway drank his daiquiris, and the Bodeguita del Medio, a tiny place with tall ceilings and stone walls on which guests scribbled their names and thoughts. It was there that actor Errol Flynn left his assessment of the restaurant, and of Cuba: "Great place to get drunk."

In sports, the famed Cuban Winter League was in full swing, drawing baseball fans to the forty-thousand-seat Gran Stadium to watch Minnie Miñoso, who played summers with the Chicago White Sox, and Tom Lasorda, an American pitcher who never quite made the big time with the Brooklyn Dodgers. Near the airport, the Oriental Racetrack was boasting capacity crowds, and two jai-alai frontons were offering matches every afternoon and evening, including Sundays. Golfers and celebrity watchers could see Johnny Weissmuller, the former Tarzan, who came down to participate in a Pro-Am tournament. Juan Fangio, the five-time champion race driver from Argentina, was scheduled to drive an 1100cc Fiat in the Havana Gran Prix, set for January.

Crowds were expected, for cars had become an obsession in Cuba. People spent hours washing and polishing them to keep off the corrosive salt spray, and if someone couldn't afford a car, he could at least look at them in the glass-walled showrooms in Vedado, where the new 1959s were just going on display: the boxy Studebaker, the space-age fins of the De Soto and horizontal fins of the Chevrolet. The automotive editor of *Diario de la Marina* examined the revolutionary grille of the new Edsel. He thought it was a winner.

At night, many stayed home to watch television. There were four hundred thousand sets in the country, which meant that Cuba ranked second in the world, after the United States, in per capita TV ownership. People could see Broderick Crawford on *Highway Patrol* shout at the bad guys in dubbed Spanish, *"Suba las manos"*—raise your hands. For women, there were the Cuban imitation of *Queen for a Day* and soap operas such as *The Woman Who Should Have Cried*. Some productions were even in color.

For the more adventurous, there was always the seamy side of the city:

the sex market that was intended primarily for Americans wanting to escape the staid Eisenhower fifties by spending a few days in Havana looking for something a little spicier, from the blue movies at the Shanghai Theater to the celebrated prostitutes.

The cheaper brothels were in Old Havana, with their linoleum-topped tables in the bar area and jukeboxes blaring Elvis Presley songs. The more luxurious "houses" were in the western suburbs, near the Rancho Boyeros international airport; here there were elegant decors and women to fit any taste. It was in one of these where the famed Superman, a mulatto with genitalia of legendary size, simulated intercourse nightly with prostitutes in a small, smoke-filled room. Ted Scott, the journalist, had talked to him once, and the man confessed that he found the work humiliating, but the pay of $25 a night was far more than he could earn in a factory.

Behind the prostitution and, especially, the numerous casinos were American mobsters. A short, frail man, Meyer Lansky, was the dominant force, and he controlled the casino at the seafront Riviera Hotel. His brother Jake was a boss at the International Casino. Santo Trafficante, a Florida mobster, had controlling interest in the gaming rooms at the Sans Souci, Deauville and the Sevilla-Biltmore. Nicholas Di Constanzo and Charles ("The Blade") Tourine handled the action at the Capri, where movie actor George Raft greeted guests at the door.

In the mornings, Cuban men sipped *café con leche* and read the newspapers, in which only international news escaped the heavy government censorship. The front pages were filled with stories on Sputniks and Atlases, on the Iron Curtain, on threats to Berlin and John Foster Dulles's responses. On the editorial pages, the prime subject was Graham Greene's biting satire of the corrupt, lazy life in *Our Man in Havana*. One columnist wrote that Havana had no more corruption and prostitution than any other major city, and he objected to Greene's portrayal of Cuba as an "underdeveloped, sleazy island, rather than the thriving metropolis it really is."

In the classifieds, many were looking for jobs. "Young colored with great references available for work in private house as cleaning boy—I am not pretentious and I know my place. Daniel—U-1688." Or: "Young—30 years—white—available for chauffeur." Scattered elsewhere in the paper were the inevitable articles of love's labor lost, which went on, revolution or no. In Vedado, a young woman, after a fight with her husband, shut the windows, turned on the gas and died holding in her lap a book of poems, *Black Pearls*. In another Havana neighborhood, a twenty-four-year-old woman attempted to kill herself by firing a .45-caliber bullet through her left breast. It came out her armpit. As she arrived at the hospital, she whispered, "I am tired and bored with life."

The revolution could have been boring as well, if one believed the articles on the fighting. Based solely on army press releases, usually just repeating them word for word, they were carried under small, one-column headlines at the bottom of page one. Oftentimes, the emphasis was on surrender: "Five outlaws were arrested yesterday after surrendering near Trinidad and saying they were sorry they ever went to the mountains." Another day, eight surrendered, saying "they were sorry they had been fighting with the rebels." Occasionally, there was a report of an actual battle: "40 Rebels, 5 Soldiers Die, Army Reports." Or: "180 Casualties Reported in Oriente." Rebel casualties were always high, army casualties always low.

A few journalists were clever enough to fool the censors. Rosiñada, the brilliant editorial cartoonist for *Diario de la Marina*, did a running series on the weather, playing on the standard joke that it was the only subject the Batista regime allowed to be discussed.

Everyone understood, as they did the cartoons in *Zig Zag*, a satirical newspaper. One famous illustration showed a long line of persons standing on a Havana street corner as they prepared to board the number 30 bus. Readers realized the "30 bus" ran to a neighborhood called La Sierra, just like the Sierra Mountains where Castro was operating in Oriente, but the censor didn't catch on for weeks. Finally, he insisted the editors change the bus number. They did, to "28 plus 2." That passed the censor without a fuss.

How widespread was Castro's support in Havana? How successful were his bearded rebels? No one in the city knew for certain. At nights, many closed their windows and turned to the one source of information that wasn't controlled by Batista: Radio Rebelde. Each night, at 7:00 P.M. and 9:00 P.M. on the 20-meter band, at 8:00 and 10:00 P.M. on the 40-meter frequencies, an announcer at the main rebel station, 7RR, began by shouting in a voice so dramatic that it seemed he was trying to overcome the limitations of his small transmitter hidden somewhere in the Sierra Maestra: "*¡Aquí Radio Rebelde, transmitiendo desde el territorio libre de Cuba!*" That announcement usually sent shivers of excitement through its listeners, even among those who were not ardent Castro supporters. Following the national anthem and the 26th of July hymn, the announcer gave accounts of rebel battles and made political appeals. Sometimes Castro himself spoke.

The people of Havana believed what the rebel announcers told them, until they heard the latest rumors from their neighbors. In Cuban slang, those were *bolas*—meaning literally a ball, but more specifically rumors, the kind that rolled through the streets, over the airwaves, in telephone lines, gathering momentum, embellishments and fabrications. In late 1958, *bolas* had become Havana's primary source of information. The people listened and repeated. They believed everything, and they believed nothing.

It was early evening when Enrique Barroso began pacing in front of the Miramar Theater. Dressed in a casual shirt and slacks so as not to attract attention, he moved back and forth past the display case containing the poster for *Around the World in 80 Days*. There were no policemen in sight, and his eyes began focusing on the local teenage girls, whose skirts that season were shorter. Their legs were pretty enough to remind him that he was twenty-five years old and single, but then he noticed the ice-cream shop next door, and that reminded him of something else: whenever he was tense, as he certainly was now, he had a craving for sweets.

Strolling into the shop glittering with chrome and mirrors, he slipped onto a stool and ordered a banana split. When he had been media director of toothpastes and soaps for Gravi-Palmolive, he had rarely eaten desserts. Now that he was a clandestine member of Castro's 26th of July Movement, he seemed to be yearning for them all the time. He wasn't worried about getting fat; the chances of dying were too great for that.

As soon as the banana split came, he took a bite from each of the scoops. While he decided what to do next, José ("Pepe") Garcerán sat down on the stool next to him. He was late.

"Hurry up," Garcerán said without looking at him. "We have some people waiting for us."

Shoveling down the rest of the dessert and leaving a bill on the counter, Barroso followed Garcerán's lean, six-foot frame out the door. A few feet away was a 1955 gray-and-white Buick Century. As they approached, Barroso saw two women inside. The one behind the wheel was a bosomy young woman with long blond hair; the one in the back was a slender brunette with a sullen expression.

Garcerán reached the car first, planting his hand firmly on the front passenger door. As he opened it, Barroso passed him, whispering, "You son of a bitch, you left me the skinny one."

Garcerán flashed him a smile the women couldn't see.

As soon as they were inside, the Buick eased out into traffic. Garcerán made the introductions. The blonde was "Olga." The short-haired brunette was "Lizzy." Following rules of the underground, both were "war names." Barroso nodded politely, trying to ignore the skinny woman sitting next to him. Like most Cuban men, he liked his women with a little heft to them.

While the Buick moved down Miramar's Fifth Avenue, headed downtown, Garcerán turned around and explained what was happening. "We are going to a meeting. You'll see some people you know. They want to talk to us about something important. These two ladies have been good enough to volunteer to help us. They will be our driver and liaison on the mission that has been assigned to us."

Olga drove them over the Almendares River into the Vedado section, past a shopping area of movie theaters, newsstands and a Chinese restaurant. The sweet smell of tobacco wafted through the air from the nearby Partagás cigarette plant.

Without saying a word, Olga parked the Buick and led them to a small apartment house, then up narrow stairs to the third floor. The blonde unlocked the door. It was an unpretentious apartment with a tile floor. Barroso walked immediately to the window. Outside was a small balcony; in the distance was the huge Havana cemetery. Everything was peaceful.

It seemed only a few seconds later that the others began arriving: Victor Paneque, known as Comandante Diego, the chief of the Movement's Acción y Sabotaje in Havana; Manuel Ray, an engineer who was chief of the Civic Resistance in the city; Luis Soto, an underground coordinator; and Sergio Sanjenís, another clandestine worker.

As soon as Barroso saw the array of leaders, he realized the meeting had to be about the weapons he and Garcerán had smuggled in from Miami a few days before. The crates had been buried at Varadero, a beach area a few miles outside of Havana. Eventually, they were to be sent to Comandante Camilo Cienfuegos, leader of a rebel column in central Cuba. The plan was for Cienfuegos to make a daring dash to the west, skirt Havana and open a new front in the westernmost province of Pinar del Río.

When all the men were seated, Comandante Diego began: "I have been notified by the Sierra that there is a change of plans. . . . It has been decided to open a diversionary front in the Madruga Hills. That can divert the attention of the army troops and start creating a peasant movement in the area. Then when Camilo crosses through the southern part of Havana Province, he at least will have a chance of making it." Barroso and Garcerán were to lead the expedition.

Barroso couldn't believe it. The hills were only a ninety-minute drive from Havana and all its military might. They were low, barren hills, not at all like the dense rain forest of Castro's Sierra Maestra.

"I think it's going to be a disaster," he said, unable to contain his anger. "There aren't enough hills in that area to support a guerrilla war. There's really no place to hide."

Ray of the Civic Resistance tried to reassure him with a smile. "It's our orders. You don't have to fight a war, just hide in there and make them come after you for a few weeks until Camilo can get through."

Reluctantly, Barroso nodded his head. Then he happened to look over at Garcerán. His friend was smiling, almost as if he relished the glory of being a guerrilla. Barroso himself felt only fear.

Part One

The Leaders

NOVEMBER 20–NOVEMBER 28, 1958

1/THE REBEL

The first rays of dawn filtered through the pines into the small, sloped clearing of the forest. A mist shrouded the trees, and tropical birds on limbs heavy with dew screeched awakening calls. From a nearby hamlet of thatched-roof *bohíos* came the bark of dogs, heralding the movement of men.

They were rebel soldiers, walking into the clearing in tattered khaki uniforms, stiff from months of sweat and mountain mud. On their heads were soiled Stetsons, black berets, red berets, baseball caps, military caps. Their shoes—combat boots, cowboy boots, store-bought dress shoes—were cracked and shriveled from sloshing through mountain streams.

Most of the men had the dark leathery faces of those who spend their lives outdoors. Many were teenagers, so young they could not grow beards. Almost all had cartridge belts crisscrossing their chests or hung from their hips, holding bullets for their Garands, or Thompson submachine guns, or fifty-year-old Springfield rifles. A few had only shotguns or pistols.

As they reached the center of the clearing, they stopped. Some nervously fingered their rosaries or the brightly colored necklace beads of the Afro-Cuban *santería* cults. Their eyes darted around the area, but only occasionally did they steal a glance toward one edge, where on a strip of parched grass stood their leader: Fidel Castro.

Castro, his brow furrowed, stared back, chewing on the stub of an unlit cigar, shifting it from side to side in his mouth. His battered khaki cap and field fatigues were as grimy as his men's, but there was no mistaking that he was the column's *comandante*. At six feet two, he towered above his troops, and his gnarled beard made him look older than his thirty-one years. Slung from his shoulders was the symbol of his rank: a Browning automatic rifle with a telescopic sight, the best weapon his forces had. Another tool, one he used more often than his weapon, was stuffed into his left shirt pocket: an American-made ball-point pen. Beside it was a three-by-five-inch dime-store notebook, its brown cover warped by sweat. All the messages he sent to his supporters and aides came from that cheap paper.

But Castro knew this was not a time for words, and he did not try to hide his concern. Most of these 180 rebels, members of his own Column 1, were new recruits. His best, mountain-hardened fighters had been sent to form columns elsewhere, and he had no idea how these inexperienced youths would react under pressure, what they would do the first time they faced a tank rumbling toward them or a B-26 swooping in to bomb and strafe. He had talked to them, explained how they had to overcome that first moment of terror. But there was no way of knowing how they would behave until the moment came.

Now, at dawn on Thursday, November 20, 1958, the moment was at hand. For months, Castro had dreamed of it. For weeks, he had plotted it. All night, he had been up, talking with his subordinates, working through every detail again and again, calculating exactly where each squad would be, deciding exactly who would man the precious mortar and the .50-caliber tripod machine gun, seeing that every possible safeguard was built into the plan. Without a doubt, it was to be the most severe test his small rebel army had ever faced: after two years of fighting from isolated mountain hideouts, he was about to launch his first attack on the plains.

If he succeeded, he was certain it would mark the beginning of the end for Batista, the man he had been struggling against for five years. For most men, that would be victory enough, but Castro was looking beyond that. He understood that the dictator's downfall might mean only a partial triumph for the rebels. As a serious student of history, he knew that in Cuba, when a totalitarian regime started to crumble, dozens of new forces inevitably sprang onto the scene, opportunists trying to steal the fruits of victory—old-time politícos, army generals, Americans wanting to intervene, even fellow guerrillas. In Cuba, something always happened at the last minute to deny power to those who had fought the hardest to overthrow the dictatorship.

As Castro watched the tense faces of his teenagers, watched them fidget in their boots on the dewy grass, he was determined that this time nothing would be allowed to betray the revolution.

Years later, when those 180 men of Column 1 had become the stuff of legend, when their exploits had made them the best-known guerrilla group in the world, Americans would still find it remarkable that it had all happened "only ninety miles away." It seems too short a distance for such an awesome difference in political systems, and even more remarkable that such an event could have happened in the nearby Caribbean, a place most Americans consider an idyllic, innocuous paradise whose sole function is serving tourists.

Yet it happened, a revolution of international significance, and no one has ever tried to explain it without emphasizing the importance of the rebels' leader, Fidel Castro. Almost everything about the man seemed to make him ideally suited to lead such a movement: his penchant for politics, his affinity for the outdoor life and, most importantly, his passion for action, *violent* action.

His father was a Spanish immigrant who owned a 23,300-acre farm in Oriente Province; his mother had been his father's household servant. They were married after Fidel was born. His early years were spent playing with peasant children on the frontier-like homestead before he was sent to board in the best Jesuit academies. At Belén High School in Havana, he became a brilliant student, an excellent debater and a champion athlete in basketball and track. But he never lost his rough, country-boy qualities, and his indifference to clean clothes earned him the nickname *bola de churre*—dirt ball. Fellow students poked fun at him when they learned he didn't know how to knot a tie or preferred to go hiking with the Explorer troop rather than attend a school dance. Yet he possessed a certain disarming charm that turned eccentricities into distinctions. "Oh, that's just Fidel," students would joke as he flicked cigar ashes on freshly polished floors. At the graduation exercises, Castro was the student who received the greatest applause.

In college, he followed the path of most hopeful Cuban politicians by entering law school at the University of Havana. Student elections there were taken as seriously as national ones, and they often degenerated into violence, with candidates trying to assassinate their rivals. *Gangsterismo*, it was called. Castro learned to carry a gun. He had some contact with Marxist students, as did most youthful *políticos*, but his own loyalties were to the Ortodoxo party, a middle-class group dedicated to ending the corruption that had permeated the country for decades.

At the same time, he was developing the Latin-American intellectual's interest in international politics, and twice he became embroiled in overseas incidents. In the first, he became involved in a plot to overthrow dictator Rafael Trujillo of the Dominican Republic; Cuban police squashed the plot before the conspirators could leave Cuba, but Castro was able to escape arrest by swimming across a bay. A few months later, he traveled with other students to a protest demonstration in Bogotá, Columbia. The city erupted in violence. Castro was arrested and detained briefly.

For a short period, he was married to the daughter of a wealthy family from Oriente Province. They had a son, Fidelito, but the experience did nothing to channel Castro's energies into the usual life of law office and country clubs. Politics was his passion, and he was just emerging as a budding leader in 1951 when a bizarre incident occurred, one that transformed even the eccentric world of Cuban politics: Eduardo Chibás, the fanatically honest leader of the Ortodoxo party, killed himself by firing a pistol into his groin at the end of his weekly radio show. Some of his followers, including Castro, thought he had committed suicide because he was embarrassed that he hadn't been able to produce the promised evidence against a politician he had accused of corruption. Others believed Chibás had simply wanted to fake a suicide to gain public attention. If so, he failed doubly. Not only did the shot prove fatal, but it came seconds after the show had gone off the air.

Irreverent Cubans joked that Chibás had always been half-crazy, that only crackpots were honest politicians in Cuba, but his death left a serious gap in Cuba's political system, a void between the military authoritarian forces and the mainstream political parties. Most of both the army leadership and the political hierarchy were corrupt; Chibás had been the only one uniting an honest, moderate alternative. With Chibás gone, many jockeyed to replace him: Castro, one of the hopefuls, became a leader for Congress.

But something else was happening behind the scenes. General

Fulgencio Batista, who had previously been the nation's leader for eleven years, was dismayed at the death of Chibás. Batista had entered the presidential election hoping that Chibás and the traditional politicians would split the vote, leaving him the winner. With Chibás dead, there was no chance of that, no chance that the military could gain control through the ballot box.

Thus, in the early-morning hours of March 10, 1952, only weeks before elections were to be held, Batista staged a coup d'etat to overthrow Carlos Prio, the democratically elected president. Students demonstrated at the university and in towns throughout the island, but Prio, whose regime was riddled with corruption, didn't put up a fight; he simply fled to asylum in an embassy. Within hours, Batista was in full control. The take-over had been almost bloodless.

It was then that Castro came to the fore. While other politicians wiled away time plotting conspiracies that led to nothing, he organized for action. On July 26, 1953, he and a small band of followers attacked the Moncada regimental garrison at Santiago de Cuba. The assault failed completely. A few youths were killed during the battle, but many others died later, shot by army soldiers when they were caught hiding in the hills above the city.

Castro himself was sent to the national penitentiary on the Isle of Pines. There, he wrote a pamphlet, *History Will Absolve Me*, explaining that he wanted to restore democracy and help the poor, especially by breaking up the massive landholdings of the *latifundistas* with indemnity to the former owners. Employees of business enterprises would share 30 percent of their companies' profits. The property of corrupt politicians would be confiscated; the telephone and electric companies, both of which had large American investments, would be nationalized. Always, Castro himself stressed that he wanted no role in the government for himself: When the dictatorship was overthrown, he would simply retire. All in all, the program was broad enough to attract young intellectuals, middle-class progressives and even some upper-class supporters. The Communists, however, condemned the Moncada attack as divisive and premature, an example of the bourgeois inclination for violence.

Yet Castro remained convinced that violence was the only way, and when he was released after two years in a general amnesty declared by Batista, he immediately began conspiring again. He was only twenty-eight, but his 26th of July attack had hurled him to the forefront of the anti-Batista forces. Hundreds wanted to join his new movement. For a few weeks, he interviewed new members and raised funds, then hurried to Mexico, where he organized a guerrilla expedition.

On December 2, 1956, he and eighty-one followers, most of them seasick, jumped off an old, leaking American yacht, the *Granma,* and waded into the swamps of the Oriente coast. The army, tipped off by a Mexican informant, was waiting for them. Fewer than twenty rebels made it to the rain forest of the mountains, an area so wild and isolated that banditry still thrived. As always, Castro's confidence was indomitable. "Are we already in the Sierra Maestra?" he asked a peasant. When he heard the answer was yes, he concluded, "Then the revolution has triumphed."

It was not, of course, nearly that easy. Ascending to the area of Pico Turquino, at 6560 feet Cuba's tallest peak, the rebels made camp. For weeks, they slept on the ground and survived by eating roots. Gradually, they gained the confidence of a bandit-patriarch and, through him, the peasants in the area helped them obtain food. The people there were poor, living in dirt-floored, thatched-roof *bohíos* with neither electricity nor plumbing, a life so primitive that it wasn't much different from that of the Indians before Columbus. Some of these illiterate peasants, deciding they had nothing to lose, joined the rebel group.

Within three months of arriving, the rebel forces received their first major break: A lanky, gray-haired editorial writer from *The New York Times,* Herbert Matthews, hiked into the Sierra for an interview. At the time, there were fewer than thirty well-armed rebels, but Castro tricked the journalist into believing he had hundreds of men. The ensuing article caused a sensation when it appeared on the front page of *The Times.* Cubans learned Castro was alive and fighting. Americans discovered a young democrat willing to risk his life in the fight against dictatorship.

As the publicity spread through Cuba, clandestine supporters from the cities began making the long trek to the mountains. They brought weapons, foodstuffs and medicines, often smuggled past the Rural Guards under the skirts of women. Some decided to stay with the rebels. Most of these urban volunteers were young, but one of the first to remain in the camp was thirty-one-year-old Celia Sánchez, a petite, plain-faced brunette. An unmarried doctor's daughter, she was considered a lifelong spinster by rigid Cuban society, a bit of an outcast, but she quickly fit in among the rebels, showing herself to be uncomplaining, intelligent and absolutely devoted to Castro. He made her his secretary. Almost from the start, she was never far from his side, day or night, even when he slept alone in a hammock, as he usually did, some distance from his men.

Castro shared the hardships of mountain life with everyone else. A tiny can of fruit cocktail was considered a luxury, but all adhered to the strict rules: food was never to be taken from a peasant without compensation and permission, and a rebel officer should never eat a larger portion than his men ate. A person could be summarily shot if he was merely suspected of being an informer. Alcohol was forbidden, and even sex was frowned upon unless the couple consented to be married by a priest.

Despite such spartan restrictions, the rebel group grew. Sleeping on the ground gave way to hammocks strung in the forest and, later, thatched-roof *bohíos*. Ramshackle wooden buildings were erected for a hospital, kitchen and headquarters. Telephone lines were strung down the hillsides to alert the rebels to army movements. Invariably, there were more men than guns; the dropout rate was high, intentionally, so that only the hardest and most dedicated remained. Those without good weapons were called the *escopeteros*, literally the "shotgun men," and they hung around to do the odd jobs and wait for better weapons.

Eventually, more guns came, sometimes from underground supporters, sometimes flown in from overseas, but most (about 85 percent) directly from the enemy itself. In the beginning, the rebels dared make forays against only the most isolated of the army outposts, and even then a rifle was so valuable that if a rebel abandoned one during a battle, he had to go back unarmed to retrieve it. As Castro used to tell his men, "We are not fighting for prisoners. We are fighting for weapons."

Always, it seemed, Castro himself outdid his men. His ability to march for hours without stopping earned him the nickname *El Caballo*— The Horse. At times, his face would turn sheepish and humorous, and he could appear as lovable as a teddy bear. But moments later, he might be pacing and bellowing in such a rage that subordinates trembled. At other times, he would withdraw, immersed in reading or thinking, but if he chose, he could talk for hours, hammering home his points again and again with a rhythmic cadence, as if he thought repeating his ideas made them more believable. Those conversations almost always centered on the tactics needed to overthrow Batista; theoretical politics and the shape of the future were almost never discussed. Those around Castro assumed that his new revolutionary government would be everything that Batista's wasn't: democratic, honest and progressive. As the civil war progressed, Castro continued to defend himself against accusations that he was too totalitarian. "Is it that we rebels of the Sierra Maestra do not want free elections, a democratic regime, a constitutional government?" he asked in the Sierra Manifesto, written in July 1957. The answer, of course, was no. "For wanting them more than anyone, we are here." Twice in 1958, he even backed down on part of the *Absolve Me* platform, telling American journalists that he had changed his mind about nationalizing the utilities, though he continued to push for agrarian reform.

By March 1958, with the rebel force still growing, Castro felt confident enough to send his brother Raúl, four years younger than himself, with a small group of men to open the Second Front in northern Oriente Province. But less than a month later, on April 9, the Movement suffered a stunning setback: the failure of a general strike, which was supposed to paralyze business throughout the island until Batista was forced to leave. It was a bold idea, badly organized. Friction developed between the urban and mountain leaders, and a certain indifference existed in the nation's economic heart, Havana. Starting in early morning, the strike sputtered as sympathetic workers kept waiting for people to lead them. The police, aided by a private army of thugs, began vicious retaliations. In Santiago alone, thirty demonstrators were killed. By midafternoon, the strike was crushed.

A few weeks later, Batista's army launched its most serious attack against Castro's mountain stronghold. More than five thousand soldiers were used in a massive summer offensive to destroy the main guerrilla group, which had only several hundred armed men. At one point, the rebel area was reduced to three square miles. But the army pushed no farther. When the soldiers were prepared for a fight, the rebels simply melted into the underbrush. When they weren't ready, the guerrillas would ambush them in the dense rain forest.

The soldiers were untrained in guerrilla warfare, it confused and frightened them, and Castro added to their confusion by treating all prisoners well. The wounded were taken care of promptly, and almost all were handed over to the Red Cross. Whenever Castro had the chance, he emphasized that he had nothing against the soldiers themselves, only their corrupt leadership. That helped demoralize the already dispirited troops. The offensive bogged down. One entire army battalion surrendered; its major joined the rebels. Castro's men gained 12 mortars, 23 tripod machine guns, 21 submachine guns, 142 Garand rifles and 200 San Cristóbal machine guns. The army leadership panicked; all forces were withdrawn from the rebel regions.

With that, Castro sensed a "great turnabout," and anti-Batista politicians everywhere began to believe the end was approaching. In July, all the major opposition groups, with the exception of the Communists, met in Caracas, Venezuela, and agreed to unite in a Civic Revolutionary Democratic Front. All disputes were to be set aside until after the dictatorship was defeated. The head of the Havana Bar Association was named coordinator of the front, Castro was recognized as commander in chief of the rebel armed forces, and an obscure judge, Manuel Urrutia, was designated "President in Arms." The judge was Castro's handpicked candidate to become leader of the new revolutionary government, and his acceptance by the other groups was a direct recognition that the youthful rebels had taken over leadership of the fight against the dictatorship. It was their proviso, issued at the end of the Pact of Caracas, that promised "full constitutional and democratic procedures" when they reached power.

About this same time, eighteen months after Castro went to the mountains, the Cuban Communists (called Partido Socialista Popular) decided to support the rebel effort. Their backing created little stir: Though they had strength in some unions and certain geographical areas, the Communists had no overwhelming popular support. Their presidential candidate in 1948 had drawn 142,000 votes, a remarkably strong showing for a Marxist in Latin America, but still he finished last. In the 1950s, after Batista outlawed the party, PSP membership was no more than 20,000 and perhaps as low as 7,000, out of a population of 6.5 million.

Castro, ignoring the politicians, kept his mind on the war. By mid-August, he decided the rebels were strong enough for him to broaden his guerrilla front by sending two of his most trusted officers, Ernesto ("Ché") Guevara and Camilo Cienfuegos, to lead groups to the central province of Las Villas. He had two motives: a desire to harass the army on as many fronts as he could, and a fear that a rival rebel group, the Segundo Frente del Escambray, was gaining too much power in Las Villas. If the dictatorship were to collapse suddenly, the group might beat the 26th of July forces in a race to Havana and attempt to establish a new government. Castro sensed the anti-Batista coalition was a fragile expediency which would fall apart as soon as any group thought it could gain an advantage.

In early November, Castro's fears intensified when Batista held an election. The major opposition groups assumed that this might be Batista's last gasp, that the voting would be rigged, and they refused to participate. Rebels in the countryside and workers in the cities harassed the voting places; candidates were considered to be revolutionary criminals. Many citizens never went to the polls, but the voting returns showed a heavy turnout. The winner was Batista's handpicked successor, Andrés Rivero Agüero,* who supposedly received more than twice the votes of the other three candidates combined. Rivero Agüero was scheduled to take office on February 24, but Castro, believing the new president would be a mere Batista puppet, continued on as if nothing had happened.

A day or so after the election, he and about twenty-five men from his headquarters troop left his rugged mountain hideout at La Plata and, after three months of inactivity, began their descent to the plains. For almost three weeks, they cautiously hiked down mountain paths and forded streams while gathering volunteers and weapons. The column had a burro for the medical supplies, and another for the troop's doctor, but everyone else, including Castro himself, walked. At a small mining village, they launched a surprise foray but retreated quickly. Castro wanted to save his forces for something more important.

Below him, on the plains, others were already harassing the regime, aided as always by the nation's geography: Cuba is a deceptively large island, stretching 775 miles between its eastern and western tips; its land mass is slightly larger than the state of Tennessee. On the western part of the island, in the provinces of Pinar del Río, Havana and Matanzas, clandestine supporters in the cities harassed the government with homemade bombs and minor sabotage. But most of the rebel action was centered in the easternmost province of Oriente, a primitive land of mountains and sugar mills hundreds of miles from the capital of Havana. The province was held together only by a two-lane paved lifeline, the

---

* A reminder to the English reader: Latins list their father's name (Rivero) before their mother's name (Agüero). Thus, Andrés Rivero Agüero's "last name" is really Rivero, or, as he preferred the combined usage, Rivero Agüero.

Central Highway. Beyond that, roads quickly degenerated into mud paths fit only for mules. A damaged bridge on the highway could halt traffic for weeks; the huge sugar-mill *centrales*, isolated in the countryside with only their tall, soot-blackened smokestacks visible from the road, were vulnerable to surprise raids and rebel demands that "taxes" be paid on each bag of sugar if the mill operators did not want their fields burned.

By mid-November, the threat of rebel ambushes had almost completely stopped traffic on the Central Highway in Oriente. The road was scarred by craters and littered with the charred skeletons of trucks and cars. In the provincial cities of Bayamo and Guantánamo, gasoline was so scarce that many residents had to resort to horse-drawn carts. The mammoth Charco Redondo manganese mine had no way to transport its ore and was forced to lay off six hundred workers. Telephone and telegraph cables to the rest of the country were out. The high-voltage electrical lines to Holguín had been destroyed, and that city of sixty thousand persons had been without lights for a month.

Such dramatic effects made the guerrilla forces seem much larger than they were. In fact, Castro's total army numbered only several thousand men, while Batista had some forty thousand soldiers in the regular army and thirty thousand police officers, who were often the rebels most bitter opponents. Altogether, Castro's men were outnumbered at least 10 to 1.*

Castro diminished these overwhelming odds by never endangering the bulk of his troop in any one battle. If a confrontation were too risky, he simply avoided it. He was not looking for a single decisive victory, but

---

* The exact size of the rebel army remains a matter of considerable debate. In the interview for this book, Castro said he had 3000 "well-armed men" in all his columns by the end of 1958; he has used that figure often in recent years, but the emphasis has increasingly been on "well-armed." In December 1958, he told American journalist Dickey Chapelle that he had about 7300 rebels. Recently, in a meticulous survey of column-by-column estimates, Professor Neill Macaulay of the University of Florida concluded that Castro had 7250 guerrillas by December 20. For those columns which we obtained estimates during interviews with rebel veterans, the figures came close to matching the Macaulay numbers. Certainly, in the last few weeks of the war, the rebel army was growing rapidly—too rapidly for anyone to measure exactly—and the new guerrillas were often inexperienced men, not always "well armed." Regardless of specific numbers, there is no doubt that the rebels were greatly outnumbered by Batista's forces.

for a series of small successes that could lead to the ultimate triumph.

It was with that in mind that he had carefully selected his first target on the plains: the town of Guisa, on the edge of the foothills. If trouble came, his men could simply slip onto the dirt-packed trails and retreat to the Sierra wilderness. Yet, if they were to get the most from their mission, they had to act quickly: Cuba's famed *zafra,* the harvest of the sugar crop, was due to begin within six weeks. Already, the rebels had much of the canefields under control, and if they could gain more, they could cripple the harvest that produced 80 percent of the country's foreign exchange. That in turn could so damage the economy that Batista's support among businessmen might evaporate.

Finally, the last of the 180 rebels strolled into the hillside clearing. As Castro studied them, he thought again of the risks involved. The army outpost at Guisa had been reinforced, but the real danger was twelve miles away, where the regiment in the city of Bayamo had about fifteen hundred soldiers ready to come to the outpost's rescue. In effect, his men would once again be facing 10 to 1 odds.

Strolling toward the center of the clearing, Castro signaled for silence. The murmurs ended.

In his intense, almost hoarse voice, he announced: "Men, we are going to attack Guisa. It has a large army garrison, but we can win. The army cannot defeat us."

The rebels shuffled nervously. In the center of the group, Raúl Trillo, the column's physician, stroked his thick black beard. He could sense the tension spreading through the men. Undoubtedly, he thought, Castro would give a long inspirational speech.

Instead, Castro walked among them. He knew how important it was at such a moment for everyone to realize how crucial his role was if they were to achieve victory. It was not a time for mere words, and so he stopped in front of each man, leaning close and fixing him with the sharp gaze of his dark eyes. To one, he whispered something personal. He grabbed another by the shoulders in an embrace. Then, moving quicker, he slapped men on the backs of their grimy uniforms and stroked their heads of greasy hair. He shook hands, examined rifles, caressed caps. As he strolled through the group, a surge of warmth and confidence spread in his wake; the men responded with small, shy smiles.

When Castro came to Dr. Trillo, he grabbed him by the shoulders and grinned sympathetically. Trillo felt a glow of pride.

A few feet away, Luis Tasi Martínez, an illiterate construction worker with a Lincolnesque beard, absently fondled a Thompson submachine gun with his crippled right hand. Castro patted him on the back. Tasi Martínez smiled; he was no longer worried about the odds facing them. He had complete confidence in Fidel.

To the man next to him, Castro whispered, "We have to win."

2/A BATTLE BEGINS

Several miles away from that rebel meeting, army First Lieutenant Reinaldo Blanco stood looking out a front window of the Guisa cuartel. The twenty-year-old commander of Company M, 23rd Battalion, had just finished shaving, and he could hear his men in the barracks slowly awakening with their usual hangovers. Pans in the mess clattered as the cook prepared breakfast.

Across the paved road and a little to his left, the manager of the Esso station, the only gas station in this small town, was sweeping dirt away from the pumps. The man had been getting little business lately. Rumors of rebels in the area had almost completely stopped traffic on the town's one paved road, which ran out to the Central Highway. Even the peasants, whose horse-drawn carts were usually laden with bulging bags of coffee beans, rarely made the trip to the Guisa warehouses anymore. What little traffic there was moved out, not in. Almost two hundred townspeople, many with close connections to the Batista regime, had fled to the safety of the cities.

Blanco and his men had been brought in to reinforce the few aging members of the Rural Guard who were stationed permanently in the

town. Altogether, he had ninety-six men, including twenty-five biv-
ouacked at the cemetery, to protect Guisa and the one-story, U-shaped
cuartel on the edge of town. On the cuartel's roof were two .50-caliber
machine guns on tripods, surrounded by sandbags.

Many senior army officers avoided posts where they might have to
face the rebels, but Blanco didn't mind. It was a chance to prove his
worth, to establish a respectable army career, as his father had. His
personal loyalty was to the army, not to the country's dictator, but many
of his soldiers felt no loyalty at all. They were teenagers recruited out of
the poor Havana *barrios* and called soldiers after four weeks' training.
Most were earning more money than they had ever had in their lives,
but they found it difficult to accept that they could be killed at any
moment for a cause they didn't believe in. So whenever they had the
money, they escaped their fears by going to the town's three bars,
especially the two where the B-girls were. Bar de Molina was the most
popular: the girls were fresher and better looking. The other was not as
good; it was run by the mayor. Blanco remembered once asking a girl
who was drinking a beer with him, "Why do you all come to lay with us?
I was told in Havana that all the girls in Oriente were Fidelistas." The
girl had laughed. "Yes, our heart belongs to Fidel, but our ass"—rubbing
her index finger and thumb together—"that belongs to Batista."

Blanco was still smiling at the thought when a squad of soldiers moved
past him to the door. They were preparing to escort the daily bus to
Bayamo. He suddenly remembered that the lieutenant who usually led
the squad was being visited by his wife. They were in a guesthouse. It
would be a rude awakening from a night of love if Blanco ordered him to
go on the patrol. Instead, he found Lieutenant Cardozo, a youth who
had just graduated from the military academy. Blanco reminded him of
the dangers, of the need to watch the hills for snipers and the bridge for
bombs. The lieutenant nodded unenthusiastically. He did not believe "a
few bandits" in the hills could cause much problem.

The squad went first to the town square, where the bus began its
route. A few minutes later, it reappeared: Lieutenant Cardozo in the
dusty lead jeep, an army pickup driven by an experienced sergeant and
then the bus. It was actually an old Chevrolet truck chassis supporting a
homemade wooden box with roughhewn benches. About fifteen townspeople were making the trip that morning. A second jeep brought up the
rear.

The convoy moved past the cuartel at a cautious thirty-five miles per hour and disappeared around a curve. Blanco remained in the doorway, basking in the quiet morning sun.

Two miles away, where the road ran between two hills and then over a stone bridge spanning a dry gully, Luis Tasi Martínez crouched in a trench, clutching the submachine gun with his crippled hand. He was one of twenty-five rebels near the top of a hill, protected by a cluster of pines. Another squad was on the opposite ridge. Farther along, a rebel lieutenant had a 60-millimeter mortar, for which there were only five shells, and a .50-caliber machine gun.

As the convoy appeared, Tasi Martínez's fingers tightened on the Thompson. The vehicles were spread out, the bus a considerable distance behind the pickup truck. At the edge of the bridge, the lead jeep stopped for a moment, then moved across. The pickup truck followed.

At exactly 8:30 A.M., the mine exploded. The truck toppled over the stone railing and crashed into the gully thirty feet below. As the civilians in the bus leaped into the roadside ditch, the rebels opened fire. Within seconds, a bullet ruptured the heart of the shocked young lieutenant, and his jeep slammed into the hillside.

When there was a brief lull in the gunfire, Tasi Martínez looked down at the gully. The sergeant had fallen out of the pickup truck. He was screaming. He had no legs.

Lieutenant Blanco was still standing in the door of the cuartel when he heard the explosion, muffled by the distance. Shouting for the radioman to notify the Bayamo regiment, he assembled a team of two medics and eight soldiers. Together, they ran down the road. When they had gone about a hundred yards, Blanco and a sergeant led a dash across a flat, barren field beside a small hill. About halfway across, a barrage of bullets slammed into the ground around them. The two men kept running, heads down, until they could dive into the protection of a canefield.

Blanco looked back. The others had retreated to the road. He motioned for them to return to the cuartel. Then he and the sergeant moved on. They found the bus passengers huddled in a thatched-roof *bohío* on a hillside. None of them was hurt, and they shouted that the two army men should stay away, lest they attract gunfire from the rebel trenches.

Blanco and the sergeant moved north, staying close to the brush and then dashing to an unoccupied, wooded hill. From there, they could see the road. The firing had stopped. Seven corpses were scattered along the pavement and in the gully. No other soldiers were visible.

Blanco was wondering what to do when he heard the rumble of vehicles. As he watched helplessly, three army trucks from the Bayamo regiment moved across the bridge. They were between the two hills when the rebels opened fire. Working quickly, the soldiers leaped from the trucks, collected the army corpses and sped toward Guisa. Minutes later, the trucks roared back down the road, the soldiers squatting below the sideboards in back, drivers slumped in their seats.

Blanco cursed. It was idiotic that the Bayamo garrison should send only three trucks and drive them straight into the ambush. Then he realized he had committed his own military blunder, the worst an officer could make. He had left his men without a commanding officer, and he was serving no useful purpose there, hiding behind a banana tree, stranded.

Behind the rebel lines, in the plantation house of a wealthy coffee planter, Dr. Raúl Trillo was receiving his first casualty, a young rebel gasping for air, his shirt front soaked with blood. Trillo told the stretcher-bearers to place him on the large, marble-topped dining table he had moved into the living room. There, Trillo cut open his shirt and went to work. Accustomed to operating in a rustic shack in the Sierra, Trillo found the villa a paradise, but his supplies, arranged on a nearby table, were minimal: bandages, a large bottle of Mercurochrome, some morphine, a few aspirin and twelve liters of blood plasma. It was not much.

He was still working on the rebel's chest wound when a guard appeared with a young army prisoner. His face was bloody. Trillo looked up for a moment. "He'll have to wait. First come, first served."

Nearby, Fidel Castro was sprawled in a hammock in a small gully, hidden by overhanging trees from the air force bombers. After a long night of planning the ambush, he was nearing the point of exhaustion, but he perked up when a lieutenant brought the first news of the fighting. In the first hour, the army had suffered seven dead, seven injured and seven captured. Three had fled into the hills. Castro chewed on a cigar and said nothing. He knew the real test was yet to come.

Early that evening, Lieutenant Blanco sneaked back to the cuartel, where his nervous young soldiers were happy to greet him. That night was quiet. The next morning, a squad hurriedly buried the seven corpses in the cemetery, erected makeshift wooden crosses and rushed back to the cuartel.

At 11:00 A.M., supported by strafing air force planes, a large army column arrived, led by a Sherman tank and several rubber-wheeled M-8 light tanks, followed by jeeps and fifteen trucks. They had met no resistance along the road. The column's commander, a major, said he had come to reinforce Blanco, but since the rebels appeared to have left, he was going back to Bayamo to get supplies for a longer stay. They would return the next day. Blanco pleaded with him to remain but the major refused to believe there was any danger. Finally, to placate the lieutenant, he agreed to leave behind one platoon and some ammunition. The column left at 2:00 P.M., waving happily to the ones remaining behind.

Fighting despair, Blanco did what he could. He placed squads of soldiers with machine guns on top of seven two- and three-story buildings, the tallest in town, and he asked Guisa's three bakeries to deliver all the bread they could to the cuartel. By sunset, several hundred loaves were stacked against a wall in the dining room. "It's not very hygienic," he said to a sergeant, "but we're going to have bread for a long time."

There was no electricity in town that night. The rebels had apparently cut the power lines. When it was completely dark, a deafening barrage of gunfire was unleashed against the cuartel. It went on for fifteen minutes, then stopped suddenly. The soldiers manning the machine guns on the roof complained they could see nothing. Blanco guessed the rebels were on a small hill, several hundred yards away. It sounded like they were preparing to attack. Waiting, the army soldiers munched nervously on sausage and bread, washing it down with milk and canned juices.

Half an hour later, the rebels fired again. It was a steady volley, followed by silence, followed by scattered shots. A strange voice, very loud, shouted, *"Chivato."* "Little goat," the rebels' slang for Batista informers. It sounded to Blanco as if the rebels had a loudspeaker.

"*Casquito*"—"little helmet," the nickname for the teenage army soldiers. Then came a chorus, singing badly out of tune: "*Ahorita va a llover, ahorita va a llover. Y si no tienes cuidado, la cabeza te vas a mojar.*" "In a little while, it's going to rain. In a little while, it's going to rain. And if you're not careful, your head is going to get wet." The voices were brimming with sarcastic sweetness.

The song was followed by a wild volley of gunfire and the boom of a mortar shell. Soldiers scrambled to their positions. Blanco strained to see through the darkness.

Nothing happened. Finally, Blanco understood. "They are going to drive us crazy in here. They are going to sing that damned song and fire their rifles all night long until they drive us crazy."

As he finished talking, the chorus began again: "*Ahorita va a llover . . .*"

3/THE AMBASSADOR

That night, the elite of Cuban society were dancing the rumba at the Waldorf-Astoria Hotel in New York. Thick cigar smoke wafted toward the silken gold and white ribbons hanging from massive chandeliers. Small palm trees, topped with golden balls, gave a touch of the tropics while sequined Cuban dancers from the Hotel Nacional strutted and swayed on the small stage.

Cuban civic organizations had complained bitterly that such an event was inappropriate in a time of civil war, but Earl E. T. Smith, the U.S. ambassador, had his own reasons for sponsoring this Cuban Gala Night. Dressed in a black-tie tuxedo and holding a cigar, he stood smiling as he watched the nearly five hundred guests who had paid $40 each to attend the party in the hotel's Sert Ballroom. It had turned out even better than he imagined and seemed certain to raise $10,000 so that a young Cuban could study commercial design in the United States.

Smith was in his element. His gray hair and six-foot-five frame made him look perfect for the role, and his background was equally impressive. A descendant of one of Massachusetts' first families, a boxing champion at Yale and an enormously successful stockbroker, he glided with ease through society life in New York and Palm Beach, where he was well known for having once told a journalist: "I have lived in two eras. One when the country was run by the classes, and now when it is run by the masses. Something in between is probably best, but I'll be honest: I enjoyed it more when it was run by the classes." He was a staunch Republican, a major contributor to the campaigns of President Dwight D. Eisenhower, and in 1957 he had been rewarded with the ambassadorship to Cuba. Cubans had told him, and he enjoyed repeating, that the American ambassador was usually the second-most-powerful man in Cuba, and sometimes the first.

For the party, he had managed to blend society, charity and politics in his own special way, to bolster the regime of Fulgencio Batista.

The publicity was certain to help. The society editor of Cuba's most prestigious newspaper, *Diario de la Marina,* had flown up for the event. A *Life* magazine photographer, laden with cameras, was prowling the crowd, looking for a cover shot. Nearby, a middle-aged man was telling a *Life* reporter: "Cats and dogs and Cubans are my charities this year."

More importantly for Smith, Cubans, especially Batista supporters, were able to mingle with American politicians like the young senator from Massachusetts, John Kennedy, who had been Smith's houseguest the previous Christmas in Havana. Smith did not agree with much of Kennedy's liberal philosophy, but he was a longtime friend of the family, and he was certain that Kennedy's instincts were good.

Nearby, holding a champagne glass, was Kennedy's quiet wife, Jacqueline, in a white Givenchy gown. Aly Kahn, Maria Callas and Mrs. Henry Fonda were there, as were Mrs. Henry Ford, Noel Coward and movie stars Dina Merrill, David Niven and Merle Oberon. Baby-faced Ted Kennedy, brother of the senator, sat near the wall with his mother Rose. They were watching the dance floor, where a vivacious young woman, her light brown hair flopping over her left eye, was doing the rumba. She was Jane Fonda, the twenty-one-year-old daughter of the famous actor.

Smith drifted through the crowd. For a moment, he stopped by the table of Porfirio Rubirosa, a widely publicized playboy and race-car driver who looked elegant, as usual, in his white tie and tails. They made innocuous comments about the size of the crowd, and Smith moved on. Seeing Rubirosa, his good friend and the Dominican Republic's ambassador to Cuba, reminded him unpleasantly of his problems, especially his continuing battle with the State Department. Seven months before, the United States had stopped shipping arms to Cuba because the weapons were intended for hemispheric defense and Batista was using them against fellow Cubans. Smith had objected vehemently, and he was delighted when Rubirosa's government filled the void by selling thousands of San Cristóbal rifles to the Batista regime.

But Smith knew those rifles were only a stopgap. No Cuban government had long survived the withdrawal of U.S. support, and he was convinced what Batista officials told him was true: the rebels were dominated by the Communists; they had to be stopped at any cost. He was enraged when the State Department disagreed, when they continued to insist that there was no solid evidence of Communism, that Castro's movement was supported by a broad section of Cubans. He believed the department's Latin-American experts were either being misled by propagandists or (as he sometimes suspected) were themselves Communist sympathizers.

Because of that, the night before the party, Smith had taken an extraordinary step. He had told Senator Jorge García Montes, Batista's former prime minister and still his canasta-playing buddy, to go to Washington to represent Batista's handpicked successor, Andrés Rivero Agüero, so that the State Department would not automatically associate the president-elect with the Batista regime. The senator could speak for Rivero Agüero; the ambassador would be the spokesman for Batista. In effect, Smith was telling a foreigner how to lobby his own country, something far beyond the bounds of normal diplomacy, but he was convinced the move was absolutely necessary. Something had to be done quickly if Cuba were to be spared a bloody debacle.

But that night in New York, such a possibility seemed far away. As the dancers left the stage, Smith simply nodded as he passed García Montes's table. This was not the time or place for confidential conversations. The orchestra struck up a cha-cha, and guests rushed to the dance floor.

That evening, 150 miles away in Albany, New York, a pert teenage girl with short dark hair was studying alone, as she did every week night, in her dormitory room at the Sacred Heart Academy. She was Rosa Rivero, the daughter of President-elect Rivero Agüero; Ambassador Smith had told her father that Rosa was welcome to come down by train to attend the Waldorf ball, but her father had said no, it would interfere with her studies.

That was merely one of the bitter frustrations she had to endure, for she had just gone through the terrible experience of turning fifteen away from home. In Cuba, that would have meant a grand *quince* party, the equivalent of an American debutante ball, but among her fellow high-school sophomores, it was simply another birthday. Her celebration had been a small one.

It was hard for her to study: all she could dream of was returning to Havana for the Christmas holidays, when she could catch up on her social life and see the handsome young Emilio, age seventeen, who was writing to her regularly. He had even promised her a surprise when she returned to Havana.

The next morning, in the State Department Building at Twenty-third and C streets in downtown Washington, a small knot of men mingled in a carpeted office on the fourth floor, overlooking an enclosed courtyard lit by a gloomy gray sky. The windows across the way were unlit: it was a Saturday, and the only reason these men, the department's Latin-American experts, had assembled was the chance to listen to, and argue with, their ambassador to Cuba. Smith was not yet there. The men waited silently, each absorbed in his thoughts; everyone knew it was going to be a difficult meeting.

Standing next to the window, arms folded across his chest, was William Wieland, the director of Caribbean and Mexican affairs. He had an unmistakable diplomatic bearing: six feet three, narrow mustache, brownish hair combed straight back and the mature face of a man in his mid-forties. Like a good diplomat, he knew how to conceal tension, but he feared he was about to reveal it now, because he disliked Smith intensely. In fact, he was convinced that the ambassador was the reason that the Cuban situation was slipping into disaster and chaos. Smith was refusing to communicate to the Batista regime how seriously the Americans viewed the situation and, therefore, postponing any possible attempts at a peaceful, moderate settlement. But Wieland's emotions were running so strong, he hoped others would do the talking.

Looking around the room, he tried to guess who else might speak up. He doubted it would be the group's highest-ranking member, the man whose office they were in: R. Richard Rubottom, assistant secretary of state for Latin America. He was a compact, composed Texan who had risen quickly through the State hierarchy by being exceedingly cautious, and he was doubly so when dealing with presidential appointees such as Smith.

Wieland, like the others, knew the pressures Rubottom had been under. Academicians and journalists had been criticizing State throughout the fifties, complaining about Washington's support of shabby military dictatorships in Venezuela, Colombia, the Dominican Republic as well as Cuba. Slowly, much more slowly than the critics demanded, the administration had been sliding toward neutrality concerning the despotic *caudillos*. Part of that policy had included the arms embargo to Batista, on March 15, 1958. That decision had relieved some of the pressure from Cuban exiles, democratic Latin countries and publications such as *The New York Times*, all of which were demanding that State stop U.S. arms from being used to kill pro-democratic insurrectionists. And, of course, when Batista's government departed, Washington didn't want the new government showing off U.S. weapons that had been used to forestall democracy.

The arms embargo had received the approval of the secretary of state, John Foster Dulles, but it was one of the very few times Dulles paid any attention to Latin America. His health was failing; his limited time was taken up by the problems of Europe and the Iron Curtain. Like most leaders in Washington, he considered Latin America unimportant, a mere American backyard. It was not where "hardball" was played. Assistant Secretary Rubottom and the others felt they were working in a vacuum.

No, Wieland decided, Assistant Secretary Rubottom wasn't going to confront Smith. He would ask the appropriate questions, but he wouldn't follow them up with probing inquiries. And none of the others in the room seemed likely to do that either. William Snow, the deputy assistant secretary, was a white-haired New Englander nearing retirement; he was conservative, perhaps even sympathetic with Smith, but he would say nothing provocative either way. Ed Little, Wieland's own assistant, was relatively new to the job, and the Cuban desk officer, Terrance Leonhardy, was preoccupied with his upcoming transfer, to Nogales, Mexico.

Wieland knew that left only himself, the man who knew more about Cuba than anyone else in the State Department. He had lived there for ten years, when he was a teenager, and his mother and stepfather had moved to Havana. He had learned to speak Spanish with a flawless Cuban accent, and in 1933, as a young reporter, he had slouched in the backseat of a car as Cuban revolutionaries rushed to police stations to free political prisoners. He had interviewed Batista and he had even considered himself a personal friend of Eduardo Chibás, the politician who had shot himself in the radio studio.

His mastery of the language meant that many of the anti-Batista exiles sought him out. Castro's own organization, the 26th of July, had a lobbyist in Washington, but so did other Cuban political groups. The younger exiles considered Castro to be their country's salvation, but the older anti-Batista politicians weren't convinced. None of them considered Castro a Communist; even Carlos Prio, the president whom Batista had ousted, denied any link between Castro and Communism. Still, many of them did not trust the rebel leader. There were stories, never confirmed, that Castro had been mixed up in violent *gangsterismo* during his university days, and he seemed so emotional, so inclined to pick up a gun, that many wondered whether they could depend upon him. There was the complaint too that Castro, while claiming he wanted no part in politics after Batista's downfall, still seemed constantly occupied in wresting power from other opposition groups.

Wieland had to concede that some of the complainers might be exaggerating problems in order to bolster their own chances, but he tended to agree with them. A year before, he had written a policy memorandum recommending that the United States avoid Castro because "his present philosophy and beliefs are not clear. . . . Even some of his prominent supporters have at times indicated their distrust of him."

Instead, Wieland recommended supporting a "third force," consisting of anti-Batista, non-Castro moderates, persons who were known to be democratic and pro-American. By November 1958, he backed wholeheartedly the idea that the third force should use violence if necessary to overthrow the regime. The longer Batista remained in power, the more likely it seemed to him that Castro would take over completely.

That was the view too of Wieland's closest Cuban contacts, men who tended to be moderates, many of them middle-aged politicians who had been the student revolutionaries of 1933. One of these, an anti-Batista lobbyist named Carlos Piad, had become a close friend who often visited Wieland's house on Potomac Street in suburban North Arlington. Together, they worked out a list of anti-Batista, non-Castro persons worthy of American support. None of the men had been informed they were on the list, nor was there any specific plan. It was merely a concept, an idea that these people should be supported in anything they tried against the regime. *

Occasionally, one of these men suggested a plan to Wieland through lobbyist Piad. Once or twice, they asked for direct paramilitary assistance, even weapons, but more often they simply wanted a "green light," a nod of approval so that customs officials in Florida would not enforce the U.S. Neutrality Act and stop their secret shipments of arms to Cuba. Castro's 26th of July people could lose several massive shipments every week to law-enforcement agencies and still get plenty of weapons to the mountains. The other groups were smaller and didn't dare risk that. Thus, Wieland took each plan, wrote it down on a piece of plain paper and passed it along to the section's liaison with the CIA. He had never received a response. "Where's the green light?" his Cuban friends kept asking. "Somewhere," he told them, "there's a big red stop sign."

Everyone knew that time was getting short, that Batista's last chance had been to hold honest elections. Of course, when the oft-postponed voting had finally come, it had been too late. The rebels, not trusting the dictator's methods, had threatened to assassinate anyone who participated. In several places, American observers reported armed Batista guards standing in front of the polling places. Voters never entered, but the precincts reported normal voting results. No one believed it. †

Yet Batista had smugly decided that the election had been accepted because Ambassador Smith had sent him and the president-elect telegrams congratulating them on the outcome. Wieland winced when

---

* The list, as Piad later presented it to the FBI, consisted of Tony Varona, prime minister under President Prio; José Miró Cardona, president of the Havana Bar Association and a leader of the pro-Castro Civic Resistance; Felipe Pazos, Prio's president of the National Bank; Justo Carrillo, leader of the small Montecristi Movement; Colonel Ramón Barquín, a military officer imprisoned in the Isle of Pines; and two minor officials.

† Years later, it was revealed how the fraud was carried out. The ballots were printed at an old two-story house called Casa Salazar, near Gate 10 at Camp Columbia in Havana, under the supervision of honest election officials. At night, when no official was watching, a second set of ballots, using the same paper and presses, was run off and marked by hand for Batista's candidates. Brigadier General Silito Tabernilla, Colonel Florentino Rosell and José Suárez Núñez, Batista's press secretary, have all confirmed this account.

he thought of that. Smith was almost beyond control, and it was no longer clear whether he was accurately reporting back to Washington what was happening on the island. The reporting issue had become particularly sensitive, and there had been several blowups about it, with Smith insisting that neither CIA agents nor his own political officers should talk to anti-Batista dissidents in Havana; he maintained such contacts simply encouraged the opposition and generated enemy propaganda. At one point, the CIA's inspector-general, Lyman B. Kirkpatrick, Jr., was sent to Havana to explain that intelligence agents had a *duty* to listen to all sources of information. Smith agreed, grudgingly. Yet Washington remained so suspicious that Park Wollam, an aide to the assistant secretary, had been sent to Cuba as the consul for Santiago, a hotbed of rebel supporters. Wollam had been instructed to take ·the extraordinary measure of bypassing the ambassador and sending his reports directly to Washington.

As Wieland contemplated the problems, Ambassador Smith was emerging from the fourth-floor elevator. Wearing a light topcoat, only slightly sleepy from the late-night party, he too was ready for a fight. All of his adult life he had detested government bureaucrats, and he considered these State Department men "lower echelon," beneath the social and economic level to which he was accustomed. It was so hard to get any decision out of men like these that he had developed a policy: he would notify them of what he planned to do, and if he received no immediate objection, he assumed he had their approval. At least that way he could get something done.

Walking with his usual brisk, long strides, Smith entered the assistant secretary's suite. A formal smile spread across his face as he quickly shook the six men's hands, gave his topcoat to an assistant and led the way to the semicircle of chairs around a coffee table in one corner of the office.

As the others sat down, Smith made a brief joke about the weather, how the day's 40-degree temperature in Washington seemed a bit harsh compared with the balmy 80-degree days of Havana. Then he turned directly to the situation in Cuba.

Basically, he said, there was an impasse. The army couldn't crush the rebels, and the rebels seemed incapable of inflicting a major defeat on the army. Most Cubans, he believed, were anti-Batista but not pro-Castro. They wanted most of all the restoration of peace and order. He added that, for the first time, he was hearing reports of economic difficulties caused by rebel activities. U.S. businesses there were likely to have problems.

A week before, he said, he had talked with President-elect Rivero Agüero, who had expressed a strong desire to restore peace and order to Cuba. To do that, he was willing to hold elections for an assembly that could make plans for a new presidential election. Batista, upon the completion of his term, would retire completely from public and political life.

Smith paused. The State Department experts eyed him coldly, but none appeared eager to talk. Rivero Agüero's main concern, he went on, was American support. He especially wanted to know if the United States would make at least a token shipment of arms to his regime as a gesture of support. Smith knew that was the main point. He was convinced that simply the symbol of America's "big stick" was enough to intimidate any dissidents into giving up.

Almost as an afterthought, Smith added that he had discussed the problem with García Montes, the former prime minister, who might be willing to help. He did not mention that he had asked García Montes to lobby the very men he was talking to.

After a long silence, Assistant Secretary Rubottom asked for specifics on the situation of American businesses.

Smith replied with what he could remember: The United Fruit Company, which had large sugar-mill holdings in Oriente Province, had suffered about $250,000 in losses. The Cuban-American Sugar Company had lost about $300,000, much of it in eleven railway bridges which had been destroyed by the rebels. Texaco was complaining. Standard Oil of New Jersey was secretly guessing that its sales in Oriente would be only about 20 percent of what they'd been a year before. And the president of the Manati Sugar Company was claiming that Batista air force bombers had caused $1.5 million worth of damage and killed ten civilians on his property.

The real problem was that the *zafra* was approaching, and one "thoroughly reliable" source was guessing that the rebels would stop at least 35 percent of the sugar crop from being sent to market. That could mean an economic disaster for both American investment and the country as a whole. "Something," said Smith, staring straight at Assistant Secretary Rubottom, *"has* to be done."

Rubottom considered that advice silently for a few moments, then glanced over at the assistant who was taking notes. He waited till the young man was done scribbling before he started speaking.

The United States, he said, was sympathetic to Rivero Agüero's attempts to bring peace, but it was still a Cuban internal matter. Only the Cubans, in the end, could provide the solution. If Batista retired and separated himself completely from politics, if Rivero won the support of the civic groups and nonviolent opposition, if the Church and the military backed his efforts, then the United States might reconsider its position toward the president-elect's regime, but American support might be something other than arms. Rubottom added that he meant Rivero obtaining the support of Cuba as a whole, but not necessarily of Castro and his 26th of July Movement.

Wieland nodded approvingly to every Rubottom "if." He was certain that the conditions were impossible to fulfill, that the time had long since passed for a Batista successor to have a chance for success. He knew that after one fraudulent election, no one would believe the promise that the next would be honest. But he could see that the ambassador was listening to each "if" as if it were a challenge, a hurdle for him to overcome.

An assistant asked Smith about Batista's role in the new government. Smith said Batista had told him he wasn't going to leave Cuba, because he didn't want people to think he was deserting his supporters. But he was planning to retire completely from politics.

Wieland shifted in his chair. To him, that was the crucial point. As long as Batista remained in Cuba, everyone would assume that he was still controlling events behind the scenes. That would prohibit any attempts at a peaceful settlement. It was *essential,* he said, for Batista to leave the country, if only for a few months, if Rivero's plan were to have any chance for success.

Assistant Secretary Rubottom agreed. Had Rivero cleared his ideas with Batista?

Smith replied he thought it unsuitable to ask Batista that question directly, but because of Rivero's close ties to Batista, he assumed that Rivero's efforts had Batista's approval.

Wieland leaned back in his chair and groaned. He had vowed to himself not to get worked up, not to allow his arrogance to show, not to reveal that he knew far more about Cuban politics than this amateur ambassador. But he could not help himself. "Listen," he said, voice rising, "this guy is purely a Batista stooge. This can't go down."

Smith jolted, his hands clenching the arms of the chair, but he kept his voice calm. "He's seemingly not a strong character, I admit, particularly in comparison with Batista. But he's intelligent and able and once he's inaugurated, he may prove stronger and more resolute than he now appears to be." He stared at Wieland for a moment, then added, "And he's the only hope there is, unless you want to witness a Communist government in the Western Hemisphere."

Wieland grimaced. The Communist specter had surfaced again. "Well, why don't you give us the benefits of your intelligence? Maybe there's something we're not seeing in the reports."

Smith tensed. He could not believe that these men were denying facts that he had accepted long ago. "I've told you countless times. Look at the men around Castro. His brother Raúl was a member of the Communist youth. And one of his top lieutenants is that Argentine, Ché Guevara. He's a Marxist; he was connected with the pro-Communist government in Guatemala. How many more connections do you need?"

Wieland shook his head. "We know all that, of course. But that doesn't make it a Communist-*dominated* movement. There are plenty of moderates in it as well. Far more moderates than radicals."

Smith's face was flushed. "What the government needs is arms."

"If you can prove," Wieland said, still repeating their longtime argument, "that there is a Communist threat to the hemisphere, that aid is coming from Moscow, then the arms can be released. Not before."

Again, Smith disagreed. He said he wasn't trying to deny the problems of Batista's government. It had been in power too long. Certainly, corruption and violence existed. But the choice now was simply between Batista's handpicked successor and Castro. There were no other alternatives.

"Sure there are," said Wieland with open anger. "Go to Miami, and you'll find dozens of moderate exiles who hate Batista and distrust Castro. It's not an either-or situation."

"Nonsense," Smith blurted.

With that, Assistant Secretary Rubottom raised his hand, open palm, in a gesture of peace. He suggested it was time for lunch.

As they trooped out the door, Wieland was convinced the disastrous meeting had been another step toward bloody chaos. If Smith would only listen, if Smith could make Batista understand that his handpicked puppet was no solution, then there might still be time to come up with a peaceful, moderate alternative.

Smith left, feeling despondent, for exactly the opposite reason. To him, the meeting's inconclusive end had been another nail in Batista's coffin, and therefore in the coffin of the entire Free World.

4/THE DICTATOR

It was shortly after noon on Thursday, November 27, when three olive-green Oldsmobiles, sirens blaring, sped down Malecón Boulevard. Near the mouth of the harbor, the convoy squealed onto a side street, rushed past a block-long plaza and stopped in front of a massive iron gate at one side of the Presidential Palace. A squad of palace guards, in white uniforms trimmed with gold, raced from the sentry house and peered into the cars.

In the center Oldsmobile, sitting directly behind the chauffeur, Lieutenant Colonel Irenaldo García Baez, the mid-thirties chief of the feared Servicio de Inteligencia Militar (SIM), impatiently drummed his fingers on the slender briefcase on his lap, his hand occasionally coming to rest on one corner, where his father's initials were engraved in gold. Inside was a report marked, "SECRET. FOR THE PRESIDENT ONLY." It contained details of a military conspiracy uncovered just that morning, a plot that was both absurd and frightening. García Baez had been up since dawn, personally handling the interrogations of the dozen or so officers involved. Several had been close friends from his military days. "*Loco*," he mumbled to himself—crazy.

Shaking his head, he stared up at the baroque palace, its three-story exterior littered with gold-painted ornamentation and topped by an elaborate golden dome. The palace had never been intended to be a fortress, but it had that aura now: the burgundy drapes on all the windows were closed over steel plates, as a protection against assassins' bullets.

At last, when his patience was almost exhausted, the palace gate creaked open, and the SIM vehicles sped through. When they stopped by the side entrance, García Baez made certain his gray suit coat was buttoned, then leaped from the car and, cradling the briefcase, ran through the door. Inside, a guard gave him a crisp salute. He waved and bounced up the broad marble staircase, his squat legs having to stretch to take the steps two at a time, each step echoing in the large hall. At the top, down a short corridor, another guard opened a steel grating which led to a two-man elevator.

As the contraption whined upward, García Baez marveled, as he always did when he was in it, that this small machine had saved Batista's life twenty months before, when a group of university students, members of the Directorio Revolucionario, had charged the palace. They had slaughtered the guards on the first floor and, in bloody fighting, managed to climb the marble staircase to the second floor. They went no farther. Batista was in his private quarters on the third floor, and the only access to him was by the elevator, locked a few feet above their heads.

Now, an aide-de-camp opened the elevator door and showed the SIM colonel to a small waiting room, lit only by a small lamp with a flowery shade. Still cradling his briefcase, he sat down on a French provincial chair. It was, he knew, an unusual time for him to come to the palace. Batista would still be in his bathrobe, reading the newspapers. Generally, the president did not get up before ten. That morning had been an exception: García Baez had insisted that Batista be awakened and informed of the aborted coup.

As he resumed his finger-drumming on the briefcase, García Baez wondered how to break the news, whether he should begin with the most startling, the most distressing news, the apparent "American connection." Perhaps, he decided, he should take it slowly: Batista would probably be short-tempered after being awakened so early.

The whole thing seemed bizarre. The officers involved, mostly majors and lieutenants, were unlikely candidates for a coup. They had no personal following, no charisma. They were nothing more than loyal drones, or would have been in normal times. But the November election had sent a tremor of fear through all army officers, a fear that Batista might abandon them and leave the country to a weak-willed nonentity. The army was in turmoil, no question about it. Fear, ambition for advancement—everything seemed to be mixed together.

To García Baez, Cuba was a land of sheep and opportunists. He was certain no more were against the regime now than had been six years ago, but movements in Cuban politics always had a bandwagon effect— once they reached a certain momentum, there was no holding back because everyone wanted to join in. That moment seemed to be approaching, because many were sensing the regime's vulnerability: the arms embargo, the failed summer offensive and then the fraudulent election.

García Baez grimaced at the thought of the election. He and many of the other hard-liners in the army, the *tanquistas*, had urged Batista to forget about the election, that it was an indication of weakness, something which would incite the bloodlust of the fickle Cubans. Maintain a show of strength, and the people would turn back into sheep. That was the attitude of his father, Brigadier General Pilar García, chief of the National Police and one of Batista's oldest followers; and that was García Baez's own attitude too. If anything, he was even more dedicated than his father, always pressing for sterner measures against dissidents, always watchful for what he considered the greatest danger, a military coup d'etat.

That had always been the most serious threat in Cuba. For decades, the enormous Camp Columbia in Havana had been the source of all power in the country. With more than five thousand soldiers, a battalion of T-17 tanks, squads of B-26s and Sea Fury fighters, 75-millimeter howitzers and .30-caliber tripod machine guns, Columbia had been able to crush any civilian opposition, usually by simply rumbling the tanks into the streets and watching the insurrectionists flee in terror.

García Baez was convinced that the real danger lay within, that some military officer might topple Batista by gaining control of Columbia. That seemed to him to be a far greater possibility than a take-over by the rebel army, and he was always suspicious when General Eulogio Cantillo, the army officer facing the bulk of the rebel forces in Oriente Province, asked for more men and weapons, as he often did, because if Cantillo collected too much power outside Columbia, he himself became a threat to the regime.

*   *   *

The man who had proved the military and political importance of Camp Columbia—had in fact proved it twice—was Fulgencio Batista himself. He was the mulatto son of a cane cutter, born in a United Fruit Company port in northern Oriente Province, raised in La Guira, the "colored section" of the company town, literally on the other side of the tracks from the American area. As a child, he had lain awake nights listening to the whistles of the trains and hoping one day to escape.

At age fourteen, he left home, working as a cane cutter, water boy, timekeeper for a work gang; he hung around railway depots and shipyards, picking up odd jobs, serving as a helper for a tailor, carpenter and barber until, at twenty, he joined the army as a private. There, he received the equivalent of a high-school education and learned to take shorthand. His quick mind and magnetic personality quickly earned him friends and admirers. *El mulato lindo,* they called him—the beautiful mulatto.

In 1933, while only a sergeant-stenographer, he received his chance when the repressive right-wing dictatorship of Gerardo Machado, beset by radical youths and economic woes, collapsed in bloodshed. Briefly, a weak, liberal regime ruled, but it could do nothing to end the violent chaos. On September 4, Batista and several other sergeants led a rebellion. Within hours, the country was theirs. Within days, Batista had emerged as the new *caudillo,* the charismatic strong man. Using a succession of puppet presidents and a strong military, he ruled Cuba throughout the thirties without serious opposition. In 1940, he approved a very liberal constitution and ran for president himself.

Elected easily, he selected for his cabinet two leaders of the Cuban Communist party, which had some strength among organized labor. It was the first time in the Western Hemisphere that Communists had received such high positions, but there was no uproar in Cuba; the party was considered too small to mount any real threat, and its leadership pledged to support the democracy.

Four years later, adhering to the constitution which prohibited presidents from serving consecutive terms, Batista dutifully left office and retired to his estate in Daytona Beach, Florida. He had become an enormously wealthy man, but he was not as wealthy as he wanted to be. His problem was romance. About the time he left office, he divorced his first wife, whom he had wed when only a corporal, and married a pale-skinned beauty named Marta Fernández. Batista told friends that they had met when his limousine knocked her off her bicycle, but some aides said that wasn't true, that they had been introduced when she and several girlfriends had gone to a party at Camp Columbia.

Whichever version was correct, there was no doubt that he was infatuated with her. The divorce cost money, and the new wife, who had blatant social ambitions, was not at all hesitant about spending more. Her closets contained hundreds of dresses, rows of shoes and handbags, shelves of hats. Her husband never complained.

In the late forties, Batista moved back to Cuba and prepared to run again for the presidency. He tried to forget his sergeant-dictator past, but Cuba's upper class wouldn't let him. His most bitter moment came when the Havana Yacht Club, the leading social organization in Cuba, rejected his application for membership. His impoverished upbringing, his mixed ancestry, his authoritarian leanings—he simply wasn't one of them.

At the same time, many officers were becoming restive. The two democratic administrations that had followed Batista's had been beset by corruption and a chaos that often led to violence. Some top military leaders had been forced to retire, because the politicians feared they might lead coups, and other officers were bitter that they had suffered a loss of status under democracy.

Thus, when the opportunity for regaining money and power presented itself, Batista grabbed at it quickly. A dozen cohorts, a few courageous moments at 2:30 in the morning at Camp Columbia, and it was all over. Army officers shouted their support, the politicians fled and within three days the country appeared to be back to normal. Colonel García Baez was not the only *tanquista* to think that reaction revealed a people who were either sheep or opportunists.

Yet, almost as soon as he established control, Batista worried about his image. He refused to wear an army uniform or even be photographed alongside military men. He tried repeatedly to gain popularity by granting amnesties, holding dubious elections and telling reporters that he considered himself "a democratic dictator."

Many of his supporters thought he was silly even to attempt to woo public opinion, especially that of the snobbish elite. They thought he should stick with his own kind, the military men, the ones who had struggled without benefit of wealthy parents or a law degree from the University of Havana.

Batista never really listened to that advice, and he continued to try to imitate the upper class by affecting a stiff formality. Even in casual situations, he replied with flowery phrases, almost a reciting of etiquette books, until sometimes his aides wanted to laugh. Always, his face maintained a stonelike expression, empty of all emotion, showing neither fear, nor anger, nor happiness. Not even his eldest son, Rubén, could penetrate his cold exterior, and a close associate, Senator García Montes, his onetime prime minister, used to joke to him, "Paraphrasing the sultans of Turkey, if one hair of your beard knew your secrets, you'd shave it off."

Each aide, each associate, received a small piece of the puzzle, a limited view of what Batista was thinking, but no one knew it all. To the politicians, he downplayed the military men. To the military, he joked about the politicians. But he never allowed his internal discipline to slip.

His self-control was especially awesome when he ate, something he could do literally for hours, eating nonstop until he took a short break and disappeared into the garden. There he stuck his head behind a tree and vomited in a short, powerful burst. When he was finished, he wiped his mouth with a white linen handkerchief and resumed eating as if nothing had happened. Only his closest aides ever saw him do that, and most admired him for it, for the degree of control it showed. Some even tried to imitate him.

His control of the government was just as tight, though it resembled more the organization of a large criminal mob than it did a traditional government. Everyone received minuscule government paychecks, but the real salaries were paid monthly in cash, distributed in plain brown envelopes. Special favors were awarded by bonuses, also in cash. The amounts varied widely. A palace bodyguard received $2500 in cash at Christmastime, but an army major who had just returned from a bitter battle with the rebels opened his envelope to find only a single 100-peso note.

The income for these payments came from nearly every sector of the government. For public works' projects, the administration paid the contractors, who returned 30 percent of the money, in cash, to the Presidential Palace. Other funds came from kickbacks on "development loans," customs duties and two types of lotteries: the legal national lottery and the illegal *bolitas*. Every regimental army commander in the provinces was required to send Batista $15,000 a month out of the countryside gambling money: that amounted to more than a million a year. An even bigger slice came from Havana's elegant casinos: $1.28

million monthly, always paid on Mondays at noon, when a representative of the Meyer Lansky–controlled mob slipped into the palace's side door with a bulging briefcase. Batista himself never met the man; a relative served as intermediary.

Much of the money went right back out again. The chief of Havana police received $730 a month for his role in gambling operations alone. Another $450,000 was given monthly for "publicity," to journalists, longtime friends and even some who were publicly considered to be mild Batista opponents. The latter were paid for simply stating that the November election had been an honest one. Most were given their money at the palace, by Presidential Secretary Andrés Domingo Morales del Castillo, but some preferred to collect their brown envelopes at the more secluded Camp Columbia, where the payments were made by Brigadier General Francisco ("Silito") Tabernilla, Batista's military liaison. Some of the largest "bonuses" went to the police "enforcers," the ones whose use of torture, beatings and murder helped keep the opposition subdued. Batista himself rarely talked to his police chiefs and was never seen with them; they knew what they were supposed to do, and it was effective, though more along the lines of old-fashioned bullying than modern systematic terror.

Despite all these payments, there was still enough money left over for El Presidente to own sugar plantations, cattle ranches, most of a small airline called Aerovías Q and many other properties which no one could trace. Like his wife, he had a special affection for clothing, and his closets were larger than good-sized living rooms. In his countryside plantation, he had one wall lined with fifty white linen suits. The other wall held fifty blue and gray suits, and each suit had a pair of brown or black shoes. He also had a wine cellar (used primarily to store French champagne), and a king-sized bed, then an extreme rarity in Cuba.

For most of each week, he stayed downtown in the palace, with his wife and the four children from his second marriage. The first floor consisted of a giant lobby and public rooms; the second, a formal Hall of Mirrors, cabinet room and official office; and the third, where he spent most of his time, contained the family's private quarters. But even that was not particularly private, with most of the rooms opening onto a courtyard that ran down to the first floor. All the rooms had marble floors and tall ceilings, chambers of echoes amidst the delicate Persian rugs and the dainty provincial furniture. It was never a comfortable place, and on weekends Batista enjoyed escaping to Kuquine, his plantation house a few minutes' drive outside the city. There, with squads of machine-gun-carrying bodyguards patrolling the grounds, he could relax.

Wherever he was, he invariably awoke about ten in the morning, read the newspapers while sipping a watered-down coffee and flipped through the four intelligence reports, each of which was twenty pages of single-spaced information. An aide, Captain Alfredo Sadulé, would sometimes read him the juicier tidbits of what they called "the novel," the transcripts of telephone wiretaps on the most prominent people in the country, both his friends and foes. About 1:00 P.M., he ate, showered and dressed, then went to the formal second-floor office for a series of meetings with politicians and outsiders; late at night was reserved for get-togethers with his cronies and military men, and it was often midnight before he sat down to dine. After that, he and his aides usually went into his private projection room, where they saw the latest American films. Batista's favorites, according to his press secretary, were Boris Karloff and Dracula movies. On Sunday nights, he went to the presidential house at Camp Columbia, where he played canasta for relatively small stakes ($10 to $50 a game) with his friends. Only years later did Senator García Montes learn that Batista cheated: aides, hovering around the table for drink orders, would signal to El Presidente what the opponents' cards were.

That petty card cheating, just like his brown-envelope bribery, his policemen's bullying, his casually opulent habits—everything about him, in fact, spoke of the era of the *caudillo*, the style which had ruled Latin America for much of the nineteenth century and the early years of the twentieth, the style in which the fattest men became police sergeants because their weight equaled power. It was a style Batista understood well. He was careful, always, to protect himself against a military coup, and he assumed his greatest political opponent was the man he had overthrown, Carlos Prio, who was in exile in Miami. The traditional army threat, the traditional political threat, were dangers he could comprehend, but he could not see beyond that. While Castro used Radio Rebelde to broadcast directly into the homes of Cubans, Batista still relied on stilted press releases. While Castro was adapting sophisticated techniques of guerrilla warfare, Batista hoarded his tanks in Camp Columbia as he had always done. For the summer offensive in the Sierra

Maestra, he had followed troop movements on an Esso road map that had only a blank space where the mountains were. More detailed maps could have been devised, but it never occurred for him to ask.

Yet he was so confident, so forceful, that those around him continued to share his vision. Even that summer, when he had suffered a stroke at his Varadero beach house, his subordinates' faith had not waned. The stroke turned out to be minor; for a month, he remained secluded until the slight twitch around the corners of his mouth and upper lip went away. It was such a small thing, and sensitive, that not even his son Rubén was told. After all, El Presidente was a mere fifty-seven, and when his health returned to normal, he seemed to be once again the *macho* leader he had been all his life. He hated humiliation above everything else, despised anything that threatened his dignity, and most of his followers, including García Baez, assumed that their leader would die fighting if it came to that.

The SIM colonel was lost in thought when an aide signaled that Batista was ready to see him. Clutching the briefcase, he marched through the door into the informal living room, where Batista, dressed in a burgundy-colored bathrobe, was semi-reclined on a sofa. The strong man was hanging up a telephone with one hand as he waved with the other for García Baez to sit down.

As the colonel selected a French provincial chair facing the sofa, he scanned Batista's face to see if the telephone call had something to do with the attempted coup, but the brownish face and high cheekbones were as immobile as ever. Perhaps he had just heard one account of the coup and wanted to compare it with the SIM version.

"Well?" Batista's voice was neutral.

García Baez slipped a typed report from his briefcase and started to hand it over. The strong man shook his head; he wanted it explained verbally.

"Do you want me to start at the beginning, Mr. President?" García Baez asked, slightly nervous as he always was in the presence of his leader.

Batista nodded.

"Well . . . early this morning, about dawn, the plot was discovered. A lieutenant from the tank corps, he had been approached by the conspirators last night. There were only about six, ten of them, mostly tank corps, none had a rank above major." The words rushed out, and he tried to slow down as he went on to explain that the lieutenant had revealed the conspiracy about breakfast time to Brigadier General Silito Tabernilla, the president's military liaison. The young officer and Tabernilla were *compadres*, godfathers to each other's children, and he had told everything he knew. Tabernilla had then telephoned the ringleader, a major, and used a pretext to meet him at the tank garages. There, he had arrested the man and ordered him to SIM headquarters.

"He was a classmate of mine at the military academy," said García Baez. "A friend. But I interrogated him myself. I told him, 'Look, we've known each other a long time. I don't want to use any "wrong methods" to get you to talk.'" The major had known exactly what "wrong methods" meant and he had talked quickly, naming others. Within an hour or two, all the plotters had been arrested, with the exception of one lieutenant who had managed to gain asylum in a Latin-American embassy.

The others talked readily. They said they had done their planning over drinks in local bars. The discussions had never been serious. Just the stuff of liquor. They had never set a specific date, never even agreed to a specific plan, but they had talked to a lieutenant who was an aide to General Martín Díaz Tamayo, and there was some indication the general was involved. He hadn't given his approval to the plan, but he certainly knew about it and hadn't reported it to the authorities as was his duty.

García Baez paused. He thought he saw Batista wince at the mention of the general, but he couldn't be sure. The general had been one of El Presidente's own co-conspirators in the 1952 coup.

The colonel decided to go on. Picking his own words with care, he said he didn't think the plotters were really a serious threat. He needed to do more checking on the general, that might just prove to be rumor, and the others were young, lower-echelon officers who had no personal following.

"But," he added, "there is one very disturbing connection." He paused. "A connection with the Americans. The chief political officer at the embassy. A Mr. Topping. One of the officers talked to him, in a secret meeting, about the conspiracy. This Mr. Topping urged the conspirators on. He was very supportive."

Batista grunted. "Do you think the officer said that just to save his own neck?" Both men knew they wouldn't dare execute someone the Americans supported; they needed Washington's help too much for that.

García Baez shook his head. "I'm convinced he was telling the truth. The whole truth." *

"It was a Mr. Topping? Not a Mr. Williamson?" The voice was still cold and distant.

"No, no." He knew Batista meant Bill Williamson, who had been the CIA's number two man at the embassy. Williamson had been extremely close to the plotters of a naval uprising at Cienfuegos more than a year before. "They transferred Williamson a few months ago. This is Mr. Topping. In the political section."

Batista stared straight at him. García Baez could sense the man's anger building, but he couldn't see it.

"This," Batista said slowly, "must be reported to the ambassador. It is not tolerable. The Americans knowing of all these conspiracies . . ." His voice trailed off. Then, after a long pause: "Thank you."

García Baez knew he was being dismissed. Sliding the report back into the briefcase, he strode out quickly, his mind spinning. His friends turning into conspirators, the Americans plotting against the Batista regime, which had always been completely pro-American. He felt a slight queasiness. Nothing seemed to make sense anymore.

That evening, Ambassador Smith, tired from an exhausting day, was playing bridge at the Havana Yacht Club. Dressed in a white suit, he was in the cardroom, where thick drapes muffled the murmurs of the players. Seated across the table was his wife Florence, a pert brunette more than ten years younger than Smith. Their opponents were an elderly Cuban couple who belonged to the club.

For Cubans, it had been just another workday, but for Americans, this Thursday was Thanksgiving, and Smith had endured the usual ambassadorial ritual, reading President Eisenhower's holiday proclamation at the Holy Trinity Cathedral, then making an appearance at the American Club in Old Havana, where families were eating the traditional turkey, cranberry sauce, sweet potatoes and pumpkin pie.

---

* Not necessarily. None of the conspirators mentioned that the group was in touch with the Havana leaders of Castro's 26th of July Movement: Comandantes Diego, Comacho, Echemendía and Sergio Sanjenís. Also, it appears probable that Topping merely listened and did not encourage.

Still full from the meal, he tried to keep his mind on the cards, but when he was dummy for a hand, his thoughts drifted back to Dispatch 292, classified "confidential," which he had received the day before from the State Department. Technically, it was a reiteration of what had been discussed at the Saturday meeting in Washington, but it went well beyond the statements made then by Assistant Secretary Rubottom. All of the ifs about support for the regime of President-elect Rivero Agüero were still there, but this time it was stated flatly that the United States would not send arms because that "would invite reprisals against U.S. and U.S. citizens and interests in Cuba, and have serious domestic and hemisphere repercussions." And, most importantly, Washington for the first time had expressed a direct concern about Batista's role in restoring peace: "Unless Batista agrees to absent himself from country after February and remain completely aloof, [the] political-scene prospects for Rivero's success would be remote."

To Smith, that whole concept seemed preposterous. He was certain Batista's presence was needed to give stability to the new regime; the only alternative was Communism and Castro. And he was convinced that the advice was beyond the bounds of some lower-echelon bureaucrats. He was not about to inform the pro-American leader of another country that the United States wanted him to abandon his fatherland.

Smith was still immersed in his worries when he felt a light tap on his shoulder. It was Mario Lazo, a Cuban lawyer who had been educated in the United States. Almost as tall as Smith, Lazo had many American clients, and he often slipped valuable information to the U.S. embassy. Leaning close to Smith's ear, he whispered, "I have something important to tell you."

Smith nodded apologetically to the other players and slipped from his chair. If Lazo said it was important, there was no doubt it was. He followed the lawyer to a quiet corner in an adjoining room.

The man seemed unusually tense. "You are to be summoned to Washington," he said in a low, careful voice. "Someone is going to be sent to Havana to talk with Batista about the appointment of a junta to replace him." Batista was to be allowed to fly to his estate in Daytona Beach. "I was told the American ambassador is not to know about it. . . . To protect you, so that if Batista asks, you can say you know nothing about it."

Smith was speechless. A Cuban had just told him top-secret information which he, the ambassador, knew nothing about. Could it be mere rumor? He was certain it wasn't. Lazo was too reliable to repeat anything that wasn't the absolute truth.

About 9:00 A.M. the next morning, Smith strode glumly out of the elevator onto the fifth floor of the U.S. embassy. As he marched past his secretary's desk, he bellowed, "Get me Topping." Edith Elverson, his loyal aide, nodded and reached for the telephone.

Smith had just received his second piece of jarring news. At a meeting in the home of Prime Minister Gonzalo Güell, he had been informed that John Topping, the chief political officer and the number three man at the embassy, had encouraged the conspiring army officers. It was astounding news, but Smith believed it. For months he had suspected that Topping was sympathetic to the anti-Batista groups. He had let some of Topping's pro-revolutionary comments pass, but this latest information required a confrontation.

Walking through the massive double doors, Smith entered his wood-paneled office. A color photograph of President Eisenhower was the only adornment on the walls, but an American flag and the blue flag of an ambassador stood on stands behind his massive walnut desk.

Almost immediately, Topping ambled into the room. With a full head of brown hair not quite combed into place, a wry smile and a light tropical suit that seemed casually Ivy League, Topping looked exactly like what he was, a mid-forties New York intellectual, a type Smith had always disliked.

Drumming his fingers on the desk top, Smith nodded him toward a chair. "Batista and Güell are very unhappy," he said, not trying to hide his anger. Briefly, he explained what the arrested army officer had told the SIM chief.

Topping's face flushed. "I didn't give them encouragement, you should know that. . . . You knew everything I was doing." He mentioned Dispatch 552, which he had written three days before, outlining everything the conspirators had told him. "You knew everything."

With a mounting anger, Topping recounted what happened. Several politicians and military officers had come to his house one morning to talk about a plan, and Topping had listened without offering the slightest encouragement, saying that the United States had a policy of strict nonintervention in the internal affairs of Latin-American nations.

Washington wanted to see "an early return to tranquillity and order," but hoped it could "be accomplished by the duly constituted and recognized government." It was the usual statement made in such a situation, and Topping had added, pro forma, "We don't want any details."

Moreover, the officers' plan had seemed unusually vague, and he guessed "they were scared of what would happen if Castro came in. They were looking to land on their feet" by being able to show the rebels that they too had been opposed to the dictatorship. Probably, they wanted a meeting with a U.S. official as a status symbol—so they could boast that they were "in contact with the American embassy"—and as a protection in case they were arrested.

Smith eyed him coldly. He didn't believe Topping's version, but rather than argue, he turned to sarcasm. He said that when Prime Minister Güell had mentioned the "American connection," Smith had to defend him, as he would any staff member, by saying, "He's an employee of the American government. I'm sure he's done nothing like that."

Topping nodded as if that settled the affair, then changed the subject. He wanted to know if Smith had transmitted to the prime minister the information of Dispatch 292, about the need for Batista to leave if peace were to be restored.

It was Smith's turn to flush. "But, John, you know I can't communicate that. My [basic] instructions come from the White House, and until the White House changes them, I've got to stick by it."

"Well, listen," Topping demanded, "go up to Washington. *Talk* to the White House. And get them to instruct you again." He said he was convinced the telegram was correct, that Batista had to leave, and if the United States played a part in his removal, it would bolster the sagging American image among Cubans. He mentioned to a close friend, Rufo López-Fresquet, a liberal attorney married to an American woman, a leader in the pro-Castro Civic Resistance. "'Trust us, John, trust us,' he keeps telling me. 'If Fidel turns out to be a problem, we politicians and moderates will be able to handle him once we get into office.'"

Smith cursed. He started to argue, but clamped his mouth shut: this was just an extension of an endless debate they had been having for months, and it was obvious to him that Topping had the same leftist sympathies as some of the Washington crowd. None of them seemed to understand that Batista and President-elect Rivero Agüero were the only alternative to Castro and Communism. With a wave of his hand, he dismissed his chief political officer.

As the man left the room, Smith scribbled a note to himself. He was going to demand that Washington transfer Topping somewhere else immediately.

5/THE GENERAL

Hundreds of feet above the Oriente hills just outside of Santiago de Cuba, the single-engine Piper airplane floated over the landscape, occasionally dipping down for a closer look at the arroyos, where dense clusters of bamboo and shrubs obscured the ground. The right door of the army plane had been removed, so that a machine gunner could strafe the hills, but on this trip, the front passenger seat was occupied by Major General Eulogio Cantillo, the chief of the Santiago garrison and the ranking military officer in Oriente Province.

Several days before, Cantillo had sent out an army convoy to reinforce the besieged cuartel at El Cristo, only a few minutes' drive from Santiago. A land mine demobilized the lead tank, and the rest of the convoy had retreated to the safety of the city. Now, all Cantillo could do was learn what was happening to the men in the cuartel. They had said via radio they were going to make a run for it.

"What's that?" The pilot pointed toward an unpaved road to their right. Cantillo signaled for him to drop down for a closer look. As the plane descended, he pulled the M-2 carbine from the rear seat and rested it on his knees.

Checking to make sure that his seat belt was tight, he leaned over to see a railroad freight car blocking a gravel road. Several army jeeps and cars were in a ditch nearby, next to a canefield. Corpses of soldiers were strewn among the cars. Nothing moved.

Cantillo motioned for the pilot to make another pass. This time, he saw a dozen rebels in the shade beside a stream, walking away from the ambush site. A rage building inside of him, he raised the carbine to his shoulder and fired off several quick shots as the plane swooped past. It was almost impossible to hit a target with a rifle from a plane, but Cantillo wanted to try. "Again," he shouted at the pilot. The Piper descended almost to the tree tops and Cantillo fired several more rounds as the last of the rebels disappeared into the underbrush.

As they climbed, he shook his head and shouted to the pilot to return to Santiago; there was nothing more they could do. Placing the carbine on the rear seat, he raised himself slightly so he could pull a pack of king-sized Chesterfields from his rear pants pocket. The cigarette, as usual, was slightly wrinkled. An aide was constantly suggesting he carry them in a shirt pocket, but he believed firmly that the telltale bulge the pack made looked unprofessional.

That dedication to appearances was indicative of the man. Fifty years old, with a receding hairline and a pencil-thin mustache that accented his high cheekbones, he had developed the bearing of a commanding officer and combined it with a more characteristic avuncular smile. His father had been a sergeant in the Rural Guards, but Cantillo, after attending the American Presbyterian School in rural Havana Province, had wanted to go to the University of Havana. That dream was killed by the Depression. He was forced to eke out a living by selling socks and Singer sewing machines; during the *zafra*, he went to the fields to cut cane. In 1933, he grabbed at a chance to join the army. It meant a guaranteed paycheck, food, housing and a free education. At the military academy, for every month of his four years, he was number one in his class, always doing the best on tests, always the most eager to please his teachers. Promotions came quickly, and three times he received the greatest plum the Cuban army had to offer: training in the United States with the American army.

The one threat to his comfortable life, and it was a considerable one, was politics, for in Cuba politics and the army were always intertwined. He had managed to survive three changes of administration by learning a small art: how to be friendly with everyone. He tried to balance himself delicately on the political fence, shunning the excessive ambition that would make people think he was a threat to the established order. His sternest test came when Fulgencio Batista and a small band of followers tried to take over Camp Columbia in 1952. Cantillo, then a colonel and chief of the air force, hovered cautiously for several hours between the Batista group and the democratically elected Prio government. Only when he had no doubt about the outcome did he agree to support Batista. Within a few days, he was promoted to brigadier general.

The civil war confused him at first. The Cuban army had never fought a real war before, and, despite all its training by the Americans, the officers were accustomed to the comfortable life in Havana and its political nuances. The art of being pleasant was not at all relevant in mountain skirmishes. Cubans were killing Cubans, and it bothered Cantillo. He told friends, "I am fighting them just because they have broken the laws, and I don't want them killed." Such thinking was decidedly limited, since Batista himself had violated the constitution with his coup d'etat, but Cantillo gradually came to realize that most people in Oriente were opposed to the Batista regime, and often for understandable reasons. From his voracious reading of history, he learned that a civil conflict could not be won by bullets alone; the attitude of the people had to be considered.

When he became commander of the Santiago garrison in September, replacing one of the most corrupt and brutal of the Batista generals, he had done what he could to eliminate police torture and mistreatment of rebel prisoners. His measures had earned him at least a modicum of respect from the opposition, and by late 1958, he was the only active field general who had not been denounced by Radio Rebelde as a war criminal. But his careful balancing act between rebel sympathizers and his own military loyalties had produced its own inner tension: Cantillo was a general with an ulcer.

Now, as the Piper descended, flying over the barbed-wire fences which lined the road from Santiago to its airport just outside of town, Cantillo felt a sharp pain in his stomach, a jarring message he had missed his afternoon nap.

The pain reminded him once again of his fear that all his moves to appease the people of Oriente might be too late. The rebel ambush he had seen near El Cristo enraged him personally; it was not strategically significant. But he had been getting reports from the neighboring military district of Bayamo about bitter fighting at the town of Guisa. From what he could make out, it was turning into the bloodiest battle of the civil war.

Part Two

The Drive
to the Plains

NOVEMBER 28–DECEMBER 16, 1958

6/"WE CAUGHT A TIGER!"

Fidel Castro moved slowly down the hill toward the scene of destruction. Behind him followed his longtime secretary, Celia Sánchez, carrying on her shoulder, as always, a nylon bag crammed with Castro's letters. On the road below, a Staghound T-17 armored carrier lay upside down in the middle of the pavement. Army trucks, their olive-green paint charred by mine explosions, were jammed into the roadside ditches, with blackened corpses spilling over the sides in back. Stray dogs and pigs nosed at other corpses strewn through the ditches, the gully below the stone bridge and the clumps of trees on the hillside. One eerie body lay with an arm sticking up, its fist clenched in silent protest.

Three times, army relief columns had moved down the road to free the soldiers at the Guisa cuartel, and three times they had been pushed back in terrible fighting. The bloodiest battle had come when mines—explosives in milk cans buried in the road—destroyed the tank and trucks at the front and rear of an army column. An entire army battalion was pinned down between the rebels' hillside trenches for two days, unable to advance or retreat. A second battalion had to rescue the survivors, and they fled back to the regimental garrison at Bayamo. They left behind a T-17 tank, still fully functional but its way blocked by the charred hulks of other vehicles. Altogether, the army had suffered 116 deaths and 80 wounded. The rebels, in their well-sheltered trenches, had only 8 dead and 7 wounded.

Castro examined the intact T-17, then walked to the overturned tank. He was elated about what his young recruits had been able to do, withstanding the daily bombings from the B-26s and the withering machine-gun fire of the convoys. He gloated that the army did not learn from its mistakes, that its officers kept thinking soldiers were safe inside tanks and trucks as they moved time after time directly into rebel ambushes.

Now, examining the charred tank and the wreckage scattered across the landscape, he rejoiced: "We set a trap waiting for a rabbit, and instead we caught a tiger!"

That night, two miles away, First Lieutenant Reinaldo Blanco paced the black-and-red tile floor in the Guisa cuartel as his men munched stale bread and awaited their eighth night of the maddening, sporadic gunfire and out-of-tune singing.

The nights and days had blended together in a nightmarish jumble. He had been forced to listen to the radio in helpless horror as the army commanders caught in the ambushes screamed to the Bayamo garrison for help. The column slaughtered in the two-day battle was the same one which had happily waved good-bye to him while promising to return the next day with supplies. Blanco wondered why the battalion hadn't simply abandoned their overrated tanks and avoided the ambush by walking through the hills. He guessed there had to be at least nine hundred rebels in the area if they could turn back an armored column of three hundred to four hundred men. *

Blanco had tried to keep the spirits of his men up, even drowning out the rebels' obnoxious songs by having soldiers play Afro-Cuban *bembe* and bongo music in the sheltered inner courtyard while others danced. But the constant, all-night harassment frayed the soldiers' nerves and made sleep difficult.

---

* In fact, with the additions of one rebel platoon and some volunteer townspeople after the Guisa fighting began, Castro's Column 1 had only slightly more than two hundred men. Their mines and hilltop trenches were more important than a simple numerical advantage.

Late that evening, so exhausted that the singing of *Ahorita va a llover* faded into a dull noise, Blanco snoozed in his office. He was still sleeping at 2:20 A.M. when a guard manning a machine gun on the roof shouted, "Lieutenant, the column made it through. They've made it. The tanks are coming in."

Instantly awake, Blanco bounded up the ladder. Peering beyond the sandbags, he could barely see the silhouette of one T-17, its large rubber tires making almost no sound on the pavement. He had heard nothing on the radio about tanks coming. "Halt," he shouted. "Stop until you are identified."

The tank slowed, but it continued to creep forward. Blanco repeated his warning. There was no response. "Prepare to fire," he ordered the machine gunners.

"But it's one of ours," a soldier pleaded.

The tank stopped about fifty yards away, near the Esso station. Its turret swung toward the cuartel.

"Fire, fire, fire," Blanco yelled.

The tank fired first, its 37-millimeter cannon hurling a projectile against the cuartel's concrete wall. The soldiers inside rushed to the shelter of the inner courtyard. Blanco and the gunners crouched behind the sandbags. He realized the tank must have been captured by the rebels at the ambush.

The shells kept crashing against the walls but seemed to do little damage. Of course, Blanco thought: They must be high-explosive projectiles, intended to destroy vehicles and people, not to knock down a building. He cursed that his one bazooka was malfunctioning. The misnamed "antitank grenades" he possessed had only a fraction of the power of a bazooka shell; they were almost worthless.

At last, after fifty shells were fired, the tank made a wide turn to leave, swinging into a ditch beyond the Esso station. There it stopped. Its engine roared, but the T-17 went nowhere. Blanco realized it was stuck. He ordered the machine gunners to open fire. Another soldier shot an antitank grenade from his M-1 rifle at the tank's tires.

That seemed to scare the men inside. Seconds later, the tank's hatch opened. The first man out was shot as he leaped to the pavement. A second jumped and began running. A third man popped his head out. Instead of fleeing, he wrestled with the .30-caliber machine gun to remove it from its mount on top of the tank. About thirty soldiers fired at him but none seemed to find the mark. Finally, he freed the gun, jumped off and ran with the weapon into the darkness.

Blanco cursed.

"Did you see that?" a soldier asked him.

"I can't believe it," Blanco muttered.

The next day, Castro personally congratulated Lieutenant Hipólito Prieto, the rebel who had so courageously removed the machine gun from the tank. Blanco was wrong: He had been hit several times, but it had not stopped him from obeying the paramount law of the Sierra, that weapons were never abandoned, regardless of the sacrifice.

At his headquarters, Castro had an even more valuable item captured from the army, a walkie-talkie on which he could listen to conversations between the Guisa cuartel and its Bayamo headquarters. That day, he heard through the crackling static that the regimental commanders had finally gotten smart. The army was going to send in several battalions on foot, walking along trails to the right of the rebel trenches.

Castro grasped immediately what that meant. This time, the army would be mobile, and his men, if they stayed in their trenches facing an empty road, would be the vulnerable ones. Without hesitation, he ordered a message sent to the squads scattered along the road and around the cuartel: Everyone was to withdraw to meet an attack along the rebel flank. They were to set up a new ambush on the trail, complete with mines and traps. "Ave María," he exclaimed to his captains, "when they come through here, we're going to demolish them."

The next morning, Sunday, November 30, Lieutenant Blanco was resting in his cuartel office when a soldier ran in. "Lieutenant, Lieutenant, the column made it."

Blanco dashed to the door. This time it was true. A battalion of about three hundred men, led by officers on horseback, were walking from the town park, the opposite direction from the paved road that led to the Central Highway. The soldiers in the cuartel erupted with a deafening shout of relief. Blanco was not sure what to think. He gazed at the hills where the rebels had been, but there was nothing, not a sound, not a stir. They had completely disappeared.

Getting off his horse, the battalion major embraced the young lieutenant. He said they had left their trucks at a town on the Central Highway and hiked to Guisa in only four hours. While the rebels were facing one battalion on the right flank, he had come through trails on the left unmolested. He ordered Blanco to get his men ready to pull out.

Blanco stared at him. He couldn't believe the command. "But, Major, if we have been able to hang on to Guisa with a hundred men, with four hundred we can beat them," he said, his anger growing.

The major shook his head. "Don't worry about that. As soon as we get out, a full-out counterattack will take place. But I have orders to pull you out."

Blanco looked around at the cuartel and the town he had been defending for eleven days. He had memorized almost every crack in the concrete at the Esso station, and now he was being told it was all for nothing. He knew, if they left, a counterattack would be impossible without running into a bloody ambush. The army had decided to give up the town.

"Well, at least," he said, looking down the road to where the T-17 was rammed into the ditch, "let's take the tank."

"No, we can't take it through the back roads."

Disgusted, Blanco ordered his men to wreck the T-17. While they pulled wires from the dashboard, took out the battery and slashed the tires, Blanco checked on the injured in the dormitory. In the cuartel itself, they had suffered only five wounded, none killed. All five were able to walk.

A short time later, a call came through from the Bayamo garrison. The commander there was abrupt: "You are to follow the orders to withdraw." Apparently, they had been anticipating his objection.

"I will," Blanco said, exasperated, "but I don't agree. This is the time to counterattack."

"Don't be a *comemierda*"—a shit-eater. "Burn the town, kill the prisoners and to hell with everything down there."

"Is that an order?"

There was no reply. That was good. Blanco had no intention of following a command like that. He looked in on his one prisoner, the man wounded when trying to escape from the stranded tank. The man was too weak to walk. Blanco ordered him left with the town doctor.

About 5:00 P.M., casting a backward glance at the cuartel that had become more than a home, Blanco led his men behind the battalion. At the town square, several families were waiting for them, their belongings in bundles at their feet. Blanco was surprised. Most people had fled into the hills during the first days of the siege. One man explained for the group: "We don't know if the rebels will think we supported you all this time by staying. We want to leave."

The civilians tagged along at the end of the column. The sun set soon after they started, and they trudged over a muddy road that was little more than a mule trail. They walked up and down hills and splashed through the water of narrow creeks. Blanco scanned the bushes for signs of an ambush, but it was impossible to see anything in the dark. At last, they reached the Central Highway at the town of Santa Rita. Less than eight miles from where he had been besieged, the streetlights were shining and young couples walked arm in arm as if everything were normal. Blanco was overwhelmed with bitterness—his tenacious struggle had been utterly meaningless.

That evening about 9:00 P.M., Castro led the way into town in a jeep. He had ordered his men not to ambush the retreating column because in the dark on the narrow trail, there was the dangerous possibility of killing civilians. Guisa was still without electricity. The darkened streets and empty buildings had a ghostly air. The rebels were backslapping-happy at their victory, and the townspeople who followed them down from the hills rejoiced that after almost seven years of Batista's rule, they were now part of *Territorio Libre de Cuba*.

Their happiness was soon diminished by another sensation: hunger. The rebel column had almost exhausted its food supplies. Cachita Montejo, a sixteen-year-old redheaded girl who had started the battle carrying hot meals to the men in the hillside trenches, was now herself famished.

Dr. Raúl Trillo watched as Castro talked with the owner of the general store in the town square. "We would like to buy supplies from you," the rebel leader said. "All will be paid for, so you take note, but let the men eat all they wish." The owner agreed gladly.

Rebels rushed into the store. They found candles, which they lit and placed on counter tops. It gave the room an intimate glow. The choices on the shelves were all canned, mostly fruit cocktails and juices. Castro himself picked up two cans of Spanish tuna and, sitting on a box, unrolled the tops.

As he ate with his fingers, he talked to his officers. His thoughts, as always, were rushing ahead. The army retreat, he said, meant that the Bayamo garrison, the main military force they had been facing for the past two years, was admitting defeat. From this moment on, they were going to turn their backs on Bayamo and push in the opposite direction, attacking the towns on the Central Highway to the east, aiming toward the prize of Oriente, the largest and best-equipped garrison in the province, the city that he had tried to win five years before when he launched his attack on the Moncada barracks: Santiago de Cuba.

7/A CITY OF TERROR AND TRANQUILIZERS

By the beginning of December 1958, Santiago de Cuba had become a city that died every night with the onset of darkness. Movie theaters were closed. Restaurants were dark. The bar under the quaintly thatched roof of the city's one modern motel, El Rancho, was empty. On the town square, the Cruz San Carlos Club was missing its old men who normally passed the evenings smoking cigars, playing dominoes and arguing politics.

The only vehicles that moved freely on the streets at night were the blue-and-white police cars, the olive-green Oldsmobiles of the SIM and the battered old autos carrying the men of a private army belonging to Senator Rolando Masferrer. Terrorist bombs exploded at unexpected moments; gunfights broke out in quiet residential suburbs without warning. Occasionally, bodies of youths in the underground appeared on mansion lawns or in the gutters of deserted streets. The police were so trigger-happy that they once fired at a doctor racing to the Centro Gallego Hospital for a late-night emergency. Another time, they shot at the company car of Swift-Armour Meats because it was painted in the corporate colors of red and black, the same as those of Castro's 26th of

July Movement. If people had to drive at night, police instructed them to put on the dome lights in the passenger compartments, but few had faith that would ensure their safety.

Instead, the city's two hundred thousand residents stayed inside their homes, their doors and shutters usually closed in even the hottest weather. Their television sets sat unused: the cable linking the city's antenna with the Havana stations had been cut by the rebels. For the people of Santiago, their one source of uncensored information, their one contact with the outside world, even their one entertainment, was Radio Rebelde and its network of shortwave stations. To the people of Havana, the broadcasts were a matter of distant, vague interest. In Santiago, they were everything, and many listened almost around the clock, even to the odd-hour book codes, transmitting messages to the underground. Sometimes, Castro talked to his brother Raúl in the Sierra Cristal, and they exchanged information.

In recent weeks, a new rebel station, Ocho Chicos Malos, Eight Naughty Boys, had begun booming a powerful signal into Santiago as it mingled news and satirical soap operas in a saucy irreverence. The signal was so strong that everyone knew it had to be coming from the hills just outside the city. For the first time, people tried to imagine what had once seemed impossible: small bands of rebels fighting the army's tanks and cannons on the streets of Santiago itself.

Some people had more immediate worries. Every day, a big, stoop-shouldered man paced through the aisles of his modern supermarket in the upper-class neighborhood of Vista Alegre. Lily Ferreiro was proud of his store, one of the two supermarkets in town, and he thought its all-window front made it look almost like its counterpart in the United States. The year before, he had grossed $500,000, but this year he would be lucky to make half that, and even then he was having to listen to customers moan about the enormous price increases. They didn't understand that when goods became scarce, he had to pay more to get them and that meant he had to charge more.

The real problem, he knew, was the war. The rebel siege had stopped almost all dairy, vegetable and meat supplies coming in from the countryside. Eggs had soared from 4 to 10 cents apiece. Yucca, once a penny or two, was now 25 cents. Ferreiro had no meat on display in his butcher's section, no milk, no potatoes and very little sugar, either brown or white. Canned and powdered milk was almost gone, and even coffee was becoming so scarce that a friend of his had bought a rare two-pound can right out of his hands, before he could put it on the shelf.

Many customers were starting to hoard. Ferreiro tried to assure them that he still had plenty of canned goods in his warehouse and that freighters were able to enter the harbor with no problem, but people were unconvinced. Ferreiro knew why. A rumor was spreading that rebels were in the hills near the western side of the bay's mouth. If they fired a few mortar shells, they could scare away the ships that were the last source of the city's food.

When Ferreiro became depressed about the situation, as often happened, he wandered to the back of the store, where businessmen gathered at a narrow counter to drink small cups of strong Cuban coffee. There, they talked about the news, speculating who in the underground had burned the municipal slaughterhouse or how many rebels were hiding on the edge of town near San Juan Hill, where Teddy Roosevelt had made his famous charge.

Usually, the men's information was accurate, for almost everyone who went to Ferreiro's for coffee was an avid supporter of the 26th of July. Miguel Lemus, who owned Tube Light, a firm specializing in electrical and neon signs, supplied wire used to detonate landmines on the Central Highway. Gerardo Abascal, the president of the Ron Alvarez Camp rum company, had delivered rebel rifles in the trunk of his car.

Ferreiro himself had allowed underground members to use his home. His family had long been friends with Fidel Castro's father Angel, but his politics went far beyond a mere family tie. Like most people in the city, he had been bitterly upset by Batista's coup d'etat. Castro had attracted first Santiago's idealistic youths, many of whom came from affluent families. When their corpses began appearing in the gutters, their elders were enraged, and each corpse brought more members to the 26th of July or its professional-businessmen's arm, the Civic Resistance Movement. Ferreiro himself had experienced his own brush with Batista justice: An army colonel with a group of bodyguards had entered his store and, in front of his customers, beaten him over the back with a large wooden plank "as a warning."

That pain, at least the physical part of it, had long since disappeared, but while he traded rumors with his fellow businessmen, he could see through the window families walking down the street that led from the hills, people with their few possessions tied to their backs or stuffed into carts pulled by donkeys. Ferreiro knew they were fleeing the fighting in the area above the city, escaping the danger and trying to find food, which was even scarcer in the outlying towns than it was in Santiago. At least in the city, families could send their children begging for handouts door to door.

One of those who came down from the hills was a short, plump housewife named Claudia Roses Monte de Oca. For her, it was a round trip of ten miles by foot from her Santiago home to the village of El Caney. It was the nearest place she could get milk for her baby. Twice a week in Santiago, she filled a large milk can with gasoline and carried it up to the hills, where she donated it to the rebels. She cleaned the can, obtained milk from a farmer and returned to her modest, lower-middle-class home. The trip took most of the day, and when she arrived back at her kitchen, she faced a cupboard that often had only spaghetti to feed her family. With soaring prices and scarcity, this pasta, so alien to the Cuban diet, was becoming a staple on her dining table.

Yet she was not complaining about the hardship. Hidden in her house were black-and-red armbands of the 26th of July and olive-green uniforms. They were waiting for the moment when the people of the city could join the rebels in a battle that would be fought house by house, street by street, until the tyranny was defeated.

On H Street, a few blocks away, was a three-bedroom house where Elias Rosales lived with his parents and ten brothers and sisters. A blond twenty-four-year-old, he had to work at a second job, making deliveries for a pharmacist, to pay off the bribe needed to get a job as a telegraph operator. Occasionally, he planted bombs for the underground, but he knew such activities were minor compared to the battle that the rebels would wage in the city. It would probably mean the brutal destruction of his neighborhood, because his house was only four blocks away from the Moncada army garrison. For Rosales, that mattered less than the defeat of the Batista regime, and he found a bitter irony in his neighborhood's name: *El Sueño*—The Dream.

Early every weekday morning, a long line formed outside the glass doors of the U.S. consulate, a modern one-story building with a front of decoratively scrolled concrete blocks. When the staff unlocked the doors, the first twenty Cubans filled the black plastic chairs in the tile-floor foyer and waited for their chance to talk to the clerks behind the counter.

The rest stood outside, in a file which often ran around the corner. Friends and relatives came to chat. Taxi drivers lounged against their fenders as they waited for customers. Outwardly, there was a festive aura of gossip and joke-trading, but sudden silences or darting eyes betrayed an underlying fear. Those near the end of the line watched carefully as the first came out. Some smiled, some frowned, a few looked as though they were about to cry, and it was all due to a simple piece of paper and a stamp on the passport: the invaluable U.S. visa.

Inside the building, in a private office beyond the counter, Park Wollam spent his days in a black upholstered chair in front of a Danish-modern desk. Behind him on a stand was a blue flag with a large white C, the symbol that he was the U.S. consul. Each day, he studied the forms the Cubans filled out and marveled at what an odd, mixed-up city Santiago was. Some visa applications were from Batista supporters, obviously worried about remaining in the city. Many others were from businessmen, seeking an escape for their children. Wollam recognized a considerable number of names. He knew the youths were working with the underground, and their parents were concerned they would either be killed by the police in the city or join the rebels and die in the hills fighting the army. Many fathers were willing to give money to *la causa*, but not the lives of their children. The smart ones requested tourist visas; the honest ones asked for residence permits, which took longer to process and were more likely to be denied.

In all his years serving in Italy and various Latin-American posts, Wollam had never seen anything like Santiago. It was the only city he knew of with a revolutionary Rotary Club. At the meetings, the top businessmen in town complained only about the badly paved streets and the city's disgraceful water supply. In private, they were all giving money to the rebels. Any Batista sympathizers in the club had long since stopped coming to meetings. The Lions Club, where younger business-men met, was the same.

The people even had a kind of upside-down racism. Countless Lions and Rotarians had told him that they never talked about politics in front of their black and mulatto maids, because they assumed most servants identified with the dark-skinned Batista. Wollam wondered if that were really true, but there was no doubt that the Santiago upper class believed it.

When he first arrived in Santiago, he had concentrated on Communism, the primary concern in Washington. At parties, luncheons and informal meetings, he asked civic leaders about the connections between the rebels and the Communists. Invariably, these businessmen said there was no connection at all. Would Rotarians support Communists? Could Fidel Castro, the son of a hardworking Oriente man who had a substantial sugar plantation, be a Communist? Didn't Wollam know that Fidel was a graduate of the best Jesuit schools in Santiago and Havana? Certainly, the Jesuits didn't train Communists.

After a while, townspeople began making cutting jokes about Communism being an American fixation, an imaginary bogeyman irrelevant to the sunny Caribbean, and, ultimately, an excuse to support a right-wing dictator. Again and again, Wollam was hounded by Rotarians, who pleaded that the United States should *do* something to get rid of Batista, restore democracy and end the terrible bloodletting.

Still, only Raúl Castro had ordered any specifically anti-American activities, and these were quickly settled. In July, Wollam flew by helicopter to the Sierra Cristal to negotiate with Raúl for the release of U.S. sailors and marines, kidnapped because the rebels thought the United States was continuing to help Batista. The U.S. military men were so well treated, and so convinced by rebel arguments, that several wanted to stay and help fight Batista. In November, Wollam had to report that Raúl's men had three times turned off the pumps that supplied water to the Guantánamo U.S. Naval Base. Some hotheaded navy officers told Wollam they wanted to send in the marines, but it was a stern warning from Washington, transmitted through an anti-Batista Cuban lobbyist, that finally caused the rebels to change their tactics. Wollam had heard Castro talk by radio to Raúl and tell him, in strict terms, that the water supply was not to be touched again. Since then, there had been no incidents.

Had Fidel been talking seriously on the radio, or had he simply been going through a charade for the Americans' benefit? Many Santiago residents had theories but, as with most information in the city, it was usually farfetched and unreliable. Wollam often said that, if he wanted, every day he could have sent fifty-page reports of "sheer horse manure" to Washington. In fact, Cubans were so eager to repeat stories that CIA agents used to joke that there were three ways of communicating in the country: telephone, telegraph and tell-a-Cuban.

That made some agents laugh, but not Robert Wiecha, the CIA's

somber-faced man in Santiago, who was listed officially as one of
Wollam's vice-consuls. Wiecha struggled to make Cubans understand
the concept of secrecy, and he raged, pacing around the consulate,
when he learned that an informer had left a confidential report with the
other vice-consul, Bernie Femminella, a legitimate member of State,
simply because Wiecha didn't happen to be in the office. Several times,
Femminella witnessed Cubans, recently returned from the hills, waving
American dollars and boasting to other Cubans, "I am working for Mr.
Wiecha, gathering information." *

For both Wollam and the CIA, it was a problem simply getting the
information to Washington. With telephone and telegraph lines to the
rest of Cuba cut, Wollam had to rely on the overseas cable or send
typewritten dispatches on the U.S. Navy plane which flew over weekly
to pick up the base's mail. He preferred the plane, because cables had to
be encoded, and Washington in its wisdom had not seen fit to provide
his lowly consulate with an automatic code machine. That meant he
had to use onetime code pads to encode each message by hand. It could
take thirty minutes to do a simple five-sentence telegram, and most of
his messages were considerably longer.

A faster, but much less private, method was to use a surplus shortwave
transmitter-receiver that the U.S. Navy had installed. It was as large as
two filing cabinets and looked as though it dated from the era of
Marconi, but it worked in establishing a network that included the
naval base and the Havana embassy. Wollam and the other operators
learned to speak a fudging double-talk which they hoped only other
Americans could understand. "El Cristo has ten angels" meant that ten
had died in a battle there. The Santiago consulate became known as

---

* Even so, four State Department officials and one CIA man state that the
CIA had no full-time agent at Castro's headquarters. It was considered
too risky. However, a number of CIA men, posing as journalists, went to
the Sierra. Some were Americans; others were Latin Americans. Even
legitimate U.S. journalists in the 1950s considered it a patriotic duty to
report to the CIA what they learned. Jim Noel, the CIA station chief in
Havana, says Andrew St. George, a free-lance photographer-writer who
made at least two trips to the Sierra, worked closely with one of Noel's
men. Castro says he suspects that some writers were not what they
seemed. After a visit by one whose name he can't remember, Castro
moved his base camp immediately; soon afterward, Batista air force planes
demolished the old site. Castro thinks this was a CIA plot to assassinate
him. His story, however, cannot be confirmed.

"Florida." The Havana embassy was "Shinplaster." That did not fool the many in Santiago who were fluent in English. Like Radio Rebelde, the U.S. network became a real-life soap opera, and they listened attentively. Sometimes, if the consulate didn't answer, people called Wollam's wife at home and told her: "Shinplaster is calling Florida, and he isn't answering."

All of Wollam's reports on the fighting were based on secondhand information, and Wollam yearned for a chance to see for himself what was happening in the hills and on the Central Highway. One afternoon in early December, he got his chance. A U.S. corporate plane was making a trip, and he wangled an invitation to go along. He made a quick call to his wife Connie and told her he would be gone overnight.

That evening, after she put their infant son and nine-year-old daughter to bed, Connie Wollam padded through their large old house on Mandulay Avenue. She double-checked the wrought iron covering the glassless windows and made sure that the large iron bar rested firmly in its brackets, spanning and locking the wooden double doors at the front of the house. With her husband gone, their five-bedroom, one-story home seemed unusually big and eerie. Its twenty-foot ceilings and the bar on the front door reminded her of a medieval castle.

She was a petite woman, with short dark hair, and her slippered footsteps made hardly any sound on the tile floor as she turned off the lights in the dining room and moved down the broad hallway which ran the depth of the house. As always, their miniature dachshund Natty trotted along behind her. Both children were sleeping soundly. The rear door by the kitchen was locked, as was the storage room, where she kept the canned milk and purification tablets for thirty-five thousand gallons of water, items that would be needed by her and all the families she could help if fighting broke out in the city.

Returning to the master bedroom, she thought of listening again to the navy-surplus shortwave receiver that sat on top of the bookcase. But it was too late for that, and she slipped into the bed, which her husband had put directly below the windows so that stray sniper fire would go above their heads and hit the wall opposite.

Connie Wollam was not one to complain about the duties of a diplomat's wife. Her husband Park was reserved, holding back his emotions even from his family; she was naturally gregarious, and she waded into cocktail parties believing they were every bit as important as a dispatch to Washington—and as demanding. To her, a two-hour cocktail party in a foreign language was as strenuous as two sets of tennis.

In Santiago, however, she could never get accustomed to the tensions. Many of the Cuban children in her neighborhood, the affluent suburb of Vista Alegre, were surviving the war on tranquilizers. She had avoided that for her own children. Her two eldest daughters were attending high school at the naval base, and her nine-year-old Janet, a freckled redhead, had learned to live with the pressures as only a child could. She boasted to Connie that she was able to detect eight different kinds of gunfire, ranging from the *pop* of a .22-caliber handgun to the *boom* of a mortar shell. During the day, as Janet rode her bicycle around the broad streets lined with oleander bushes, she simply raced home at the sound of a minor *pop*. If it were a *boom,* she jumped off her bike and hid behind the nearest tree.

Other tensions in Santiago were only a little less subtle. Every night, shortly after sunset, Connie saw five or six henchmen of Senator Rolando Masferrer go by in an old sedan, their machine guns sticking out the car windows. They always turned off their engine at the top of the gently sloped boulevard and coasted past her house in complete silence. She wondered why her street deserved such special treatment; it was worrisome, at least, because she had heard the stories about Masferrer's men, demanding protection money from businessmen, robbing homes and banks in broad daylight, beating those who didn't cooperate and sometimes murdering them as well. Even a Protestant missionary had complained to her that he was forced to give a car tire to the gang.

Nestled in her bed, Connie strained to hear those innocuous sounds—a car door slamming, a bush rattling—that would indicate the start of trouble. But all was quiet, without the usual gunfire that brought forth an ungodly roar from the mangy lion at the small zoo and inevitably awoke her eighteen-month-old son, Chip. At least her husband had chosen a peaceful night to be away.

She was almost asleep when it began: a horrible rattling at the front doors. Someone was trying to get in. She lay still in the bed, her heart pounding frantically against her nightgown. The sound went on and on, and she could imagine the huge iron bar banging against its brackets.

The telephone was beside a window at the rear of the house. If she tried to reach it, she would be exposed and, besides, whoever was out there could have easily cut the phone line.

For a time that seemed like an eternity, the rattling continued. She wondered if someone was trying simply to frighten her. At least her two children were still quiet; she was thankful for that.

Suddenly, the noise stopped. Then it came again, from the back door, a banging this time. She thought of her baby Chip, asleep in the next room in his screened-in crib. She wanted to see how he was doing, but she was too frightened to move.

The banging ended at the back, only to be renewed at the front. Were they really trying to break in? If they were, how long would the iron bar hold up? She couldn't imagine they were rebels, but she couldn't think of anyone else who would do something like this.

The rattling stopped. She thought maybe they had succeeded in bouncing the iron bar from its brackets. They could be standing in the front hall at that moment, trying to figure out what to do. She decided she had to act. At least she could reach the men before they got to the children. A .22-caliber Italian pistol was on top of her wardrobe, but a gun might only encourage the intruders to violence.

Sliding silently out of bed, Connie put on her white-lace robe. She drew her eighty-five pounds up to their full five-foot-one-inch height and marched into the house's long hallway. No one was there. The iron bar rested firmly in its brackets behind the door. She looked through the large, barred windows onto the front porch. It was empty.

Rushing to the telephone, Connie called Bernie Femminella, the vice-consul. He arrived a short time later, with a squad car. Three officers—one from the police, one from naval intelligence and one from the army's SIM—listened intently to her story. She wasn't certain if they thought it was simply the frightened imagination of a woman alone, but for the rest of the night, a patrol car circled the block. Connie lay awake until almost dawn, listening to the reassuring return of the car every few minutes and wondering who might have known her husband had left town on such short notice.

Connie Wollam did not realize it that evening, but she had seen something new when the police came to investigate. Major General Eulogio Cantillo had decreed that all squad cars were to carry one member of each law-enforcement agency. His theory was simple. Agents from one group might be loyally quiet if one of their own committed an act of brutality, but they were less likely to cover up for men from other agencies.

It was a small but important step, one that Cantillo had pondered long during his lonely nights in Santiago. His wife and children were still living in Camp Columbia in Havana, far from the war, and his three-bedroom house at the end of the Moncada garrison parade ground contained only a single bed and a few pieces of goverment-issue furniture, including a rocking chair on the porch. Cantillo was a great believer in rocking chairs, and sometimes, to younger officers, he gave long monologues on why a rocker had the perfect shape and motion to promote both physical and mental well-being. At the very least, it seemed to soothe his ulcer.

Sometime in early December, as he rocked on that porch, facing the green lawn of the parade ground and the light-yellow, two-story concrete barracks that stretched for almost a city block, Cantillo came to another, bolder decision.

Rolando Masferrer was one of the most powerful men in Cuba. He was chief of the Senate Armed Forces Committee, and he had his own private army, the Tigers, in the hills of Oriente, as well as innumerable henchmen in the city. Often the Tigers put up vigorous struggles against the rebels; Cantillo had no objection to that. But Masferrer's men were young and "overly enthusiastic." If Cantillo were going to gain the confidence of the people, Masferrer and his Tigers had to be kicked out of Oriente Province.

Rolando Masferrer was at the office of his newspaper *Libertad* when he received the call from one of Cantillo's aides. The officer told him that he wanted to come over for a talk. Masferrer said fine and turned back to his perpetually cluttered desk to examine the page proofs of the next edition, which would boast of another army victory. He knew what was really happening, but the truth in this case was not going to help his cause.

Masferrer was an odd man, and even his friends had a hard time understanding him. He had a penchant for Country and Western music, Stetson hats and cowboy shirts with pseudo-pearl buttons. All of that was a legacy from his teenage years spent in San Antonio, Texas, where his uncle was a captain in the U.S. Army, but it had nothing to do with his bizarre politics. As a youth, he had fought with the Republicans during the Spanish Civil War and become a Communist. At the University of Havana law school he was a student leader and never far removed from violence. Later, like so many other Cuban politicians, he became more interested in money than leftist ideals, and that led to a drastic shift to the right. He worked his way up the political system until he owned a farm in Pinar del Río Province and two newspapers, including *El Tiempo* in Havana. A confidential U.S. memorandum stated that once "he was caught forcing two men at gunpoint to dig their own graves."

He built his private army with unemployed youths, paid them a salary and had them trained by two friendly army officers. They were called the Tigers because Masferrer had the flag of a Havana baseball team with that name and the group needed an emblem. By December, there were about 120 men in the outfit, plus many "associates" around town. But he thought the people of Santiago had an exaggerated sense of his power. Some of his associates were no more than acquaintances to whom he gave slips of paper to help them carry on their business.

When Cantillo's aide arrived, Masferrer had him shown immediately into his paper-strewn office. The army man was nervous as he sat down, and Masferrer realized what he was about to say. Rumors had been circulating for weeks that Cantillo was going to make a move, and it no longer mattered that Masferrer considered the general too weak-willed to cope with the problems of Oriente Province.

The officer approached the subject cautiously but directly. The general wanted to "soften" the situation in Oriente. He explained at length, careful not to insult Masferrer, but his tone was firm. The decision was inarguable.

Keeping his face emotionless behind his black-framed glasses, Masferrer agreed reluctantly. When the aide left, he decided the best choice was to fly the Tigers to his farm in Pinar del Río and close down the Santiago newspaper. He himself would go to Havana. As for his other associates in the city, he was certain they could take care of themselves.

8/THE APPLAUSE OF LEPERS

It was about 7:00 A.M. in the hills above Santiago when a young rebel officer with blue eyes and blondish hair emerged from a white wooden house in San Vincente, a one-street village of fifty houses and two general stores. He was Raúl Varandela, a former construction worker from a small Oriente town. Joining him on the small porch was a city underground man who had stayed overnight.

Down by the road, a husky man in his mid-forties was just getting off his motor scooter. Rebels rushed up and began pulling loaves of bread from his side cart.

"Who's that?" the underground worker asked, frowning.

"Oh," Varandela said, "he's just our baker. He brings up bread every day from the city."

"Well, your baker happens to be a Masferrer henchman. He is known to have killed a lot of people."

Varandela was distraught. "That can't be," he insisted. "He is a very good man, gives us a discount on the bread. He's a friend."

The underground worker shook his head. "The man is a Masferrerista.

I tell you, I'm sure. You should arrest him now. Search him. I'm certain he'll have a weapon or something in his motor scooter."

Varandela marched down to the road and confronted the baker, who was handing a loaf to a rebel. "Listen, what's your name?"

Calmly, the man gave his name, address and the name of his bakery. Varandela thought he was more of a pussycat than a Masferrer Tiger, but he had to continue. "I'm sorry. We'll have to search you."

"You can do as you wish," the man said smoothly.

Varandela ordered a rebel to hold the baker at gunpoint while he looked through the scooter and side cart. He found nothing, but he began thinking of all the jokes they had traded with this stranger and how much information the rebels must have let slip in the two weeks the baker had been showing up.

He ordered the man to take off his shirt and pants. He did. That revealed nothing except that any man can look pathetic in only his underwear and socks. A crowd of rebels and townspeople were gathering. The man tried to appear unruffled.

"OK," Varandela said. "Take your socks off."

For the first time, the baker looked upset. "You only said my pants. What else do you—"

"Do as you're told."

Slowly, the baker slipped off his socks. Varandela saw it immediately: a piece of paper taped to the sole of his foot. He ripped it off and unfolded it. The note was short: "The bearer of this document is a faithful servant of the government and is authorized to cross the siege lines to obtain information useful to the government." It was signed by Senator Rolando Masferrer.

Varandela felt his face flush. He had allowed a spy to operate in their midst. Immediately, he ordered the man escorted to the headquarters of his chief, Húber Matos, the *comandante* of Column 9.

That afternoon, the baker was executed.

By early December, the forces of the Santiago siege had become an odd mixture of rebels, civilians and new volunteers who were able to move with some ease between the city and the hills. Including Juan Almeida's Third Front and those companies of Raúl Castro's Second Front that faced the city, the rebels had about a thousand men watching the roads, and their ranks swelled daily as city youths slipped past army barricades and walked up the parched-grass hills to the rebel-held villages. Some brought food and supplies. Others, especially women, seemed to come out of simple curiosity, and they had a horrible tendency to stand in the open to watch gun battles, as if they were looking at a Cinemascope movie that posed no threat. Even prostitutes made the trip; they took their heroic young rebels, isolated for so long in the mountains, into the shrub-covered gullies for quick bouts of lovemaking.

Many small rebel groups were less than an hour's drive from the Moncada army garrison, but their commanders thought it far too dangerous to launch a direct attack. Their mission was simply to stop armored convoys from reinforcing and supplying the outlying cuartels and, if possible, to so choke the city's economic life that it would weaken Batista's support.

Army caravans were still able to move, with considerable difficulty, on the Central Highway, but almost all other roads out of Santiago were controlled by rebel checkpoints. If there were the slightest suspicion that a vehicle was on a government mission, it was burned immediately. When the rebels needed gas, they siphoned five gallons from each car, ten from each truck, paid for with cash or revolutionary bonds, redeemable upon victory.

The gas was needed for rebel jeeps, most of which had been captured from the army or confiscated from sugar mills. Almost all were in terrible condition. Many rebels had never driven before, and they negotiated the winding, steep roads by constantly riding the brakes. Before long, the brakes gave out, and drivers managed to slow their descent only by downshifting and caroming against boulders and trees, a feat accomplished with a certain *macho* élan, occasional minor injuries and frequently smashed headlights. The headlights bothered no one because security precautions prohibited the use of lights in any case.

As he did almost every night, Captain Dunney Pérez Alamo paced restlessly in front of the general store in the hamlet of Villalón, only fifteen miles from downtown Santiago. Some of his men were even closer, entrenched at the edge of the golf greens and sand traps of the El Caney Country Club.

For several weeks, they had seen no real action, and, as with most drawn-out sieges, their days had been reduced to a numbing tedium, sitting around their headquarters at the general store, which had been lent to them by its black owner. Because of Castro's orders, they couldn't even relax by having an occasional beer.

At nights, they had only one small entertainment, and when Pérez Alamo grew weary of his pacing, he decided it was time. Walking to the zinc-covered concrete patio beside the store, he slid into the front seat of a black Oldsmobile 98, stolen from the Santiago police chief by a rebel supporter.

Pérez Alamo turned on the engine to conserve the battery and waited until his men gathered around the car. Then he pressed the transmitting switch on the radio microphone.

"Listen, Haza," he said, calling the police chief by name. "We still have your car up here. When are you going to come get it?"

He released the switch and waited. The reply came seconds later: "You son of a bitch—I'll get you." The voice sputtered more obscenities, but the rebels couldn't hear them. They were laughing too hard.

One afternoon about this time, three rebel jeeps bounced along a narrow, rough road in the Santiago hills. Every time the driver in the lead jeep, a Toyota, hit a chuckhole, he winced as the dirty, bloody medical tape pulled on his tender ribs, broken in a jeep accident some days before. He was Napoleón Bequer, a captain in Column 9, a onetime grocery-store owner who had not seen or heard from his family in more than six months.

Leading a patrol on an inspection of the area, Bequer reluctantly decided it was time to explore the one place in the rebel-controlled hills that all the other patrols had avoided: the El Cristo leper colony.

Forcing his jeep up a steep incline, he led the patrol through aged gates into the grounds, where a large Spanish-style farmhouse was surrounded by smaller buildings. Bequer saw the lepers in the distance, vague shapes of humanity, and he tensed involuntarily.

Before he could say anything, the lepers broke into cheers. Some clapped with misshapen hands as they ran to the jeeps. Bequer watched in horror; he had expected them to keep their distance. Many of their faces and bodies were badly disfigured. There must have been three hundred of them, and they shook his hand, caressed his grimy uniform and even stroked his beard. Bequer kept a smile plastered on his face.

Politely, he and his men followed the leper leaders on a tour of the hospital. It appeared to be well kept, with old but comfortable furniture.

The lepers talked happily about how they listened to Radio Rebelde and supported wholeheartedly the struggle against the dictatorship.

When they reached the infirmary, one leper asked if they needed medical supplies. Bequer admitted they were always in short supply, and the hosts passed out boxes of plasma, penicillin and bandages. The rebels took the boxes, but they gave Bequer nervous winks. They wanted to leave, quickly. Bequer did too, but he didn't want to appear rude.

At last, mumbling thanks, their hands filled with supplies, the rebels walked back to their jeeps. The lepers cheered as they left, but Bequer hardly noticed. He raced the Toyota back to headquarters, where his men opened the precious one-gallon bottles of gasoline. Dipping their handkerchiefs into it, they scrubbed their hands, faces and beards. For many, it was the first time they had washed in weeks. Everyone was afraid of "falling apart."

Bequer knew little about leprosy, other than the usual old wives' tales, but of one thing he was certain: The lepers of El Cristo were "100 percent Fidelistas."

About this same time, several hundred miles away, Bequer's wife, Vitalia, paced in front of the gate of a stucco schoolhouse in the village of San Miguel de Los Baños. She listened nervously as the children inside recited in unison a poem of the Cuban martyr, José Martí. *"No me pongan a lo obscuro a morir como un traidor . . ."* Do not place me in the darkness, to die like a traitor. . . .

She was planning something special for that afternoon, something she knew was dangerous, not so much for herself as for her ten-year-old son, Napoleón, Jr. She vowed to make certain he never found out.

Pacing beside the dusty schoolyard, she wondered how many times there had been like this one in the family's two-year fight against the dictatorship. Of course, they had never realized how much it would hurt the boy. When it had begun, her husband Napoleón had been a partner in a prosperous general store in the town of Manzanillo, Oriente Province, at the edge of the Sierra Maestra foothills. There, he had become a leader of clandestine activities. During the day, underground contacts brought messages to their house, and Vitalia slipped them into the boots of their young son, who took them to his father at the store. The boy never showed any signs of nervousness, and the parents thought nothing about his small role in the struggle.

But then the father, hounded by police, had fled to Costa Rica, and the boy became sick, losing weight, refusing to eat, even to talk. Vitalia had taken him to medical experts in Havana and Boston before doctors reached a verdict: emotional trauma had caused a severe case of colitis. The boy needed an operation to install an artificial colon or he would die within months.

But the thought that her child would have to suffer with a tube in his body for the rest of his life was intolerable. "It would be better that he died than to do that to him," she had told relatives. "We have already ruined his short life." Rejecting the operation, she took him and her two other children to a place far from the war zone, this village in Matanzas Province. To people who didn't know her, she professed indifference to the strife as she followed the daily routine of a typical housewife, going to the butcher's shop, bakery, vegetable stand and *bodega* to gather food for the nightly meal. She listened to Radio Rebelde on her shortwave set only when her son was soundly asleep. The war was never mentioned in their house, and Vitalia kept assuring Napoleón, Jr., that his father was safely in Costa Rica, though she knew he had flown with a planeload of weapons to the Sierra some months before. Since then Vitalia herself had no way of knowing whether he was still alive.

The boy, thankfully, had stopped asking, and in the tranquil setting, his health improved. He no longer awoke screaming in the night, color returned to his cheeks and he gained weight.

Everything seemed peaceful until the afternoon before, when she was approached by the boy's fifth-grade teacher, one of the few who knew her real sympathies. The woman had whispered to her: "There are rebels in the hills near town. I'm going to make a food run tomorrow. Would you like to go?" Without hesitation, Vitalia had said yes.

Now she found herself pacing at the schoolyard gate as the children inside put away their books. She wondered why the decision had been so easy. It was like a fever, a compulsion, something she couldn't resist. The doctors had warned her that the boy shouldn't be upset again, and he surely would be if she were captured by police. But, she decided firmly, nothing bad was going to happen.

Just then, the school door popped open, and the children exploded past her, running and chattering down the dusty street. Her son, with the teacher, was one of the last out. Vitalia gave him an intense hug as he babbled happily about what he had done in school.

"Yes, yes," she said, with a forced smile. "Very good. Now, your teacher and I have something to discuss. Run on home to Grandma, and I'll be there for supper."

The boy skipped down the street as the two women wordlessly hurried to the car. The teacher slipped behind the wheel, and they sped out of town, with Vitalia occasionally peeking through the rear window. No one was following them. When they were safely in the countryside, she opened her purse, and keeping the contents below window level, showed the teacher the religious medals she was taking to the rebels. Suddenly, she felt a surge of excitement. There was no way of directly helping her husband, but at least she could do something for his comrades-in-arms.

Within a few minutes, as the setting sun brushed the tops of the trees, they arrived at the side of a stream. The teacher beeped the horn, and several rebels appeared from the bushes. They helped the women carry the groceries from the trunk to a small clearing, where there were more men, about thirty-five in all. Some had week-old beards. They had initiated no military actions, but still Vitalia beamed with pride.

As the men gleefully examined the food, their leader talked to the two women. He said it would be some weeks before they were trained enough to start any actions, but when they were, they would attack the small army cuartel in their town.

"I don't want to scare you," he said somberly, "because the cuartel should be easy to take. But there will be shots, and someone could get hurt. And when the army finds out, they will try to take it back." He promised to warn them a day in advance so they and their friends could leave town.

Walking through the tall grass back to the car, Vitalia tried to control her panic. If her son had to go through a battle, the tension could kill him. For once, as independent a woman as she was, she wished she could consult her husband. If he were still alive.

Three Americans trudged along a narrow, muddy road beside a railway track in southern Oriente Province. They were fleeing the war, trying to walk to the safety of the Guantánamo U.S. Naval Base. Originally, the Canadian whom they worked with at the Ermita sugar mill had planned to drive them past the village of Boquerón to the little-used Northeast Gate of the base, but they had found the road blocked by an overturned bulldozer, surrounded by mud, rocks and logs, undoubtedly the work of a rebel ambush squad.

Daymond Elmore, the mill's assistant manager, turned for a moment to watch the Canadian's white 1957 Chevrolet disappear into the distance. Then he moved on, his eyes scanning the shrubs and trees in the gently rolling hills for signs of an ambush. Beside him walked the mill's short, chunky manager, Albert Wadsworth, and his son, whom everyone called Albert, Jr. The father was already breathing heavily, and Elmore worried that the man did not spend enough time exercising. Elmore himself played golf, and he imagined the hike would be no more than a few rounds on an American course. Even if it were, he *had* to make it. There was no turning back.

After thirty years of living peacefully in Cuba as a sugar-mill supervisor, he had recently become a pawn for both sides in the civil war. In July, the rebels kidnapped him, along with a busload of U.S. sailors and marines. During his ten days as a prisoner, he was well treated, and the rebels even passed along a medicine he needed for his glaucoma, but still, it was not an experience he wished to repeat.

Later, the Batista army had managed to do something even worse: An officer forced him and Wadsworth to go in front of an army patrol sweeping the area for rebel sympathizers. They became, in effect, hostages, a guarantee that the rebels wouldn't shoot at the soldiers. When the patrol came across a group of five, including a young boy, the group fled in panic. All were killed. Rumors spread through the community that the Americans had pointed the group out. That was ridiculous. Elmore was no fan of the Batista regime; he considered it as corrupt as all the other Cuban governments. But the rumors persisted, and the mill's absentee owner finally called from the States to tell them to leave.

Now, as they walked down the road, Wadsworth waved at him. He was gasping, his face a bright red in the harsh sunlight. "I've got to rest," he managed, slumping onto a large boulder beside the road.

Elmore and Albert, Jr., sought the shade of a nearby tree. As Elmore pried the mud from his shoes with a stick, he cursed the muddy road. He knew there were modern, paved highways around Havana, but nothing seemed to get done in Oriente. Even the water supply in Ermita was an embarrassment: they had to boil their drinking water. "Do you know what's wrong with Cuba?" Elmore asked rhetorically. "The damn politicians. They've stolen the country blind."

Albert, Jr., nodded numbly, obviously not interested in discussing politics at that moment. They sat in silence until Wadsworth grunted that he was ready.

As they walked on, Elmore's thoughts turned to what he was leaving behind. Cuba had given him a good life, he couldn't deny that. The mill provided him with a spacious home rent-free and a membership in the company's country club. He had a full-time maid and another who came in to do the washing. The company's sixty thousand acres of choice meadowland were available to him without fee; at times he had up to a hundred cattle. To him, Ermita was home, and he thought most Cubans enjoyed it too. "I've never met anyone," he was fond of saying, "who would leave an American-owned mill to work for a Spanish-owned one."

On the road, Wadsworth, wheezing and puffing, was falling behind. "Wait, wait. I have to rest again." This time he sat in the shade.

When he stumbled again to his feet, they had to walk only a short way before, rounding a bend, they saw the town and, beyond, the wire-mesh fence and wooden guardhouse of the naval base. They thought they were safe at last.

The next afternoon, Elmore saw things suddenly worsen. It happened after the navy put them on the edge of the base, in one of a cluster of Quonset huts, where other American refugees were staying. Sitting in the small hut with nothing to do, the exhausted Wadsworth became oddly quiet and distant. He fell asleep, and slept so long that the others grew worried. Finally, Elmore poked his boss on the shoulder to awaken him.

Wadsworth sat up with a start. He began trembling uncontrollably and babbling words Elmore couldn't understand. Then he lapsed into a long silence, refusing to speak even to his son. A navy doctor told them what was wrong: Wadsworth was suffering a nervous breakdown. The tensions of the civil war had claimed another victim.

9/A NEW PRESIDENT IN SUNGLASSES

Eight thousand feet above the Caribbean Sea, a twin-engine C-47 lumbered through the chilly nighttime air at a speed barely faster than what was needed to keep itself in the air. The wing lights were off. Its tail had a three-inch-long Venezuelan flag, tiny identification numbers and, as a wry joke, the words "Motilón Corporation." The Motilones were cannibalistic Indians from Venezuela.

Inside the plane, heading north toward Cuba, passengers huddled among the heavy wooden crates that were responsible for the C-47's slow speed. The crates contained 100,000 rounds of ammunition, 210 grenades and 30 .30-caliber tripod machine guns. They were being sent to the 26th of July rebels by Admiral Wolfgan Larrazábal, the leader of Venezuela's liberal-oriented junta.

Manuel Urrutia crouched on a crate, his legs drawn up to the chest of his crinkling-new, olive-green uniform to conserve as much body warmth as possible. He was a silver-haired man in his mid-fifties, and even in the dim cargo hold, he wore his black-framed sunglasses that were as much a part of his face as his thin, graying mustache.

Urrutia had spent weeks in Caracas helping arrange the arms shipment, but he believed his own presence on the plane was at least as important as the weapons, for he was the designated president-in-exile, so named by the anti-Batista coalition that had signed the Pact of Caracas. Suggested by Fidel Castro, a man whom he had never met, Urrutia had been an acceptable compromise because he was not closely identified with any political group. In fact, he was not a politician at all, simply a career civil servant, a judge who had made only one major political comment in his life. That had come at a trial when he declared that the 26th of July prisoners were not guilty because they were defending their inalienable rights against an unconstitutional regime. Soon after that, he retired and, from the United States, began working actively to oust Batista.

Now, he was returning to Cuba to set up a provisional government in the rebel-held area of Oriente Province. The Movement had assured him there was no danger involved, and Urrutia's wife, Esperanza, a strong-willed woman, insisted on coming along, even though it meant leaving their third child, born only three months before, with relatives in New York. With them was their second son, fourteen-year-old Jorge, who viewed the trip as a great adventure.

But none of them realized how cold the flight was going to be until after takeoff, when a bitter wind started to whistle through holes in the floor. The pilot, Humberto Armada, decided not to turn on the heat, because it came from the engine exhausts. A small gas leak and a spark could ignite all the explosives they were carrying.

To compensate, several men tried to move the crates so they could huddle together on the floor and share each other's body warmth, but the boxes were too heavy. The men sat on top; Esperanza and the boy managed to squeeze between two crates and escape most of the chill.

Her husband muttered oaths about the cold while others traded jokes. "What do you think our chances are of making it?" one asked. Another replied: "Whatever happens down there is going to be better than freezing up here." They all knew that many gun-running planes had crashed while trying to land on the short mountain airstrips.

For more than three hours, they shivered in the dark compartment. The cold numbed their bodies and minds. Talk stopped. The danger of landing in Oriente was forgotten.

At last, in an area of gently rolling hills above the city of Niquero, Urrutia saw two parallel rows of flickering purple lights. As the plane circled, the lights flashed off, then on, then off again. The pilot turned the wing lights on for a moment, and that caused the ground lights to be turned on for good.

The pilot yelled back at them: "Hold on tight. It's going to be a bumpy landing. And keep absolutely quiet once we're on the ground." Then he whispered to his copilot: "If we crash, the fireworks will be seen in Havana."

The plane hit the airstrip with a jarring bump, skipped and banged against the ground again. Passengers screamed as the wooden crates slid across the floor. Mrs. Urrutia thought it felt like an earthquake.

The C-47 stopped a bare hundred feet from the trees at the end of the airstrip. Immediately, the pilot taxied to the other end, so the plane would be ready for a quick takeoff if an army patrol showed up.

Someone opened the cargo door. There were no stairs, and the Urrutias had to leap to the ground. Several dozen rebels, their uniforms dusty and sweat-stained, were running toward them from the surrounding darkness. Wordlessly, they began unloading the crates.

The Urrutias, all three in their spotless uniforms, watched uncomfortably. No high-ranking rebel commander came to greet them, and the president-in-exile recognized no one. The rebels seemed more interested in the guns than they did in their new political leader.

10/MISSION A-001

Manuel Fajardo, wearing the insignia of a rebel captain on his tattered khaki uniform, strode purposefully down the street toward a large gray house beside the Romelie sugar mill. He was a squat, broad man, and his shoulder was encased in a heavy white cast, mending a collarbone broken in a jeep accident. Workers greeted him with smiles and waves as he walked past. Some fell into step behind him.

They knew what he had come for. A workers' congress, organized by the rebels, was backing a law on "wage differential," which meant that if a sugar mill earned a larger profit than anticipated, the workers were going to get part of the additional money. Most mills were paying; the Central Romelie was not, and Fajardo was considered the ideal man to apply pressure. He was an illiterate peasant, born in a dirt-floor *bohío*, and one of the first to join Castro after he had gone to the mountains.

Fajardo led the way into the gray house, where his group was shown immediately into the administrator's office. The man, rising from behind his desk, greeted them with a thin smile, and after strained introductions, ordered his secretary to bring them coffee. As Fajardo and the workers sat down, he produced from a desk drawer a full box of Bauzá cigars and a Parker pen and pencil set.

Fajardo took them, but he let his face reveal his disgust. He knew this was the kind of bribery administrators had used for years—giving trinkets to army sergeants to escape taxes and regulations—and apparently this man assumed that he, a rebel captain, could be treated the same way. To show that he couldn't, Fajardo looked carefully around the office and remarked that it was interesting that the room was much better maintained than the workers' houses. He suggested that, before anything else, the administrator should first clean and paint his employees' dwellings.

The man said nothing, and Fajardo came directly to the reason for his visit. The rebels were calculating that the wage differential entitled workers to an extra 8 percent in their paychecks. There was an uneasy silence, marred only by the squeaking of chairs, until the administrator finally replied: "The only laws I recognize are the ones promulgated by the Batista government. This so-called law about a wage differential is not a law at all."

Fajardo was startled. The mill was in territory controlled completely by the rebels. "Well," he said firmly, "if you do not recognize our law, I will do something so that you *do* recognize it. Either that, or the government which you say is the legal one will have to defend your mill. I can order my men to burn it at any moment. And if the Batista troops aren't here within twenty-four hours, I *will* burn the mill."

Not giving the administrator time to reply, he announced he was leaving two platoons at the mill to stop "the army of the tyranny" from coming to his rescue. With that, he drank the coffee in one gulp, lit a cigar, tucked the box under his arm, slipped the Parker set into his pocket and said, with an easy arrogance, "Tomorrow I am going to sign the new contract with this pen."

The following day, the administrator told Fajardo that the mill owners had "reconsidered their position." A contract was waiting. After several labor leaders checked it for accuracy, Fajardo pulled out his new Parker pen with an exaggerated flourish. "I am going to use the pen you gave me," he said, not bothering to hide his sarcasm, "so that you can see how well it writes."

He scrawled his mark, then said with finality, "Don't make that mistake again. We are officers of an army of a very different nature, and there is nothing in the world with which you can bribe us."

Fajardo was the second in command of Column 18, which was part of

Raúl Castro's Second Front, the most organized—and most radical—of the rebel groups. Raúl had arrived in the Sierra Cristal with only seventy-seven men, fifty-three of them armed, but he quickly established control over broad stretches of eastern and northern Oriente Province.

Compared to the rugged isolation of Fidel's Sierra Maestra, Raúl's area was far tamer, with better roads, more hamlets and farms, and far easier access to the cities. By early December 1958, Raúl had built up an army of two thousand rebels, with another thousand willing to fight as soon as they had weapons. Hand-laid telephone lines connected fifty-five checkpoints in the mountains, so that rebel squads knew almost instantly of any army patrols entering the area. Fourteen meadows had been cleared to make airstrips so that planes could bring in weapons from other countries, especially the United States.

Scattered among the hamlets, the rebels had a tailor shop, where seamstresses made olive-green uniforms; a small bomb factory, which produced land mines out of air force bombs that failed to explode on impact; and even a primitive weapons shop that fabricated such odd devices as rifle grenades, conical pieces of metal fired from the end of carbines. Sometimes the homemade grenades worked, but they had a dangerous tendency to explode just a few feet from the person who shot them.

Most of the hierarchy, especially the women with the front, were able to sleep in comfortable houses and eat canned meat, codfish and vegetables purchased from the *campesinos*. They could take showers, and the women were able to wash and iron their rebel uniforms.

Travel to rebel territory became so easy that even relatives came up for brief visits. The army stayed away, and the only threat was from the air force, which used U.S. munitions to bomb the mountains daily from the safety of the skies. To evade the bombs, the rebels worked nights and in the early mornings, when the mountain fog was too thick for bombing runs; they slept during the day.

The headquarters was located in the hamlet of Mayarí Arriba, but Raúl Castro traveled often in his gray Toyota Land Cruiser as he kept in touch with his forces. Twenty-seven years old, he was shorter, thinner and quieter than his brother Fidel, and absolutely devoted to him. His shoulder-length hair was pulled back in a ponytail, topped by either a light-colored cowboy hat or a black beret, and he had a wisp of a mustache with a few scattered hairs for sideburns. During the early

1950s, Raúl had been a member of the Communist youth group, but after joining Fidel in the attack on the Moncada barracks, the party, then dedicated to nonviolence, expelled him. Still, he had attracted some of the 26th of July's most radical followers, men like Manuel Piñeiro, known as "Barba Roja" because of his reddish beard, who had come in contact with Marxism during encounters with other foreign students while studying business administration at Columbia University in New York.

Piñeiro, one of Raúl's chief aides, helped organize the Second Front into what was, in effect, a functioning government, with departments for health, education and justice. The groups were so structured that their periodic reports to Raúl were even typewritten.

The director of education was Asela de los Santos, a young divorced woman from a poor Santiago family who became close to Movement members while attending the University of Oriente. Raúl explained to her that teaching the illiterate *campesinos* had a political as well as a social function. If the rebels worked for the people's benefit, the *campesinos* would support the revolution.

Some teachers were rebel volunteers working without salary, but others were career *maestros* who simply continued teaching in their old classrooms after the rebels took over their territory. Oddly, they continued to receive paychecks from the Batista regime.

During the day, they held classes for the children in huts and schoolhouses scattered throughout the Second Front. At night, Asela could look down the hillside from her headquarters at Tumbasiete and see flickering kerosene lamps clustered together, signs that adults were gathering to learn how to read.

Her main problem was the illiterate rebel soldiers, who rarely showed interest in entering classrooms. "What is it you want?" she used to ask them. "Just to *tirar tiros* [shoot shots] and not be able to read?" Such rhetoric failed to impress even her driver and bodyguard, who disappeared one time and did not return for days. When she went to see what happened, she found he had joined a rebel fighting group, which he considered far more important than simply escorting a woman to classrooms. He came back with her, but not willingly.

Not far from Asela's headquarters, Dr. José Ramón Machado Ventura had set up the Second Front's health department in the village of Majimiana. The son of an accountant from Las Villas Province, he had torn down the inner wall of a general store to make room for a hospital of twelve to fourteen beds. The operating room was thirty yards away, in a wooden house with a zinc roof. Altogether, in the scattered hamlets and towns, he had 150 persons working for him, including 19 doctors, 4 dentists and 2 pharmacists.

Since rebel or army wounded arrived only once every twenty days or so, there was plenty of time to take care of *campesino* families, many of whom had never been treated by a doctor before. Machado Ventura's carefully kept records, typed by a female pharmacist, showed that in one six-month period, Second Front doctors treated 3180 *campesinos*. The worst were the children, who suffered from gastroenteritis and other diseases caused by parasites. The *campesinos* responded gratefully to the rebels' help. When their wounded were brought in, they often came with fruits, honey and chickens to feed the men.

The hard life of the *campesinos* in the Sierra Cristal made a strong impression on Vilma Espín, a twenty-eight-year-old woman who had grown up in Santiago in the liberal Rotarian-Lions Club milieu that permeated the city's upper class. Her father was an executive with the Bacardí rum company, a man who possessed basically traditional ideas, but who saw no harm in giving his daughter an education as good as any male received. After her early years in Catholic girls' schools, she majored in chemical engineering at the University of Oriente, while picking up from her progressive professors a sense of moral outrage about what had been happening to her country. For a year, she did postgraduate work at the Massachusetts Institute of Technology, but then she visited the Castro brothers in Mexico and decided to dedicate herself full time to the struggle. Returning to Santiago, she became one of the most daring leaders of the underground, working out of safehouses, always keeping just one step ahead of the police. At last, when several of her co-workers had been killed, friends convinced her that the city was too dangerous and she fled to the Second Front headquarters, where she quickly became a top administrative assistant, a liaison to the underground and Raúl Castro's fiancée.

Even in the mountains, she never abandoned the fastidiousness of her girls' school upbringing. She kept her long black hair clean and pulled back in a ponytail. Her rebel uniform was tailor-made and she managed, even during bombing attacks, to brush her teeth and put on lipstick each morning.

When she had arrived in the Sierra Cristal, she shared the progressive attitudes of most young Cuban intellectuals. She was opposed to corruption and dictatorships, she wanted the poor to have a better life and, most importantly, she believed that Cuba had never had a decent government.

To her and most other young idealists, Cuba seemed to oscillate between frail democracies and rigid military tyrants. Countless times, revolutions had failed. Worse, young revolutionaries tended to become old, corrupt cynics. And always, the United States was part of the process. In the nineteenth century, Cubans had fought three bloody civil wars against the Spanish, stretching over thirty years, but in 1898, just when it appeared the Spanish were about to collapse, the United States entered the conflict. Cuban military leaders were ignored in the surrender negotiations, a slight which no Cuban intellectual could forget. American newspapers even called it the Spanish-American War, leaving out any hint of the Cubans' participation. The people had been denied the honor of achieving their own freedom, and it made the word "revolution" some kind of magical promise still waiting to be fulfilled.

In 1902, when the United States granted Cuba what was supposed to be its independence, it forced the island to accept the Platt Amendment, allowing U.S. troops to intervene whenever Washington thought chaos threatened the economy. For the first thirty years of the republic, Cuba did not even have its own currency: it used U.S. dollar bills.

The Platt proviso was eventually eliminated, but intellectuals suffered another bitter defeat in 1933, when the brutal Machado dictatorship was collapsing. As student revolutionaries and their professors struggled to overthrow the regime, an American emissary, sent by Washington, orchestrated a change in governments. Order gave way to chaos, and a few days later, Batista's establishment of a new dictatorship defeated the revolutionaries once again. When Batista relinquished power peacefully, two democratically elected regimes followed. Both were made up of many of the student revolutionaries from 1933, but they had lost their dedication to idealism; the two administrations were as corrupt as Batista's.

Vilma Espín, like so many others, wanted to overthrow Batista's second regime without returning to the failures of previous administrations. She was not certain what kind of government that meant, but whatever it was, it had to herald a new era, something that would wipe out the past and eliminate completely the American dominance of Cuban affairs.

To her, there was nothing wrong with Marxism, but it was a theory she knew little about, one which seemed removed from her Cuban nationalism. When Raúl asked her to teach Communist principles at the rebel political school, she objected: "I don't know anything about Marxism." Raúl assured her that it was simply a logical extension of what they were fighting for, a framework strong enough to fulfill their goals, but if she wanted, she could teach instead the sayings of José Martí, the Cuban poet-revolutionary from the nineteenth century. She did that, while pouring over the few Communist pamphlets she could find and trying to interject a little Marxism into her talks.

In the rebel camps, however, political theory was always secondary to the military struggle, and in early December, Vilma Espín found herself working nights in a small house at the end of the 4800-foot grassy runway at Mayarí Arriba as she helped put together the rebels' most daring project yet: a plan to drop a napalm bomb from a plane on an army cuartel. It was called, rather formally and optimistically, Mission A-001 of the Rebel Air Force.

At first she hoped her background in chemical engineering was sufficient to allow her to make the bomb herself, but she discovered that napalm was a tricky substance. One needed exactly the right blend of soap and gasoline to obtain the maximum explosion on impact. To help, she asked one of her former professors to come up from Santiago. Together, they experimented, using a fifty-gallon can as a mixing tank and a small outboard boat motor for a blender. Luis Silva, a short man with receding hairline, hovered anxiously behind them. He was the one who was to fly the plane.

There was one problem: the plane wasn't operating. The rebels had experienced mechanics, but almost no spare parts. To compensate, they devised an ambitious plan that bordered on the incredible. At one airstrip, they had a King-Fischer fighter from the Batista air force. It had been forced to land with engine problems. The plane was intact, but the engine was useless. At another airfield, a similar plane had crash-landed while delivering rebel weapons. The fuselage was destroyed, but the engine appeared to be all right.

A group of teenagers were working frantically, day and night, to remove the good engine, transport it sixty miles over mountain roads and install it in the King-Fischer. Then the pilot would have to see if the plane could fly and the bomb work against its target, the cuartel at La Maya.

* * *

La Maya was an oddity in Oriente, a bastion of Batista support. Many soldiers' families lived there, and people in the coffee business were closely allied with the regime. Over time, they were joined by Batista sympathizers and informers from outlying villages abandoned by the army. When the rebels attacked the town, two hundred of them had retreated with the three hundred soldiers into the cuartel.

It was the largest concentration of soldiers the rebels had ever faced in one place. Ordinarily, they would have avoided such a serious risk of defeat, but the town was in a crucial position, located on the highway east of Santiago. If it could be taken, the Second Front would be united with the forces of the Santiago siege and, through the mountains, with Fidel's Column 1 in an unbroken line of rebel domination stretching almost the width of the province.

One column had surrounded the La Maya cuartel while the Santiago siege groups were blocking all reinforcements from the west. The rebels' greatest worry was that an army convoy would break through from the other direction, coming from the garrison at Guantánamo City. To stop that, Raúl had assigned his second-in-command, a slender mulatto named Efigenio Ameijeiras, to prepare the largest ambush of the war.

Ameijeiras went about the ambush with a vengeance. He had seen three of his nine brothers killed in the struggle against Batista, and he was not going to let anything stand in the way of victory. His men planted several two-hundred-pound land mines in the road about ten miles east of La Maya. A bulldozer dug a hole large enough for a tank to fall into, and two hundred men were stationed in the hills above to cut down those still living after the bombs exploded. To act as a decoy, a squad of forty men was sent ahead. They were to fire on the army convoy for fifteen minutes, then retreat quickly, luring the convoy into the main ambush.

For thirteen days, Ameijeiras had waited. Finally, one day shortly before noon, as he prepared to eat lunch at his headquarters in the hamlet of Yerba Guinea, he heard gunfire rumble in the distance like weak thunder. Two B-26s appeared overhead, flying figure-eight patterns at a thousand feet while strafing the site where the advance squad was located. A messenger rushed up to tell him that it was a huge convoy, led by a jeep, an armored car and a tank, followed by three busloads of soldiers and another jeep as rearguard.

Ameijeiras waited for the convoy to reach the real ambush. Minutes went by. The firing continued as strong as before. The advance squad wasn't retreating. An hour passed, then two. Suddenly, the gunfire stopped. Ameijeiras tensed, waiting for the booming explosion of the mines to tell him that his trap had worked. But there was only silence.

After a long delay, a sweating, grinning rebel ran down the road to explain. The advance group had shot the driver and officer in the lead jeep, as well as three officers in the first bus. When the squad was going to retreat as planned, the B-26s opened fire and pinned them down. All the squad could do was fight back. They were almost out of ammunition when the convoy suddenly turned around and went back to Guantánamo City. The army had never gotten near the real ambush.

Ameijeiras cursed. The advance squad had done its job too well. Then he realized what it meant. A large convoy, supported by the air force, had fled when confronted with only forty rebels. Obviously, he decided, the army was losing its will to fight.

Early the next day, Comandante Antonio E. Lussón, chief of the rebels' Column 16, climbed to the flat roof of a two-story dance club in La Maya.

About 150 feet below him, at the bottom of a small hill, were the horse stables at the rear of the cuartel his men had been besieging for almost two weeks. Even from this distance, he smelled the stench of the dead horses, shot by the rebels to demoralize the army soldiers. Overhead, dozens of turkey buzzards circled, vague shadows against the still-dark sky.

On the ground, Lussón could barely see his men getting in position for the attack. He checked to make certain that some were next to the stacks of wood, which were to be lit at 5:30 A.M., to show the way for the King-Fischer fighter that was going to bomb the cuartel.

Lussón hoped the attack would demoralize the army men enough to surrender. He knew their spirits were already very low. With a captured army radio, he had heard an air force pilot ask them how long they could hold out. The commander, in a rage, shouted back, "Many days ago, I informed you that La Maya was 'burned' by the rebels, and now you come with that shit-eating question. We are besieged and they are going to kill all of us because of your abandonment. We have four dead, twenty-three injured. There is no food or medicine. We will fight until the death."

Lussón was less impressed with the commander's bravado than he was that an officer had used an obscenity in a formal army communication. It revealed how demoralized the men were.

The only support the cuartel received were packets dropped by parachute, but almost all fell into rebel hands. Some contained personal letters, including one to the cuartel commander from his wife in Havana. She sent a photo of their two children; one was blowing out candles on a cake. In a poignant letter, she told about the birthday party and lamented that her husband was so far away, unable to talk by telephone, risking his life while the privileged ones were safe in Havana and living luxuriously on government money. Impulsively, Lussón had flipped the photo over and written a note on the back, begging the officer's pardon for opening such a personal letter but hoping he understood the need for military censorship. He mentioned how he himself had abandoned his job as a truck driver, leaving his wife and four young children to join the rebels, and he could imagine how the army men felt being separated from their own loved ones. He explained that the rebels were not enemies of the soldiers themselves, only of their corrupt leaders, and while a military man had to fulfill his duty, Lussón hoped he would read the letter from his wife carefully. During a truce, the letter and photo were taken to the cuartel. Later, when Lussón talked to the army captain, the man appeared confused and indecisive.

Lussón hoped the rebel fighter plane would end his indecision. Shortly before 5:30 A.M., he started to listen for the drone of the plane. There was only silence. Lussón paced. He wondered if something had gone wrong.

At 5:45 A.M., he saw it: the silhouette of the King-Fischer against the dark-blue sky. He gave the signal to light the bonfires.

At 5:47 A.M., the plane made a low pass over the town. The soldiers in the cuartel saw the insignia of the air force on its wings and shouted with joy. They believed the plane had come to bomb the rebels. Some stood up to wave.

As the plane began its second pass, rebels opened up with a massive barrage of gunfire against the windows and machine-gun emplacements of the cuartel. Soldiers ducked for cover. The King-Fischer swooped down and dropped two homemade bombs. They exploded in the cuartel's patio in a burst of flame, followed by a pillar of smoke.

With the army men crouched behind their walls in numbed silence, the plane made three more passes, firing every one of its 750 rounds from its .30-caliber machine gun. Lussón, from his observation post atop the dance hall, saw that the plane had caused no serious damage, but he guessed the psychological impact had to be enormous.

He was right. Moments later, the army signaled for a truce. Lussón and the cuartel captain met in an open space between the lines. The officer was willing to surrender, if he and his men were handed over immediately to the Red Cross. Lussón agreed.

The soldiers walked out, hands on top of their heads, without their weapons. A rebel escort marched them down the main street while others raced into the cuartel to find what spoils victory had produced. As after every successful battle, each piece was meticulously counted and recorded. The rebels now had 275 more rifles, 62 grenades and 48,000 rounds of ammunition. Each rifle meant that another man could be added to the rebel army, ready to capture more cuartels, gain more weapons and add even more men.

11/REVOLUTIONARIES IN A BUICK

It was a clear, warm night as the 1955 Buick Century drove out of Havana, moving east at a cautious speed along the four-lane Vía Blanca—the White Way. In the backseat, underground worker Enrique Barroso sat uncomfortably. Underneath his sports shirt and slacks was a crisp new olive-green uniform. After days of planning, he was about to help open a guerrilla front within ninety minutes of Havana.

His friend, Pepe Garcerán was once again in the front seat, seated next to the blond Olga. Lizzy was in the back. This time, she looked a little better, dressed in a low-cut white dress with thin shoulder straps. If they were stopped by police, the presence of the women could make it appear that they were simply on a date.

Even until the last, when Lizzy and Garcerán were moving the weapons from the beach to the Madruga Hills area that was their destination, Barroso had thought about balking. He was a city boy with no military experience, the hills were too close to Havana, too small for a real chance to hide. He had even more doubts about Garcerán, a close friend but a wild romantic who wrote brooding poems to his wife about his own death and who thought that his best contribution to his country would be to die for it.

Barroso knew such thoughts did not make for a hardened guerrilla, but it was too late for them to back out. Trying to overcome his nervousness, he turned to Lizzy. The white dress was becoming, even if she was somewhat skinny. He decided to try a small compliment: "Pepe told me it was a dangerous mission to bring back the weapons from the beach."

"Oh," she mumbled, "I'm used to that."

They lapsed into silence as the Buick moved past two ridges. Near a bridge, Olga turned right onto a narrow dirt road. She flicked off the headlights and slowed down.

In the backseat, Lizzy leaned back, arms crossed, a little angry. She had sensed from the start that Barroso liked Olga better, and she resented his phony compliment. She despised men who rejected her because of her looks, especially Cuban men who had such an attraction for full-bodied women that many teenage girls stuffed themselves with weight-gaining pills. That male-dominated craziness was not for her, and at the age of twenty-two she "did not feel romantically inclined." Her passion was the revolution, and she acted as messenger, lookout or whatever else the underground needed to have done.

The Buick came to the end of a small valley and began to climb. Lizzy tensed. She had bought the car with Movement funds and she knew it was two months overdue for a tune-up.

The Buick started to cough. It stalled on a steep curve.

The men cursed silently. Everyone climbed out. Barroso raised the hood and peered angrily into the dark engine compartment. Lizzy started to say something, but Barroso quieted her: "Sssh. Don't make any noise." She marched away, fuming, her broad white skirt fluttering in the nighttime breeze. Once again, she thought, she was the victim of men who didn't pay any attention to her.

Only when Barroso had given up did she pull a Coca-Cola bottle filled with gasoline from under the front seat. Calmly unscrewing the air filter, as she had done countless times before, she poured a little gasoline into the carburetor. The men watched in astonishment.

"Turn it on," she told Olga.

The engine roared. Lizzy, with the rage of triumph, slammed down the hood. Barroso screamed. She had slammed it on his left hand.

His howl filled the night, echoing through the hills. For a moment, she thought it served him right, but then she saw how much pain he was in. Tenderly, she took his hand. It was badly bruised, and there was a little blood. The thick graduation ring, on his fourth finger, was bent. She realized the ring had probably saved the finger.

As Olga drove on toward the farmhouse, Lizzy cuddled Barroso's hand in hers and murmured apologies. She felt sorry for him, and he in turn was thinking that despite all her drawbacks, she was showing an unusual tenderness.

Neither had long to think about it. The Buick soon pulled up to a small wooden farmhouse. A squat peasant named Manolo came to greet them. The women said hurried good-byes and drove off, their dim parking lights disappearing quickly.

"And where," Garcerán asked the peasant, "is the group that is fighting in this area?"

Manolo smiled broadly. "Fighting? They aren't fighting. There are five or six of them, sometimes less when they're off with their wives. They hide in the caves in the hillsides near the sea. There are lots of caves up there."

Barroso swallowed hard. How, he wondered, were they supposed to turn this into a guerrilla front?

12/WHEN A DICTATOR SAYS "MAYBE . . ."

It was shortly after midnight when Lieutenant Colonel García Baez, the chief of SIM, was allowed to see Batista. Under his arm was his leather briefcase, containing only some mildly interesting reports from the top-secret "K" files. It had been a relatively quiet day.

Batista, dressed in a white linen suit, was in the dining room. "García," he said casually, "sit down." He waved to the opposite end of the dining table. "I want to eat."

Knowing of his leader's prodigious eating habits, García Baez ran through the report quickly, hoping to leave so that he didn't get involved in a marathon eating session. He was just about to stand up when Batista asked, "Did you see the newspapers today?"

"Yes. What about it?"

"Those photographs of Díaz Tamayo."

"Oh . . . yes." General Díaz Tamayo had been linked to the Thanksgiving Day military conspiracy, which insiders had nicknamed *Los Borrachos*—The Drunkards—because the officers involved had done their conspiring in bars. It was obvious that the general had been at least peripherally involved in the plot, but Batista had shown an odd gentleness by simply retiring him, according to the press release, "for reasons of health." Yet that day a Havana newspaper had carried photographs of Díaz Tamayo at a beach club with a caption: "See how sick I look?" (Díaz Tamayo has always denied that he participated in any conspiracy.)

"You know," Batista said as he stuffed a forkful of food into his mouth, "he's pushing us to arrest him. Maybe we should arrest him." His face, as always, was emotionless.

"Yes, sir," García Baez said. He fell silent. Any time Batista said "maybe" something should be done, that meant only one thing to the chief of SIM. Excusing himself, he hurried to an anteroom, where he called SIM headquarters. "Listen," he told the duty officer, "I want you to take your best men and arrest Díaz Tamayo right away. I am at the palace. Call me as soon as you've done it. Take him to headquarters."

Within thirty minutes, the call came back. The general was confined at SIM.

García Baez, proud that SIM efficiency had come through once again, walked confidently back into the dining room. Batista was still eating. "You know," the president said pensively, "he's been a good man for me over the years."

"Who's that, sir?"

"Díaz Tamayo."

"Oh."

"He was with us on the tenth of March," Batista said, mentioning the date of his 1952 coup. "He's always been a good military man. You know, maybe it's not a good idea to arrest him."

García Baez felt sick. "Mr. President, I'm afraid it's too late." He explained what he had done. "He's already at headquarters."

Batista's face soured slightly, the closest he ever came to showing emotion. "Well," he said slowly, "as long as you've done that, maybe you better talk to him. But go easy."

García Baez understood what that meant. None of his "special" methods of interrogating prisoners were to be used. He rushed from the room, embarrassed by his mistake, but concerned too about Batista's sudden gentleness with his opponents.

Batista's handpicked successor, Andrés Rivero Agüero, was preoccupied with his own fears. Thirteen policemen roamed the grounds of the president-elect's house in the Biltmore area. Twenty-two army soldiers were on the terraces or inside the sprawling five-bedroom, two-story home, looking through the windows for snipers. Rivero Agüero's brother, a foreman at the Bacardí rum factory, had been killed by the underground while sitting on his front porch during the election campaign, and he knew that he himself was an even more likely target.

Still, the protection sometimes seemed worse than the danger. Each day, it seemed, the edgy bodyguards fired a shot or two, then explained it was an accident or they thought they had spotted an intruder. The gunfire was driving his wife Isabel almost to hysteria, and it did nothing to calm his own nerves.

One day in early December, his fears came to a head when Freddy Fernández, dressed in his gardener's clothes, came into his office in the three-room library wing. Fernández looked through the windows to make certain no one was listening and then eased himself into an upholstered chair. Unknown to the guards, he was a longtime friend who was acting as a spy, tending the lawn as he listened to the talk among the soldiers and police.

In a whisper, Fernández told about a conversation he had just overheard between an army officer and some soldiers about the accidental shots. "If you men are not careful," the officer had said, "one of these days a shot is going to kill the president." Fernández reminded Rivero Agüero of other conversations, of soldiers mumbling, "He could be killed any day now," and, "No one knows how many rebels are waiting to kill him."

The danger, Fernández said, was that the army men could be setting up an "accident" and blame it on an unintentional shot or an underground sniper. If the captain of the army guards was part of the conspiracy, no one would be able to prove otherwise.

Rivero Agüero leaned back in his chair. He knew that no one in the army felt any loyalty to him personally and many would feel threatened. It was obvious that, after his inauguration on February 24, 1959, he was going to have to change some of the military commanders, trying to find some that would be *his* men, and the deposed officers certainly were not going to take kindly to that. He knew he would be vulnerable to a coup d'etat, and he had pleaded with Batista, his only real source of support, that he stay on as the minister of war or chief of the armed forces, to keep the officers in line, but Batista was being vague about his plans, promising assistance but making no real commitment.

After a long silence, Rivero Agüero told his gardener-spy that it made no sense to be protected by people he couldn't trust. From now on, no soldiers were to be allowed inside the house. He was going to bring in ten close friends; they would alternate sleeping in the house, and Fernández was to find submachine guns for them and his two sons. Fernández himself should never leave the premises, and he had to make certain that the soldiers' machine guns were replaced with rifles. That way, his friends and relatives could serve as a counterbalance to the army men.

Fernández agreed. As he left, Rivero Agüero turned back to the paperwork atop his desk, but he could not concentrate. He realized that now it was going to be a struggle simply to survive until his inauguration as president.

About that same time, on Long Island, New York, attorney Paul Tannenbaum made a decision: After reading so much about the Cuban civil war in *The New York Times*, he decided he wanted to see the country for himself. Tannenbaum, a slender man who looked almost professorial in his black-framed glasses, arranged for his wife, two sons and his in-laws to take a two-week cruise aboard the British ship *Mauretania*. It was scheduled to arrive in Havana harbor on New Year's Eve.

13/LIFE INSURANCE FOR THE UNDERGROUND

A Havana tourist brochure described El Principe, an old Spanish castle converted into a prison, as a place where "convicts, when they have done their 'time,' come out well fed and as red as boiled lobsters. Tropical sunshine does the trick, as there are ample terraces at the prison."

No tourist, however, was able to look inside the thick, gray-stone walls of Havana's main prison, crowded with men awaiting trials that never seemed to come. The three hundred activists among the political prisoners were crammed into Cell 21, a room about sixty feet by thirty feet. There were only seventy-six bunks—one for every four persons— and most slept at night on the damp stone floor. Makeshift boxes were attached to the walls, so that each prisoner could store a few books, clothes and canned food brought by relatives. The one toilet was located in the back, separated from the room by a curtain. The "ample terrace" was really a small courtyard, with two shower stalls and a concrete tank for washing clothes. The prisoners' one entertainment, almost a tantalizing torture for the younger ones, was to peek over the stone wall and watch a lascivious guard's daughter making time with the baker or milkman.

Such had been the home for eight months of Julio Fernández León, a youth in his early twenties who came from a blue-collar neighborhood near the Estrella Cookie Factory. It was his seventh or eighth time in jail—he had forgotten which—and it was his longest, and worst, stay. He had been arrested in early April, caught bending nails to be thrown in the streets and gathering explosives for use in a general strike. The strike had failed miserably, but by that time he was already in the precinct station, his body badly beaten by police, who used rubber hoses and vicious *telefonazos,* hard slaps against both ears simultaneously that continued until he thought his head was going to burst.

In Cell 21, Fernández León had seen the prison population grow almost daily. Some were thrown in for minor offenses, such as the fifteen-year-old boy caught carrying a 20-peso bond of the 26th of July Movement. Almost all arrived bruised and bloody. If a prisoner came in unharmed, the others ostracized him because they assumed he had talked to escape punishment.

Many, probably most, of the prisoners were 26th of July men, but there were also students from the Directorio and Auténtico followers of the democratically elected president whom Batista had overthrown. Starting in late summer, when the Marxists' Partido Socialista Popular began supporting Castro's rebels, there were Communists as well. Fernández León himself was a member of a small Directorio splinter group. Occasionally, the prisoners argued political theory, but mostly they just waited for something that would overthrow the Batista regime and allow them to be freed.

Fernández León had vowed to himself that if he did get out while Batista was still in power, he would begin immediately working against the dictatorship once again, no matter what the personal cost.

The clandestine movement in Havana was always an amorphous group, because friends joined together in small bands with only tenuous ties to the Movement's hierarchy. Some scholars say there may have been as few as four hundred active clandestine workers in those last weeks of 1958, while others believe the figure should be closer to two thousand, the number of dedicated 26th of July and student Directorio

men willing to risk their lives to take over the police stations when the
Batista government collapsed.

Mere figures, however, are misleading, because Havana residents had
varying degrees of commitment to the cause. Many, especially the
young, listened to the distant voices of Radio Rebelde and cheered for
the rebels the way they did for cowboy heroes at the Saturday matinees,
but their support was about as helpful as their shouts at the silver screen.

Among the active supporters, the largest group, with the smallest
commitment, were the countless thousands who contributed money for
26th of July bonds, theoretically redeemable upon victory. The smallest
group, and the one which Castro always emphasized most, was Acción y
Sabotaje, made up of those willing to shoot or plant bombs for the
cause. Almost always, the unit's members were completely "underground," using fictitious war names as they hopped from safehouse to
safehouse to keep ahead of the police.

In between the bond buyers and the sabotage unit, in both
commitment and size, was the Civic Resistance, a group created by the
26th of July to attract businessmen and professionals. Most of these men
led a twilight life, working at their regular jobs during the day, doing
their Movement activities at night. They were led by one of Havana's
most successful architect-engineers, Manuel Ray, and many were driven
to the cause out of a profound sense of embarrassment, a feeling that
while they could boast of their air conditioners and television sets that
seemed to put them almost on a par with the Americans, they had as a
government a shabby military dictatorship that seemed more worthy of
an old banana republic than a country aspiring to join the modern
world.

They played the game cautiously. Cuba was a small enough country
that "connections" could be used, and there was the Latin emphasis on
family, in which even a distant relative was important. That meant
almost everyone had a friend or relative in the government, a person
who, if worse came to worst, could be counted on to vouch for someone
taken to jail. Such a connection might not be enough to free a prisoner,
but it usually guaranteed that at least his body would not appear on a
street corner. The Batista police could be brutal on occasion, but there
was a certain haphazardness to their enforcement, a softness that
allowed some (especially the affluent and well-connected) to go into
exile and bumbling detective work that helped others to escape arrest
altogether.

Emilio Guede understood how oddly the police worked. He was an advertising executive and the propaganda chief of the Civic Resistance. On Sundays, he went to the empty Gimnasio Parera studios in the Vedado area, where among the exercycles and the barbells he produced posters denouncing the dictatorship. As a professional, he wanted to make them as elaborate and as beautiful as possible, even to the point of using a new printing process called Ektagraph. The ink and paper for the system were sold at only one store in Cuba, but the police never carried out even an elemental investigation, which would have led directly to him.

Guede had come to feel somewhat secure when suddenly, in early December, as rebel gains mounted in Oriente, the Havana police began a widespread campaign of repression. Bodies of Movement supporters started appearing on country roads outside of towns. Many others were being arrested. The message was clear: Beyond the polite diplomacy of connections, it was still possible to die. Supporters of clandestine activities began taking additional precautions, never saying anything significant on the telephone, avoiding suspicious meetings, perhaps making a quick contact during an all-night wake at a funeral home. There, they could keep track of their compatriots, find out who had been questioned, who was missing, who was thinking of fleeing to Miami. It was obvious that the police were getting serious.

It was about 10:00 P.M. when Ismael Suárez de la Paz walked nervously out of a house in the blue-collar neighborhood of La Vibora. A slender, olive-skinned man whose perfect white teeth were offset by a crooked nose, he had been for hours in a meeting trying to find volunteers to take medicines and supplies to the rebels hiding in the hills of the central province of Las Villas. Many were willing to donate goods, but few wanted to risk the trip, and the meeting had dragged on, violating all principles of the underground. It had gone on so long that neighbors could grow suspicious, and there had been far too many people there, about twenty, for them to pretend it was a mere social gathering. Now, he would have to appear on the streets with a group of men at night, a sight that always aroused the interest of police.

Suárez de la Paz had become a hardened veteran of Acción y Sabotaje by avoiding such risky situations. Few even knew his real name, or that he had gone from a street-wise, blue-collar childhood to being the top salesman for Ferro National Foods, or that now, in his late thirties, he was almost penniless as an underground man while hiding in a luxurious safehouse apartment in the high-rise FOCSA building. Most contacts knew nothing about him but his war name: Comandante Echemendía.

Outside the house, he followed three other men into a 1954 brown Chevrolet Bel Air. The driver headed the car toward the Vedado area, moving along a broad thoroughfare until they came to the traffic circle facing the modernistic, saucer-shaped Sports Palace.

Suddenly, Echemendía saw three police cars blocking the road. "Hide this," the driver mumbled to him as he handed over a .45-caliber automatic pistol. Echemendía cursed. The man had broken an underground rule by even bringing the pistol along. Not only was it incriminating evidence, but it gave police a chance to shoot them on the spot and claim they were responding to "criminals'" gunfire.

As the car stopped, Echemendía slid the pistol under the cushion the driver was sitting on. "Don't let the cushion slip when you get out," he whispered. The driver nodded.

About a dozen policemen, some carrying submachine guns, surrounded the car and ordered the four men to stand on the sidewalk. As Echemendía climbed out, he realized he had in his pocket a list of names and telephone numbers of persons who had volunteered to transport the supplies to the rebels. That was the worst security violation of all.

Waiting for the search, Echemendía stood facing a large fountain in the center of the circle, where water bathed in colored lights gushed four or five stories into the air and crashed back into the pool with a terrible roar. A little to one side, people were staring at them from the cars parked in front of Havana's only drive-in restaurant. A sign advertised American hot dogs with Cuban seasonings.

The police patted the men down, looking for weapons, but they asked for no identification and didn't check their pockets. Echemendía realized they were simply making a routine search of a suspicious car carrying four men.

As an officer moved to inspect the trunk and engine compartment, Echemendía slid into the driver's seat and sat on the cushion concealing the gun. A policeman checked under the seats, but he didn't ask Echemendía to move.

"OK," the officer said when he was finished, "you're lucky that you're clean, so stay clean."

As the Chevrolet Bel Air pulled away, Echemendía started sweating and shaking. It had been a close call. Quickly, the driver dropped the men off at different street corners, where they could catch buses and disappear into the night.

In the town of Bauta, on the western edge of Havana, Julio Duarte was doing something he had no interest in: listening to a life insurance salesman. The man had wandered into his law office unannounced, sat down and begun talking about the virtues of security. He seemed to have a lot to say.

Duarte had far more important things to do. He was trying to take care of the legal work that had been piling up because of his clandestine activities. On the surface, he was a respectable member of the Establishment, son of a conservative politician, an affluent attorney with two law offices, and the secretary general of both the Havana and Cuban Bar Associations. Yet he was the one who had arranged for passports so that men could go to Mexico to join Castro's expedition to Oriente Province and he was the Movement's star money collector, sometimes from businessmen who believed in the cause, other times from sugar-mill owners forced to contribute because their lands were in rebel territory. Out of caution, he had stopped going to his Havana law office, but he still occasionally used the one in Bauta, confident that he, as a leader of the bar association, was almost immune to arrest.

The insurance man droned on. There were all sorts of advantages, he said, if Duarte signed up now. He could be eligible for a lottery to be held in mid-January, among other things. The prize was $5000. Duarte said he had plenty of insurance, but the salesman didn't take the suggestion.

He was still talking when the telephone rang. It was Duarte's wife in Havana. "Can you talk?" she asked. Her voice was tense.

"There's an insurance salesman here," he said casually.

"Oh, then don't say anything. I've just had a call from Mrs. Dorticós."

"Yes?" That was the wife of the head of the Cuban Bar Association, Osvaldo Dorticós, who was also chief of the 26th of July underground in the city of Cienfuegos.

"She says the police have arrested her husband, and she doesn't know where they've taken him."

"I see," said Duarte, staring across the desk at the insurance man. "Well, I'll have to talk to the other members of the bar about that."

He hung up the phone slowly. If the police dared arrest the leader of the Cuban bar, then no one was safe.

"Yes, I guess you're right," Duarte said to the salesman. "I *could* use some more life insurance." He searched for a pen to sign the contract. The salesman smiled triumphantly.

Shortly after that, about 3:00 P.M. on a Friday afternoon, a close friend of Duarte's, Danilo Mesa, drove down the broad Malecón Boulevard as gentle Gulf waves lapped against the seawall. It was the end of the traditional two-hour siesta break, and he was returning to open his store, California Alta Fidelidad, which specialized in selling Scott, Fisher and Garrard hi-fi equipment at La Rampa shopping center.

A short man with curly black hair, he was a money collector for the 26th of July, but for a time he had held one of the most dangerous jobs, serving as the public contact for the Movement's underground chief in Havana. Each day, people would come to him to find out the location of the safehouse the chief was using that day, and that meant too many knew who Mesa was. In turn, he had an enormous number of names and addresses in his head, but the police had never bothered him, not even when they arrested his sister Lilian and kept her for three months in an SIM cell. She had not been tortured, but she was now a nervous shambles, gulping tranquilizers and hiding out with Cuban friends who lived at the U.S. Guantánamo Naval Base.

Mesa turned right off the Malecón and drove up a gently sloping hill, past the modern stores where tourists and the area's middle class shopped, until he found a parking spot in front of his own store.

As he climbed out of the car, five or six policemen appeared. Mesa recognized the insignias on their uniforms immediately: They were from Servicios Especiales, one of the antisubversive forces that reported directly to Batista. "You have to come with us," an officer told him.

Mesa fought back a feeling of panic as police led him to a squad car and pushed him into the backseat. There, he saw the familiar face of his building's parking-lot attendant.

"Yes, this is the one," the attendant told the police officers.

"What are you talking about?" Mesa tried to act enraged.

"Oh, you know a lot."

"What? You're crazy."

The officers didn't listen. Two climbed into the front seat, and the driver pulled the squad car into the traffic by the CMQ Radio Center.

Mesa tried to sort things out. There were hundreds of people who could have identified him as a clandestine worker, but this parking-lot attendant? It didn't seem possible. The man lived in the blue-collar area of Marianao, and sometimes after work Mesa gave him a ride home. He was a talkative fellow, always asking Mesa what certain people were doing and describing his own vague schemes to undermine the regime. Mesa, cautiously, had never explained his own underground connections.

Now he looked at the attendant carefully. The man was nervous and pale. Perhaps he had been tortured to talk, but he couldn't have been beaten much because Mesa didn't see a mark on him. Once, an underground member had boasted to Mesa, "If the police ever catch me, they will never be able to make me talk, regardless of what they do." Mesa wasn't certain about himself. "My parents never beat me as a child," he told his friend. "I don't know what I'd do. How can you say something like that when you don't have any experience?" Now he thought grimly that he was about to find out.

The squad car stopped behind the 10th Precinct Station in the El Cerro neighborhood. In the back was the headquarters of Colonel Conrado Carratalá, one of Batista's most feared officials. Mesa was led into an office, where there were a desk, sofa and chairs. It did not seem like an interrogation room, and Mesa relaxed a little as four or five policemen leaned against the walls and watched him.

An officer asked him to talk about his underground activities. Mesa said he knew nothing and hoped they couldn't hear the fear in his voice. The man repeated the request. Again, Mesa refused.

Without warning, a policeman slugged him in the jaw. He crumpled to the floor and felt a sudden sickening sensation. The others began beating him on the back and around the head with their fists and rubber hoses. Some kicked him, and with each blow he felt more nauseated.

"Talk, talk," the policemen demanded.

Mesa said nothing. It was impossible to speak.

"Talk, talk! You know a lot."

He curled into the fetal position for protection. His mind was numb, but he realized they were accusing him of nothing specific, not mentioning one of the industrialists he had blackmailed for contributions or any of his underground connections. All they had was the idiotic accusation of the parking-lot attendant.

They kept pounding his back. It could have gone on for half an hour, or only ten minutes. Time seemed to have no meaning. At last, he blacked out. Vaguely, as if in a dream, he heard the men leaving. "We will try again later," one said.

About an hour after his arrest, Mesa's wife Rosa received a telephone call at their sumptuous home in the El Country Club subdivision. It was Mesa's partner, a former Belgian count, and he said he had just arrived at the store to find the doors still locked. A chauffeur standing nearby told him what had happened.

Rosa knew immediately what to do. She was a big-boned woman so dedicated to the struggle that the day before she gave birth to their third child, she had transported a car filled with Ping-Pong balls injected with explosive chemicals for the burning of canefields. Now, her husband's life was at stake, and it was critically important that they find out within hours which precinct station he had been taken to. If they could learn his location, that meant specific officers were responsible for his treatment, and they wouldn't dare kill him. If they couldn't discover where he was, then no police officer could be held responsible and his body might easily turn up on a country road.

She first telephoned a friend who was a member of a woman's group that specialized in calling government officials at times like this, begging for mercy and threatening exposure unless the prisoner was released. At least one member of the group knew John Topping, the political officer at the U.S. embassy. A politely phrased American "inquiry" to the Cuban foreign ministry was one sign to the regime that a prisoner deserved special consideration.

Then, with Mesa's sister, Nelia Galíndez, she hurried to the hi-fi shop, where they talked to the chauffeur. He had not seen the policemen's insignia, but he did add a single fact: One of the officers was wearing a white bandage, maybe a cast, on one of his arms.

Rosa returned home to wait for phone calls. The sister went on to the office of the Italian monsignor who was secretary to the papal nuncio. The representative of the pope was officially neutral, but he hated brutality by either rebels or the police, and he was known to have saved perhaps sixty police prisoners by making "inquiries."

The monsignor quickly agreed to help. Together, they spent the afternoon and early evening going from one police station to another. At each, Nelia let the priest do the talking: "We understand you have Mr. Mesa here." Each denied it.

At the 10th Precinct Station, it was the same story. A sullen captain said he had never heard of the man. But Nelia spotted an officer behind the waist-high partition that separated the public area from the policemen's desks. He had a bandage on his arm.

"That's him," she shouted, pointing to the man. "That's the one who was there." She repeated the chauffeur's story. The captain asked the officer, but he said it was all a lie. The monsignor wasn't so certain. "Well," he told the captain, "I will have to take this to the diplomatic corps, so they can be informed."

That night, Nelia talked to her husband, Ignacio Galíndez, a retired army general who in 1933 had been one of the sergeants who had helped Batista take over the government. At one time, the two were so close that they became *compadres*, godfathers of each other's children. They had split in 1952, when Galíndez objected bitterly to Batista's second coup d'etat, but the retired general was still on friendly terms with some of the family. About 11:00 P.M., as the family listened anxiously, Galíndez telephoned Rubén Batista, the eldest son. Mesa would be safe with one word from him, but Rubén refused to go along. "Well, General," he said, "I'm sorry to hear your brother-in-law is mixed up with those bandits. But if he's not guilty, he has nothing to be afraid of." Those were the last words the family wanted to hear.

The next morning, realizing it already might be too late, the Mesas tried again. They convinced one of the country's most prominent businessmen, Julio Blanco Herrera, owner of the Tropical brewery, to make a respectful call at the 10th Precinct Station. The entrepreneur was a neighbor of the Mesas and, secretly, a major contributor to the 26th of July. To the police captain, Blanco Herrera asked politely about the welfare of his friend, Danilo Mesa. He received no answer, but the family hoped the inquiry was enough.

Mesa's wife Rosa decided to try one last ploy. Her brother was married to a daughter of Colonel José A. Martínez Suárez, the territorial inspector of the Fifth Military District, based just outside of Havana. He was a diehard Batistiano, but he was worth a try.

Martínez Suárez was at home when the call arrived. He was being asked to help his daughter's husband's sister's husband. In a non-Latin culture, that would be stretching the idea of family beyond all limits, but Martínez Suárez didn't hesitate. He had two phones in his house, a regular one and a special microwave set which linked him to the nation's military and police installations. The microwave network implied the call was official. That was the set he used now. He started with SIM, the military intelligence service; they had never heard of Mesa. Then he called Lieutenant Colonel Esteban Ventura, the most active chief of the antisubversive squads. Ventura was an old friend, and Martínez Suárez believed him when he said that Mesa wasn't at his station.

At last, he called the 10th Precinct. "Oh, yes," Colonel Carratalá told him, "Danilo Mesa. I have him here." He said he knew that Mesa was one of the 26th of July mainstays in Havana, but he didn't have solid proof. Martínez Suárez assured him of Mesa's basically good character, he was an honorable man who had made some mistakes, and he promised that if Mesa were released, he would personally guarantee that Mesa engaged in no more subversive activities.

"But I have 'this way,'" Carratalá objected, referring obliquely to his beating of prisoners. "If I let him go, pretty soon he will start talking about everything."

Martínez Suárez promised that Mesa would speak to no one, especially not to foreign journalists who might publish his story. Carratalá consented, but he said he couldn't let Mesa go for several days, until the wounds had healed.

That night, Rosa was allowed to see her husband after an agonizing two-hour wait. An officer led her to the end of a large room, where a black policeman holding a rifle guarded a door. The officer opened the door, revealing a dimly lit corridor.

Mesa was walking down it, accompanied by a guard. His wounds still ached, but after the inquiries, the police officers had covered the worst bruises with ointment and stopped the interrogation. He had told them nothing.

The guard made him stop just before the end of the corridor. Rosa strained to see if he had been beaten, but he was hidden in the shadows, standing there stiffly.

With the guards beside them, the conversation was unnaturally formal.

"Hello, how are you?" she asked.

"I'm fine."

"Did you eat the food I sent?"

"Yes. How are the kids?"

"They're fine."

"Well," Mesa said distantly, "good night."

Rosa asked a guard if she could kiss him. He said yes. Mesa took a step forward and they embraced as she whispered, "Did they beat you?"

"No," he said, but when she drew back, while his head was still bent forward into the light of the main room, she saw that his ear was badly bruised. She left, fighting back tears.

That same day, police chased a twenty-two-year-old rebel sympathizer named Francisco J. Gómez Mejumir into the Central Hotel, at the corner of San Rafael and Consulado in Old Havana. He raced to the third floor and, there, leaped to his death rather than be captured.

A scrawny underground man named Max Lesnik, wearing a T-shirt and blue jeans to make him look younger than his twenty-eight years, rode up an elevator in a high-rise apartment building on the edge of the Vedado area. He was the Havana leader of the fledgling group called the Segundo Frente del Escambray, which had several hundred followers, most of them unarmed, in the mountains of central Cuba.

At the penthouse floor, Lesnik stepped off and, peering through the fake eyeglasses he used as part of his disguise, found the apartment of Jack Stewart. Almost as soon as he knocked, Stewart opened the door. He greeted Lesnik in fluent Spanish, with only a hint of a Texas twang, and led him into a large living room, which overlooked the Vedado Tennis Club and the Gulf of Mexico. It was the first time Lesnik had been to the apartment and, as he sat down in a comfortable easy chair, he remarked how luxurious it seemed compared to his own safehouse apartment, which had no electricity and only a pillow for furniture.

Stewart smiled, then asked what he wanted to drink. Lesnik, following the code of the underground, requested something non-alcoholic, and the American disappeared into the kitchen to get it.

The two had met some months before, introduced by a Cuban friend who had whispered to Lesnik afterward, "I think this guy is with the FBI." Neither had ever heard of the CIA, but they knew that Stewart, who talked vaguely about having a lowly paper-pushing job at the U.S. embassy, spent much of his time in cafés, talking to men who could tell him about anti-Batista activities. Gradually Lesnik had come to trust Stewart, and the American, in turn, had become quite helpful to the Segundo Frente. Some weeks before, he had even used the embassy's diplomatic pouch to smuggle a letter from Lesnik's group to Carlos Prío, the president whom Batista had overthrown, who was in exile in Miami. The Segundo Frente, desperate to achieve recognition, wanted Prio to go to their hideout in the Escambray Mountains and set up a government-in-arms. Then Prio could legitimately claim that he was the one who should succeed Batista, because he was the last democratically elected president. They knew that Prio was making huge contributions to anti-Batista groups, but he had become accustomed to a luxurious life-style, and to woo him, the Segundo Frente promised to provide a large farmhouse, called El Mamey, complete with telephone, television and an air-conditioned room. An airstrip was nearby, and a plane could whisk him away quickly if danger threatened.

When the American returned and handed him a glass of ginger ale, Lesnik said he had seen the name of Santo Trafficante, the mobster who ran several casinos, on a mailbox in the lobby. "Is he here to watch you?" Lesnik joked. "Or are you here to watch him?"

Stewart laughed, but his face turned serious quickly. He asked if Lesnik had heard anything from Prio in Miami.

Lesnik fidgeted. He had to admit that Prio was being reluctant about returning to Cuba. The man obviously did not relish the idea of living in the mountains, of risking his life, but he was at least helping on another plan, by donating $100,000 to buy weapons that the Segundo Frente needed badly. And that, Lesnik said, subtly making his tone more serious, is what he had come to Stewart to talk about.

"It appears our man is about ready to come back, but we are having trouble getting a 'green light' so that the plane can take off without any problems. We can't afford to lose those weapons. The 26th of July can lose a planeload and have another ready to take off the next night. We're not in that position. We would have to spend six months making arrangements for another shipment, and we have no time to waste. If we don't act now, then Castro will take over."

Lesnik had talked to Stewart many times about why his group was opposed to Castro, but now that he was asking a crucial favor, he wanted to repeat the reasons: "If Castro should win an absolute victory, it is not only Cuba that is threatened, but liberty. Regardless of what he is, a Communist or a fascist or whatever, he is a totalitarian. If the United States stands by and lets Castro take over, then it is going to have headaches. Now, this is a conversation man to man. I am not just playing a political game."

Stewart asked if Lesnik was saying that the weapons would make the

Segundo Frente the military and political equal of the 26th of July.

"No, no," Lesnik said. "I'm not saying that, but there are many unarmed men with our guerrillas, and I think that if we get those weapons, we could race them to Havana. All we are asking is that the plane be a safe bet."

As Lesnik drained the last of his ginger ale, Stewart made a sympathetic reply, but he promised nothing. The message would have to be passed along to higher authorities, and they would make the decision. Lesnik understood, but he asked him to hurry.

14/AN EMBASSY DIVIDED

At 8:30 A.M., the last of the senior staff members took his place at a long wooden table in the conference room of the U.S. embassy. They were on the building's top floor, but the walls of windows, which usually offered a spectacular view of Malecón Boulevard and the Gulf of Mexico, were covered by curtains to prevent anyone in the nearby Vedado high-rises from seeing what was happening.

It was time for the daily briefing, and Ambassador Smith, sitting in a white suit at one end, his long legs stretched out under the table, began by talking about an early-morning meeting he had just had at the house of Prime Minister Gonzalo Güell in Miramar. It was one in a series of discussions in which the two of them were attempting to reach a secret agreement, so that President-elect Rivero Agüero could take office early and form a coalition that might be able to end the war. Smith said he was making progress, but they still had a way to go.

When he asked for other reports, Colonel Samuel Kail, the army attaché, and Jim Noel, the CIA station chief, discussed the information they had been receiving about the 26th of July rebels in the hills of central Las Villas Province. They didn't seem to have many men yet and, except for a few annoying ambushes, they were not doing much fighting, but the Cuban army appeared unwilling to confront them. According to the best information available, their leader was Ernesto ("Ché") Guevara, a young Argentine doctor.

As the discussion moved around the table, most agreed that if Batista could not "wipe out" these rebels less than three hundred miles from Havana, his government was probably doomed.

Then Smith asked, in an unusually quiet voice, "Is Guevara a Communist?"

There was a long silence. Paul Bethel, the press attaché, saw the staffers fidgeting in their chairs. The specter of Communism was becoming an almost daily argument at the briefings. Sometimes it centered on Raúl Castro. Now it was Guevara.

"So," Smith continued, his voice rising as he tried to answer his own question, "what the hell else would an Argentine be doing there? He was in the Communist revolution in Guatemala, and the Reds must have put him here as the international link."

Political officer Topping broke the staff's silence with an undisguised sigh. "Look," he said in his crisp New York accent, "we *know* he's from Argentina. We *know* he's been in Guatemala, but we don't have any signs that he was such a red-hot instigator there. And there's no sign he's ever joined the Communist party."

"Baloney," Smith grumbled.

"But, Mr. Ambassador," Topping went on, obviously trying to control his temper, "you say he's an agent of an organized Communist conspiracy, and we can't say that. We don't have any proof."

"So what is he doing in a Cuban revolution?"

"Maybe," Topping shrugged, "they just needed a medical man in the mountains. Simple as that."

Disgusted, Smith turned to Eugene Gilmore, the economic counselor, and asked him what he knew. Gilmore, surprised he was being called upon, said he knew nothing.

Smith, anger building, looked at Noel, who had become the CIA station chief only weeks before. Uncomfortably, Noel repeated what he had already said several times before, that an agent who had been in the Sierra for a while reported that Castro "had no intimate contact with people we suspect" of being Communist.

Smith persisted. He wanted information on Guevara specifically.

Noel admitted uneasily that he knew little about the man. He would have to check the agency's information and report back.

Hearing that, Smith leaped from his chair. "What the hell is this? Top career officers and not one of you can tell me whether Guevara is or is not a Communist?" He picked up the telephone and buzzed his secretary. Holding the receiver against his chest, he almost shouted: "Well, I know that Guevara is a Communist even if you don't. And I'll tell you what I'm going to do. I'm going to burn up the wires to Washington and tell them that the Communists are marching through Cuba like Sherman's march to the sea. Now, how the hell do you like that?"

The staff was dismissed. They walked out sullenly, realizing that still another embassy meeting had degenerated into chaos.

If Smith had disagreements in Washington, his problems inside his own embassy were even worse, and by the last weeks of 1958, the rancor was so intense that the ambassador and some of his staffers refused even to talk to each other outside of the formal meetings. Daniel Braddock, a mild-mannered man who as deputy chief of mission was the number two official in Havana, often had to serve as mediator between Smith and the others. Braddock considered it the most divided embassy he had seen in his long career in the foreign service. So did Paul Bethel, the press attaché, who arrived in mid-1958 to find that almost everyone on the staff had chosen sides in the civil war. Bethel had never seen diplomats' emotions run so high about another country's problems.

Ambassador Smith distrusted almost all of his staff, except the military attachés and the commercial specialists, who he assumed were "pro-business." In midsummer, he had managed to oust the CIA's longtime station chief and the man's deputy because he was convinced they were too sympathetic to the anti-Batista groups. In November, when political officer Topping had been accused of encouraging the military conspiracy, Smith had wanted his recall too, but Washington had simply ignored the request. The ambassador received a modicum of satisfaction by making certain the complaint was entered into Topping's personnel file.

Even with more neutral staff members, Smith insisted on seeing every cable they wanted to send to Washington. Sometimes he changed the content to keep it in line with what he thought was the real situation, but still he suspected some staffers were "going behind my back" by slipping their own views into the diplomatic pouches sent to the State Department.

The problem, of course, was that different Cubans had different views. Smith, who spoke no Spanish, was getting his information primarily from Prime Minister Güell and Senator Jorge García Montes, a former Batista prime minister. Both Güell and García Montes spoke fluent English, and each convinced Smith that the Cuban people craved a *caudillo*, a charismatic strong man, whether he be of the Right or of the Left. The United States could either support Batista, who had always been pro-American and catered to foreign investment, or, inevitably, it would have to face a take-over by Fidel Castro, who they were certain was a Communist and anti-American. Sometimes, they provided Smith with what they said was documentation of the Communist menace.

But CIA officials doubted the evidence, and sometimes even laughed at it, especially when the Buró de Represión Anti-Comunista, known as BRAC, held press conferences in which they produced confiscated copies of a weekly underground Communist newspaper. It did not take the CIA long to realize they were showing the same stacks of newspapers each time, and it became obvious that the organization was only using Communism as a pretext when it raided the offices of wealthy Cuban lawyers simply because they were opposed to Batista. Worse, BRAC agents sometimes used brutality in their interrogations, a severe embarrassment to the CIA, which had urged the Cuban government to set up an anti-Communist agency and had even trained its officers, the same way that the U.S. Federal Bureau of Investigation had trained many officers of the feared SIM group.

Despite those connections, many anti-Batista Cubans sought desperately to talk to American officials, who had always been the focal point of power when chaos threatened. Both conservatives and certain kinds of progressives considered it an unbeatable status symbol to boast they were "in contact with the U.S. embassy." To fellow Cubans, that implied a man was getting secret information and even approval for his own conspiracies, though in reality it usually meant an American staff man was pumping him for information and promising nothing. Andrés Suárez, a member of the small, liberal Montecristi Movement, used to choose a table in the center of a fine restaurant when he lunched with Basil Beardsley, a redheaded young CIA agent. That way, all of Suárez's friends could see he was talking to a U.S. official, and if Batista's police noticed, it was almost a guarantee against arrest. The image was more important to Suárez than the meetings themselves, for the earnest young Beardsley kept asking about Communism, especially about Carlos Rafael Rodríguez, a leader of the Communists' Partido Socialista Popular (PSP), who was rumored to have joined Castro in the mountains. Suárez was annoyed by the persistent questioning. He suspected Castro had totalitarian tendencies, but he believed Marxism was irrelevant to the Cuban situation, and he kept telling Beardsley that the members of the PSP had never thrown a bomb or imported a rifle in the fight against Batista.

Many anti-Batista Cubans were telling American officials the same basic story, and it was this interpretation that enraged Smith. Jim Noel, the new CIA station chief, was more circumspect in dealing with the ambassador than had been his predecessor, but he was obtaining the same information. On a trip to Santiago de Cuba, a Catholic priest had told him, "Oh, no, they're not Communists. Listen, Castro even has two Catholic chaplains with him in the mountains, and a Communist wouldn't have chaplains. Look at Batista: he doesn't have chaplains."

Political officer Topping was hearing similar viewpoints, but he was more emphatic when passing the information along to Smith. Unlike the ambassador, Topping spoke fluent Spanish, and he moved easily through several sectors of Cuban society as he listened to academicians, professionals and businessmen preach about corruption and violence in the Batista government. Even his American neighbors in Miramar were aiding the underground with money and supplies.

Time and again, Topping had been confronted by Cubans who asked, "How can you," meaning the United States, "be so stupid as to support this man Batista?" That question stung Topping, and every time the ambassador pointed to some link between the mountain rebels and the Communists, Topping mentioned the many middle- and upper-class Cubans who were supporting Castro, people who certainly would have nothing to do with a Marxist revolution.

Yet Topping and his ambassador agreed that Washington was "shoving a doctrine of nonintervention down our throats." Both men believed the American economic and political presence in Cuba was so pervasive that simply to do nothing had a major impact on the country. To Smith, it meant allowing the Batista regime to crumble. To Topping, it meant de facto support for the dictatorship.

Often, repeating the same experiences Director Wieland was having in Washington, Topping and the CIA chief were approached by Cubans who had plans to oust Batista. Some suggested replacing him with pro-American moderates. Others, more sophisticated, wanted to put democratic officers in charge of the army, then let all the political groups—including Castro's—vie for power and public support. Democracy could return and flourish, but the army leaders would ensure that the new regime wouldn't step beyond the bounds of the 1940 Constitution. Each of these plots was passed along to Washington on the CIA's top-secret radio channel, over which Smith had no control. But there they were simply lost in the bureaucracy, never to be heard of again.

Washington's passivity enraged Topping, because he knew that the talk of a new regime under Rivero Agüero was a farce. The "president-elect" wasn't even doing his own negotiating with the ambassador; that was the duty of Güell, Batista's prime minister. And there seemed absolutely no chance of establishing a genuine coalition. Washington's Dispatch 292 had said the pro-Castro "civic organizations" were necessary for unity, but Topping was convinced these civic moderates would never support a Batista puppet. Without them, no regime could succeed. Yet morning after morning slipped by in the staff meetings without Smith mentioning the dispatch or saying that he had relayed its demands to the regime.

The delay was astounding on such a crucial issue. If the United States formally stated that Batista should leave the country, the dictator would have to obey, because the United States was his last hope. When the hope was smashed, his regime was finished. But every time Topping started to ask Smith about the dispatch, the ambassador turned away. The two men rarely spoke anymore.

There was one other matter that Topping and Smith could agree upon: the state of the Cuban economy. Even in the last tumultuous weeks, memorandums were streaming from the embassy's commercial section showing that U.S. investors still had faith in Cuba. One American announced plans to build a $6-million resort near Havana that would offer a casino, a nightclub, bowling alley, riding stables and hunting lodge. The Cuban Goodrich Rubber Company was preparing to start work January 1 on a $2.4-million plant, and General Electric was developing a $3-million light-bulb factory. Chrysler had begun confidential discussions with the embassy about building a Cuban factory that would assemble all its cars for Latin America. In Oriente Province, where the U.S. government had already constructed a $100-million nickel mining operation at Nicaro, the Freeport-Sulphur Corporation was developing a $75-million project to mine even more nickel.

U.S. investment in Cuba was already more than $1 billion, and that included projects by the giants of American enterprise, such as Republic Steel, Esso Standard Oil and Texaco. The American and Foreign Power Company, which provided much of the country's electricity, had a $221-million investment. IT&T owned more than a third of the $85-million Cuban Telephone Company.

Yet in recent years American dominance of the country's business had been decreasing, especially in the important sugar industry. Over thirty years, the Americans' share of sugar production had shrunk from 55 percent to about a third, as Cuban-owned output soared from 20 percent to more than 60.

Until the civil war depressed the economy, Cuba had prospered under Batista, and it ranked as one of the most affluent countries in Latin America. In 1957, when sugar prices were high on the world market, Cuba's per capita income was $374, making it second only to oil-rich Venezuela. It had the lowest infant mortality rate and ranked among the best in the number of doctors, literacy rate and percentage of homes with baths and electricity. Tourism tripled during the Batista years. Construction soared.

Cuba was no longer a predominantly rural society. Slightly more than half the people lived in the cities and towns, but the economy remained gravely unbalanced. The overwhelming portion of development was confined to Havana. From 1954 to 1958, the city, with less than a quarter of the country's 6.5 million population, accounted for about three-quarters of all construction, and the bulk of that was in hotels and luxury apartments.

Making matters worse, each year thousands of rural peasants were moving to Havana, attracted by the glamour and dreams of wealth, causing an enormous housing shortage for the lower classes and creating the *barrios* of plywood shacks. Even those slum dwellers, however, considered themselves better off than their rural brethren who lived in dirt-floor *bohíos*. Throughout Cuba, 20 percent of the population was illiterate, but in the countryside, 42 percent could neither read nor write.

The government did little to improve matters. The income tax on $1 million a year was only 10 percent, and even that was rarely paid. Most of the wealthy found it easier to slip a small bribe to the tax collector. Of the thirty thousand members of Havana's top country clubs, only one in six was a registered taxpayer.

But both the rich and the poor shared a certain vision: the American Dream. Many of the upper class spoke fluent English and feverishly copied American customs, from eating hamburgers to attending drive-in movies. They considered it a status symbol to send their children to college in the United States. The poor could see the signs of American wealth every day, in the showroom cars, the television shows and movies and, most visibly, in the tourists who came down to spend their money. Compared with Latin America, the Cubans were an affluent people, or so the statistics showed. Compared with the United States, only ninety miles away, the people were, on the average, very poor. Their annual per capita income was less than one-seventh of the U.S. average, and many Cubans continued to yearn for the American Dream, which seemed so near yet so far.

The subtleties of all this were lost on the American business leaders, but they still had a rather comprehensive grasp of the political situation of the country, and Ambassador Smith respected their opinions far more than those of the career diplomats.

In early December, Smith listened to what the managers had to say at the monthly meeting of his businessmen's advisory council. Gathered in the penthouse conference room, the heads of Cuban operations for Portland Cement, the Moa Bay Mining Company, Esso Standard Oil and the First National Bank of Boston agreed that the "Castro movement is Communist-inspired and dominated," but they could offer no more proof than the CIA men could. They believed that "unless strongly supported by U.S., Batista cannot last until February 24 and maybe not beyond January 1. Even with this support, it is doubtful whether he can hold out to end his term." To avoid the worst bloodbath in Cuban history, the businessmen suggested that the United States help create a civilian-military junta, including the "best elements" of the present government and the political opposition. It was a cautiously conservative stance, but even these businessmen echoed what the State Department had said, suggesting that the junta include "civic groups now supporting Castro. Batista should have no role in government."

Smith was not content with that proposal. After the meeting, he called his longtime secretary, Edith Elverson, into his office. As always, he dictated to her at machine-gun speed, pausing occasionally so that she could read it back, allowing him to make insertions and deletions.

Pacing, he added his own comments to the businessmen's suggestions. He was bothered, he said, by how Batista and the military leaders could be convinced to accept a junta. He thought Batista might consider it unconstitutional because "it disregards results of elections." And he wondered about accepting pro-Castro civic organizations since "Castro's group would still have to be dealt with," and he wanted to keep Castro out of a new government at any cost.

As a counterproposal, Smith suggested that Batista be urged to turn over the presidency to his successor, Rivero Agüero, as soon as possible, well before the February inauguration. Rivero Agüero could then form a "national union government" consisting of "respected elements," call a constituent assembly and hold new elections within two years.

Again, Smith ignored the problem of Batista's role, and he did not mention to the State Department one key point: that his proposal was exactly the agreement that he and Prime Minister Güell had hammered out at their early morning meetings, held secretly at Güell's house so that no one would accuse him of interfering in Cuba's internal affairs.

The day after the cable was sent, Smith received a crisp telephone call on the scrambler system: Washington wanted him to fly up for "consultations." He did not mention it, but he suspected that the information he had been given on Thanksgiving Day was true. It was time for the secret emissary to fly to Havana.

A few hours before Smith arrived in Washington, three men gathered in a fourth-floor office of the Old State Department Building. Sitting in chairs on one side of the coffee table were Assistant Secretary Rubottom and William Wieland, the director of Caribbean and Mexican affairs. Opposite, on the sofa, lit by the gray light from the enclosed courtyard, was William D. Pawley, a thin, gray-haired man who had spent his life involved in big business and secret government projects.

Wieland had seen him flitting between offices for the past several days, and he guessed that something was up. It usually was when Pawley was around. In the 1920s, Pawley had formed Cuba's first national airline, which he later sold to Pan American. In the mid-1930s, he built three aircraft factories in China and, after the Japanese invasion, helped organize the Flying Tigers. He had met both Mao Tse-tung and Chou

En-lai, but his sympathies were always with the Chinese Nationalists, and he believed bitterly that the U.S. State Department had abandoned China to the Communists. Later, he became the negotiator who carried on secret conversations with dictator Francisco Franco, so that the United States could obtain military bases in Spain. He had also been ambassador to Peru and then Brazil, where Wieland had been a junior member of his staff.

Almost from the beginning, the two men had disliked each other intensely. Pawley thought Wieland was a leftist sympathizer and Wieland considered Pawley an ultraconservative who didn't really understand Latin America. Both spoke fluent Spanish and both had spent years in Cuba; Pawley still had large investments there.

Now, Pawley was being carefully polite as he explained to Wieland what he was planning to do. It had begun, he said, at his home in Miami, where he had hosted a late-night meeting with CIA and State men who happened to be in town for a Latin-American conference. All agreed that something had to be done quickly about the Cuban situation. Pawley had decided he was the man to do it. He talked to the CIA and then went to the White House to meet with Eisenhower, whom he knew well.

The president, he said to Wieland with some drama, supported his plan completely. Pawley was going to Cuba to tell Batista that he should leave so that a military-civilian junta could be appointed to end the fighting.

Wieland grimaced at the mention of a junta. Clearing his throat, he said that except for a few days in 1933, Cuba had never had a junta, and group leadership seemed to fit the Cuban psyche "like a snowball in hell."

Pawley's face flushed as he explained that the junta would be only temporary, until the country could be quieted down. Then elections would be held. "This damn thing is all screwed up," he said, staring directly at Wieland. "And I can straighten it out. I have a lot of influence with Batista, and I'm going to use it. I'll lay it on the line."

With that, Pawley stood up and walked out. Wieland turned to Assistant Secretary Rubottom: "Is he a Smith substitute?" Both were concerned that the ambassador was not passing along State's viewpoints to Batista.

Rubottom shook his head. "Not of our choosing," he said slowly. "Apparently, he got this idea into his head, and you know the clout he has with the agency and the White House." Christian Herter, the undersecretary of state, was going to make it clear to Pawley that he should make the trip merely as a private citizen; he could not claim to be representing official policy. Even with that restriction, Rubottom was confident that the blunt-spoken Pawley would not hesitate in telling Batista how serious the situation had become.

"If he falls flat on his face," Rubottom said, almost as a whisper, "he won't embarrass anyone in government." Then he added, unnecessarily, "Anything in this room does not go beyond this room—to *anyone*. Do you understand? Absolute silence."

Wieland nodded.

That afternoon, Ambassador Smith strode into Wieland's corner office, which overlooked a small triangular park at Virginia Avenue and E Street. It had turned out to be an unseasonably mild day, with temperatures in the mid-fifties, but the gray sky gave the leafless tree limbs the forlorn look of winter.

As soon as Smith was seated, Wieland asked if Batista had made any plans to leave the country after Rivero Agüero's inauguration.

Smith shook his head. Batista wasn't going to leave because he didn't want to abandon his followers. But he would retire completely from politics.

Wieland said bluntly he doubted that. He couldn't imagine a man like Batista simply sitting quietly in his country villa, doing nothing.

Smith, a little self-righteously, replied he had no reason to distrust Batista. In any case, the main concern was that the United States support the president-elect "or it's an end to a free Cuba."

"Look," Wieland said, "*give* us a reason to get behind this guy. What's he doing to create a government with broad support?"

"He says he will."

"But what's he *done* about it?"

"He's waiting for guarantees, for the United States to resume arms shipments."

Wieland said he hadn't seen any indications that Rivero Agüero had made any overtures to form a genuine coalition that would end the fighting.

"Look," Smith said with an edge to his voice, "you have your choice. Castro or Batista. Now, which do you want?"

"Let's not polarize it. You can deal with the rest of the people. Keep Castro in the damn hills. Find a middle ground."

"Impossible," grumbled Smith. He started to explain again his theory about the Communist conspiracy.

Wieland interrupted, stopping an argument he had heard many times before, and asked about the solution Smith had proposed in the cable. He wanted to know what "respected elements" Smith wanted to see in the new government.

"I'm talking about people like Márquez Sterling," Smith said, mentioning the conservative who had run against Rivero Agüero in the November election. "The ones who are willing to follow the laws."

"The laws of Batista?"

"Of course."

"But what about all those doctors, lawyers and businessmen who are helping the underground in Havana?"

Smith's face flushed. "There aren't that many."

"Yes, there *are*. Are they 'responsible opposition'?"

"Not if they're helping the rebels."

"So you're saying they should be kept out of a new government?"

"I'm not saying that. I'm saying they shouldn't be included among the leaders. We shouldn't go overboard to get their approval."

The argument dragged on until Wieland cut it off by saying he had arranged for Smith to attend a number of meetings, over the next several days, with CIA and State officials. He said nothing about the secret emissary, and Smith carefully did not reveal that he knew anything about it.

As the ambassador left, Wieland's mind drifted back to his pet project, the idea of a "third force." Several new suggestions had come in recently; he had forwarded all of them to the CIA, and once or twice the section's liaison with the agency had whispered to him, "I think something's cooking," departmental slang to indicate that the CIA was working on it. Another time, Wieland had been told to avoid a would-be conspirator: "Don't give him a yes. Don't give him a no. If he calls, you're out."

Still, nothing concrete ever seemed to happen, and Wieland began to wonder if it were getting too late for a third force to work. Castro's popularity among Cubans was continuing to soar, and few others showed any hint of doing anything for themselves. Sometimes, he grew weary of timid Cubans looking for that magic "green light" from the United States. It appeared as if they wanted a stamp of American approval in their passports before they took any action.

Why, he wondered as the neon signs came on near E Street, did the American influence have to be so important?

15/A MESSAGE FOR BATISTA

When William Pawley arrived in Havana on his secret mission, stray signs of Christmas were starting to appear in store windows. One place boasted of Lionel electric trains "at Miami prices," and the huge El Encanto department store was selling "Nordic pines just unloaded from freezing ships" at 85 cents a foot.

Few, however, rushed to buy presents, for a vague sense of gloom was smothering the holiday spirit, a gloom assisted by front-page stories about Smith's sudden departure for "consultations." When the embassy announced his return was being postponed for several days, that too was front-page news. Knowledgeable Cubans, those who understood how serious the situation was in Oriente Province, wondered if the trip would lead to an American orchestration of a change in the Cuban leadership. It had happened before, and they saw no reason why it wouldn't happen again.

Yet, while Cubans looked northward, the secret emissary was already in Havana, meeting with the one American official in the city who had been formally told he was coming: Jim Noel, the CIA station chief. In the house of an American who had temporarily left the island, Pawley paced the floor and fumed that the State Department had double-crossed him at the last minute by forbidding the use of Eisenhower's name. State officials were so concerned about preserving their precious image of neutrality, he complained, that they were willing to allow Cuba to slide into chaos. Without being able to say that his message came straight from the White House, he feared that Batista might simply ignore the plan.

Yet, he told the CIA man, every detail had carefully been worked out in Washington. He could offer Batista the chance to live in Daytona Beach, where Batista maintained a mansion. He could promise that Batista's associates would not be harmed in Cuba. Most importantly, he was certain that a junta would stop Castro from coming to power, because if the rebels kept fighting, it could only mean that Castro was seeking power for himself, rather than merely trying to overthrow Batista, as he claimed he was doing. Under such circumstances, Castro would lose all popular support.

When Pawley rattled off the names of the proposed junta, Noel recognized them immediately as the ones "on everyone's list" of pro-American moderates. None had been told their names were being suggested. None had any real political experience nor a widespread popular following. They were to serve only as a caretaker government until elections could be held. *

Pawley's plan, so carefully crafted, ran into problems as soon as he met with Prime Minister Güell in the library of Güell's Miramar home. In a four-hour session, Pawley explained exactly why he wanted to see Batista and, ignoring his State Department instructions, implied clearly that the message was coming directly from Eisenhower. Güell rushed to the Presidential Palace, but after Batista heard what the American wanted to say, he refused to see him.

When Güell passed the news along, Pawley argued angrily. He demanded a personal confrontation with Batista, and he underscored the point that no Cuban leader could ignore the wishes of the president

---

* The junta was to include Colonel Ramón Barquín and Major Enrique Borbonnet, both imprisoned on the Isle of Pines; General Martín Díaz Tamayo, the officer forced to retire for "medical" reasons and then arrested briefly by the overenthusiastic SIM chief; and Pepín Bosch, head of the Bacardí rum company, who had contributed large amounts of money to the 26th of July Movement.

of the United States. Without the United States, what other support could Batista count on? Reluctantly, Batista agreed.

On the night of December 9, as Pawley rode to the palace, the first cold front of the season was heading toward Havana. Temperatures were still in the mid-seventies, but waves were splashing over the Malecón seawall and dribbling across the sidewalk into the gutter lining the boulevard.

Dressed in the manner of an old-fashioned plantation owner, with a white suit and broad-brimmed straw hat, Pawley strode into the Presidential Palace and up the marble staircase to Batista's formal office on the second floor. Major Cosme Varas and several other aides looked at Pawley with worried expressions. They knew he had business dealings with Batista's predecessor, and they considered Pawley an enemy.

For three hours, Batista and Pawley met behind closed doors. Aides lounged around outside and, after a while, Brigadier General Silito Tabernilla arrived with the army reports of the day's fighting. When he heard whom the president was meeting with, he wondered aloud if Batista had begun the conversation by saying, "Last night, when I lay in bed reading *The Day Lincoln Was Shot,* I got to thinking . . ."

The aides laughed. Everyone heard Batista say that to Americans at varying times; it was his favorite opening line.

At last, the presidential door opened. Pawley marched out grimly. Tabernilla walked into the office. Batista, usually stone-faced, was scowling. As Tabernilla lay the reports on the desk, Batista muttered, "I wanted to kick him out of here with my foot."

A short time later, Prime Minister Güell came in. When the two were alone, Batista explained that he had rejected the proposal completely. He was bitter that Pawley had the gall to suggest some of his worst opponents, but, he added, there had been something oblique about Pawley's idea, something odd. It had not been exactly "a message from Eisenhower," as Güell said it would be. "A little something was missing," he said, puzzled.

Though neither Güell nor Batista knew it, Pawley had retreated to his State Department instructions for the formal meeting with Batista. He had hinted at certain influential supporters he had in the United States, but he spoke only as a concerned private investor.

The next evening, December 10, while Smith was still in Washington, Daniel Braddock, the deputy chief of mission, drove his ivory-colored Oldsmobile 88 to the home of Prime Minister Güell. A servant greeted him at the door and led him into the book-lined library, where Güell was waiting for him. They shook hands with bland smiles and exchanged small talk until coffee was served.

Their meeting had been arranged on the spur of the moment that morning when the two had met for one of those dull diplomatic functions, a casual conversation with a visiting U.S. senator. When it was over, Güell had asked to see Braddock later for a more substantial discussion. Braddock, acting ambassador during Smith's absence, checked with Washington, which leaped at the opportunity to get a direct message to the Cuban government.

Both men were professional diplomats, accustomed to acting pleasant even when delivering the toughest communications. Güell was erect, gray-haired, with an aquiline nose and a large mole on his cheek. Braddock was short, slender, with thick glasses which caused fellow staffers to joke that he looked like the meek Wally Cox, star of *Mr. Peepers*, a television show then popular in the United States.

The appearance was misleading. Braddock possessed a tough mind, and as the servant disappeared with the empty coffee cups, he started by asking Güell a crucial question. Would the new Rivero Agüero government include "responsible elements now supporting Castro, such as the civic organizations?"

Güell paused for a moment, as he always did when speaking English, and his tongue flitted across the roof of his mouth as he sought exactly the right words. His answer was yes, "provided they are willing to negotiate."

Braddock, also choosing his words carefully, said that a firm statement of U.S. policy had to await the return of the ambassador, but it seemed to him *personally*—he emphasized the word—that the Rivero government must gain the support of the pro-Castro moderates.

Güell, sliding beyond that problem, insisted that "to consolidate a new government, especially to retain support of military forces and police," it was "indispensable that Batista remain in an active role for three to six months after the administration takes over . . . Without Batista, even if there should be a military junta, there would be a breakdown of internal order, accompanied by much bloodshed." Castro would come into Havana "hailed by the populace as a victor, since nothing succeeds like success." The regime, he said, desperately needed more U.S. arms if the Communists were to be stopped.

Though Braddock knew nothing about the Pawley proposal, he had just heard the official response to what Batista thought of a junta. Ignoring that, Braddock concentrated on the role of Batista. For the first time, an American official told the Cuban government that Batista's presence was a "basic difficulty . . . a bone of contention." As long as Batista was in power, "it seemed unlikely that responsible elements now adhering to the 26th of July could be won over to Rivero Agüero." He suggested that "any possible active support" of the president-elect by the United States might "begin simultaneously with the departure of Batista from the scene."

The entire conversation was carried on in polite, cautious tones. At the end, the two men shook hands cordially, and Braddock repeated that he was stating his own opinions.

That was a mere diplomatic nicety. He had, in fact, told Güell exactly what Washington had decided two weeks before about Batista's presence in Cuba, a message that Smith had delayed transmitting. Pawley, too, had emphasized Batista's departure, but only as a "private citizen." As the rebels continued conquering towns in Oriente Province, no one had yet told the regime directly and officially that the United States was going to do nothing until Batista left.

That same evening, six hundred miles away at the Moncada army garrison at Santiago de Cuba, General Eulogio Cantillo sat in his rocking chair on the porch of his house. He was feeling a little groggy, having just awakened from a late-afternoon nap, prescribed by his doctor to soothe his ulcer, and he watched listlessly as the last enlisted men returned to the barracks after dinner. Slowly, he tried to focus on a report that the rebels had made a major advance that day west of the city, moving down the Central Highway and attacking a well-equipped army company at the town of Maffo. It was in the operating area of the Bayamo garrison, outside his direct control, but still it was worrisome.

He was still thinking about it when he saw a Catholic priest, his black cassock fluttering in a gentle breeze, walk toward him in the company of a sentry. The soldier introduced him as Father Francisco Guzmán and said the Jesuit had an important message that he refused to divulge to anyone except the general. Cantillo dismissed the guard and motioned for the priest to sit down in an adjoining rocker.

Guzmán, slightly nervous, eased into the conversation by saying that the guards had not wanted to let him through, and he had to make a small speech about how priests sometimes had confidences they couldn't reveal.

The general laughed. "Well, I receive anyone who wishes to see me."

"But your soldiers don't see it that way." Without waiting for a reply, the priest slipped an envelope from his cassock and handed it to Cantillo. "General, this letter was given to me by people whom I trust."

Cantillo put on his reading glasses. The letter was difficult to read, handwritten on lightweight letter stationery, the type in which each sheet is glued together to form an envelope. Flipping to the last of the twelve pages, he saw the signature, in blue ink, of José Quevedo. He knew the man well: an army major who had surrendered his battalion to Castro during the summer offensive and then joined the rebels.

At first, Cantillo had a hard time determining how the pages turned, and he tried holding the sheets several ways before he understood the system.

It was an exceedingly polite letter. Quevedo explained he was with the rebels because he could no longer support the dictatorship and that the 26th of July Movement simply wanted "a free Cuba without corruption and favoritism." He knew Cantillo was an honorable man who had done what he could to stop police violence in Santiago and had always treated rebel prisoners fairly. But it was obvious that "militarily, the army is lost." He listed the towns the rebels had taken and asked how Cantillo could possibly imagine a reversal of the trend. At the end, he suggested that the general meet with him and Castro on neutral ground to discuss ways to end the bloodshed.

The letter did not surprise Cantillo. For some time, a number of former army officers had been writing similar messages to officers and sergeants they knew. It was obviously a propaganda campaign, and when an officer handed such a letter to Cantillo, he forwarded it to Camp Columbia in Havana. He would do the same with this one.

Stuffing the letter into his pocket, he looked more closely at the priest. He knew that many Jesuits were Red Cross volunteers, tending to the wounded on battlefields and helping exchange prisoners. It was an open secret in Santiago that many of them sympathized with the rebels, and they often served as messengers between the mountains and the city. Cantillo realized that if the need arose, this priest could serve as a valuable contact with the rebels. It might be good to get to know the man better.

"Excuse me," he said, when he noticed the priest was puzzled by his stare, "the letter was a little long." He asked if Guzmán smoked. The priest nodded, and Cantillo went into the living room, returning with a carton of Winstons, which he handed over.

Guzmán thanked him, opened a pack and lit up.

"You know, Father," Cantillo said, swaying in his rocking chair, "I love Oriente. It is a province that knows how to defend itself. I am from the country, and I admire the determination of the people of Oriente. I am sorry that I didn't come here three months earlier."

The priest disagreed. "General, you should have come a year earlier, and many deaths would have been avoided."

For two hours, the conversation drifted on, with Cantillo talking about his young daughter in Havana, whom he was rarely able to see, and his love of flying, the soothing silence of the air, the joy of seeing a peaceful sunset. At the end, he handed Guzmán his card. "It has my private number here. Don't hesitate to call me about anything at any time. I am always available."

The priest thanked him and left, the carton of Winstons tucked under his arm. As he watched him from the porch, Cantillo realized he had established a contact, a line of communication for that delicate balancing act he had done all his career between opposing sides. But he had no way of knowing then how important the contact might become.

16/EXILES ON FLAGLER STREET

Flanked by two pilots, Dr. Armando Fleites walked across a concrete runway in a remote section of Miami International Airport. The area was nicknamed "Corrosion Corner," home of dilapidated cargo planes usually used for the minor Caribbean runs, but that didn't bother Fleites. The Segundo Frente del Escambray had sent him to Miami to obtain weapons for its small guerrilla band in Las Villas Province. The guns themselves were no longer a problem: Carlos Prio, the president whom Batista had deposed, had donated $100,000 worth of hand grenades, Garand rifles and ammunition. Now, what they needed was a plane.

Just then, the Venezuelan pilot tugged at his arm. "There it is," he said, pointing toward a dark hulk in one corner. The American pilot beside them grinned.

Fleites stopped. He wasn't certain if his mouth fell open or if it just seemed that way in his mind: the plane, an air force surplus B-26, looked more like a pile of junk than a flying machine. Its camouflage paint was faded to the color of dried mud, its steel exterior marred with scrapes and dents. On its side, a U.S Air Force insignia was so faded that it was almost invisible.

As they approached the plane, the Venezuelan pilot assured him it wasn't as bad as it seemed. The B-26 hadn't flown regularly for three years, but with a couple of hundred dollars for maintenance, it would be "as good as new."

Fleites grimaced. Watching the two pilots climb through a rusted door into the cargo hold, he decided he couldn't expect much for $4500, which is what the plane had cost. At least now they had a plane. All that remained was the "green light" from Washington—the approval that would allow them to take off without fear of being stopped by customs officials. Fleites knew time was running out. If the OK didn't come soon, it would be too late: each day, shortwave sets in Miami were picking up new reports of rebel victories.

As he looked over the plane's battered exterior, the American pilot stuck his head through a cockpit window. "The radio works," he said, smiling, "but I don't know if it can fly."

By late 1958, there were between four thousand and five thousand political exiles in Miami, and they spent their time collecting money for the cause, hiding weapons in their rented homes until they could be smuggled into Cuba—and, as with exiles everywhere, wasting hours upon hours arguing politics.

Such arguments had long been a Cuban passion, even the subject of a joke told by Cubans themselves: If you put three Cuban politicians in a room, you would end up with three different philosophies, seven political parties and innumerable arguments. The Pact of Caracas had been intended to end the bickering, or at least postpone it until Batista's downfall, but in fact it was only a temporary cosmetic as the factions kept jockeying for power.

Castro's 26th of July Movement was by far the most powerful and influential. Never concerned about waiting for a "green light" from the U.S. government, its leaders had the boldness of youth; they were the most active and, therefore, attracted the most members and the largest contributions, much of which came from Cubans who had emigrated to the United States years before. Those donations had even allowed Eduardo ("Guayo") Hernández, a photographer, to make a propaganda film for the Movement. Later, when he needed money to feed his wife and children, the group's Miami leader, Haydee Santamaría, simply opened a desk drawer and handed him $1000 in hundred-dollar bills.

Compared to that, the other anti-Batista groups had to struggle along, sometimes losing members to the 26th of July. People from such organizations as the student Directorio Revolucionario, the AAA, and the remaining remnants of the old Ortodoxo party sat in downtown Miami diners and discussed the ever-increasing reports of rebel successes in Oriente. Many feared that Castro's movement had become so strong that there would be no place left in a new government for anyone else, and they began plotting to find ways to grab a share of the glory—and political clout—for themselves.

One of the major schemers was Antonio ("Tony") de Varona, a squat, balding man who had been prime minister under the Prio administration. Most of those close to Prio, members of the Auténtico party, had been discredited by the regime's corruption, but Varona was known to be impeccably honest, so much so that fellow exiles joked that he had to be a little stupid not to have profited from his years in government.

In Miami, Varona spent his days wandering, going to homes and having lengthy meals at restaurants, gleaning rumors and seeing if he could find some kind of contact, something that would give him and the Auténticos a piece of the action, or at least the ability to boast that he had done more than his share in helping overthrow Batista. Occasionally, he went to Washington, to urge the State Department to withdraw support from the dictatorship and, not coincidentally, to back some plan of his own, to give him the almost mystical *luz verde*—the green light—that American sign of support which, Varona was certain, would guarantee the success of any plan.

Another Miami exile, Justo Carrillo, was working on a scheme of his own, one he had been developing for months. The leader of the obscure Montecristi Movement, composed of a few liberal intellectuals, Carrillo was one of the 1933 revolutionaries who was firmly convinced that Cuban history showed that the only way to overthrow a military tyrant was from within the army. And he was certain the one man who could do it was Colonel Ramón Barquín, imprisoned on the Isle of Pines for having attempted a coup d'etat against Batista.

Barquín was both a professional soldier and a liberal. Outside the army, he wasn't widely known, but many military officers respected him. Carrillo was certain that Barquín could control the military and allow democratically oriented politicians, such as himself, to run the government.

His plan was bold and nearly incredible: He wanted to free Barquín and his followers from the national prison in a daring commando raid. Two C-47 planes, carrying fifty armed men, would land at an airstrip near the prison, catch the guards by surprise and take Barquín's men to selected military garrisons, where officers were known to be sympathetic to their cause.

Carrillo's group had already purchased the planes and $70,000 worth of weapons and explosives, most of it from the black market in Argentina. The commandos were ready. All they needed was a place to leave from. *That* was a problem. Venezuela and Honduras leaders were friendly, but both were reluctant to get directly involved. Carrillo had gone to Washington several times, to meet with men in the Departments of State and Defense, but nothing had happened until, suddenly in late November, an intermediary told Carrillo to fly to New York and see Willard Carr, the aged president of Carr Aluminum Corporation and a former college classmate of Allen Dulles, director of the CIA.

At an exclusive men's club in Manhattan, Carr told Carrillo that he represented a "group of Americans who love Cuba . . . some of whom have a lot of interests in Cuba. We are worried about Castro." The industrialist listened carefully to Carrillo's plan and sent two men to look at the weapons. They examined the guns with the trained eyes of experts, not like businessmen from an aluminum company. Carrillo assumed they were CIA men; he did not ask.

After that, there had been occasional contact, but no specific promises. Carrillo grew edgy. Castro rebels were gaining ground rapidly in Oriente, and he feared it was getting too late. For days on end, he pestered New York and Washington with phone calls. They all led to nothing.

Then suddenly, one afternoon when he was in his two-bedroom house on Mary Street, he received a call from the New York industrialist.

"Listen, about that business matter of yours . . ."

"Yes?" Carrillo could feel his heart pounding. It seemed like months of effort were about to be rewarded.

"It seems you can't leave from Florida because it would backfire. It would be too risky, and it would violate U.S. neutrality laws."

Carrillo cursed in Spanish and translated his curse. Here, Castro and his radical friends were winning battle after battle, were threatening to bring an anti-American government to a country which had always been pro-United States—and the most powerful government in the world was worried that the takeoff of two small planes was "too risky." He couldn't believe it.

"Now, here, here," the New Yorker objected. "We are going to build a runway in Mérida, in the Yucatán Peninsula, so that you can do it from there."

Carrillo sputtered a protest. There was no time for that. "The situation in Cuba is very bad, and we are afraid that Batista will leave at any minute. Then Castro will be unstoppable."

He insisted Carr make contact with his "friends" and try again, to see if a faster plan could be worked out. The industrialist said he would see what he could do.

Carrillo hung up and cursed again.

17/CONSPIRACY OF "THE PURE ONES"

In Circular Building 4 at the Isles of Pines penitentiary, Colonel Ramón Barquín was sprawled on the bunk of his third-tier cell. He was wasting away yet another afternoon, staring at the ceiling and listening to the metallic echoes of his fellow political prisoners as they moved along the walkways surrounding the round courtyard at the center of the six-story building. All he could do was wait once again for nightfall, when he would pull the small transistor radio hidden beneath his mattress and place it next to a steel beam, which served as a large antenna. That way, he could listen to Radio Caracas's uncensored reports of the Cuban fighting.

The listening was always bittersweet. As much as he wanted to see the downfall of Batista, each broadcast reminded him that others were gaining the glory for the struggle—a glory he thought should have been, *could* have been, his. In April 1956, he had been only hours away from staging a coup d'etat, supported by many of the younger officers, when an informer had tipped off the regime. *Los Puros*, his conspiracy had been called—the Pure Ones—but that was little consolation for the thirty months he had spent in prison. In his mid-forties, he should have been at the peak of his career, instead of seeing his family pile up debts to survive, as he spent day after day simply trying to fight off jail rot by clinging to the vestiges of his former life: the crisp crew cut and the ramrod bearing of a commanding officer. That was not easy to do when wearing the humiliating blue-denim prison garb with its large white *P* on the back.

Like every prisoner on the Isle of Pines, he knew that telltale uniform was only one problem if they managed to escape from the cellblock. A barbed-wire fence surrounded the compound, watched over by machine-gun towers, and a second fence lay beyond. If by some miracle a prisoner got past both fences, he still had no way to get off the small island and back to the mainland of Cuba.

Barquín had given up all hope of escape, and he waited in mounting frustration for something to happen on the outside that would free him and his fellow Puros. He had no way of knowing that his name was being mentioned in Washington as a leader of a possible "third force," or that his friend Justo Carrillo was trying to free him in a commando raid, or that a secret American emissary had mentioned his name to Batista as one of those who should form a civilian-military junta.

For him, all the news had been discouraging, and as the months passed, with the number of political prisoners growing to five hundred, the 26th of July men had gradually become the majority, dominating the prison group as they were the anti-Batista movement everywhere. One of them, Jesús Montané, a former accountant with General Motors' Cuban subsidiary, had spent most of Batista's regime in jail, first for his part in the 1953 attack on the Moncada garrison, then for having landed with Castro in the *Granma*.

Several of the military Puros had become openly sympathetic with the 26th of July. Major Enrique Borbonnet had his wife and children living on the Isle of Pines with a 26th of July leader's parents. Lieutenant José Ramón "Gallego" Fernández had been named "mayor" of Building 4 with 26th of July support. Barquín himself was cautiously friendly with the rebel sympathizers, but he kept a certain distance, hoping for something that would thrust his own name to the forefront.

That afternoon, as he half-dozed on his bunk, his dim hope was realized when several of the Puros, their faces flushed with excitement, squeezed into his small cell.

One of them, barely able to control his enthusiasm, stammered out the story: He had just been visited by his father, who had passed along a message from Colonel Florentino Rosell, the chief of the army corps of engineers. Rosell was preparing a coup to overthrow Batista. He wanted the Puros to take part.

Barquín sat up with a start. He asked how serious the plan was.

The details were still vague, an officer told him, but Colonel Rosell claimed he had the backing of General Alberto Del Río Chaviano, commander of the army in central Las Villas Province, and General Cantillo, commander of Oriente.*

The officers all began talking at once. Lieutenant Fernández complained that he thought Rosell was corrupt. He had used his position in the engineering corps to profit his own private construction company. Others objected to Del Río Chaviano, whom they considered both corrupt and brutal, the general most hated by the rebels.

Barquín himself was worried about Cantillo. The two had been classmates at the military academy, and for every year and every month that Cantillo had been first in the class, Barquín had been second. The imprisoned Puro was bitterly convinced that Cantillo had stayed ahead of him by always being a cautious conformist, never taking risks, and Barquín wasn't certain that he could trust him to carry out any kind of conspiracy.

The plot itself was only an outline, based on the fact that Colonel Rosell's engineering corps had been ordered to prepare an armored train, which was to go to the central provinces to repair rail and highway bridges damaged by the rebels. The train would be used by the coup leaders to take control of some areas, while a plane picked up the imprisoned Puros and carried them to the central city of Santa Clara, where they could take over the regimental garrison. Then they would demand Batista's resignation and form a junta. When Batista left, those objectionable to the Puros would retire.

The officers kept arguing. They had no way of knowing whether the conspiracy was simply another fuzzy dream, as most military plots were, and the persons mentioned seemed most unlikely to stage a coup.

---

*Cantillo later denied any part in the plot, and Rosell, in an interview for this book, admitted that he had used the names of Cantillo and some other officers without their permission.

Colonel Rosell was a close friend of Brigadier General Silito Tabernilla, the president's military liaison and a loyal Batistiano. General Del Río Chaviano was related by marriage to Silito's father, General Francisco ("Pancho") Tabernilla, the joint chief of staff and one of Batista's oldest allies. Nothing seemed to make any sense except that the army leaders had to be getting very nervous. If what they said were true—that they were willing to retire after Batista's downfall—then that meant they thought Batista's collapse was inevitable, and they were looking for an in with the new leaders, seeking some credit for overthrowing the dictator and, therefore, a chance to keep the wealth they had gained during his regime.

Finally, Barquín became impatient with the debate. "Gentlemen," he announced, "we are at the bottom of the well. We need to get out of prison, and then we can argue. We won't be worse off on the outside than we are here. This is a critical moment. They need our prestige and support."

No one disagreed. What good was it to remain the Pure Ones if it only meant remaining in prison? Someone suggested they send a symbol indicating their support.

Barquín noticed Colonel Manuel Varela's graduation ring from the military academy. He asked Varela to give it to him: It was a heavy ring, eighteen-karat gold, with Varela's initials on one side of the academy insignia and "47," the year of his graduation, on the other. The Puros decided the ring would be the perfect symbol of their approval.

As the officers filed out of the cell, Barquín decided he was feeling better than he had in months. If there was any truth to the Rosell plot, with the names he mentioned, they could dump Batista easily, then negotiate with Castro. Like the secret American emissary, Barquín was sure that once Batista was toppled, Castro would not dare oppose a new government. If he did want to continue the war, he would lose all popular support, and Barquín was willing then to fight him with all the military might he could find.

18/LAS VILLAS: WAITING FOR DISASTER

That evening, as he did almost every night, Guillermo Domenech emerged from an Otis elevator into the tenth-floor bar-restaurant of the Gran Hotel in downtown Santa Clara, the city that the imprisoned Puros were hoping to take over. The restaurant was nearly deserted, except for the cluster of poker players sitting on beige chairs around a table near the bar.

Domenech, a teenager who had rejected his family's funeral business to become a hotel clerk, paused for a moment to watch the cardplayers. Their betting seemed to be getting steeper each night, and they played grimly, with almost no conversation. He had come to think of them as strangers thrown together on a cruise ship, reluctant to talk about anything controversial since they didn't know the others' political opinions. Most were traveling salesmen. They had made the year-old hotel almost a headquarters, because beyond the city, in the countryside of Las Villas Province, blown bridges and the threat of ambushes had made travel all but impossible.

As a salesman raked in a pot of pesos, Domenech walked across the gray-and-white tile floor to the windows overlooking the Central Park. From this, the tallest building in town, he could see most of Santa Clara, the bustling commercial hub of central Cuba. In recent weeks, there had been a subtle, but unmistakable, change in the city. It was partly caused by the bombs the underground occasionally placed around town, but there was something more than that: a sense of foreboding, a feeling that worse times lay ahead.

Below him, in the park, everything seemed quiet, far too quiet for normal times. Only a few lights shone past the four Grecian columns of the Lyceo men's club, which was usually filled with men arguing politics and watching television. The nightlight of the Banco Núñez, with its traditional Spanish architecture, fell on an empty sidewalk. In the park itself, the parade of young men and women was a thin one, but they were following the custom: the whites walking around the center, near the bandstand; the mulattoes in the middle lane; and the blacks on the sidewalk bordering the edge of the park.

Domenech liked to think that his city had the prettiest girls in all of Cuba, and in normal times, they gathered in the park to see and be seen and, if there was a proper introduction by a mutual acquaintance, perhaps take a trip to the Central Hotel's coffee shop for a chocolate shake. It was a ritual Domenech often followed, though he considered himself a modern young man, avoiding the traditional piropo—a flirtatious, slightly naughty wisecrack to a girl—and using instead the more sophisticated "cool, sensual glance." But recently the prettiest girls had stopped coming to the park, and that meant, gradually, fewer boys came too. At least for Domenech, it made it less difficult having to go to work while others played.

That thought reminded him he should be getting something done. He descended in the elevator, stopping briefly at the fifth floor, where in the room of the hotel electrician, a secret rebel supporter, some men surrounded a shortwave set tuned to Radio Rebelde. Nothing much seemed to be happening, and he returned to the lobby, going to the small telephone switchboard behind the counter.

The switchboard was quiet, but it would start lighting up quickly, as it did every night. Some calls came from Suite 515, which the army commander of the province, General Del Río Chaviano, used as a hideaway so that his Oriental secretary could bring girls up to him two or three times a week. But most of the telephoning was done by fifteen to twenty nervous men, Batista officials who had moved into the hotel from the small towns threatened by the rebels. They usually stayed in their rooms, except for meals, and spent their time making anxious calls to the Leoncio Vidal regimental headquarters to learn of rebel activities and seek assurances they were safe in the city.

Domenech was a cautious sort, he wanted to make the hotel business a career, but he couldn't stop himself from violating the manager's regulations and listening in on some of the calls. That was how he learned the army was refusing to patrol large parts of the Escambray Mountains to the south and that traffic east of Santa Clara was almost nonexistent. The army officers, however, assured the politicians that the city itself was absolutely safe, that it had far more soldiers than there were rebels in the entire province. Yet despite such a soothing guarantee, Domenech learned something else, something highly disconcerting: The army assumed the rebels' ultimate objective in the province was Santa Clara itself.

That evening, some sixty miles east of Santa Clara, Captain William Gálvez and the other men in Column 2 of the 26th of July rebel army were at a camp in a clearing of mango trees and palms in the hills near the town of Mayajigua. Nearby was a cluster of wooden huts, which served as their supply rooms, infirmary and kitchen, but they slept in hammocks in the safety of the woods.

For weeks, Gálvez, the son of a small shopkeeper, with a blondish goatee that made him look younger than his twenty-five years, had helped carry out ambushes and make raids on small Rural Guard outposts, but their primary mission was to gather manpower and weapons so they could make a dangerous trek across half of Cuba, going westward, skirting Havana and setting up a new guerrilla front in the westernmost province of Pinar del Río.

That had been the plan formed by Castro when Column 2 left the Sierra Maestra to make the long, risky trip across the open grasslands of Camagüey Province. Some sixty men had survived to reach the Las Villas hills, where they were joined by seventy-five badly armed Marxist guerrillas of the PSP, led by Félix Torres, a onetime congressman from the area, which had traditionally been a bastion of Communist support.

The Column 2 leader, Comandante Camilo Cienfuegos, had decided to help arm the PSP men, a move that aroused bitter arguments from some of his own rebels and a leader of the 26th of July underground,

Victor Paneque, better known by his war name of Comandante Diego. They wanted nothing to do with the Communists, whose goals they thought were different from their own hopes for a purely nationalistic revolution. Finally, Comandante Cienfuegos had stopped all debate by calling together the PSP and 26th of July leaders in the area and explaining to them "the necessity of consolidating a revolutionary unit in which, in order to fight Batista, it had to have an abandoning of ideological discrepancies and religious beliefs, because the fundamental part was the combat against the enemy, and after the revolutionary victory, one could discuss those questions."

That made sense to Gálvez, a man of typically progressive ideas whose main concern was the overthrow of the dictatorship. If anyone wanted to join in the battle, he saw nothing wrong with that. In fact, once agreement had been reached, the PSP had been particularly helpful, and Gálvez had worked with the party's labor leaders in organizing a conference, attended by five hundred workers' representatives who had gathered in a hillside clearing. Gálvez had listened to their complaints about working conditions and elicited in turn their support for the rebel cause.

With that kind of backing, Gálvez was confident Column 2 could easily take over the few aged Rural Guards and the lone army company in the area.

That night, as he did every night, the commander of the army company facing Gálvez's column patrolled the dirt roads in the area. He rode in a jeep, with two or three of his soldiers, past the farmhouses and the unnaturally dark countryside. The rebels had cut the electricity lines. He never saw the rebels themselves, but informants had told him they were in the nearby hills, and he could almost sense their presence.

His name was Alfredo Abón-Ly, a military academy graduate in his mid-twenties. His almond eyes, high cheekbones and olive-yellow skin were unmistakable signs of his Chinese ancestry—El Chino, the townspeople called him behind his back—and he wanted desperately to show that, despite his minority standing among Cubans, he could be as brave and as tough as any other officer, and better than most. He was especially determined not to repeat the mistakes other commanders had made in fighting the rebels.

His base was in the town of Mayajigua, where the Rural Guard cuartel was so small it could house only twelve men. He used it only as a place to serve his men's meals, in shifts. The rest of the time, they stayed in their trenches scattered outside of town. Abón-Ly knew that other army commanders had made the mistake of holing up inside cuartels, where they were easily surrounded and besieged by the rebels, or choosing the tallest buildings in town, which encouraged the guerrillas to sneak through side streets and backyards until they were right next to the buildings. Abón-Ly wanted to face the rebels in the open, where they would have to charge across open fields to reach his lines. It was a sound plan, but he had no way of knowing then that he, an obscure army captain in a little-known village, was going to put up the fiercest defense that the rebels would face during the entire civil war.

Three groups had made the Escambray Mountains of Las Villas Province their base of operations, but the Segundo Frente del Escambray was by far the most divisive, even at one point kidnapping a local 26th of July *comandante* in an attempt to prove its superiority in the area. For more than a year before Castro's rebels had arrived in the Escambray, the Segundo Frente men had been hiding out there. Roger Redondo, a young carpenter, was one of the group's founders, fleeing to the safety of the hills with about twenty others when police pressure became too intense in their small Las Villas hometown. They had roamed about, frightened, confused and poorly armed, for months before a leader appeared. He was Eloy Gutiérrez Menoyo, a twenty-two-year-old former university student who was a natural leader and possessed what they did not: weapons, including ten rifles, nine machine guns and ten thousand rounds of ammunition. That was enough for Redondo's group, and they quickly accepted him as their *comandante.*

He was soon joined by a tall blond American named Willie Morgan, a former Marine who spoke almost no Spanish but showed great prowess with weapons and delighted the Segundo Frente guerrillas with his cowboy-style displays of drawing from the hip. He quickly became a leader, teaching the rebels how to aim a rifle and throw a knife, and he showed considerable bravery the few times the badly armed group launched hit-and-run attacks against small army cuartels. Redondo and the others assumed that he was a CIA agent, though he never claimed he was and his limited Spanish would have made intelligence gathering difficult. But his men believed it to be true, and for these pro-American guerrillas, that was a status symbol.

The men themselves often mingled with friends in the 26th of July and the student Directorio, but both their leaders had a profound distrust of Castro's group. Gutiérrez Menoyo was suspicious of the rebel leader because his elder brother had had serious political disagreements with him at the University of Havana in the 1940s. Morgan was worried about Marxism, which he talked about incessantly, and he called Castro and Ché Guevara *"ñángaras,"* Cuban slang for Communists.

Neither Segundo Frente leader wanted to undertake any joint actions with the 26th of July rebels, but with few weapons, there was little they could do on their own except sit around their campsite and make plans—hoping to do something with the navy in Cienfuegos, waiting for weapons from Miami, dreaming that former President Prio would join them and thinking that if Batista should suddenly flee, they would be the guerrilla group closest to Havana. In a race to the capital, they just might be able to win.

19/CHE GUEVARA AND HIS TEENAGERS: LEAVING THE BACKPACKS BEHIND

Those power-hungry dreams of the Segundo Frente del Escambray had preoccupied Comandante Ernesto ("Ché") Guevara for weeks, throughout most of the autumn, and had paralyzed rebel activity in much of the province. It was a political problem more than a military one, but Castro had instructed Guevara when he left the Sierra that the Segundo Frente situation should be one of his primary responsibilities.

The trip to Las Villas had been bitterly difficult, the men eating only twenty times in forty days, so many dropping out that only 140 of them, 110 armed, had managed to make it to the safety of the Escambray Mountains. Yet, as soon as a campsite was found, Guevara and Lieutenant Oscar Fernández Mell started concentrating on the dissension in the mountains.

They began by visiting the other guerrilla groups and urging them to unite in the common struggle. A small band of local 26th of July men agreed readily to put themselves under Guevara's leadership. A column of student Directorio guerrillas, led by Faure Chomón and Rolando Cubela, was somewhat more reluctant, but at least they consented to cooperate. The Segundo Frente, however, even after numerous meetings, refused to go along. Guevara and the other 26th of July rebels began thinking of these obstinate guerrillas as *comevacas*—cow-eaters—meaning they lived off the peasants and did nothing for the cause.

Finally, after weeks of conferences, a vague compromise was reached when the guerrilla groups gathered at the hamlet of El Pedrero. There, in a dirt-floor *bohío*, the three bands agreed to divide up the province. The Directorio was to launch attacks in the southeastern part of Las Villas and work together in some operations with Guevara's men, who were to make the main thrust northward, toward the city of Santa Clara. The Segundo Frente, without joining the other groups, agreed to harass the army in the southwestern area.

It meant that, at last, rebel operations in Las Villas could begin.

Ché Guevara was an unlikely man to negotiate such an agreement; in fact, he was a highly unlikely candidate even to be a guerrilla: a shy introvert, a scrawny asthmatic who often wheezed after the slightest physical activity, and an Argentine with a distinctive accent immersed in a heavily nationalistic revolution.

Yet, through an intensity of will, intellect and hard work, he had become a top rebel leader and one of Castro's most influential advisers. Like Castro, he came from a comparatively affluent family, in the city of Rosario on the River Plate. Like Castro, he had a passion for sports, beginning at an early age; in his case, he wanted to counteract asthma. In college, Guevara specialized in allergies for his medical studies, but he never set up a practice. That seemed too staid, he was attracted more to a bohemian life-style—a Latin version of the fifties American beatnik. Bumming through Chile, Peru, Bolivia, Venezuela and Panama, he practiced a little medicine, but mostly he just lived, and read. In his politics, he was a romantic leftist, a free-lance Marxist adventurer who was a staunch opponent of the U.S. "big stick." He read Marx and Mao, but he never joined the Communist Party or allowed his thoughts to be restricted to Leninist dogma.

In 1954, Guevara was earning a living as a salesman in Guatemala City when the CIA orchestrated the overthrow of a pro-Communist regime. Enraged, Guevara rushed to do what he could, serving as an air-raid warden and helping transport weapons. It was a decidedly minor role, and he quickly abandoned it for the safety of Mexico. There, in 1955, he met Castro. The two were the same age, and they immediately established an uncommon rapport, talking for ten straight hours at their first meeting. A few months later, leaving behind his Peruvian wife, Guevara joined the *Granma* expedition.

In the Sierra, he never talked politics. Instead, he led by example. On long marches, even when he was gasping painfully from a severe asthma attack, he never asked another rebel to carry his backpack; he simply took a pill and moved on. He never ate more than his men, and often less if food were scarce. He was never heard to complain, and he expected his men to be equally as stoic. When they stepped out of line—talked when they should be quiet, or fell asleep on guard duty—punishment was immediate, whether the offender be common soldier or rebel captain: twelve hours extra guard duty or a day without food.

One of the rare times he displayed emotion was when he saw famished mountain children. The sight visibly depressed him, and he often sent rebel doctors out to examine them. Before long, rebels were joking that he was an Argentine who cared more for the Cubans than did most Cubans.

Like most bohemians, he cared nothing for materialistic possessions, but he had a passion for books, and he always managed to find room in his knapsack for something to read. In the Escambray Mountains, his favorite was a long history of the Roman Empire, and even during an air attack, he would become so immersed in reading that an aide would have to ask him something twice before he could focus on it. When he did respond, his orders were crisp, without explanation of the reasons behind them, as if each action formed part of a whole that only he himself understood.

To his men, he always seemed to be thinking far ahead, and that applied even to his asthma, the debilitating disease that affected his entire life. Sometimes, he would say, "In a little while, I am going to have an attack," and he was always right. In the Sierra he tried to be careful with what he ate, but often there was so little that he had no choice. His sickness was even worse in urban areas, but in the Escambray, something odd happened: the asthma attacks stopped. To his men, it seemed almost like a sign.

For his Column 8, Guevara had selected some of the youngest Sierra rebels to be his officers. They were strong enough to make the trip, they followed him without question and they showed uncommon bravery in battle. For one of them, Lieutenant Rogelio Acevedo, a seventeen-year-old rebel veteran, the trek to Las Villas Province was almost like returning home: He came from the town of Remedios, in the northern part of the province.

Son of a Spanish immigrant who owned a drugstore and gas station, Acevedo had learned politics at the family dinner table, where his mother insisted that Batista was an assassin while his father maintained that as long as business was good, he didn't care who ruled the country.

At the age of sixteen, Acevedo decided his mother was right. With his brother Enrique, two years his junior, he started participating in school strikes and performing minor acts of sabotage, which were usually little more than cutting telephone and electric lines. When his girlfriend told him that her father didn't want her to have anything to do with "activists," he told her good-bye. He was a revolutionary.

In early 1957, the police arrested his fourteen-year-old brother and held him incommunicado for fifteen days, an action which angered their father and turned him too against the regime. After the boy was released, the two brothers decided to join the rebels in the Sierra Maestra, which they imagined to be rather like a cowboy movie, with a well-armed, well-supplied group of men dedicated to eliminating evil.

Telling their parents they were merely going to a nearby town for "clandestine activities," they obtained an Esso road map and took a train to the city of Bayamo, then a taxi to Baire, a town on the edge of the Sierra. From there, they were led by peasants on a walk which lasted a month before they found the rebel camp. The place was nothing like their movie dreams. Food was scarce, arms were few and some rebels didn't even have shoes. Guevara at first didn't want to accept them; they seemed too young. But they insisted they could adapt, and they did so quickly, following Guevara's examples.

By the late-summer march to Las Villas, the brothers were among Guevara's most valuable men. But then, in a skirmish in southern Camagüey Province, fifteen-year-old Enrique was wounded in both arms and had to be left behind. For weeks, Acevedo didn't know what had happened to him, until Enrique unexpectedly showed up at the Escambray camp, wearing a short-sleeved white shirt which revealed the greenish tint of skin grafts on his arms. Enrique explained that rebel sympathizers had hidden him in a nuns' hospital, and he joked that he was sorry that as children they had never learned to pray, because his ignorance had angered the nuns, who gave him an unwanted religious education. The nuns had also notified their parents, who had gone all the way to the hospital to take him home. Enrique had refused. He wanted to rejoin the column. When he arrived, Guevara gave him a squad of his own to command.

Both boys, of course, were unusually young for such a task, and Acevedo continued to be profoundly embarrassed by his scrawny 125-pound body and the fact that he was too young to grow a beard. To compensate, he let his brown hair lengthen until it touched his shoulders, he wore a black beret just like Ché's and—most importantly—he carried a Garand rifle and a Colt .45 handgun, weapons earned in battle, symbols that he was among the rebels' toughest fighters. His men respected the weapons; they ignored his age.

By mid-December, Guevara's squads were making occasional hit-and-run attacks against the villages on the edge of the mountains. The army rarely chased them and, except for air force bombings, they were allowed to roam through the mountains at will. The atmosphere became almost festive, with the rebels enjoying the status of celebrities as townspeople came up to the rebels' ambush sites and took photos of themselves with the guerrillas. Even Acevedo's parents came, by taxi, guided by an underground worker. They treated their son just like a boy who had been away at school, giving him a fine-quality watch and a transistor radio, inquiring about his health and worrying that he might catch a cold in the chilly mountain air.

Acevedo was just getting comfortable with the new informality when Guevara suddenly ordered him to guard a demolition crew which was to blow up the Falcón Bridge, spanning the Sagua River on the Central Highway. It didn't make sense to the teenage lieutenant. He thought a rebel's duty was to fight the army, not to worry about bridges and railway tracks, but he never questioned Ché's decisions.

Thus, shortly after midnight on December 15, Acevedo stationed his men next to a small cemetery on the highway, about a half-mile from the bridge. They set a land mine in the road and waited, hidden behind the tombstones.

Acevedo was just beginning to relax when a single rifle shot shattered the nighttime stillness. He tensed, expecting an army convoy to appear, but nothing happened. After a while, a rebel from another squad ran down the road and told him that a youth, checking out a rumor that army soldiers were hiding in a nearby shack, had banged on the door with his rifle butt. The gun discharged; he was wounded, but not seriously. Of course there had been no army men inside.

Acevedo gave a high-pitched, sarcastic laugh. Then, since everything seemed quiet, he wandered down to the bridge to watch the welders, workers from a nearby sugar mill who had volunteered for the assignment. About 3:00 A.M., they began, their torches uncommonly bright in the complete darkness of the countryside, as they knelt on the 150-foot-long bridge and began to cut through the steel trusses. The rebels had few explosives, and they wanted to save them for land mines. The welders' torches worked just as well, if they had enough time to finish their work.

For about two hours, Acevedo watched the men cut through the thick steel. At times, he had to fight the desire to keep his eyes on the searingly bright torches, and he would look away, down to the nearly dry riverbed, where the ghosts of the torches seemed to form blue-green images on the dark water.

The workers were about two-thirds of the way across the width of the bridge when one of them gave a sudden shout. The bridge was slowly collapsing, and the welders leaped off it so quickly that one left his torch, still burning, behind. Acevedo saw it fall down with the steel trusses, which churned up a cloud of murky dust as it hit first the riverbank and then made a gurgling splash as it settled into the river.

It was almost dawn, and Acevedo hurried back to his men, expecting they would be ordered to pull out immediately and return to the mountain hideout. But his captain told him the squad was to remain by the cemetery and ambush any army reinforcements trying to reach the town of Fomento, which Guevara was planning to attack in force. The only way now for the army to approach the town was to go past the ambush and ford the river.

Acevedo made a mild objection. He and his men had been told to leave their backpacks behind at the camp in El Pedrero. He had almost no provisions for his men.

There was no more time for backpacks, he was told. They were going to be moving fast, grabbing food and supplies where they could in the towns, charging forward and abandoning completely the safety of the mountains. Now, there was no turning back.

The next morning, well before sunrise, Ché Guevara and Lieutenant Fernández Mell halted the *comandancia* platoon at the Santa Lucía sugar mill and called the army post at Fomento. A lieutenant answered.

"Are you the chief of the cuartel?" Guevara asked.

The officer said he was.

"The cuartel is surrounded," Guevara announced in his unmistakable Argentine accent. "We invite you to surrender so there will be no bloodshed. If you do so, no actions will be taken against you."

"Under *no* circumstances," the lieutenant replied. He said he was a graduate of the military academy, and he had to uphold the code of the professional soldier to do his duty. Then he cursed.

Guevara slammed down the phone. The battle for Las Villas Province had begun.

Part Three

A Regime in Ruins

DECEMBER 17–DECEMBER 23, 1958

20/A MEETING AT KUQUINE

Staring at the American flags fluttering from the front fenders, Ambassador Smith slumped morosely in the backseat of his limousine as the car sped through the Havana streets. It was the evening of Wednesday, December 17, and Smith was headed for a crucial showdown with Batista at his Kuquine country house, the only place where the two could meet without causing dozens of rumors.

The streets were still glistening with water, the remnants of the first severe *Norte* of the season, which had swept over the city with forty-mile-per-hour winds and torrents of rain, flooding neighborhoods near the Almendares River, forcing the evacuation of hundreds and knocking out power-relay stations, including one which provided electricity to the two hundred thousand people in the suburb of Marianao. A cold front had followed the storm, and the limousine windows were rolled up tight to keep out the chilly evening air.

Smith stared straight ahead; his thoughts were far removed from the weather. He believed what he was about to do was the most difficult task he had ever faced. It was going to sound the death knell of the Batista regime, and for him that meant only one thing: "Soon we would be faced with Castro."

Seven days of conferences in Washington had not swayed the State Department at all, and finally Robert Murphy, the deputy undersecretary and the highest-level official to get directly involved with the Cuban situation, had told him formally about the secret emissary and stated bluntly that Batista had to leave the country if peace were to be restored.

Reluctantly, Smith had come to the same conclusion. It was no longer possible for Batista to remain, even as a behind-the-scenes force. But he continued to argue vehemently that the United States had to show support, including new arms shipments, for President-elect Rivero Agüero. In that he failed. Washington refused to provide any backing to a man who had shown no mass appeal among the Cuban people.

When Smith returned to Havana, his arrival was reported on the front page of the English-language *Havana Post*, though he had no comment for reporters. He knew everyone was waiting for the Americans to take some action. On his desk at the embassy, the usual stream of staff reports on advice from Cuban politicians had turned into a flood. Both conservatives and moderates were pleading for the United States to end the strife. Even some loyal Batista followers were admitting that if the Cuban president didn't leave, a bloodbath was inevitable. One conservative politician predicted that if the United States did nothing, up to fifty thousand men, women and children would die. A more cautious suggestion was made by two leaders of the Catholic Youth Association who urged the formation of a civilian-military junta that would ask Castro "to lay down his arms and cooperate on the political level in restoring peace and constitutional government."

Smith himself had been meeting with the papal nuncio in Havana, but despite the Vatican's desire for peace, the Church, like everyone else, expected the United States to lead the way in solving the problem. He knew that Washington was making confidential contacts with the ambassadors from the Organization of American States (OAS), urging them to apply political pressure to both the rebels and the Batista regime so that a provisional government of moderates could take over. Smith thought that plan naive, and even if it had a modicum of promise, the OAS was moving far too slowly to counteract the rapidly deteriorating military situation.

Seeing no hope in changing Washington's mind, Smith had held an awkward meeting in his living room with Senator Jorge García Montes, the Batistiano whom Smith had urged to go to Washington as a separate lobbyist for the president-elect. The senator told him he was ready to make the trip. Smith, in despair, told him it was too late. He couldn't explain why, but it was too late.

Finally, his frustration and anger mounting, Smith had fired off a crisp telegram to Washington: "The danger, which we must always bear in mind, is that any action taken on our part to weaken Batista without setting up a strong replacement backed by U.S. would automatically strengthen Castro and thereby benefit the Communists."

The reply came the next day. Smith had to be firm and tell Batista, directly and emphatically, that he should leave and that there would be no support for his president-elect. Until that was accomplished, nothing could be done to straighten out the situation.

At last, three weeks after the State Department had first enunciated the policy, Smith realized that he had come to the end of the line. Any further argument would be futile, no matter how bad he thought Washington's decision was. Hurrying to the home of Prime Minister Güell, he announced, "It is my duty to inform the president of the Republic that the United States will no longer support the present government of Cuba and that my government believes that the president is losing effective control." Güell paled when he heard the news, but he promised to set up an appointment with Batista.

Now, as the ambassadorial limousine arrived at the gates of Batista's sprawling country estate, soldiers shone flashlights into the car, first at the chauffeur, then at the backseat. They waved the driver on, and the car moved up a long driveway to the tan, two-story mansion with a red-tile roof. It was bathed in floodlights. Guards with machine guns patrolled the lawn. It was, thought Smith, an ominous sight.

The limousine sped past the main double-doors, and stopped at the entrance to the library wing, where Batista's office was located. A military aide opened the car door and escorted Smith into the *biblioteca,* where Prime Minister Güell was seated in one of four overstuffed leather chairs around a low table. He smiled politely, but Smith could see the strain in his face.

Slowly, trying to master the distaste he felt for having to be there, Smith looked around the room in which he had had several other meetings with Batista. He had come to know it well: the walls lined with books, the busts of Ben Franklin, Gandhi, Montgomery, Churchill, Joan of Arc, Dante and Homer, each on its own pedestal. A rare 1822 edition of *Vie Politique et Militaries de Napoleon* rested on a special table.

Moments later, Batista appeared from a small inner office. Smith, towering above the squat Cuban leader, shook his hand, and the two of them sat down, Batista beside Güell, Smith in a facing chair on the other side of the table.

As usual, Batista's face revealed no emotion. In fluent English, he made a vague comment about the recent storm, then he fell silent. It was Smith who had to do the talking.

The ambassador began with agonizing slowness, stumbling over his first words. He could be blunt with his embassy staff, but that would not do for speaking to the head of a foreign country. He tried to start softly, talking about Batista's long friendship with the United States, the contributions he had made to Cuban history, the historical bonds between the two countries.

As he rambled on, he thought to himself how absurdly evasive he was being. It was "like applying the Vaseline before inserting the stick." At last, he came to the problem. In considerable detail, he explained how he had fought to persuade the State Department to back Rivero Agüero's coming administration with arms and support. He had failed. Washington had decided that Cuba was in danger of being drowned in a bloodbath. But if Batista acted quickly, the State Department believed there were "Cuban elements which could salvage the rapidly deteriorating situation." It was necessary to obtain the broad support of Cuban leaders, persons who could come up with a national solution.

Smith paused for a moment. Now came the crucial part of the message. Washington, he said slowly, viewed Batista's presence in Cuba as itself a central stumbling block that would impede any hopes for peace, and it "would view with skepticism" any plan if he remained in the country.

He stopped. He had not said exactly that the United States was kicking the president of Cuba out of his own country, but he knew that was the underlying idea. Batista's face was still without expression; his body, erect in the chair, had not shown the slightest sign of movement. But Smith could detect a slight irregularity in his breathing, "like a man who was hurt."

When he saw that Batista was going to say nothing, he plowed on. He said he was not allowed to discuss specific solutions, or to recommend persons for a junta. The United States did not want to be accused of intervention. As he said that, he realized how hypocritical it must sound. Telling a foreign leader to resign was the most blatant form of intervention.

Finally, Batista spoke. Using slow, measured phrases, he said the army would collapse if he left the country and no military junta could survive without his backing. If the army was given U.S. arms, if it had political backing, then he could leave and the president-elect could assemble a coalition. A political amnesty could be declared. But without that backing, the only victor would be Castro. He asked if the United States was willing to stop the fighting. Smith repeated simply that there would be no intervention.

As the conversation drifted on, Batista continued to cling to the idea of a Rivero Agüero coalition, the plan which Smith had already proposed to Washington and had seen rejected. The ambassador gave him no encouragement.

Suddenly, Batista changed the topic. He asked if he and his family would be allowed to go to his mansion in Daytona Beach.

Smith suggested he try Spain or some other country instead. The important issue was that he should not postpone leaving Cuba any longer than it took to organize an orderly transition of power.

With that, Batista stopped arguing, but he insisted their conversation be kept absolutely secret. If word of the meeting got out, it would mean the instant end of his regime. Not even his president-elect should be told. Smith assured him that, with the exception of the cable he had to send to Washington, he would tell no one. They agreed it would be too dangerous to meet again, even at the secluded Kuquine. From then on, Smith would communicate with Batista only through Prime Minister Güell.

Two hours and thirty-five minutes after the meeting began, Smith shook hands with the two men and left. As he emerged into the chilly nighttime air and walked to the waiting limousine, he realized that the crucial point of the meeting had come when Batista asked about going to Daytona Beach. Obviously, he was seriously contemplating leaving.

As Smith's limousine sped away from Kuquine, Enrique Barroso and thirty rebels were slipping into their hiding places in a ditch next to the

Central Highway, about an hour-and-a-half's drive east of Havana. Barroso's mouth was dry, and his whole body seemed nearly paralyzed with fear. He reached into his pants pocket, where he felt a reassuring handful of candy bars. When he was tense, he always became hungry, and chocolate was the perfect balm. But now there was no time to eat. Their tiny 26th of July group was about to undertake its first military action, in an area where no rebel group had dared operate before. And Barroso was not at all confident they could do it.

Ever since he and his friend had been driven by the two underground women to the Madruga Hills, their plan to open a new guerrilla front had merely stumbled along. About twenty-five peasants, after hearing they had weapons, had joined the six who were there to greet them, but even after some training, they showed little regard for discipline. Often, they disappeared at night to see their wives and girlfriends. Barroso had argued with them but it did little good.

The only break in his frustration, and the tedium of living in the hills, came when the two women drove the Buick up to deliver messages from the Havana underground. Barroso and the group's leader, Pepe Garcerán, would take the women about a half-mile down the dirt road, to an avocado tree where they would sit and chat about the Movement in the city and the war in Oriente. Barroso viewed those talks as "business conferences," unlike the peasants running off to their girlfriends, but he had to admit that he was becoming attracted to Lizzy, the brunette who knew how to repair a car, even if she was a little slender. And she had seemed more than vaguely interested in him. They had started talking about personal things, what led them into the Movement, what they hoped to do after Batista was overthrown. Her visits had made life in the hills almost bearable, but then, three days before, she had brought a shattering order from the Havana underground. They were to blow up a bridge at Ceiba Mocha on the Central Highway, to prevent any army reinforcements going from Havana to the central province of Las Villas. But the plan was more complicated than that. First, they were to hijack a truck, mine the bridge and stage a quick raid on the city of Matanzas. Then, when the army chased them out, they were to speed back to the bridge and blow it up at exactly the moment the soldiers' trucks passed over it.

Barroso had objected vehemently. "We're in no shape to do something like that." They were simply two city men, untrained in guerrilla warfare, leading a band of badly organized peasants.

Garcerán disagreed. He had been hungering for something to do for weeks, something that would duplicate the imagery in his poetry of romantic fighting and heroic death. "Listen," he had said, "we either fight, or we are going to get to the end of the war without having fought."

Now, as Barroso crouched nervously in the ditch, he looked over at Garcerán. The poet seemed unnaturally buoyant, and Barroso felt as if he hardly knew his longtime friend.

His worries were interrupted by the rumbling of a truck in the distance. The rebels strained to see its headlights, but as it approached, they could tell it was too small to carry all of them. They stayed in the ditch, heads pressed against the moist earth until it passed.

Another truck appeared, but they heard the rough sound of its engine and decided it was too undependable for the mission.

When a third came into view, Garcerán studied the sound and the width of its headlights. He nodded approval.

Several rebels, waving their rifles, ran to the middle of the road. The truck stopped, and a peasant shouted that they needed to "borrow" his truck for a while. Everyone tensed, clutching their rifles, fearing the driver might gun the engine and try to escape. But the man simply smiled and said, "Fine, the truck belongs to the company. You can take it. I support you."

The rebels climbed into the back of the truck and took off. Five minutes later, they arrived at the steel bridge of Ceiba Moca. Garcerán leaped down first, standing on the highway at the rear of the truck as he shepherded the men down.

Barroso was just climbing off when machine-gun fire shattered the stillness. He dashed across the highway and dived into the ditch on the north side. About ten men leaped in after him.

Peeking over the trench, Barroso saw the vague shadows of several army jeeps and trucks at the opposite end of the bridge. Probably, he thought, they had been on a routine patrol, checking the drivers' licenses of suspicious late-night travelers, and had happened on the rebels by accident.

He could see that most of the rebels had jumped in the ditch on the opposite side of the highway, nearest the truck. Garcerán was partially hidden behind one of the tires.

He did not stay there long. Cradling his carbine, Garcerán rushed to the front of the truck, toward the bridge and the army patrol, about two hundred feet away. Then he started a dash across the highway. The soldiers unleashed a barrage of machine-gun fire.

Garcerán, stopping in the middle of the road, turned and started lifting his rifle as if to fire. The weapon never reached his shoulder. As Barroso watched in horror, the rifle slipped to the pavement. Garcerán clutched his chest as he fell backward. He did not even cry out.

Barroso, panicked, thought of running over to drag him to safety, but the shooting did not let up. As his eyes adjusted to the darkness, he could see a pool of dark liquid forming on Garcerán's chest, exactly at the area of the heart.

Moments later, the army patrol began advancing on foot across the bridge, and the rebels on the opposite side of the highway disappeared into the darkness. Barroso signaled to the men with him to follow as he ran along the steep riverbank away from the road. The sound of gunfire melted away until, slowing to a jog, they heard rushing water coming from the river, about sixty feet below them.

Fifteen minutes later, they reached a cluster of hills at a bend in the river. One of the peasants told him there were caves in the hills, almost invisible from the riverbank and known to only a few people. He led them up a steep slope until they found a narrow cave opening. They crouched inside just in time to hear, about 150 feet below them, army soldiers shouting to each other, asking if anyone had spotted the rebels.

Leaning back against the cave wall, Barroso tried to figure out what had happened. The appearance of the army patrol was probably just rotten luck; and maybe Garcerán had tried to dash across the highway to consult with him about what to do. But why had he then stopped in the middle to fire back? It made no sense, unless Garcerán had a death wish; that was entirely possible.

As the sounds of the soldiers faded away, Barroso focused on the problems ahead. He fished into his pockets and pulled out the chocolate bars. There were six of them, and he remembered that he had given others to some of the peasants before they left camp. He whispered for the others to count their supply. It worked out that they had enough so that each could have half a chocolate bar a day for three days. They had no other food.

21/FIDEL ORGANIZES

Lounging in a hammock, shifting a well-chewed cigar from side to side in his mouth, Fidel Castro listened to his Oriente commanders report on what their columns had been doing. Occasionally, he smiled and gave a short, rough laugh when some particularly stupid army action was described to him. The atmosphere was relaxed. For the first time in eight months, since he had started sending columns to other areas, Castro and his principal Oriente officers were reunited. Most had sailed with him on the *Granma* and shared the hardships of the early days in the mountains. Now, they were gathered together almost as if it were a family reunion, trading anecdotes and jokes as they took a few minutes off from the worries of war to bask in the marvel of how far they had come since their small band had started.

It was Thursday, December 18, the day after Ambassador Smith talked to Batista, and the rebel leaders were holding a meeting of their own in a small clearing in the woods, next to a cluster of boulders, not far from the Central Highway. Though they had yet to take a city with more than twelve thousand people, their control of the countryside was so absolute that the officers had been able to come to this forest near the Charco Redondo manganese mine with only minor security precautions.

Raúl Castro crouched on the ground beside the hammock. His fiancée, Vilma Espín, wearing a black beret that matched Raúl's, sat behind him on a log. Near her was Juan Almeida, the black leader of the forces at the siege of Santiago, and one of his subordinates, Comandante Húber Matos, chief of Column 9. Matos sat carefully on a rock so as not to jar the cast on his leg, which had been broken in a jeep accident some days before.

When the anecdotes subsided, Castro asked for the *comandantes* to report on the present status of their columns. Raúl went first. The main battle of his Second Front, he said, was at the city of Sagua de Tánamo, near the northern coast. The attack had begun two days before, but the army was putting up strong resistance, with their forces scattered around thirteen positions in the city. He was hoping his men could again use the King-Fischer fighter plane, to bomb the city and perhaps speed up the surrender. It was almost impossible for the army to get reinforcements through; the rebels had set up ambushes on all the main roads.

Comandantes Almeida and Matos discussed the Santiago siege. Four days before, the army had made its most serious attempt yet to get a column out of the city, and it had failed completely. Three companies of infantry, three tanks, five trucks and a large gasoline tanker had been trapped in the Puerto de Moya hills west of the city. With land mines, the rebels had destroyed the lead tank and two trucks; the convoy suffered sixty casualties before the soldiers fled back to the city.

But in another area near Santiago, the rebels had been forced back. An army battalion with about two hundred men, several tanks and at least one cannon, had managed to retake most of El Caney Country Club, and the rebels were re-entrenched by the club's horse stables, on a ridge above the main clubhouse. Some of the army men had reinforced El Viso, an old Spanish fortress near the club. Comandante Matos had ordered more rebels into the area, because if they retreated any farther, the siege would be broken.

Castro's face turned grim, and he bit down hard on the cigar before he said that it was absolutely vital that the siege be maintained. There were only two major army posts left on the Central Highway between his Column 1 and Santiago, and if the soldiers were not reinforced, he was certain he could take both rather quickly. One of them, at Maffo, had already been besieged for a week, but he had to admit that the two army companies there were being unusually tenacious. They had set up a nearly impenetrable defense, with trenches and hundreds of sandbags topped by sheet metal to protect several two-hundred-foot-long Quonset warehouses. The soldiers were well armed, and they had even built a tunnel under the adjoining road so that they could get water from the basement of a nearby house. The rebels had dug trenches about 120 yards away, but the bazookas and mortars captured at Guisa did little good against the sandbag fortress.

Castro said he had learned during a truce that the soldiers were willing to give up if they could leave the area, but he turned down the offer. Some inside the warehouses were thugs associated with Senator Rolando Masferrer; they had committed crimes. He promised them a fair trial, but he wouldn't let them go. From what he could tell, the major in charge of the troops was willing to accept that, but a captain was being obstinate, and many of the soldiers supported him.

Castro paused, lost in thought, as his eyes followed the cigar smoke floating upward toward the tree limb above him.

An officer suggested they simply bypass Maffo. It was two miles off the Central Highway and presented no danger to their transportation. They could leave a few rebels there to make certain the soldiers went nowhere, and the rest of Column 1 could move on.

Castro grunted. He couldn't accept that. For Santiago, they were going to need all the arms they could get, and he desperately wanted those weapons at Maffo before he moved any farther. After that, the only place remaining on the Central Highway would be Palma Soriano, a mere thirty miles from Santiago. There was a large army garrison there, and he would need not only arms, but also all the rebel troops available.

Comandante Almeida said he already had troops near the city, and they could easily join in. Raúl volunteered to send at least half of one of his columns.

Castro nodded. For what seemed like a long time, he stared up at the tree leaves, waving in a gentle breeze. When at last he spoke, his voice had become rather distant and philosophical. He was certain, he said, that the Batista government was on the verge of collapse, and that meant they were entering a very dangerous time for the civil war. He reiterated that, countless times before, Cuban revolutionaries had met failure at the last moment. He was not going to allow that to happen again, under any circumstances. They were the ones who had been fighting the tyrant, and they *had* to be the ones who made certain the new government was the revolution's own, not some small group of opportunistic politicians who had done nothing for the struggle.

He suspected that Batista was trying hard to find a pretext for American military intervention. Every rebel officer had to be warned to be "very careful not to fall into any provocation or trap. We should not provoke the American enterprises, which would create incidents between the United States and ourselves." He doubted American public opinion would tolerate direct intervention, but he wanted to be certain "to avoid incidents that would lead to it."

There were two compromises he would not tolerate, he said, repeating what he had announced often on Radio Rebelde: a military junta replacing Batista and outside intervention. Other matters were negotiable; these were not. Already he had been hearing that some groups were trying to use the Organization of American States (OAS) to bring about a negotiated settlement. *

"At a fine hour," he had said sarcastically on Radio Rebelde a few days before, "these people with intentions of intervention or of calling in the Organization of American States are coming out of the woodwork. When the dictatorship here was breaking the heads of dozens and of hundreds of men, they worried absolutely not at all about that. They do not have the right to worry now."

Castro explained to the *comandantes* that he was starting a series of meetings with the underground leaders throughout the country. Originally, he had wanted the meetings to tighten the Movement's organization in the cities, which had grown rather lax in recent months, but now there was no time for that. They had to prepare for the possibility that the Batista government might topple at any time, and he was ordering them to prepare for a general strike that would shut down every store in the country, every hotel and office, every part of the economy, if the regime fell and any organization other than their own tried to form a new government.

Castro swung his legs over the side of the hammock and sat up, pulling the cigar from his mouth and studying the well-chewed end. It had gone out, as it often did, and he relit it before going on. The real

* Castro's knowledge of Batista's diplomatic maneuvers—as well as some of those of the State Department—was always quite good because the sergeant in the communications room at the Cuban embassy in Washington was a 26th of July spy.

reason, he said, that he had asked them there was to plan the attack on their ultimate target in the province: Santiago. For that, he would need almost every column. First, they would attack the outlying army posts, the microwave tower on the Puerto Boniato heights and the El Viso fortress near the country club. Then they would seal off the airport from the city.

When that was done, they would move into the city itself at night, from the area around San Juan Hill, going through the sprawling lawns of the mansions in the Vista Alegre section. From that point on, each squad would be on its own, fighting block by block until they reached the Moncada army garrison. He said that he was already making preparations to ship a hundred weapons into the city so that the underground could join in the uprising as soon as the rebels arrived.

Comandante Matos mentioned that if the army fought back tenaciously, they could be burned with "all the gasoline at Texaco." Its refinery just outside the city was already under rebel control. Others made suggestions and reported how many men they could provide for the battle.

Castro listened, occasionally interjecting a crisp question when he thought an idea too vague. When they were done, he said he figured they would be facing about four thousand to five thousand army soldiers in the city. It would mean they would have their best numerical chance of the war: Only 4 to 1 odds against them.*

The *comandantes*, who had faced far worse odds, thought nothing of that. They went on to discuss a timetable. They were guessing, but assuming it took a week or so for Maffo and Sagua de Tánamo to surrender, they figured they would be ready to attack in about two weeks: in the first days of January 1959.

---

*Comandante Matos, speaking to the Santiago Rotary Club in early January, said the rebel force prepared to attack the city was "about half" as large as the army garrison.

22/THE REBELS PUSH ON

At 4:30 in the afternoon of December 18, as Castro met with his subordinates, Captain Alfredo Abón-Ly of the Cuban army dejectedly led his seventy soldiers down a narrow paved road, leaving behind Mayajigua, the town he had worked so hard to defend. His men were on foot, followed by three empty army trucks. Abón-Ly had no desire to repeat the mistake made by so many other army officers, of driving a vehicle straight into a homemade land mine. He wanted to proceed cautiously, on foot, his eyes scanning every inch of the dusty pavement ahead of him, every shrub on the parched, low hills on either side. It seemed like a perfect place for an ambush.

All his plans in Mayajigua, all his perfect defenses had come to naught. True, his men had not been trapped inside the cuartel, but mobility had turned out to be their only advantage. The promised reinforcements from the Santa Clara regiment had never arrived. That dawn, about a hundred rebels had attacked his positions, outnumbering his own small platoons. Five of his soldiers had died before the regiment ordered him to retreat to Yaguajay, fifteen miles away. Abón-Ly had sputtered a protest—all he needed was a company of soldiers, perhaps some of the tanks resting at the regimental parade ground—and he could throw the rebels out. He was certain of it.

The regiment had said there would be no reinforcements of any kind, but they had at least granted his demand for a B-26 to fly escort service. It was now above him, doing lazy figure eights over the hills, occasionally hurling volleys of machine-gun fire into the barren slopes. The soldiers were walking in two columns in the ditches beside the road. The trucks, groaning in first gear, rumbled along behind.

They had marched about a mile when a soldier spotted a hillside trench. Abón-Ly, fighting back the fear that they might be encountering a major ambush, ordered a squad to crawl up to it on their stomachs. They did. It was abandoned.

Several hundred yards farther on, they found a crudely made mine only partially buried in the highway. If they had been speeding along in trucks, they undoubtedly would have hit it. But as it was, they and the trucks slipped past it easily.

As the sun set, Abón-Ly worried that a nighttime ambush would be impossible to defend against, but nothing more happened. About 8:30 P.M., exhausted from a day of fighting and walking, they arrived at the cuartel in Yaguajay, a sleepy town of 5200 located in an area of sugar mills. About a hundred soldiers, most of them aged members of the Rural Guard, met them with nervous smiles.

As Abón-Ly searched for something to eat in the cuartel's kitchen, he realized what their concern was. Undoubtedly, the rebels were going to be attacking Yaguajay next, and he would have to start the next morning organizing the defenses of the town.

If he could get support from the regiment in Santa Clara, there would be no problem. Even without reinforcements, he had a strong position. There were several two-story buildings in town where he could station men, and the cuartel itself was an ideal situation. It was a large one, located about a mile from the town, surrounded only by flat, barren fields which made it impossible for rebels to approach without being seen.

As he ate dinner that night, he decided he would defend the town as best he could, with or without support, and that is all that could be asked of him. If he had to retreat again, the northern coast was only a few miles away. He tried to think in solid, tactical terms, as he had been taught at the military academy. It was not his intention that his plans—

and the fate of circumstance—were to make him the last hero of the old Cuban army, which had dominated the republic for almost fifty years.

Throughout the war zones, a pattern was developing. As had happened at Mayajigua, the large army garrisons in the cities were refusing to break through ambushes and reinforce their compatriots besieged in the small towns. The air force continued strafing and dropping bombs, but that was the only support that most isolated outposts received, and sometimes the rebels, despite their overall numerical disadvantage, outnumbered the soldiers at individual garrisons.

Almost nightly, Radio Rebelde was broadcasting reports of new victories. The information was true, though the intensity of the fighting was often exaggerated. Sometimes, the men in the army cuartel gave up after only a few shots, now that they knew the rebels would treat them fairly.

The day after Abón-Ly made his retreat in northern Las Villas Province, Ché Guevara's men to the south captured their first major town, Fomento, population eight thousand, on the edge of the Escambray Mountains. His Column 8 had cut off the water supply to the cuartel and were about to burn down the movie theater adjoining it when the 130 soldiers surrendered. Their commanding officer said he would rather join the rebels than be handed over with the other prisoners to the Red Cross. Guevara agreed.

Rogelio Acevedo, the seventeen-year-old rebel lieutenant, had remained outside of town, manning the ambush site at the cemetery. He had taken elaborate precautions, with mines and trenches to block tanks and reinforcements, but none had come. Instead, he himself was reinforced, with new recruits from the area, armed with some of the weapons captured at the Fomento cuartel. Most of the new men were older than Acevedo and they grumbled that their weapons were not as good as the others had, but Acevedo silenced dissent by telling them that the best weapons, the Garand carbines and the Thompson submachine guns, were always given to the most experienced fighters. If they wanted better arms, they would have to win them in battle.

Again, Acevedo assumed they would hurry back to the safety of the mountains, but Guevara passed along an order for them to push toward the towns of Cabaiguán and Guayos, which were located on the Central

Highway. He was committing them irrevocably to the plains, to win or to die.

About this same time, a small band of guerrillas from the Segundo Frente del Escambray attacked a squad of army soldiers stationed at the Tope de Collantes sanatorium, located on a mountain peak in southern Las Villas Province. Eloy Gutiérrez Menoyo, the group's leader, arranged for a hospital orderly to help him sneak into the building. Holding a BAR submachine gun, he burst into the office where the army captain was alone. Gutiérrez Menoyo told him that most of his men were already captured and that he and the soldiers manning the machine guns on the sanatorium's roof should surrender to avoid further bloodshed. That was a lie. Most of the soldiers were still in their trenches, but the captain chose to believe the man with the machine gun. The Segundo Frente quickly took over the hospital.

In northern Oriente, the going was considerably tougher for the rebels in the city of Sagua de Tánamo. The residents had fled to the countryside, and the army soldiers had retreated back to the cuartel and the city hall only after burning most of the town behind them, including the movie theater, the main department store, the Hotel Saratoga and the local newspaper, *El Tanameño*. They had done that to have a clear line for gunfire if the rebels decided to approach their positions.

Shortly after midnight on December 19, Comandante Antonio Enrique Lussón, the onetime truck driver who had taken La Maya with the help of the Rebel Air Force's only fighter plane, climbed with another officer to the flat roof of the church's bell tower. They were four stories above the ground, and to the east they had a clear view in the moonlight of the cuartel, a light-yellow concrete building, almost as tall as the church.

They were waiting for what was to be called Mission A-002 of the Rebel Air Force. A scout had studied the area the previous afternoon, to make sure of the cuartel's location, and the plane was due to attack just before sunrise. Lussón, unable to sleep, sat on the top of the tower and explained to his fellow officer the panic the first mission of the King-Fischer had caused at La Maya. He was feeling supremely confident.

About 5:00 A.M., when the first rays of dawn were beginning to lighten the sky, Lussón heard the distant drone of the plane. The other officer saw it first, coming from the east, from behind the cuartel.

"Look at it!" Lussón shouted. "Now you'll see how scared the soldiers are going to be. Are they in for a surprise!"

The surprise, however, was on Lussón. The plane swooped down, flew past the cuartel and kept coming toward the church.

Instantly, Lussón realized the pilot was going to attack the wrong building. He and his friend flattened themselves against the rooftop as two napalm bombs exploded below them.

As the King-Fischer roared into the distance, Lussón surveyed the damage. Mission A-002 had just destroyed the park bench in front of the church. Lussón cursed, but he had little time to be angry. The rebel pilot was coming back for a strafing run.

Again, the two officers fell, stomachs down, to the flat roof. The plane zoomed in, splattering the front of the church with machine-gun fire. Several minutes later, it came again. And then again. Altogether, the King-Fischer made four runs against the church.

The next afternoon at 5:00 P.M., after Lussón had berated the pilot and the pilot had explained that the church and cuartel looked so alike in the dark, the Rebel Air Force tried again. Mission A-003 started with rebels on the ground setting a wooden cart on fire beside the cuartel, sending a tall column of smoke billowing into the sky. This time, the King-Fischer buzzed so low over the army post that Lussón feared the pilot was trying to atone for his earlier mistake by crashing into it. As it was, the wings almost touched the roof as the plane swooped by. The bomb exploded inside the cuartel, but did little damage, and, unlike La Maya, the soldiers were not frightened into surrendering. The siege went on.

23/A BATTALION GIVES UP

Arms folded across his chest, Major General Eulogio Cantillo stood looking out the window of his second-floor office at the Moncada garrison. Through the treetops, he could see a sliver of the shimmering waters of Santiago Bay. Almost directly below him, on the edge of the parade ground, mechanics were doing routine maintenance work on the Staghound T-17s and rubber-wheeled M-8 light tanks.

His problem was not the machinery, but the human beings who had to operate it. That fact was presenting him with a critical situation. Almost all of Battalion 17 was refusing to carry out orders. He had already transferred the group's commanding officer, and he had to decide what to do next. It was a mobile-armor battalion, the one with which he hoped to break the rebel encirclement of the city. Without it, crushing the siege had only slim chances of success.

Turning from the window, he walked across the black-and-white tile floor to his scarred wooden desk and sat down. What he needed, he decided, was for someone to see exactly how demoralized the battalion was, someone who could be sympathetic but firm. The best man, perhaps the only man, for an assignment like that was his territorial inspector, the man in charge when he was out of the city, Colonel José Rego Rubido. He had been chief of the national police under an earlier, democratically elected regime, and Batista had forced him, along with many other officers, to resign following the 1952 coup d'etat. Two years later, faced with mounting bills and a seriously ill daughter, Rego had asked to be reinstated, and he was. But his assignments had all been inconsequential, and Cantillo knew that the man harbored an intense, though unspoken, bitterness toward the Batista regime. There seemed little doubt that Rego hoped a new government would appreciate his talents more, but he was not the type to start a conspiracy on his own. All of that made Rego the kind of man who would be understanding with the balking soldiers but who would nevertheless carry out orders.

Cantillo picked up the phone and told an aide to send Rego in.

The colonel's office was just next door, and he appeared within seconds. With dark-framed glasses and a bland face, he looked a bit like a schoolteacher.

Cantillo wasted no time. "Colonel," he said, "Battalion 17 has come in this morning. It's been ordered to camp at the new hospital because we have no space here at the Moncada." He paused. Rego was slightly older than Cantillo, and the general was reluctant to give cut-and-dried commands. "It would be a good idea," he went on, making it indirect, "if you went over to inspect this battalion. We have had some problems with discipline, and I have had to relieve the major who was in command. A captain is in charge now."

Rego did not look enthusiastic, but he said crisply that he would check into it. Running downstairs, he jumped into a jeep and drove to the military hospital, a short distance from the garrison. In an unused wardroom, which had yet to be supplied with hospital equipment, he found the soldiers. Most were lounging on the floor. The captain, seeing the colonel enter, shouted, "¡Atención! ¡Atención!"

About half the soldiers got to their feet. The rest remained on the floor. They stared at him sullenly.

Rego repeated the order. "¡Atención!" The bellow reverberated through the still room. Most of the others, hostile looks on their faces, stood up, but they moved so slowly that even their obedience implied insurrection. Five remained on the floor.

The colonel gave a short speech. He could understand, he said, what they had been going through, and the difficulty of being asked to fight against their fellow countrymen in a civil war, but there was such a thing as military discipline, and it had to be maintained. The five men did not move. Rego ordered them arrested.

The captain, a relatively young man, took the colonel into a corner. Apologetically, he said that many of the soldiers in Battalion 17 were refusing to fight. They had gone through some bloody confrontations with the rebels during the summer offensive, and since then they had been given no leave time. As a mobile unit, the men were simply breaking under the strain of thinking that they could be unexpectedly ambushed at any time.

Rego rushed back and reported to Cantillo. The general listened, then decided to give the battalion one more chance. The men were to be ordered to form on the grounds of the hospital at six o'clock the next morning and practice marching within its confines. If they were still accepting any discipline at all, they would have to carry out the order.

The next morning, about sunrise, Rego slipped out of his small bedroom in the third-floor tower of the barracks and walked through an adjoining door onto the building's main roof. Putting the field glasses to his eyes, he saw an absurd sight on the hospital lawn several blocks away. The captain was barking orders to one other officer and five enlisted men. They were marching, left, forward, right, to the rear, like a tiny boy scout troop. More than ninety soldiers were missing.

Rego hurried to Cantillo's wooden house at the end of the Moncada parade ground. They talked on the porch, standing, neither bothering to use the rocking chairs. Both realized that the demoralization could quickly spread through the entire garrison if something wasn't done quickly. Cantillo said he had to punish them in some way, but he didn't like the idea of jailing them. That might only start a rebellion among the other soldiers. The best solution was to get them out of Santiago.

Summoning an aide, he dictated a telegram to Camp Columbia in Havana: "Dir Opns G-3 EME—Stgo de C 201045 Dic 958—MSW: Upon being ordered to go out on operations, 97 officers and soldiers Battalion 17 refused to leave. STOP. Request from you urgent air transport to order to take them out of the Command. STOP. Request authorization from you to shave their heads before putting them on the plane so they can serve as an example. I repeat: Urgent evacuation right away."

The telegram was sent at 11:40 A.M., December 20. There was no reply from Camp Columbia.

24/CONNIE'S VISITOR

A few blocks away from where General Cantillo was worrying about Battalion 17, Park Wollam took Connie into the master bedroom of their home in Vista Alegre and closed the door so that the maids couldn't hear. Sitting together on the side of the bed, facing the old shortwave radio atop the bookcase, the American consul told his wife that a U.S. corporate plane was about to fly to Havana, and he was taking it. He wanted a chance to talk to Ambassador Smith in person and urge him to call for the evacuation of American residents from Oriente Province.

Wollam could feel his wife tensing. They had talked about evacuation many times in recent weeks, and both knew it could be a life-or-death decision. At the very least, it would affect his whole career, for the pressure in Santiago was becoming almost unbearable as the city waited for the rebels to attack. Almost every afternoon now, Connie sat on the balcony of a friend's apartment and watched the single-engine army Beavers and Pipers strafe the hills above the city. Army machine-gun nests had even been set up in the heights near their suburb. Already Texaco had sent the families of its U.S. employees to Jamaica by tanker, and the U.S. Navy had evacuated the American families at the Nicaro nickel mine on the northern coast. The Nicaro operation had almost been a disaster, with Cuban navy gunboats firing on the rebels in the town as the Americans waited at the pier. It was just pure luck that they weren't cut down in the cross fire, and Wollam didn't want to see a risk like that again.

Connie asked him how much a threat the rebels represented.

Not much, he said, at least not directly, because they seemed to be increasingly concerned about U.S. citizens and their property. An American with a chicken farm near the city, in rebel-controlled territory, had complained to the rebel commanders after he missed sending his weekly shipment of eggs to the U.S. naval base. The rebels had offered a compromise. They would allow a plane to land, pick up the eggs and take them to the base and to the American-owned Moa Bay mining company on the northern coast. In return, the American promised not to ship any eggs to Santiago itself.

Wollam laughed as he recalled another incident, at the Texaco refinery on the western edge of Santiago Bay, which the rebels were visiting almost nightly. One evening, they had taken an auto from the sales department. It was returned several days later with a note, in English: "Dear Sr: I send you the car that we tooked the other night, because some of my men got shut in a leg and it was impossibilite to walk. Thank a lot for every things you have been doing for us. Sincerely yours, Cap. Humberto Rodríguez, M-26-J." Wollam told his wife that Texaco officials were angered at the suggestion that they were cooperating. They "helped" only when faced with armed men, and the company had lost about $125,000 in gasoline and equipment to the rebels.

But, Wollam added, the Cuban air force might be more of a danger. An American rancher, an aged fellow, had walked seven miles, from El Cobre, to show him a leaflet which the air force was dropping. It ordered all civilians to leave the rebel-controlled areas, or they would be considered rebel sympathizers and might be bombed by the air force. Wollam had complained to General Cantillo, but he was told there was nothing that could be done. They were at war, the rebels had to be bombed, "and you can't tell an American from the air."

Wollam stopped talking and stared at the shortwave set for a moment as he tried to sort out his thoughts. It helped for him to talk to Connie, helped clarify the options. "The real problem," he said slowly, "is that if we wait too long to evacuate, it might be too late." Airline flights couldn't carry all the Americans, and the rebels were certain to shut down the airport, just outside of town, before they attacked the city.

"And if you try to take them out by boat, that bay is a bottleneck. If anyone wanted, they could seal off the mouth with a few cannons. And if we try to get to the naval base, which might be the easiest way, there would be at least two rebel roadblocks to negotiate, plus figuring out what the army would do. And, last, if we had to get out on foot . . ." He let the words hang, trying to imagine Americans walking into the hills during a battle. "Well, that could be so dangerous that it probably would be best to keep them inside the city."

He added that almost every day Americans were coming into the consulate and asking him whether the area was safe. He was telling them what he was telling Washington, that the rebels now controlled 90 percent of Oriente Province, that attacks on the city seemed imminent, but that there was no formal advice about whether to stay or go. He knew Ambassador Smith would be reluctant to make any statement about evacuation. Such an announcement would be a blatant admission that the American government thought Batista was no longer able to control the situation, and to Smith that was almost the same as withdrawing recognition.

It was possible, Wollam said, that he could issue a warning on his own authority, as the U.S. official closest to the situation, but with the ambassador opposed, that could ruin his career if it turned out that evacuation wasn't necessary. Yet, how could he weigh that against the idea that dozens, maybe several hundred, American lives were at stake?

"Listen," he said, becoming even tenser, "whatever I decide, I want you to take Janet and the baby, and stay at the naval base until this is over."

She shook her head. "I know you plan to be the last American out of town, and, well, I'm going to be the last American woman out."

He stared at her for a long moment, then stood up. She was a stubborn woman, and there would be no changing her mind. Quickly, Wollam packed an overnight bag, kissed her good-bye and drove away in the consulate's 1957 black Ford.

As Connie watched him disappear down Mandulay Avenue, she started thinking about the night to come. She hadn't wanted to worry Park about it, but she hated the idea of her and the kids staying in the house by themselves.

Walking down the great hall, past the kitchen and pantry, she found Anselmo, the gardener, working in the backyard. He was a tall, muscular black man who looked about thirty but was probably closer to sixty. He rarely spoke as he went about his duties, and Connie suspected that he was helping the 26th of July underground, but he seemed like a stable sort. When she explained that her husband was out of town, he readily agreed to spend the night in the vacant servants' quarters.

After dinner, her daughter Janet took a shower and then she bathed the baby, as she always did, in bottled water, shunning the dirty liquid that came out of the taps the color of weak tea. When the children were in bed and she was certain the doors were securely bolted, she retired to the master bedroom. There was little new on Radio Rebelde that evening, and she sprawled on the bed, only half listening. She was starting to doze when she heard voices coming from the side yard, between the servants' quarters and the garage.

Rushing down the hall, she looked through the iron grating of the kitchen window and saw Anselmo on the lawn.

"There's a man," he told her. "He's going to the back door. I'm going to stop him."

Moments later, she heard Anselmo talking to someone she couldn't see. The stranger mumbled a low reply. Then there was silence.

Someone knocked at the door. "It's me. Anselmo. Let me in—it's all right. I'm alone."

She opened the door. Anselmo came in looking more puzzled than alarmed. "The man was pretending to be drunk," he told her. "But he wasn't. He said he came looking for the maid."

Connie frowned. "But everybody knows our maids don't stay overnight."

Anselmo shrugged. That's what the man had said. He described him: a fellow of medium build, slightly Oriental features, wearing a white suit. He had a .45-caliber revolver in his belt.

As Connie had done before, she called the vice-consul. He and a squad car arrived within minutes. Again, she described the situation as the officers took notes, but when Anselmo mentioned the man's appearance, they frowned and exchanged glances. Soon after, they put their notebooks away, thanked Señora Wollam for calling them and said they would look into it.

That night, they did not patrol the block. Connie lay awake, straining to hear the sound of the patrol car circling the area, but it never came. She wondered if the police thought she were merely a frightened housewife, imagining things. No, she decided, that couldn't be. The gardener had seen the man this time. At least the neighbors would be happy. They were angry the first time, when the police car spent the night patrolling the block. No one in Santiago wanted the police so nearby.

Park Wollam returned from Havana feeling disgruntled and "not very forceful." Ambassador Smith had found it hard to believe how serious the situation was in Oriente, and Wollam was forced to admit that, as of then, not a single American had been killed in the strife.

In a way, Wollam could understand Smith's thinking, because there was such a profound contrast between the atmosphere in Havana and the terror in Santiago. To Wollam, the capital had seemed remarkably tranquil, the land of "tourists singing and cha-cha-cha."

When Connie told him about the strange nighttime visitor, Wollam made a call. A police official and SIM army officer came to see him at the consulate. The two assured him that the intruder had been neither a policeman nor a soldier, and they were quite confident the man wasn't connected with the rebels. "But there's a third force in town," they said, "over which we have no control." Wollam understood that could mean only one group: the thugs of Senator Rolando Masferrer. But what would they want at the home of the American consul?

About this same time, another kind of "third force" was getting under way in Miami. Meeting in an old downtown hotel, Tony Varona, the prime minister of the democratic regime that Batista had overthrown, had finally come up with a possible conspiracy after weeks of searching.

Sitting on a bed in a small hotel room, Varona listened to an old friend, Abel Loredo, whom he knew from his days in his native province of Camagüey. The man spoke in hushed tones, as if he feared a secret microphone was in the room. He said there was an army captain who was chief of the cuartel in the town of Guáimaro. The fellow was highly dissatisfied with the Batista regime, but he refused to do anything to help the 26th of July rebels. He would, however, be willing to join with Varona, as a representative of the last democratically elected regime, in an uprising.

Varona leaped from the bed. The situation couldn't have been more perfect, he told his friend. The town was strategically located on the Central Highway. With some army men on their side, they might be able to rally the soldiers in the Agramonte Regiment in the provincial capital of Camagüey City. That would give them control of the province. When Batista fell, as seemed inevitable, Castro's troops would have to move through Camagüey to get to Havana. With Varona controlling the province, the rebels would have to negotiate with him, and he could successfully demand a major role in the new government for his Auténtico party.

Telling his friend to stay in Miami for a few days so that he could make some plans, Varona hurried to the Miami Beach home of his mentor, former president Carlos Prio. Prio had given large sums of money to the 26th of July, but now he, as did Varona, saw this as a last-minute chance to grab some power for the Auténticos. He agreed to provide the plane for the trip.

That night, Varona called Carlos Piad, the anti-Batista lobbyist, at his suite in the Roosevelt Hotel in Washington. He explained the plan and asked if Piad could arrange for U.S. permission so that a planeload of weapons and men could leave Florida for Camagüey.

As soon as Piad hung up, he hurried over to the North Arlington home of William Wieland, State's director of Caribbean affairs. "This looks definite," Piad said hopefully, "but Varona has to keep this very quiet. If the Batista people found out, or the Castro people . . ."

Wieland said he understood. "I'll pass this up the line," he said, "and maybe this can get some support."

He did not need to mention all the other times he had said the same thing, and it had led to nothing. Piad already knew that, but there was something he didn't know and that Wieland couldn't tell him. He had seen the ambassador's report of Batista inquiring about going to his Daytona Beach home. Undoubtedly, the government was about to collapse, and it seemed almost too late for any "third force" to work.

Still, as Wieland watched his Cuban friend drive away, he decided that while any chances remained, no matter how slender, they had to be tried.

That evening in the Madruga Hills outside of Havana, Enrique Barroso waited impatiently beside a flickering kerosene lamp in the hut of Joseito, the peasant who was his contact with the city. For four days, Barroso had been living with the vivid, sickening memory of his small rebel group's failure at the bridge, and now he could only wait for Lizzy to arrive from the Havana underground so that he could tell her the news. Through the glassless window of the hut, he saw clouds obscuring the moon and stars. A storm was coming.

He was thankful it had not arrived earlier. For two days, he and his ten men had hidden in the cave above the river and listened to the ground patrols and a single-engine army plane searching for them. All they could do was sit quietly and take mouselike bites from their few chocolate bars. When the patrols had finally disappeared, they sloshed across the river and made a two-day march, sleeping one night on the bare ground, back to their base camp.

He was wondering how to break the news of Garcerán's death when he heard the familiar sound of the sputtering Buick, still needing a tune-up, as it climbed the last hill. Moments later, Lizzy appeared, her short brunette hair waving in the growing wind as she walked up the path toward the hut.

Barroso ran down to meet her. Taking her hand, he led her under a mango tree. The fact that they had become more than "revolutionary *compañeros*" made his task even more difficult.

"Where's René?" Lizzy asked, using Garcerán's war name.

Barroso didn't know how else to put it. "The attack on the bridge was a disaster," he said bluntly, almost as if spitting out his bitterness. "René was killed."

She began trembling. Her legs buckled and Barroso grabbed hold of her by the shoulders as she sobbed. The wind was rising, swirling dust around their legs, while she clung to him.

At last, she was able to speak. "We had been hiding together, bringing weapons together," she said, tears forming rivulets on her cheeks. "If we had been at parties all this time, it wouldn't have meant so much, but . . . I had met his wife so many times. I took messages to her." She paused as they both thought of Garcerán's wife, who was due to give birth within a couple of weeks. That brought more tears. "He was such an idealist, so sure. Such a fighter. Are you sure he is dead? Couldn't it be that he was only injured?"

"No. He was only twelve feet away from me. They shot him in the chest, and he dropped dead." He wanted to spare her the bloody details.

Just then, a shower burst upon them. Even under the tree, they quickly became soaked, their clothes sticking to their skins, as they hugged each other, oblivious to the rain.

Vitalia Bequer sat idly listening to rebel radio transmissions on her Zenith Transoceanic in a small room at the rear of her rented concrete-block house in the town of San Miguel de los Baños. She kept the volume low, so that her son, asleep in the front room, couldn't hear.

Ever since doctors had told her about his psychosomatic colitis, she made certain he never heard the broadcasts for fear that they would bring back memories of the terror he had suffered. But she couldn't help listening herself, hoping she would learn something about her husband, Captain Napoleón Bequer. The last time she had heard about him was six months before, when a woman had told of seeing him in the Sierra Maestra. He had a broken leg then, but he seemed in good spirits.

The rebel announcers droned on, giving their nightly reports of battles and propaganda speeches. There was no sensational news, and she was getting drowsy as the regular program ended and the radio operators began exchanging information and chitchat between the different columns.

She heard only vaguely when a rebel in Las Villas Province put out a general call, asking anyone in Oriente to respond. He received a reply from Column 9, which the operator said was located in the hills near Santiago.

"Oye," the Las Villas man said, "if Húber or Napoleón is there, let me talk to them."

Instantly, Vitalia was awake. She couldn't believe it. Did they mean her husband? There weren't that many Cubans with the name Napoleón.

Moments later, she heard her husband's voice saying, "Hello, how are you?"

"Fine," the Las Villas rebel answered. "We're pushing the army around here. We're in good shape."

Napoleón described what had been going on at the Santiago siege.

Vitalia wanted to scream. He was alive! Then she slapped a hand over her mouth. She didn't dare to wake her son.

In Havana, at the Rancho Boyeros international airport, Rolando Amador, the lawyer who was going to Paris to close a business deal, kissed his new bride Carmen good-bye at the gate leading to the plane. They had been married the night before, in his firm's stately law offices in Old Havana. About twenty-five friends and relatives had gone with them to the Sevilla-Biltmore Hotel for a small reception of champagne and cold cuts. They had spent their one-night honeymoon at the Riviera Hotel.

Carmen's eyes brimmed with tears as they said good-bye, and Amador tried to comfort her. He was only going to be gone for two weeks or so and, as he had said countless times before, the business deal was important for his career—closing a very large contract for the building of several casino cruise ships that were being financed by the Batista government. "In January," he said soothingly, "when I get back, we will have all the time in the world."

That same day, another Havana man was leaving Cuba too, but for an entirely different reason. Danilo Mesa, the high-fidelity store owner who had been beaten by the police, dressed himself in flashy tourist clothes and went with his wife Rosa right to the heart of Batista's power, Camp Columbia. The army officer who had helped free him, Colonel José Martínez Suárez, had passed along word that the police wanted him out of the country or his next encounter in a precinct station might be even more injurious to his health.

That was warning enough for Mesa. He had spent four days in jail before the bruises had disappeared enough for his guards to let him go, and after his release, a dentist had to treat his mouth for an infection caused by a tooth jarred loose during the beating.

In planning his departure, Mesa decided to avoid the main airport at Rancho Boyeros, where SIM officers were always on the lookout for suspects. There was still a possibility that the police might want to pick him up, and so he did the unexpected, choosing Aerovías Q airline, which was owned by Batista and some of his cronies. It flew to Key West from the Camp Columbia airfield. Mesa figured that no one would imagine that a clandestine Movement member would dare walk right into the camp, and he worked out a careful cover story, about going fishing in the Florida Keys. But no one at the Aerovías Q ticket counter bothered to ask. There was an agonizing wait in the plane, as it seemed to sit forever on the concrete apron, but eventually it took off.

For the first time, Danilo Mesa realized he was doing what so many Cuban activists had done before him, going into exile. He guessed it would be only for a short time.

While others were leaving Cuba, fifteen-year-old Rosa Rivero returned. The daughter of the president-elect was surprised to see her father's friends carrying machine guns as they patrolled the house, but her mother assured her it was just a precautionary measure, and Rosa quickly dismissed it from her thoughts.

On her first afternoon in Havana, she put on one of her prettiest dresses, checked her stylishly short pageboy hairdo in a mirror and went downstairs to the living room to meet Emilio Posada, her seventeen-year-old boyfriend.

Her green eyes flashed as the tall, curly-haired boy shyly handed her a navy-blue leather diary, the present he had been promising in his letters.

She looked at it carefully. The pages were edged in gold, and on the right lower corner of the cover were the initials of her full name—RRC—Rosa Rivero Collado. It had a leather strap with a lock.

He handed her a small golden key and she opened it. The first page was for December 31.

"I will wait until then to write my first entry," she said, blushing.

He smiled. "I hope we will be able to celebrate that date together. New Year's Eve."

She nodded shyly. It would be her first formal date.

25/"LIFE IS A RISK"

It was early in the morning when Ambassador Smith's black limousine swung off Seventh Avenue in the Miramar neighborhood and moved down the driveway to the house of Prime Minister Gonzalo Güell. Not bothering to wait for the chauffeur to open the door, Smith let himself out and walked briskly across the front courtyard of the old-style Spanish house. A servant opened the door and showed him into the book-lined library, where Güell was already seated in an overstuffed chair. Smith sat down in a matching one, facing him.

Ever since he had delivered Washington's message to Batista, the ambassador and the prime minister had been meeting daily, always at Güell's home before Smith went to the embassy so as not to attract attention. At the first meeting Smith had simply reiterated everything he had told Batista. The Cuban president had been so astounded at the news that he wanted it repeated, to make certain he understood it correctly.

Güell's face was somber this morning, but, as always, he asked Smith in a pleasant voice if he wanted a cup of coffee.

Politely, Smith refused. He had developed a genuine admiration and affection for this aging diplomat who, even in the face of enormous adversity, could keep such a cool demeanor.

Güell waved the servant away, and the man closed the door behind him. Then the prime minister picked up a legal pad from the end table. It was covered with scribblings. Smith knew they were notes taken by Güell at his daily briefing with Batista.

Speaking with deliberation, Güell said he had just been informed of a new army offensive, into the central province of Las Villas. Troops were to be sent from Havana in an armored train, its passenger cars protected with reinforced steel plating. The army corps of engineers would be in charge. Its men and weapons would easily enough defeat the small bands of guerrillas in the province, and then the mechanics would repair the damaged bridges.

Smith nodded and said that would be good news, if it proved to be true. He was about to say something more, but he stopped, for he saw that Güell was not finished.

"I have been told," the prime minister said, "that because of this new military development, the situation is not nearly as serious as some had previously believed." With that in mind, Batista had authorized him to suggest again that President-elect Rivero Agüero could take over the government before his February 24 inauguration. In fact, Batista was willing to step aside immediately, and it could all be done legally, within the constitution. There was only one condition, the same one he had always had—that the United States support the new government, especially with arms.

Smith nodded. Except for Batista offering to resign immediately, there was nothing new so far.

But Güell was not finished. "With that support," he said, "then the new president could form a coalition cabinet and have elections within *one* year."

That was new, and Smith leaned back in his chair. Before, Güell and Batista had been suggesting a two-year wait. Now they were cutting the time limit in half. The ambassador cleared his throat, then said that while it seemed like a generous offer to him, he doubted if Washington would accept even a year of a Rivero Agüero government. He asked if the timetable could be advanced.

Güell said he would have to ask Batista, but it might be possible to have voting in, say, six months.

"Make it four months," Smith said, knowing that even that promise would be difficult to sell to the State Department.

The prime minister said he would see what he could do. Smith would have an answer by the next morning, after Güell had talked to the president.

As Smith walked back to his waiting limousine, he decided that the State Department now had a perfect opportunity. It could dictate almost anything to Batista, and he would have to accept. But he doubted that Washington would seize the chance, even if it would mean new elections within months. After all, State had already turned down every suggestion that he and Güell had come up with.

As Smith climbed into the backseat of his limousine, he realized he might be seeing the climax of a Greek tragedy, and he, supposedly the second-most-powerful man in Cuba, could do nothing about it.

That afternoon, President-elect Andres Rivero Agüero walked slowly up the marble steps to the second floor of the Presidential Palace. At the top, a military aide showed him to a sofa facing a marble railing that overlooked an enclosed courtyard. The officer said the president would see him shortly.

Since his election in early November, Rivero Agüero had been accustomed to meeting Batista every Saturday evening for dinner at the president's home in Camp Columbia, but he had requested a special session at the palace because of the recurring rumors he was hearing.

Batista had been telling him little. He knew nothing about the Americans' attitude, except Batista's continued assurances that the United States wouldn't dare abandon them. The only reports he received on the fighting were the same press releases, boasting of army victories, that were sent to the newspapers. From friends, he knew that the real military situation was not nearly that rosy, that some army commanders had been shirking their duties and should be replaced, but his real concern—far more important to him than the rebels or the Americans—was what to do if he did kick the generals out. He was especially worried about the Tabernilla clan: General Francisco ("Pancho") Tabernilla was joint chief of the armed forces, his son Winsy was chief of the air force and another son, Silito, was commander of the Havana infantry division and Batista's military liaison. If they chose, the

Tabernillas could topple Rivero Agüero's government with a snap of their fingers.

The aide's return jarred Rivero Agüero from his worries. He was led down the hall and into the president's formal office, where Batista, dressed in a white linen suit, his thin black nylon socks showing under the desk, sat studying some papers. He did not look up right away, and Rivero Agüero stood there uneasily for a moment. The wooden desk was oddly ornate, with carved pseudo-Oriental goddesses, bare-breasted, forming the eight legs. Behind Batista, staring down at him, was a white marble bust of José Martí, the Cuban martyr, and the national flag, its red, white and blue colors symbolizing, as Rivero knew well, its nineteenth-century creator's hopes that Cuba would one day be annexed by the United States.

The president-elect felt a momentary burst of pride when he realized the office would soon be his own, but then he noticed the burgundy-colored drapes concealing the steel plates that covered the windows. That symbol of danger brought him back to reality.

At last, Batista looked up from his documents and signaled curtly for Rivero Agüero to sit in a French provincial chair facing the desk.

Rivero did so. It appeared Batista didn't have much time, and the president-elect plowed straight into his concerns about army conspiracies: "I think that you should change the military commands right away, so that when I come into office, it is already taken care of. I wouldn't have to be concerned with that. Otherwise, I don't know what the Tabernillas would do. I consider them quite capable of staging a coup against me if I force them out."

Batista's face was as expressionless as ever, but his voice snapped as he said, "No, that is your job. It will be good for your image. You will come across as your own man if you make the changes yourself. It may even be good for the morale of the army."

"Yes, but . . ." Rivero Agüero paused. He had never seen Batista this brusque before, this willing to delegate authority. "I am afraid they would rebel against me . . . because I have not developed any loyalty among the military. . . . It would be a risk."

"Look, it's your job," Batista said, even more brusquely. "Don't bother me again with the idea. It's yours to carry out. It would enhance your national stature, and it would indicate that you are not Batista's sidekick, but that you are carrying out your own desires."

"But the risk—"

"Andrés," Batista said, calming a little, "life is a risk. Government is a risk. What is more of a risk than our own situation, where our lives are at stake every minute? . . . You know, there was just discovered a plan among some young army officers to take both of us prisoner."

Rivero Agüero was shocked. He had heard nothing of this, and he waited for Batista to explain.

But the president simply went on: ". . . There is a risk with every move we make, and in my own present situation, I do not feel I should start playing with the military commands just two months before the end of my government."

That last statement was said with finality, and as Batista looked back at his papers, Rivero Agüero realized the meeting was over. He wanted to ask about the conspiracy to kidnap them, but he knew that Batista explained only what he wanted to.

Thanking him for the discussion, Rivero Agüero said he would think about changes in command. He left, not feeling at all certain that he was capable of the task and wondering why Batista had made such a point of emphasizing that he needed to boost his own public image, as separate from Batista's. It was the first time Batista had ever mentioned that.

Batista had said nothing to Rivero Agüero about Ambassador Smith's message that he should leave the country and that there would be no support for the president-elect's proposed government. Nor had he discussed the frantic negotiations between his prime minister and Smith.

But, at a midnight meeting in Camp Columbia, Batista had revealed many details of the Smith meeting to three of his oldest and closest friends, the chief of the navy, the chief of the army and General Pancho Tabernilla, the joint chief of staff for the armed forces.

That revelation made the military leaders realize that their last hope had disappeared. Forced at last to face the reality of the civil war, something for which they had no experience, they started to do what they knew best: planning conspiracies and counterconspiracies, forming vague alliances for coups d'etat and offering to bargain for power. The highest officers had begun to scramble for themselves, to see what they could salvage personally from the situation.

26/THE ARMY PANICS

Well after midnight, Major General Eulogio Cantillo climbed down the stairs from his C-47 transport plane at the Camp Columbia airfield in Havana. The spotlights on the air force headquarters' roof glared in his eyes, and only with difficulty could he see the small group of officers waiting for him on the concrete apron, as they always did, hoping for tidbits of news on the fighting in Oriente. Sometimes he stopped to chat, but tonight he simply waved as he stepped into the olive-green Oldsmobile that was waiting for him.

"Estado Mayor," he said to the driver, naming the building that was headquarters for the Cuban armed forces. Ordinarily, he would have stopped first at his home, located only a block from the Estado Mayor, but he had been summoned to Havana for an emergency meeting with General Francisco ("Pancho") Tabernilla. Pancho Viejo, they called him—Old Pancho—the first officer to join Batista in his Sergeants' Rebellion in 1933 and still his closest associate. Cantillo despised the man. He had never taken a single class in the military arts and had no real experience, except showing a steadfast loyalty to Batista, whom he always called "Chief," in English. It was widely rumored that Tabernilla had amassed a fortune by using air force planes to smuggle appliances from Miami, avoiding Cuban customs and making large profits on the black market.

Exhausted, Cantillo slumped back against the seat. He had ordered a cot installed on his C-47, to grab some rest during his frequent trips to Havana, but it was always hard for him to sleep during flight, and he had never been able to adjust to the differences between the two military garrisons. The Moncada in Santiago, like most army installations, started its day early, about sunrise, and stopped in early evening. Camp Columbia, or at least its highest officers, did the opposite. Since Batista slept late and did most of his work at night, his military commanders did the same. Only rarely did a Columbia meeting begin before midnight.

As the Oldsmobile sped through the gate separating the airfield from Military City, Cantillo reflected how different, especially now during the civil war, Columbia seemed from Oriente. The military police in their shiny white helmets stood guard as they had always done, and the late-night repair crews from the air force strolled across the vast parade ground as if nothing were happening. The war had touched Columbia not at all, and that set off in Cantillo a wave of bitterness. There was squad after squad of tanks in Havana, and howitzers, and fighter planes—for weeks he had been begging for some of that equipment to be shipped to Santiago, where it could be used, but Batista had refused. He wanted the best armaments kept in Havana to protect himself. That was always his number one priority; the fight against the rebels was secondary.

Cantillo's car sped past his small house at one corner of the parade ground and stopped in front of the Estado Mayor. Trying to overcome his exhaustion, he bounded up the long staircase leading to the second floor of the light-yellow building. Inside, he took another stairway to the third floor and walked down the hall. The joint chief's aide waved for him to go in.

Tabernilla put down some papers on his desk and stood to shake Cantillo's hand. He was a haggard-faced, stoop-shouldered man with thinning white hair. At least six inches taller than Cantillo, he bent forward a little to look him in the eye as he asked him how the war was going in Oriente.

Cantillo sat down and lit a king-sized Chesterfield. He described the military situation briefly and then asked why the Estado Mayor had not replied to his telegram demanding evacuation for the rebellious soldiers of Battalion 17 and allowing him to shave their heads as an example.

Tabernilla shrugged. "Well, under the circumstances," he said, "we can't be too strict with discipline."

Cantillo couldn't believe it. He was not a strict disciplinarian himself, but simply to ignore a battalion's refusal to fight was an invitation for chaos. "What then do you want me to do?"

Tabernilla shrugged again. That was not important now, he said, walking over to a large wall map of Cuba, with little electric lights indicating the various regiments and Rural Guard outposts. He stared at it thoughtfully.

The map only increased Cantillo's anger. It was Pancho's toy, nothing more, absolutely useless for military planning, and many of those tiny lights indicated posts now in the hands of the Oriente rebels. Cantillo, with all his military education, was continually astounded at the ignorance of the men who ran the Cuban military. It was in this same room, during the summer offensive, that General Rodríguez Avila, chief of the army, had told him where to position his men by putting a pen mark on an Esso road map of Cuba; Cantillo had muttered, "General, do you realize that a company could not walk from one end of that dot to the other in a single day?"

Tabernilla turned away from the map and looked squarely at Cantillo. "The war is going terribly," he announced matter-of-factly. "It is time to find a 'national solution' to end the bloodshed."

Cantillo sat up in his chair. "What do you mean, 'national solution'?"

"It is necessary to speak with Castro," Tabernilla said as calmly as if he were suggesting a meeting with an old friend, "to see if he will accept a military-civilian junta. To see what his thoughts are."

Cantillo leaned back and took a long puff of his cigarette as he tried to sort things out. At the end of the summer offensive, Castro had suggested a meeting with him, to talk about the war and exchange prisoners. At that time, Batista had personally summoned Cantillo to his Varadero beach home and told him that he was too high-ranking an officer for such a meeting. A colonel had been sent instead. Now, *he* was being asked to do it, and the request had not come directly from Batista but from his longtime friend. For days, Cantillo, like everyone else, had been hearing rumors of conspiracies inside Camp Columbia, and he wondered if he could any longer trust even Pancho Tabernilla. No, he decided, such a thought was absurd. Tabernilla was not only Batista's ally, he was also a glorified lackey who had neither the charisma nor the fortitude to run the country.

Choosing his words carefully, Cantillo said, "First, I just don't like the idea. It's a surrender mission, no matter how you put it. If you ask to speak to the enemy, then you are admitting you are defeated.

"Second, I don't want to speak to someone like Fidel Castro. Third, I don't even know where he is. It is difficult. I don't know how to get in touch with him."

Returning to his desk, Tabernilla reminded him of the priest who had brought the letter from the officer who had defected to the rebels. Surely, the priest could easily set up a meeting. But it had to be done "right away," before the army collapsed completely. He added that "we" in Camp Columbia had talked about the meeting and decided it was absolutely necessary.

Cantillo left the Estado Mayor bewildered. He felt a gnawing fear. When Pancho had said that "we" had discussed it, the implication was he had talked it over with Batista, but he hadn't said so directly. Perhaps Batista didn't want to get personally involved, so he could deny knowledge of it if he had to. Or perhaps he didn't know. Whoever was behind the idea, it was absolutely clear that a change in governments was about to take place, that the army was thinking of giving up and that he was the one being asked to handle the negotiations.

As he cut across a corner of the parade ground toward his house, he thought of all the times before he had balanced himself so carefully on the tightrope, but he wondered if this time he had the stomach for it, literally. His ulcer was protesting with a sharp spasm of pain.

At 3:00 P.M., Monday, December 22, Comandante Echemendía of the Havana underground walked into the living room of an old two-story house in the Vedado area, on a shaded street about two blocks from the Gulf of Mexico. The man who had been stopped by police at the Sports Palace water fountain was accompanied by Comandante Diego, chief of Acción y Sabotaje for the 26th of July in Havana. Through a byzantine series of contacts, they had heard that General Cantillo and Colonel Florentino Rosell, chief of the army corps of engineers, wanted to meet with them to discuss a plot to overthrow Batista.

For long minutes, they sat nervously on a frayed sofa and waited. Echemendía knew they could easily have been set up for a trap, but he was willing to risk it for the chance to talk to two high-level officers of the Batista army.

His worries were groundless. At 3:15, Colonel Rosell, carrying a slender leather briefcase, strode in briskly, followed by an aide. Both were in full military uniform. The squat, fair-skinned colonel shook the underground men's hands and said in a smooth businessman's voice, "I'm sorry General Cantillo couldn't come today. He has been terribly busy. But I have his full backing."

Comandante Diego nodded. "Well," he said with a certain coldness, "we are willing to listen to what you have to say, but we really came here as liaisons. To listen. We cannot offer any agreement, because that has to come straight from Fidel."

Rosell said he understood. Quickly but without any sign of nervousness, he walked to the dining-room table and pulled from his briefcase a large map of Cuba. Echemendía was impressed: the less time they spent together, the less chance they had of being caught.

"As you may or may not know," the colonel began, as if he were conducting a military briefing for subordinates, "we have a fully equipped and manned armored train that in two days will leave Havana for Santa Clara.

"We are proposing to you that on Christmas Eve at six P.M. there will be an uprising in the army, and we will distribute all the weapons from the armored train to the revolutionaries there. The troops who do not join us will be arrested. Then, the army and rebels together will march toward Havana and take over Camp Columbia."

Rosell pointed to the map, where he had marked several locations with rebel circles. These, he said, were bridges that the rebels had to blow up, so that troops loyal to Batista could not interfere with their plans.

When the combined forces took Havana, he went on, they would set up a military-civilian junta. It would include General Cantillo, who would lend his Oriente soldiers to the cause; one of the Puros, the imprisoned military officers on the Isle of Pines, who had sent a graduation ring as a sign of support; and three civilians, including Manuel Urrutia, president-designate of the anti-Batista groups, and two others to be chosen by Castro.

General Alberto Del Río Chaviano, commander of the troops in Las Villas Province, would cooperate, as would the military chief of Camagüey Province. Those two would then be allowed to leave the country. All the others involved in the 1952 coup d'etat, including Batista himself, would be arrested.

Looking up from the map, Rosell added that they had discussed his plan with the American embassy, which had given its approval. The United States would recognize the junta as soon as it took over.*

Echemendía listened, his face void of expression. He was surprised at some of the names dropped, and he wondered what Rosell, who had not proposed himself as part of the junta, wanted out of it. But he repeated simply that he would transmit the plan to Castro and contact the colonel later.

Rosell nodded. He folded the map quickly, slipped it back into the briefcase and left, trailed by his silent aide. The whole meeting had taken only a few minutes.

Echemendía watched through the window until the colonel's car disappeared around a corner, then rushed to a nearby safehouse, where an underground contact had a powerful shortwave set in his den. Flopping in a chair beside the radio, he scribbled a note to "Alejandro," Castro's war name. After describing the plot, he concluded: "They want to talk to you or Comandante Ché Guevara within the next 24 hours. I have simply listened to their propositions and sent them along to you so that you may resolve them as you wish. I await instructions."

The radio operator transcribed the message into a simple book code and, after Echemendía's notes, added some of his own about rumors concerning plots to assassinate Batista and other plans for coups d'etat. He ended the transmission with these words: "We are living through decisive moments."

At that moment, several miles away, Brigadier General Silito Tabernilla, the president's military liaison and the son of the armed forces chief, was watching Fulgencio Batista pace over a black-and-white

---

* Rosell was exaggerating. As he later admitted, he had outlined his plan to the CIA's Jack Stewart, but he had been given only mild encouragement and a promise that the idea would be passed along to Washington. There, the plan disappeared into the bureaucratic maze, like so many others. Rosell was also mentioning officers' names without their approval, and General Cantillo had no idea that the colonel was meeting with the underground. Rosell and Cantillo had talked, but Cantillo, with his usual balancing act, had only agreed in vague terms that it would be good if something happened to stop the bloodshed. Finally, it is highly unlikely that Rosell would really have allowed the arrest of the Batista hierarchy, since the Tabernilla clan were among his closest friends. All in all, Rosell was spinning a complicated web of intrigue.

tile floor. They were in an office across a narrow, covered walkway from Batista's house at Camp Columbia. Outside, through a narrow window, Silito could see soldiers marching in the golden glow of late afternoon on the grassy parade ground. But Batista's attention was fixed on the framed black-and-white photographs lining the office walls. They were all photos of himself, taken at the high points of his career: The 1933 coup, the 1940 election in which he was formally voted into the presidency and the 1952 coup.

Now, Silito thought, the smiling, sometimes gloating images in the photos seemed to be looking down at their older twin in mockery. The Association of Cuban Landholders had just met and decided to ask Batista to resign, as a patriotic gesture, to save the *zafra* of the sugarcane and protect the economy. Batista had refused to see the association's two representatives, but the landholders' decision had come as another bitter blow.

Turning away from the photos, Batista looked straight at Tabernilla, who was sitting at a desk. The situation, he said, was becoming grim. It was time they prepared a list of persons to be notified "in case we have to leave."

"Well," Silito replied, with momentary bravado, "why don't we fight to the last man?"

"Silito," Batista said, staring at the floor, "that's not possible."

"Well, then you should leave." Silito had been worried for weeks that they might be caught by a bloodthirsty mob if the government fell suddenly. "As the Americans say"—he switched into English—"'the sooner the better.' Because people are giving their lives to defend your government."

Ignoring that, Batista asked him to check with his brother Winsy, chief of the air force, to see how many seats were available at a moment's notice.

Dialing a number he knew by heart, Silito found out. Three airplanes, two from the Aerovías Q airline that used the Columbia airfield, and Batista's personal plane, the *Guáimaro*, could be used any evening. There would be a total of 108 seats.

When Batista heard the number, he said, thoughtfully, "Silito, those hundred and eight persons whose lives we save—someday they will thank me for it."

He resumed his pacing, staring at the walls as he began rattling off from memory the names of those who should be notified in an emergency and asked to leave with them. Silito scribbled on a notepad. When Batista saw he was having a hard time keeping up, he would pause for a moment, then continue.

The list was remarkably detailed, including who should go on which plane. On the first would be Batista himself, his wife Marta, his brother-in-law and his closest political associates, including Prime Minister Güell and President-elect Rivero Agüero, along with a few military leaders. The Tabernilla clan, offspring of Batista's first marriage (and his ex-wife) and the top police officials would go on the second. The third was reserved for several of his youngest children, some servants and the mistress of one of his generals. On each plane, a few seats were saved for unnamed aides and bodyguards, and he assumed most of the leaders would want to take their wives along. Silito wrote the names down on three pieces of paper, one for each plane.

"Keep the list in your pocket," Batista said when he was finished selecting the names. "Never separate yourself from it." Any hint that he was thinking of leaving could topple the government. And Silito's brother Winsy was to have the planes on constant standby alert, pilots ready, engines checked.

Silito slipped the notepaper into the thin leather wallet that held his military identification card. "Where will you be going?" he asked.

"I'll decide that in the air," Batista answered, pulling a brown envelope from his suit pocket. He handed it to Silito. "This is for you," he said and walked out the door.

Silito opened it. Inside was $15,000 in cash. He was accustomed to receiving money for special favors, but this was an unusually large one. It showed how important Batista considered that list to be.

That evening, well after midnight, the leading military officers gathered in the third-floor office of General Pancho Tabernilla in the massive Estado Mayor. The lights of the garrisons still shone on the wall map, but no one looked at them.

The officers sat glumly in chairs around Tabernilla's desk and the nearby conference table as they reviewed how badly the war was going. After a while, Lieutenant Colonel Irenaldo García Baez, the youthful chief of the SIM intelligence service, slipped in and listened, leaning against a wall.

Everyone in the room was a longtime associate of Batista, his most trusted friends, but each now was hiding information from the others.

Silito Tabernilla did not mention the list in his pocket. His father Pancho said nothing about the message from Ambassador Smith. Colonel Rosell gave no hint that he had met with two underground 26th of July *comandantes* the previous afternoon.

But everyone knew that the government and the army were crumbling. General Del Río Chaviano said his troops in Las Villas Province no longer seemed willing to do battle. Colonel Rosell of the corps of engineers agreed: "Within hours or days, Las Villas is going to collapse. The headquarters can't resist anymore. The army doesn't want to fight." They thought the situation was just as bad, if not worse, in Oriente.

Silito Tabernilla complained that the rebels were using "unfair tactics . . . Every time we send a battalion out, they never find a rebel. Send out a patrol, and the rebels kill two or three."

The discussion turned to Batista. What would he do if the regime collapsed? They knew he placed an enormous emphasis on his pride and dignity. There was a good chance he would commit suicide, they decided. Even Silito, with the list in his pocket, agreed. Batista still might choose to stay and fight until the bitter end.

Considering that, one of the generals said, where did that leave *them*? In Cuba, when a government started to collapse, everyone wanted to leap on the bandwagon and claim part of the victory. It might be filthy opportunism, but it meant that after a certain point, the end would come very quickly. Then they would be at the mercy of the mobs.

Pancho Tabernilla, sitting at his desk, spoke for the first time. He said he had explained to "the chief" how bad the military situation was, and Batista had said, "'OK, bring me a proposal to solve the situation.'"

That was an opening for Colonel Rosell, and he jumped into it. Ignoring his meeting with the 26th of July, he told about his contacts with Colonel Ramón Barquín and the other Puros on the Isle of Pines. The only way, he said, "to avoid total disaster is to give power to Barquín and the other jailed men, because they are close to the Americans, and they would be acceptable to the army and to the people."

The colonel had just admitted to Batista's closest cronies that he had been plotting to overthrow the regime, but none of them voiced any immediate objection. They were all beyond that now, and one general even agreed that Barquín was the best solution, but he added, using an old Cuban idiom, "Who is going to bell the cat?" Meaning, who had the courage to suggest that to Batista?

Pancho Tabernilla ignored that, but he suggested someone had to contact the American embassy, to see what kind of a proposal Washington would accept. He might do that himself. Someone else, he went on, would have to contact Castro, to see what he would approve. Cantillo was the best man for that, because of his impeccable reputation.

In a corner, García Baez, the SIM chief, had heard all he could tolerate. He was young enough to be the son of several of the generals, and his ties to the "chief" were secondary, through his father who was commander of the national police, but he felt he had to say something.

"It's impossible to bring Barquín back," he announced with growing anger. "How can we support him? We're the ones who found him guilty of treason and conspiracy. . . . The situation is not as bad as you believe. It's bad in Las Villas. It's bad in Oriente. All right. But what's happening in Havana? What's happening in Matanzas, Camagüey, Holguín? We have control of seventy-five percent of the country."

"Sure, García," one of the generals retorted sarcastically. "You're talking that way because you're head of SIM. Your organization is behind the president one hundred percent."

That enraged García Baez even more. "And do you know why it's that way?" he demanded. "Because no one in SIM has any other choice. Because if one single agent is doing something wrong, he knows what's going to happen. You know that in the middle of the SIM building is a courtyard. And if one agent betrays his president, we would kill him in that courtyard. Everyone knows that." It was time to get tough, he said, time to stop thinking of defeat and actually start fighting. If soldiers didn't want to fight, they should be disciplined so severely that everyone else would fall into line.

The group fell into an awkward silence. The generals stared at the floor. Finally, General Pancho Tabernilla, the joint chief of staff, stood up, drawing his usually stooped frame to its full height, and announced, "Gentlemen, gentlemen. We have to die next to the cannon like good military men. We shall follow Batista in whatever fate he chooses."

The words rang hollow, but no one said anything more. The meeting was over.

It was almost dawn as García Baez rushed back to the SIM

headquarters in a corner of the camp, next to the military hospital. Summoning his department heads to his second-floor office, he decreed that from that moment on, all three hundred of the SIM headquarters staff were to be on twenty-four-hour alert and remain in the building. Cots were to be brought in, so they could sleep in the hallways. Special agents were to start following General Del Río Chaviano and Colonel Rosell, especially Rosell. It was, he said, an unpardonable betrayal that the man in charge of the armored train, intended to relieve the besieged forces in Las Villas, was conspiring against the government.

In fact, he added, unable to contain his rage, he had a mind to take the entire SIM staff and arrest the military high command immediately.

A SIM veteran shook his head. "You are a young man. You are angry, but you have to think about it. Go see your father, and see what he has to say."

García Baez took the advice. He sped in his Oldsmobile across the camp to his father's house facing the parade ground. The sun was just rising above the buildings when his father, who had been ill for some months, came to the door in a bathrobe. They talked in the living room. The old man, one of the original conspirators of Batista's 1952 coup, told his son to do nothing until he had talked to the president.

It was still early morning when García Baez was shown into a small waiting room on the second floor of the Presidential Palace. But then came hours of frustration. First, the aides refused to wake Batista, who had just gone to bed. Then the president had a rare morning cabinet meeting. And finally, as the SIM chief raged, General Pancho Tabernilla himself slipped into Batista's office for a long conference.

When Tabernilla emerged, García Baez confronted him: "General, did you speak about all the things that happened last night?"

"Yes," the general said somberly, "and, García, you were right. We need to support the president. We need to die for the president. It is the best way."

When at last García Baez was able to get into Batista's formal office, he poured out his anger and frustration, rambling through Rosell's plot with the imprisoned Puros, Tabernilla's desire to speak to the American ambassador and the suggestion that General Cantillo should talk to Castro.

Batista showed no reaction. "This is a conspiracy against me by the highest-ranking people in the army," he said in a low, measured voice.

Apparently, thought García Baez, Tabernilla had not explained everything after all. That realization gave him the courage to go on: "Mr. President," he said firmly, "I think we should arrest them all. Right away."

Batista leaned back and emitted a gentle, ironic chuckle. "García, I don't have too many friends right now in the army." He told him to do nothing.

The SIM chief left stunned. The whole regime seemed beset by impotence and defeatism, and they still had most of the country under their control. Batista appeared to have given up.

Shortly after lunch that afternoon, General Cantillo walked back from the mess hall at the Moncada garrison in Santiago and sat down in the rocker on his front porch. For once, the chair failed to soothe his nerves, and he realized he was going to miss his afternoon nap again: The Jesuit priest was coming at any moment.

His mind in turmoil, Cantillo tried to sort out the situation as he waited. Before leaving Havana, there had been a second meeting with General Pancho Tabernilla, but it was even vaguer than the first. Again, Tabernilla had said "we" had discussed it thoroughly, including Cantillo's objections, and still "we" thought it absolutely essential that he meet with Castro to discuss the possibility of a junta. Cantillo wanted to know what kind of junta. Who was to be included? Castro himself? Tabernilla offered no specific answers, only saying that he was to "feel out" Castro on what the rebel commander would accept.

The whole situation had become very odd. Almost always, Batista asked to see him when he came to Havana, for a firsthand account on the fighting in Oriente, but on his last trip, the president had never contacted him. Did he know what was happening but wanted to pretend he didn't? Was Old Pancho Tabernilla preparing a trap, a plan to kill Castro (and incidentally Cantillo himself) when Cantillo unknowingly led the assassins to the rebel leader? Or was there some plan at Camp Columbia to discredit him, to have him meet with Castro and then claim the meeting was unauthorized, to set the stage for a Tabernilla coup?

The options seemed too complicated to contemplate, and for once in his life, he saw no middle ground to walk, no way to please all these divergent forces. Obviously, the Batista regime was ending, and it was time to stop the fighting and dying. But, he decided, that was as far as he would go. This was going to be his last act for the Cuban army, which he had served for so long and which had rewarded him so well.

Moments later, Cantillo saw the priest, Father Francisco Guzmán, walking in his black cassock across the parade ground. He stood up to shake his hand and, carrying the rocker, led him into the spartan bedroom, which had only a bed, a chest of drawers and a small night table.

Closing the door, Cantillo sat in the rocker as the priest took the bed. He was about to speak when Father Guzmán spotted his Bible, bound in red leather. Guzmán picked it up and flipped through its heavily underlined pages.

Cantillo, blushing, said, "I read this book every day."

The priest smiled. "Good reading, General."

But Cantillo was not in the mood for small talk. He suspected the priest was a rebel sympathizer and he wanted to be careful about what he said to him, so he made the message simple. The nation, he said, had been marred for too long by bloodshed. It was time to end the fighting. "I would like to have an interview with Castro as soon as possible."

The priest did not seem surprised. "I think I can arrange for that. Any conditions?"

"The only condition I would demand is that right away, in the very moment we are able to come to an agreement, I be retired. . . . Father, this step I am about to take is the end of my military life. My father was a sergeant in the army. It is extremely hard for a soldier to determine when his pledge to uphold the flag no longer binds him."

The short speech exhausted him. Wearily, he pulled a 50-peso bill from his pants' pocket and handed it to the priest. "Here, Father, I don't want you to incur any expenses over this."

Father Guzmán tried to refuse, but Cantillo insisted, and at last he put it in his wallet.

Calculating out loud, the priest guessed it would take several days to pass through the rebel and army lines and then find Castro, who was now moving about often. Cantillo said he had to return to Havana, but he would be back in four days, by Saturday, December 27. Anytime after that would be acceptable.

The priest said he would be in touch as soon as he knew something definite.

Cantillo showed him to the door. As he watched Guzmán walk back toward the main gate at the far end of the parade ground, he wondered if events were slipping completely out of his control.

Castro was at a new headquarters, in the engineer's house of the Central América, a large sugar mill next to the Central Highway, when a young messenger from Radio Rebelde ran up the steps to the porch. He handed the rebel leader the decoded message from Comandante Echemendía in Havana.

As the messenger watched, bewildered, Castro erupted with an angry shout as he read the details of the conspiracy suggested by Colonel Rosell.

Pacing and ranting, he bellowed that the plot had everything wrong with it, everything he had been fighting against for the past six years. The connection with the American embassy, the idea that military officers at Camp Columbia were involved—every detail seemed to indicate that once again the traditional powers of Cuban politics were trying to thwart a revolution at the last minute.

Intuitively, he sensed that Colonel Rosell's offer for him to appoint members to the proposed junta was simply a cosmetic subterfuge to make him stop the war. His small rebel group would be disbanded, and Camp Columbia, controlled by army officers, would remain the bastion of power. The military could overthrow the 26th of July junta members anytime it felt like it.

But when he calmed down, Castro realized there were two notes of optimism. First, the officers at Camp Columbia were obviously panicking even to suggest such a plot. Second, the name of General Cantillo offered possibilities. Cantillo had never committed any war crimes, and his troops were in Oriente, far from the insidious control of Columbia. It might be possible to persuade Cantillo that he and his men should join with the rebels in a united front.

Pulling his ever-present notebook, warped and sweat-stained, from a shirt pocket, Castro scribbled: "Echemendía: Reject conditions. Organize a personal interview between Cantillo and me." He signed it with his war name: "Alejandro."

27/THE $450,000 BRIEFCASE

That same day, December 23, as Castro and General Cantillo each worked to arrange a meeting, Rosita Ferrer peered out the window of a twin-engine Cubana Airways prop plane as it taxied toward the Cienfuegos terminal, on the southern coast of Las Villas. An attractive young woman with light brown hair, wearing a fashionable gray suit, she tried anxiously to see her friend Carmen Gutiérrez, who had invited her to spend Christmas at her home. But the open-air terminal seemed deserted.

Rosita's father, a wealthy Havana doctor, had demanded that she not take the flight, because of rumors of rebel activity in the area. But she had argued vehemently, pointing out that he himself didn't believe the absurd propaganda broadcasts of the few "bandits" in the hills. Reluctantly, he had given in. The family chauffeur had driven her to the Havana airport.

The plane stopped on the concrete apron, and a steward opened the door, which fell down to form a staircase. She picked up her gray suitcase, trimmed in green, and climbed down the steps. She was the only passenger getting off. It wasn't like the Gutiérrez family not to send someone to meet her, but she shrugged it off as she walked toward the terminal. They were probably a little late, she decided.

Suddenly, by some bushes at the end of the runway, she saw some bearded men emerge carrying submachine guns. Rebels! Her heart quickened, then she realized how silly it was. She was on the edge of a large city, impossible for the rebels to capture. Undoubtedly, they were police intelligence officers, participating in a war exercise.

Inside the terminal, Rosita found no one, not even an airline employee. She placed her suitcase on the tile floor and waited.

Moments later, a bearded man carrying a rifle ran up to her. Perplexed but polite, he asked if she were driving into town.

"No," she said without terror, "I'm waiting for someone to pick me up."

The man pointed to the other side of the terminal, near the driveway. "They'll find you there. I want you to stay away from the plane."

She thanked him and followed instructions. It seemed like an odd kind of war game, but she wasn't one to question authority.

After a long wait, a car raced up the driveway and stopped. It was her friend's brother, Pedrín.

"Rosita," he yelled, "what a day to arrive! The rebels have taken over the airport. Let's get out of here quickly."

She threw her suitcase into the open door and jumped in after it. As the car sped away, she asked, "Are you *sure* those are rebels?"

Late that afternoon, Julio Duarte, the secretary-general of the Cuban Bar Association who had bought additional life insurance because of his role in the Havana underground, parked his two-tone 1956 Chevrolet on a narrow street in Old Havana and walked quickly into the stately headquarters of one of Cuba's largest sugar companies.

Inside, he was shown immediately into the office of the president. Several executives were sitting around the high-ceilinged, wood-paneled room. They greeted him pleasantly, and said the aging patriarch of the company would join them shortly.

Duarte sat down in a chair facing the main desk and waited, hoping he was showing no sign of his nervousness. In June, after the general strike had failed, the Movement had been able to raise only $700 in the entire city. In November, they had collected $30,000. Now, he was waiting for a delivery of hundreds of thousands of dollars, "taxes" that the rebels had imposed on the company's sugar mills in rebel-held areas. This sugar company had been one of the last great holdouts, with three hundred thousand acres in sugarcane and $40 million invested abroad. The family that ran it was highly conservative, with close ties to the Batista government, but the president had arranged this meeting because he believed making a "contribution" was "the right thing at the right time."

Duarte was just starting to get edgy when the gray-haired patriarch hobbled into the room and took a seat beside his own. Duarte stiffened. He didn't want to listen to this ancient Batistiano, but he had no choice.

"I'm very much concerned about the political situation," the old man said. "It is a shame for Cuba to be torn apart like this. There must be a way to stop this bloodshed." He offered to serve as a mediator, because he was close to the government leaders.

"Well, that is a very generous offer," Duarte said politely, lying. He was only thinking of the money, but he had to let the old man drone on. Which he did. Only when it appeared he would speak for hours did Duarte mumble something about getting in touch with him later. Then the corporate president cleared his throat. The old man fell silent.

Reaching behind his desk, the president pulled out a large leather briefcase and placed it on the desk. He flipped it open.

"Here is the money," he said blandly. "Four hundred fifty thousand dollars."

Duarte stared at the cash. It was stacked neatly, 100-peso notes tied into groups of 10,000. That was the most money he had ever seen in his life, but he tried to conceal his excitement.

The president counted it by the bands of 10,000—$450,000. It was all there. Duarte knew that was exactly the amount the company owed, but he had expected them to cheat at least a little. They were playing it absolutely straight, apparently because they wanted an in with a future 26th of July government.

"Of course," the president said, putting the stacks back in the briefcase, "we are going to need a receipt."

"Of course," Duarte replied, realizing he would have to use his real name, which would make for a very incriminating document if this were a trap. "Listen," he added, "there are some people who know I am here, and if I don't return shortly with the money, I'm afraid they will take steps. Perhaps we could speed things along."

That was a lie. Outside of one man in the Civic Resistance, no one knew where he was, but it was his standard dodge, a not-so-subtle suggestion that if anything happened to him, there would be retaliation.

The president handed him a handwritten piece of paper, listing the tax per bag and the total contribution. Duarte scribbled at the bottom, "Received by Julio Duarte, delegate for Raúl Chibás, treasurer of the 26th of July." Chibás was no longer the treasurer, but he was safely in the Sierra, out of the policemen's reach.

He returned the receipt, took the briefcase and, after quickly shaking hands with the executives, walked out the door. The Movement now had more money than it knew what to do with.

28/WAGING SEMIPEACE

Tuesday, December 23, was officially the second day of winter, but in Washington it was unusually warm, with temperatures rising by midafternoon into the upper fifties. William Wieland, the director of Caribbean and Mexican affairs, could look out of his corner office on the fourth floor of the State Department building and see people in shirt-sleeves scurrying to finish their Christmas shopping.

The town's mood was buoyed by the impending holidays, the delightful weather and the quiet pride caused by the United States successfully launching a four-ton Atlas, which newspapers boastfully called the "largest satellite in the skies," giving America some kind of equality with the Russian missile program.

That news, however, had done little to cheer Wieland, whose overwhelming concern, the Cuban problem, remained on the "back burner," as the State Department cliché went. Not once so far in December had Cuba even made the front page of the *Washington Post*.

On his desk was more depressing news: the latest dispatch from Ambassador Smith, with a new proposal for President-elect Rivero

Agüero to take office early and hold new elections within six months. Wieland found it incomprehensible that Smith was offering even this slim ray of hope to the regime. If everyone had assumed Rivero Agüero's election in November was a fraud, how could anyone trust his promise for new elections? The proposal seemed simply to be delaying the inevitable, Batista's departure, and each day of delay meant that the rebels were gaining more control of the country.

Even worse, Smith was reporting that Prime Minister Güell had told him that Batista refused to seek out moderates, persons allied with neither Batista nor Castro, to serve on a junta. Batista claimed such efforts would immediately leak out and cause the bloody overthrow of his government. To Wieland, that meant only one thing: Batista was going to flee with no warning and leave behind a horrendous vacuum. There was going to be a chaotic, perhaps murderous, race for power.

Wieland tossed the dispatch back on his desk and, as he often did, stared out the window, his eyes fixing on the Christmas decorations at a restaurant across Virginia Avenue. It was probably no longer possible, he thought, to keep Castro out of a new government completely. His popularity and his military victories, even if they were achieved against an army that didn't want to fight, meant he had to have *some* role in the future administration. The only chance for the moderates, he believed, was a "third force" in politics and some maneuver to keep the Cuban army out of Castro's control.

Time was running out, and Wieland's only hope was that the State Department's highest echelons, including the office of the secretary, had suddenly begun to show an interest in Cuba, barraging him and Assistant Secretary Rubottom with requests for details about the country's situation.

Wieland didn't know it, but the details were for a memorandum that was sent that day to the White House by Christian A. Herter, the acting secretary of state. Marked "TOP SECRET," "SPECIAL HANDLING" and "Sensitive," it was a concise, three-and-a-half-page summary of the entire Cuban situation, including Batista's 1952 coup and Castro's 1956 landing in Oriente. The memo assumed its reader knew nothing at all about Cuba.

On that warm winter day, President Dwight D. Eisenhower sat at his desk in the Oval Office and read that the State Department was placing increasing emphasis on Cuba because of "the advent of the sugar harvest and the rapidly deteriorating position of the Batista government." The memo estimated that Batista had "alienated some 80 percent of the Cuban people . . . [who] seem not to have forgiven him his interruption of democratic processes despite the bad reputation of the Prio Government which he overturned."

But State showed no sympathy for Castro either. Mentioning the kidnapping of the thirty U.S. seamen and the shutdown of water to the Guantánamo Naval Base, the memorandum added that "there are other clear indications that irresponsibility and a degree of anti-American sentiment are characteristics of the Castro movement. We also know that the Communists are utilizing the Castro movement to some extent, as would be expected, but there is insufficient evidence that the rebels are communist-dominated." That's why it was impossible to use the sanctions of the Organization of American States to intervene directly.

"The Department clearly does not want to see Castro succeed to the leadership of the Government. It believes that the majority of Cubans likewise share that view.

"Therefore, we have been attempting in every appropriate way, through all means available, without openly violating our non-intervention commitments, to help create a situation in which a third force could move into the vacuum between Batista and Castro."

The goal was to "keep the Castro movement from power," get Batista and his family safely out of the country and establish "a government broadly based on popular consent and support. Above all else, we want to avoid the appalling mob violence which attended the overthrow of Machado in 1933, and which Cubans fatalistically expect to occur again."

Eisenhower placed the memorandum back on his desk and called in his foreign-affairs advisers. He told them he was deeply bothered by the report and even more perturbed by a message from Allen Dulles, director of the CIA, who had just informed him that "Communists and other extreme radicals appear to have penetrated the Castro movement. If Castro takes over, they will probably participate in the government."

The president was angered that he hadn't been given this information before, but an adviser told him that earlier reports on Communist threats had come from Batista supporters and were therefore suspect.

One aide suggested that the United States support Batista "as the lesser of two evils."

Eisenhower decided against that. As he wrote later, "If Castro turned out to be as bad as our intelligence suggested, our only hope, if any, lay with some kind of non-dictatorial 'third force,' neither Castroite nor Batistiano."

More than a year after the middle-echelon men of the State Department had first proposed a "third force," the president of the United States had at last made it a reality.

But now only eight days remained in the year, and each of those days was assuming an immeasurably critical importance. Now it was only a question of how many people would die when the regime fell, and what group—or groups—would succeed it, what kind of power plays could be concocted, what type of political bargaining could grab at least a piece of the victory and the power that went with it.

Part Four

The Race for Power

DECEMBER 24, 1958–JANUARY 8, 1959

29/DECEMBER 24: CHRISTMAS EVE

In an old hotel in downtown Miami, Tony Varona paced the floor of the small room as he explained to his friend, sitting on the bed, all that he had been arranging for their plan to stage a joint uprising with an army garrison in Camagüey Province. The former prime minister had received no word from Washington about a "green light" for takeoff, and he had decided not to wait. Time, he said, was too precious. Already, he had managed to find weapons, an airfield in northern Florida for the departure and a small group of men willing to make the trip.

Now, he was worried about the Cuban part of the plan. His friend was to return to Camagüey shortly, and Varona tried to imagine the problems if they were able to persuade hundreds of the province's soldiers to join their cause. "You should arrange," he said, still pacing, "to purchase about one thousand blue shirts, the kind that workers use. . . . Make the purchases in various sizes, because we're just planning to change the shirts of the soldiers. There's no time to order full uniforms made, so . . . we'll have an army of blue and khaki." The next problem, he said, was to find a place to land.

His friend suggested an airstrip in the central part of the province, near the village of Santa Lucía, but he added, "The army has dug it up with tractors so it can't be used. It's abandoned."

"So much the better," Varona said enthusiastically. "Just find yourself a good crew, cover it with dirt, patch it up as best you can . . . Then cover it with branches and leaves so the army won't see it. We'll get there sometime Sunday."

That was four days away, on December 28.

That morning, at ten o'clock, Paul Tannenbaum, the forty-year-old lawyer from Long Island, stood with the five members of his family on the deck of the British cruise ship *Mauretania*. He watched as other passengers tossed confetti toward the waving crowd on the New York dock while tugboats slowly pulled the ship toward the channel.

His two young children, seven-year-old Paul and ten-year-old Rich, waved back with unbridled excitement. Tannenbaum felt merely relieved. The last few days had been hectic, clearing up his law work, buying tropical clothes, getting the kids out of school, but now it was all taken care of and they were under way. Their first stop was Trinidad, in the southern Caribbean, and then it was on to Havana and a chance to see the country he had been reading so much about. The cruise ship company had told him there was no danger whatsoever. The fighting was still far from the capital, and Havana was safer for tourists than any other port in the Caribbean. Besides, Cubans were considered very pro-American.

In Havana that morning, Daniel Braddock, the U.S. deputy chief of mission, drove his ivory-colored 1957 Oldsmobile past the large tourist hotels as he headed for work. Chilling winds were sweeping down from the north, and the broad Malecón Boulevard was made impassable by the huge waves crashing over the seawall, but Braddock simply took inland streets in the Vedado area as he made the quick check of the hotels that had become a daily routine, part of his job as coordinator of the embassy's emergency plans, in case violence broke out in the city. Already at the embassy were hundreds of American-flag decals, ready to be put on the homes and cars of U.S. citizens who lived in the area. The decals seemed a perfect guarantee, since even in their wildest moments, Havana mobs had never intentionally destroyed American property.

Tourists, however, were another matter. They didn't speak the language, and they were more likely to panic at the first hint of trouble. For a while, Braddock had thought they wouldn't be much of a problem, because news stories of the strife had caused a sharp decline in visitors.

But now, as he had for several days, he noticed an unusually large influx for the holidays. The driveways of the Riviera, Nacional and Hilton hotels, even on this overcast day, were filled with taxis dropping off American tourists, who looked mildly absurd in their flower-print shirts and broad-brimmed straw hats, purchased no doubt at the Rancho Boyeros airport. It was almost as if, Braddock thought, these tourists *wanted* to have a brush with danger, to experience the excitement of a Latin-American revolution.

Some of the store windows Braddock drove by that morning showed no signs at all of the holidays. That was a subdued recognition that a civil war was no time for celebration, but many other businesses had installed their traditional displays of Santa Claus and the Three Kings. One store advertised Christmas costumes for children: Indian chiefs, El Zorro, Superman and even U.S. Confederate soldiers. The King American Circus was in town, playing at the Sports Palace, and the Tropicana Nightclub, attempting to appeal to both Cubans and Americans, was preparing a Christmas Eve feast so that a guest could have either stuffed turkey with cranberry sauce and crème de asparagus, or roast suckling pig with rice, black beans, ice cream, coffee and *turrón*, a traditional Spanish cake, thick and sweet, made in the shape of a brick. Either dinner cost $8.

Over the years, Cubans, especially those in Havana, had tried to combine the best of two worlds for the holidays. Santa Claus put gifts under a pine tree on Christmas Day and, following the Spanish custom, the Three Kings brought presents on January 6, the Epiphany. Christmas Eve was known as *Nochebuena*—the Good Night—a time of family get-togethers and great feasts.

But for the *Nochebuena* of 1958, most families were planning only small, subdued gatherings, for the vague aura of anxiety that had permeated the city for weeks had turned into a patina of dread.

In such an atmosphere, many had cut back on their Christmas purchases, and the Movement was attempting to extend that antibuying mentality one step further, into a complete boycott of purchases that would make the economic pressure on Batista unbearable.

The campaign was being carried out by a method that amounted to a bizarre practical joke on the Batista censors. In the days leading up to the holidays, readers opened the pages of newspapers like *Diario de la Marina, El Mundo, El Crisol, El País*, the satirical paper *Zig Zag* and the nation's most popular weekly magazine *Bohemia* to find advertisements, white letters on black backgrounds, asking simply, "What is 03C? What is 03C?"

Emilio Guede, propaganda chief of the Civic Resistance, had dreamed up the campaign, and the ads had been placed by an American businessman sympathetic to their cause. The American, Henry Wolff, had told the newspaper salesmen that the ads were teasers for a campaign for a hair tonic. A later ad would explain that "03C" stood for zero *calvicie* (baldness), zero *caspa* (dandruff) and zero *canas* (gray hair). He even showed them a black-and-white glossy photo of the hair-tonic bottle, which had a label stating the stuff was produced by MORECI Laboratories, an insiders' joke no one noticed: the letters stood for Movimiento de Resistencia Cívica.

When the ads began appearing, Radio Rebelde started broadcasting an explanation: "What is 03C? What is 03C?" the rebel announcer asked in a booming voice picked up by sets in Havana. "Now Radio Rebelde brings you the answer. Pay attention! Because 03C is a matter of life or death for you!"

Second announcer: "What is 03C?"

Third announcer: "What is 03C?"

Fourth: "03C?"

Fifth: "It is the watchword for public shame! Zero cinema. Zero consumer purchases. Zero cabaret. Movement of the Civic Resistance."

Then the rebel announcers broke into a chorus of verse, chanting short, catchy verses, ending with:

> "If all of Cuba is at war,
> Don't you go to the cabaret!"

The radio spots were as professionally slick as any commercial station's, but Radio Rebelde had botched the timing, beginning before all the ads were published. Guede was thrown into a panic, fearing that the censors would withdraw the rest of them. He was wrong. They appeared right on schedule. The Batistianos had other things to worry about this holiday season.

Lieutenant Colonel Irenaldo García Baez was in his second-floor SIM headquarters that morning when he received an unusual phone call from the SIM sergeant assigned to watch civilians using the Aerovías Q airline at the Camp Columbia airfield. The man humbly apologized for bothering the colonel personally, but he had been seeing something he thought he should report directly.

"Colonel García, there are two Aerovías Q airplanes here in a corner. The pilots are sleeping here, and the planes seem ready to leave at any time."

García Baez thanked him. As soon as he hung up, he shouted for an aide to come in. With all the chaos and betrayal permeating the camp, he was certain the planes were part of a Tabernilla plot to abandon the army at its most critical hour. To the aide, he explained the situation, then ordered: "Take a car with a full crew, and put it right in front of the planes. No one is to be allowed to take them."

Minutes later, his telephone rang. It was Colonel Winsy Tabernilla, the son of Old Pancho. "García," he shouted angrily, "this is *my* headquarters. I am the chief of the air force, and I want that SIM car out of here."

García Baez paused. He didn't have the authority to directly disobey the man, and so he agreed. But by radio he ordered the squad car to remain just outside the airfield boundaries. "And tell me everything about who gets close to those planes."

Soon afterward, Batista called. It was an extraordinary event for the president to telephone personally.

"García," Batista said, his voice as calm as always, "what's happening with those planes over there? I understand you ordered a SIM car to stop the planes from leaving. Is that true?"

"Well, Mr. President—"

"What did you *do?*" His voice was firmer.

"Well, I've taken the car away. But I don't like it. Those airplanes are ready because people of our government are going to leave at any moment."

Batista mumbled something noncommittal and told the SIM chief to keep his men away from the planes. Confused, García Baez hung up. He was becoming less and less certain about what Batista really wanted.

*   *   *

That noon, at the plush Havana Yacht Club overlooking the Gulf of Mexico, Senator Jorge García Montes hosted a lunch for the Colombian ambassador, Guancho Calvo, and his embassy's first secretary, a small, blond man who had just been transferred to Cuba from the Orient.

Sitting at a small table in the corner of the dining room, García Montes approached the subject indirectly. He was a former Batista prime minister and still his canasta-playing buddy, and he wanted to be careful. After they ordered from the menu, the senator began, as he had when Ambassador Smith had come to Cuba, by lecturing the new arrival on the Communist domination of the Castro Movement. Subtly, he eased the conversation into the worsening condition in Las Villas Province. He admitted that, until a few days ago, he had believed that the new Rivero Agüero regime would be able to take office on February 24 as scheduled. Now, he was no longer confident.

Then, looking around to make certain no waiters were present, he leaned forward and whispered to the ambassador, "If worse comes to worst . . ."

"Yes?"

"Well, do you go along with the idea of offering political asylum to those who need it?"

"Of course," the ambassador said, adding he lived in the Rosita de Hornedo, a high-rise apartment hotel on the waterfront in the Miramar suburb. García Montes was welcome to come there if there were any trouble.

The senator thanked him politely. When the meal was over, he made certain to pick up the check.

Just west of Havana, at the Barlovento docks, Senator Rolando Masferrer, dressed in an immaculate white linen suit, stepped out of his limousine. Trailed by his usual entourage of policemen, military aides and bodyguards, the newspaper publisher who had his own private army walked over to a pier, where his PT boat had just arrived.

The sixty-two-foot-long craft, dubbed *Olo-Kun II*, was sagging in the water, its paint faded and peeling. He had bought the boat that summer at the Guantánamo Naval Base, where it was listed as surplus, for about $2500.

Several of his men made wisecracks about how old the ship was, and

Masferrer nodded tolerantly. "We can fix it up," he said. "Paint it, renovate it. It will be just like new."

He turned to his most trusted bodyguard, El Indio, and told him to have two men guard the boat full time. He was going to purchase an airplane, a two-year-old Piper Apache, red and white, with space for six passengers.

"Are things that bad?" El Indio asked.

"No," Masferrer answered evenly, "I expect we'll fight here, but this is just in case we have to leave. By that time, the airport might be closed."

Five hundred miles away, in Oriente, *Nochebuena* served as an interruption to the usual battle routine. In the village of Jamaica, rebel captain Manuel Fajardo ambushed an army troop trying to get meat and ended up with five freshly slaughtered cows to feed his men and the townspeople. In Caimanera, next to the U.S. Naval Base, the rebels in charge of the town sent four roast pigs to the two Batista navy frigates in the bay; the sailors, apparently content to sit out the war, had stopped firing on them. In the town of Maffo, where Castro's Column 1 was facing the obstinate company barricaded inside the coffee warehouses, a brief truce was called to share *turron* with the soldiers; the army captain took the food but refused to surrender. To the north, in Sagua de Tánamo, the rebels had better luck; the King-Fischer fighter plane had done little to frighten the soldiers, but their food supplies ran so low that they were forced to surrender to Comandante Antonio E. Lusson.

Just outside Santiago, in the Puerto Bonato heights, the army platoon defending the base of the microwave antenna fled down a steep slope, away from the besieging rebels. To celebrate, a youth with Column 9 took a black-and-red flag the size of a bedsheet, climbed halfway up the tower and fastened it to the metal struts.

Within minutes, word of the 26th of July flag spread throughout Santiago, and everyone walked into the streets, staring into the late-afternoon sun toward the barren, brown-gray hill where the flag was clearly visible. Lily Ferreiro ran from his supermarket and looked at it with his customers. There was little food in the city for a traditional *Nochebuena* celebration, but the flag was a fine replacement. It sent a shiver of joy through Ferreiro and those around him. Some women began crying. After six years of struggling against the dictatorship, their own flag was now flying openly, defiantly, and for once there was nothing the police could do about it.

More than three hundred miles away, in Las Villas Province, Rogelio Acevedo walked into a small store in Placetas, where Ché Guevara was making his temporary headquarters. The Argentine *comandante*, his left arm in a black sling, was bending over a table, looking at a map as he talked to his aides. The seventeen-year-old Acevedo waited, lounging against a counter top.

He was a captain now, promoted after his platoon commander had lost an arm in the battle of Cabaiguán. That was where Guevara himself had been injured, his arm broken when he tripped over a fence while trying to avoid a B-26 bomber.

But none of the injuries had stopped the rebels from pushing on. In only a week's time, Guevara's Column 8, with occasional minor assistance from the student Directorio, had nearly cut the province in half, capturing the towns of Fomento, Guayos, Cabaiguán, Placetas and Sancti Spíritus. Placetas had a population of almost thirty thousand, Sancti Spíritus, forty thousand—the largest cities the rebels had ever taken. Both were on the Central Highway.

The Column 8 campaign had started off a bizarre domino effect. When Fomento surrendered, the army weapons were given to new recruits and the captured soldiers turned over to the Red Cross, which had deposited them at the cuartel in Cabaiguán. When the rebels attacked that town, the recently released prisoners urged their associates to surrender quickly, to avoid bloodshed and with the certain assurance they would not be mistreated. When Cabaiguán gave up, this new expanded group of prisoners was sent on to the next cuartel, where their demoralized attitude quickly caused another surrender. Each time, the rebels gained more weapons for their eager Las Villas volunteers and more dispirited soldiers. Captain Oscar Fernández Mell, the column's physician who was in charge of prisoner transfers, even had one soldier tell him, "I have already handed over three weapons to you."

Now, the headquarters was in Placetas, less than thirty miles from the province's commercial hub of Santa Clara. Acevedo assumed once again that Guevara was calling a halt to the march, to give them time to regroup and train the recruits, but when the *comandante* signaled for him to come over to the table, he had something else in mind.

On the map, Santa Clara lay off to the northwest, but Guevara said the column was going almost due north, toward the towns of Remedios and Caibarién, each of which had about 150 soldiers. The towns had access to the sea, and he wanted them taken before Batista could send reinforcements by ship. He had already sent another commander west of Santa Clara, to make certain no troops from Havana could reach the province by road.

Acevedo's job was to set up an ambush north of Santa Clara, so that the city's regimental garrison could not cut off the bulk of the rebel column moving toward the sea.

Acevedo asked a couple of brief questions, took a quick look at the map and left with a new exuberance. He was being sent within a dozen miles of his hometown, Remedios. Perhaps, he thought, there could be a reunion with old friends, his high-school classmates who would be shocked to see that he was now a hardened captain in the rebel army. It was something to look forward to.

A few miles away, Captain William Gálvez of the rebels' Column 2 lay, stomach down, in an open field just outside of Yaguajay. His eyes were fixed on the one-story cuartel in the distance. The concrete building had a front porch, protected by a wall that was four feet high, interspersed with three-foot-wide columns. A stone fence, slightly less than waist-high, surrounded the U-shaped structure, including an open yard in back, where there was a wooden horse stable. A faded Cuban flag was flying from a flagpole near the porch.

A sixteen-year-old boy, Paneque, and five other rebels crouched in the grass beside Gálvez, but the rebel captain kept his eyes fixed on the cuartel, trying to find a weakness. There were plenty, especially the large glass windows in front, but the problem was how to approach it. The cuartel was surrounded by barren fields.

Gálvez put his head down, his blond goatee pressed against the ground as he tried to think. He was exhausted. For several days, Column 2 had been harassing the town with sporadic gunfire, but the order to attack had not come until Comandante Camilo Cienfuegos had organized all their forces, about 280 men, including the Communist PSP guerrillas, and another 30 or 40 volunteers armed only with shotguns. The fighting had started shortly after two that morning, when Gálvez and the others slipped into the town, moving from house to house, street to street, toward the three locations defended by the army and police: the electric plant, the two-story city hall and the Gran Hotel, each of which had about fifteen soldiers.

Gálvez's squad had attacked the hotel, a two-story stone and wood building with a tile roof. The fight was over quickly. When several rebels sneaked close enough to hurl Molotov cocktails into the ground floor, the soldiers rushed out the back. By 10:00 A.M., the soldiers and policemen were fleeing from all their town outposts toward the cuartel, about a mile away. The rotund chief of police was killed as he ran down the main street. Seventeen others had been killed, wounded or captured.

Now, the problem was the cuartel itself. Regaining a bit of energy, Gálvez whispered to the others that they should test the army defenses by creeping closer, into the middle of the open field. If they came near enough, they could "soften up" the soldiers by shouting requests for surrender, suggesting they could all spend *Nochebuena* together, eating a fine meal instead of fighting.

Gálvez was just about to begin his propaganda speech when his men spotted soldiers, the upper parts of their bodies visible above the stone wall, moving in the rear yard toward the horse stables. It looked as though they were trying to escape.

One rebel, not waiting for orders, opened fire. The cuartel responded with a machine-gun barrage.

"Stop, stop!" Gálvez yelled to his men. "What's going on?" To attempt a fire fight when they were exposed in the field was suicidal.

But he had no time to react. An 81-millimeter mortar shell came screaming down on them. Gálvez never even heard it explode. He lost consciousness.

When he awoke, he found that the others had dragged him to safety. His head ached terribly, but he was told he had suffered only superficial shrapnel wounds. Two other rebels had been injured, and the sixteen-year-old boy with them had been killed instantly. Then came the worst news of all: his men had opened fire during a truce. The soldiers they had seen running were only going for water.

Several hundred yards away, inside the cuartel, Captain Alfredo Abón-Ly watched as a priest and a man with a Red Cross insignia on his sleeve removed a wounded soldier on a stretcher toward an old ambulance parked beside the flagpole.

The truce was allowing his injured to be taken to a hospital, but it did nothing for the soldiers still able to fight. Ever since Abón-Ly had evacuated his troops from the village of Mayajigua, he had been dreading this possibility. His troops were cooped up in the cuartel, without mobility, completely surrounded. It was the way all the other cuartels were falling to the rebels. Several times, he had requested the regimental garrison in Santa Clara to send reinforcements, ammunition and food. There had been no response, and he couldn't even complain directly. The telephone lines had been cut, and his Magnavox shortwave radio could reach only to the closest cuartel, at Remedios, where his messages were relayed to the regiment.

He had done what he could, stationing the three .30-caliber tripod machine guns on the roof. Altogether, the cuartel had about 250 men, 200 of them young army soldiers and 50 Rural Guardsmen, most of whom were in their fifties. But ammunition was already running low, and the previous night the cook had stewed the last of the meat.

After the third, and last, of the wounded soldiers was carried to the ambulance, the priest told Abón-Ly that the chief of the rebel forces wanted to see him for a conference. Abón-Ly said he had no objections.

A short time later, as the army captain watched from the cuartel porch, Comandante Camilo Cienfuegos and an aide walked down the dusty road toward the cuartel. He was twenty-six years old, the same age as Abón-Ly, but there the similarities ended. Abón-Ly was wearing a clean khaki field uniform, his black hair closely cropped, his black shoes highly polished. Cienfuegos had long, brown hair hanging to his shoulders, a flowing beard that completely hid his neck, muddy boots without shoelaces and a broad-brimmed cowboy hat. An ammunition belt was slung low on his hips. His two shirt pockets were bulging with papers.

The rebel leader greeted Abón-Ly with a large, good-natured smile. They shook hands on the porch, then Abón-Ly escorted him into his office at the front of the cuartel.

"Listen," Cienfuegos said casually, "we'd like to make a good *Nochebuena* dinner for everyone. You and your men can eat with us. We could have a celebration."

Abón-Ly shook his head. "I'm not going to permit that," he said tersely.

The *comandante*'s face lost its smile. "There are too many persons dead already," he said, then repeated Castro's argument that the rebels were fighting the tyranny, not the soldiers themselves. He said he knew Abón-Ly had committed no war crimes, that he had nothing to fear. If he surrendered, the rebels would put him and his men on trucks and take them to wherever they wanted to go. That was the same deal that

Ché Guevara had been offering other army commanders, and so far all had accepted.

Abón-Ly refused. He said haughtily that he was expecting reinforcements by land and sea, with air support. "I obey the orders of the president. That's not political. That's my job."

Cienfuegos tried to persuade him that it *was* political, that by doing his "job" he was supporting a corrupt, unpopular dictatorship.

Abón-Ly merely shook his head. He was trying to think. His boasting of reinforcements had been sheer bravado, and he knew that if his men had to hold out in the cuartel, they would eventually be starved into submission. With that in mind, he made a counterproposal. He was willing to abandon the cuartel, he said, if his men were allowed to leave with their weapons and ammunition.

Cienfuegos rejected that idea immediately. He said his troops already had complete control of the town, and the only reason they were bothering with the cuartel at all was the need for his weapons.

The two commanders glowered at each other for a few moments in silence, then Cienfuegos turned to his aide, the smile returning to his face. Pulling 200 pesos out of his shirt pocket, he told the rebel to run into town and get cigars and cigarettes for the soldiers, as a *Nochebuena* present of goodwill.

For a while, the rebel *comandante* chatted idly with Abón-Ly's enlisted men, asking them about themselves and where they were from. When the aide returned, Cienfuegos passed out the smoking materials and even gave one soldier his watch.

Again, he suggested that Abón-Ly give in. When the army captain repeated his refusal, Cienfuegos turned grim. "From this moment on," he said, "the responsible one is you. Really, I lament it, because I would have invited some of your soldiers to eat roast pork with us tonight."

Soon after the *comandante* left, the firing began again. Abón-Ly slumped in his office chair, growing depressed as he tried to imagine a way out of his predicament. He was still thinking when at dusk a soldier ran in to tell him some good news: an air force plane had just dropped two large cardboard cartons from parachutes.

"Our ammunition has arrived!" a sergeant shouted. Soldiers embraced and yelled with joy, but as Abón-Ly reached the window, he groaned. One of the cartons had fallen into rebel territory, and the other was drifting down toward the open field in no-man's-land.

He knew it was absolutely essential to get that ammunition. As soon as it was dark, four volunteers snaked along on their stomachs into the field.

Within yards, the rebels spotted them and began shooting. The men crawled on, until they were almost to the crate. Then, as Abón-Ly watched, they stopped and whispered among themselves. Something was decided. They turned around and sneaked back to the cuartel.

Enraged, Abón-Ly demanded an explanation. They told him the crate had cracked open on impact and they had seen what was inside: food, nothing else. They thought it wasn't worth risking their lives for, and their captain had to agree.

That night, the soldiers listened over the Magnavox radio as rebels made loud smacking noises and boasted about the food found in the carton that had dropped into their territory.

"Ah, we are eating your food and loving it. What's this? A leg of lamb?" More smacking noises. "And here is some rice. And black beans. And roast pork. And look what we have here for dessert."

The army soldiers pecked glumly at their meager helpings of rice covered with a thin black bean soup. They all agreed it was the worst Christmas Eve of their lives, but none suggested they surrender.

At that moment, sixty miles away in the regimental garrison in Santa Clara, the twenty top army commanders in the province sat at a long, formal dining table eating an elaborate meal off a set of fine china. There were large bowls of pork, white rice, black beans and yucca. A steward kept the crystal glasses filled with Spanish wine. Three or four of the men had brought their wives.

On one side of the table, next to Colonel Florentino Rosell of the army corps of engineers, was Comandante Echemendía of the Havana underground. The colonel had introduced him as a relative, and no one questioned it.

Echemendía was almost beyond fear. It was so inconceivable that he should be sitting there, sharing a meal with these corrupt Batistianos, that the dinner seemed to take place in a dream.

Only that morning, he had been in Havana, going about his normal life, when he had received Castro's message rejecting Colonel Rosell's proposal and asking for a meeting with General Cantillo. He had flown to Santa Clara and delivered the message to Rosell at the barracks. Rosell had shown him into the plush office of the provincial commander, General Alberto Del Río Chaviano, where Echemendía had sipped coffee and studied photos of the general and Batista on the wall. Rosell disappeared, saying he was going to contact General Cantillo. For what had seemed like hours, Echemendía had sat there, waiting. Nothing had happened, except for brief, frantic visits by the colonel to announce he couldn't get in touch with Cantillo in either Santiago or Havana.

Echemendía began to suspect a trap. Surely, he decided, a colonel should be able to talk to a general fairly easily. Maybe Rosell was lying. The underground *comandante*'s fears grew even greater when Colonel Rosell introduced him to General Del Río Chaviano as "a relative," and the general shook his hand with a sly smile that made Echemendía realize the general knew who he really was. He was starting to think about fleeing when Rosell had invited him to the dinner. If they were going to arrest him, he decided, certainly they wouldn't eat with him first. Now, as he listened to the officers talk around the dinner table, he discovered that they were almost to the point of panic. One captain said intelligence sources were estimating that twelve thousand rebels were in the area near the city. "It is an ironclad siege," he moaned. "They've got us surrounded." *

The wife of an officer added, looking at the general, "Listen, Chaviano, the way things are going, those people are going to be seated right where we are within a month."

No one contradicted that, and Echemendía cautiously did not even give Colonel Rosell a knowing look. The dinner lapsed into a painful silence, broken only by the clanking of silver against the china.

When they were finished, Rosell took Echemendía back to the general's office. After closing the door, the colonel, for the first time looking a little nervous, said he hadn't been able to find Cantillo anywhere, and their plan for an uprising, which had already missed its 6:00 P.M. schedule, had to be postponed some more, because the armored train had been late in arriving in Santa Clara. "Do you think you can negotiate a cease-fire with Ché?" Rosell asked, almost whispering. "It would take some of the pressure off and allow us to carry out the uprising."

Echemendía said he would try, but he needed a way to get through the army lines. The colonel asked him to wait. Ten minutes later, he

---

* In fact, at that moment there were less than eight hundred "well-armed" rebels in the entire province.

returned with a handwritten pass from General Del Río Chaviano.

Slipping the pass into his billfold, Echemendía promised, "I'll be in touch with you in the morning."

Nearby, at the edge of Santa Clara's Central Park, Guillermo Domenech, the young hotel clerk, stared morosely down on the city from the tenth-floor restaurant. Even the least attractive girls had stopped coming to the park and with them had gone the last of the boys.

The Gran Hotel was almost deserted, its guest list down to forty-two. The only recent arrivals had been a well-to-do farmer's son and his pudgy, thick-lipped wife who had brought along a week-old baby girl. After getting out of the hospital, they hadn't been able to travel back to their farm in the southeastern part of the province.

Almost all roads out of the city were closed. Cubana Airways had stopped its regular flights, and after dusk the residents stayed inside their homes, their doors closed, their windows shuttered. A commercial radio station, just a few miles away in a town taken by the rebels, was boasting it was part of *Territorio Libre de Cuba*.

Only in the hotel's rooftop bar were there any signs of normalcy, and even that was tinged with tension, as the marooned salesmen played their nightly poker game with unusual intensity, their drinking and betting escalating to ever-higher levels. They were gambling, thought Domenech, as if there were no tomorrow.

In his prison cell on the Isle of Pines, Colonel Ramón Barquín, leader of the Puros conspiracy, lay on his bunk, listening to the battery-powered radio leaning against the steel beam. A Venezuelan station was broadcasting reports of new rebel victories in Las Villas Province. Each triumph the announcer mentioned renewed his despair. He had heard nothing more about Colonel Rosell's conspiracy, and he had decided that, like so many officers' plans, it was simply idle dreaming. Here he was, the famous, moderate Barquín, being left to rot while the dictatorship and the radicals fought it out.

The holiday season seemed to intensify his bitterness. In a nearby cell, he could hear the gurgling noises of other prisoners, recipients of a cheap wine that had been smuggled into Circular Building 4 under phony labels. They had mixed it with fruit to form a watery *sangría,* and as they drank, they debated what Batista was going to do. Some thought he was so *macho* he would fight to the end, but an imprisoned lieutenant argued, "As soon as he hears four shots, he'll be gone."

Down in the courtyard, a group had formed a chorus to sing Christmas songs, tunes that made Barquín think of happier times, of his children and wife whom he had not been able to see for months.

"Silent night, holy night. All is calm, all is bright . . ." The chorus was badly out of tune, but Barquín could detect the emotion in the men's voices. Some were obviously crying.

About that same time, Fulgencio Batista was walking into his formal office on the second floor of the Presidential Palace. There, in the center of his ornate desk, was an olive-green uniform. The marble bust of José Martí appeared to be staring at it.

Batista looked at it carefully. It was a full military uniform, with stars inside circles, indicating the "Supreme General in Chief." Beside it was a small pistol taken from his desk drawer.

Several of his most dedicated officers, including SIM chief García Baez, had talked Batista's wife Marta into giving them his measurements. An aide, Captain Alfredo Sadulé, had rushed the order through the tailor shop of the national police. The uniform was a not-so-subtle suggestion that the president himself should lead the soldiers into battle against the rebels.

Batista refused to try it on.

Batista's handpicked successor, Andrés Rivero Agüero, sat alone that evening, brooding in the library of his spacious Biltmore home. He had wanted to issue a statement about peace and brotherhood on *Nochebuena*, but Batista had vetoed it as a sign of weakness. To Rivero, it seemed as if no one cared about him. That day, the newspapers didn't even mention his name.

More than five hundred miles away, in the mining town of Charco Redondo, Rivero Agüero's equivalent among the anti-Batista groups, President-designate Manuel Urrutia, walked to a small wooden house. There, with his wife and three rebel doctors, he ate a simple meal of canned Spanish codfish, rice and black beans.

Castro almost never talked to him, but Urrutia was buoyant about the impending victory, when he and the politicians could take over the government. For a while during the dinner, the men talked about who should be in the new cabinet, but the discussion broke up as soon as the meal was finished. All went to bed early.

In La Yaya, another town in Oriente, Vilma Espín, the woman who had helped make the napalm bomb, chatted with her father at an informal gathering in the temporary headquarters of the Second Front. The elderly man, a onetime executive with the Bacardí rum company, looked oddly out of place among the bearded, sweat-stained rebels, but the atmosphere was relaxed, and he mingled with them easily.

It was the first time Vilma had seen him in more than a year. She had asked him to bring her birth certificate, because for a while she and Raúl Castro had been planning to get married on *Nochebuena*. But events were moving so rapidly, the end seemed so near, that they had decided to postpone the ceremony. Soon, she thought, she could have a real wedding in Santiago itself.

About ten that evening, Fidel Castro and his secretary Celia Sánchez drove up in a green Land Rover jeep to Castro's childhood home in Marcané. Trailing him on the dusty road were two more jeeps, filled with bodyguards.

It was Castro's first trip home since he had gone to Mexico to organize the *Granma* expedition, and as soon as the Land Rover appeared in the driveway, the family dashed from the porch to embrace him—his mother, sisters and older brother Ramón, who had been running the plantation since their father died.

Marcané had become "Liberated Territory" only two weeks before, but Ramón had been keeping a twenty-four-pound turkey in the freezer for a year and a half in anticipation of this moment. They ate a huge meal as Castro recounted his exploits. He felt so secure that when he heard about a skirmish starting not far away, he ordered his twelve-man escort to go and help. He didn't need their protection.

30/DECEMBER 25: TOY CARS AND CONSPIRACIES

About 3:00 A.M., Castro and Celia Sánchez returned to the rebel headquarters at Central América sugar mill to find Father Guzmán waiting for him in a small wooden house. Sitting at a living-room table, the priest seemed exhausted, and the two did not talk until a woman brought them *cafés con leche* and a basket of crisp Cuban crackers.

When she left them alone, Guzmán said simply, "Cantillo wants a meeting with you."

Castro leaned forward in his chair. He sensed immediately that this was the chance he had been waiting for, a way to conquer Santiago without enormous bloodshed. He asked what the general had said exactly, and the priest repeated the conversation as best he could remember it.

Ignoring his coffee, Castro stood and paced the polished concrete floor. Cantillo's offer seemed genuine, but it would be an unnecessary risk to have the meeting at his headquarters. There was, however, a nearby abandoned sugar mill. "The meeting," he said, looking at the priest, "will be at Central Oriente. Cantillo can come by helicopter."

Guzmán nodded. "The general will need to know where to land. Why don't you put four bed sheets on the ground, held down by rocks?"

Castro stopped pacing. Between his headquarters and Santiago were two towns under siege: Maffo and Palma Soriano, a city of thirty thousand, only thirty miles from Santiago. It was not going to be easy for the priest to travel. "Will it give you enough time to get back if we set it up for December twenty-eighth? Three days from today?"

"Yes, yes."

"Well, he can come anytime after eight A.M. Tell him we'll have a landing area set up next to the mill's main building."

Pulling the small notebook from his shirt pocket, Castro scribbled a note to the general about the arrangements.

As the priest set off, Castro watched him from the doorway. Events, he realized, were starting to move with incredible speed.

Shortly after sunrise in Santiago, the entire Wollam family was awake. The youngest children were begging to see their Christmas presents, and it had been a particularly difficult night for sleep in any case, with sporadic gunfire crackling in the distance and the mangy lion at the zoo roaring in protest.

Sleepy-eyed, the family gathered around the sixteen-foot-tall spruce tree in the living room, set well back from the large French windows so that it could not be seen from the street. Most of the attention focused on eighteen-month-old Chip, whose "big present" was a red pedal car. As soon as he ripped off the wrapping paper, his father put him on it, showed how the pedals worked and let him go *zoom-zoom* down the great hall. The rest watched as he squealed with delight, trying to run them over on his ever-faster trips up and down the corridor.

Connie Wollam, still dressed in her bathrobe, watched with satisfaction from the sofa. She was accustomed to being overseas during the holiday season, and no matter how much she wanted her children to learn foreign customs, Christmas was something special, a day to bring back a bit of America. For the first time in months, the family was reunited, with the two eldest daughters returning from high school at the naval base. The oldest, Barbara, had brought along her boyfriend, a young navy lieutenant.

The family seemed happy, but Connie herself was gripped by

depression. The day before she and the vice-consul's wife, armed with dozens of cheap presents from a local dime store, had visited the pediatrics ward of a Santiago hospital. It was a huge room, so crowded that sometimes two children were sharing a bed, and there were not enough hospital gowns to go around. Her most vivid memory was of a girl, no older than ten, lying silently on a bed. Under her sheet, where her legs should have been, there was only a flat space. A doctor explained that the girl's parents were schoolteachers, who had been traveling by jeep on the Central Highway when the rebels, expecting an army convoy, detonated a mine.

With incidents like that, hardly anyone in Santiago felt like observing Christmas, and the 26th of July had decreed that not even Christmas trees should be displayed in this time of strife. Most persons were complying, because it was difficult to plan even a modest Christmas meal. Meat was almost impossible to get at any price, and Connie's two greatest presents had been two turkeys flown in from the naval base and, through an American pilot who flew to the States, eight or nine pounds of ground beef wrapped in white butcher paper, which looked prettier to her than any Christmas wrapping. Counting her two maids and the gardener, she had ten people to feed.

About the time that young Chip abandoned his pedal car and began playing with his small plastic cars on the tile floor, Bernie Femminella, the Brooklyn-born vice-consul, walked up to the front of the Wollam house with Father Jorge Bez Chabebe, who was well known as a rebel sympathizer.

For a moment, they stood beside the wrought-iron fence and talked about a message from the Santiago archbishop that had been read at *Nochebuena* Masses the night before. Taken by itself, it had seemed an innocuous sermon, a plea for peace and an end to the horrors of the "civil war." But the Batista regime was denying that any civil war existed, stating that the army was simply involved against "small bands of outlaws."

Femminella asked the priest if the Church had felt any repercussions. Bez Chabebe told him he had heard rumors of anger among police officials, but nothing specific.

The vice-consul suggested the priest join him at the Wollams for a Christmas drink. Bez Chabebe was starting to decline when a 1957 four-door Oldsmobile screeched to a halt at the curb. It was filled with SIM officers.

"Get in the car," one of the military men barked.

The priest hesitated for a moment, then moved nervously to the open rear door.

"You too," the officer said to Femminella.

Femminella was taken aback, then he realized that with his *guayabera* shirt and his dark Italian features, the officer had mistaken him for a Cuban.

"Wait," he said, "not me. I am an American consul." He showed them his diplomatic identification. That and his heavily accented Spanish convinced the officers. They slammed the door and sped away with the priest.

Femminella rushed into the house. As Chip played with his toy cars, he explained what had happened. Wollam called the archbishop. The monsignor, enraged, promised to investigate immediately.

A short time later, the priest was released.

Earl E. T. Smith, dressed in a white shirt, stood beside his wife Florence on the sprawling lawn of the ambassador's residence. In front of him, 160 Cuban children, selected by sixteen local welfare agencies, ran squealing across the grass from attraction to attraction. In one corner of the backyard was a carousel, in another a tent for Mickey Mouse cartoons. Nearby, "Professor Derka," boasting to the kids in Spanish that he had come "all the way from Vienna," was performing magic tricks.

Later would come hot dogs, ice cream and Coca-Cola, followed by the embassy staff handing out presents: toy cars and service stations for the boys, dolls and purses for the girls, along with stockings of candy for everyone.

For months, Smith had held no social functions in Cuba, considering them inappropriate in time of strife, but he had made an exception for the ambassador's traditional Christmas party. Yet even among the children, Smith's mind drifted back to politics. That morning, Prime Minister Güell had told him he was making a three-day trip to the Dominican Republic, supposedly to repay a visit made earlier by Dominican officials. Though Güell had explained no more, Smith suspected that the "officials" had been Dominican army officers. His own military attachés had reported that several days before, a delegation of army men had come to Havana to offer Batista more weapons and the use of two thousand to five thousand Dominican soldiers, who could land in northern Las Villas Province and crush the rebels' offensive in central Cuba.

Comandante Echemendía of the 26th of July underground was sharing the back of a jeep with Colonel Rosell as they sped out of Santa Clara toward the spot where the armored train was located. To their left was a series of low-lying hills, covered with parched-brown grass, the highest topped by a repeater antenna that was part of the nationwide CMQ radio-television network.

It was sunny, but a little chilly, and the only time the colonel spoke during the ride was to comment on the weather. He had been smooth and self-assured when Echemendía had first met him three days before. Now he appeared haggard, unshaven and wearing wrinkled combat fatigues.

Their relationship was reduced to a strained civility. Early that morning, Echemendía had found Ché Guevara in a captured army cuartel. The Argentine had shown a thin smile when he heard of the panic inside the regimental headquarters, but he refused to grant a cease-fire, which could only give the army time to regroup. He said that this revolution was going to make no last-minute compromises. When Echemendía passed the message along to the colonel, Rosell had visibly sagged, but he asked Echemendía to stay with him. Apparently, the army man still hoped for some kind of 26th of July approval, though Echemendía was now serving as nothing more than a spy.

Several miles outside of town, the jeep driver swung left onto a narrow gravel road. They bounced along between an opening in the hills for a few hundred yards until they passed a baseball diamond and came to the railway tracks. There, gleaming in the cool sunlight, was the armored train, a mixture of freight and passenger cars, guarded by patrols armed with machine guns and rifles. Several hundred soldiers were mingling about in battle fatigues, some scrubbing the dark-brown cars, others simply lounging on the parched grass. Echemendía tried to calculate the number of machine guns, bazookas, antiaircraft guns and rifles hidden behind the closed doors of the freight cars. It boggled his imagination. There might be enough weapons there to double the size of the rebel force in the province.

Colonel Rosell stepped down first, managing a smile as he walked among his troops, patting backs and asking how the trip had been. He led Echemendía to the officers' dining car, where they sat on wooden benches by a window. The colonel ordered a late breakfast for both of them, and within moments a steward appeared with two plates of steaming ham and sunny-side up eggs, followed by toasted Cuban bread and cups of *café con leche*.

As they ate, a captain ran in. He too looked harried as he reported that of the 373 soldiers that had left Havana on the train, 27 were being listed as deserters and another 21 were absent. Many of the others, he stated, were getting jittery about the idea of fighting, especially the carpenters, electricians and plumbers in the corps of engineers, who had no combat experience.

The colonel gulped down the rest of his food. Telling Echemendía to wait, he dashed out the door. The underground man finished his breakfast at a leisurely pace. When an officer asked him who he was, he said casually that he was a relative of the colonel's.

After a long while, Rosell reappeared, without explaining what he had been doing. Together, they sped back to the regimental headquarters, where Echemendía was again told to wait, this time in a soft leather chair in the general's office. Occasionally, the colonel popped his head in the door to say he was still trying to locate General Cantillo, but he never seemed to make any progress. Rosell was playing some kind of game, but Echemendía couldn't figure out what.

At one point, the army commander of the province, General Del Río Chaviano, came in, smiling nervously, carrying a plastic tray with a Coke and sandwich. As Echemendía ate, he had to listen to this general whom the rebels considered responsible for the slaughtering of Castro's compatriots after the 1953 Moncada attack. The man spoke on and on, lamenting that he was misunderstood, that he himself was "one of the greatest victims of this process." It seemed surreal.

Finally, about dusk, Colonel Rosell dashed in again. "I can't seem to find Cantillo anywhere," he said in dismay. "We must fly to Havana."

They hurried to the airport, where an air force plane, a twin-engine C-47, was waiting for them. Rosell told Echemendía to get on board, he would be along in a moment. When the underground man climbed the stairs, he found several officers already inside, sitting silently on the military-style benches facing the center of the plane. Through the open door, he could see the colonel and General Del Río Chaviano having an animated, almost angry, conversation on the concrete apron. After a while, the general stalked off, and Rosell ran up the stairs. Moments later, the door was shut, and the C-47 took off.

In the air, the colonel whispered to him, "Do you have any compromising documents on you?"

Echemendía panicked. "I've got Fidel's message to you, in code."

Rosell took the paper and, untying the gleaming army boot on his right foot, slipped it beneath his sock.

An hour later, when it was completely dark, the C-47 landed and taxied to the front of the air force headquarters at Camp Columbia. Echemendía was gripped with fear as he followed Rosell down the stairs. It seemed inconceivable to him that he was inside the bastion of the Batistianos' power.

A reception committee, including at least one of Tabernilla's sons, was waiting, lit by the headquarters' floodlights, and when they saw the colonel, all began shouting questions about conditions in Las Villas.

For about fifteen minutes, wondering if he were about to be arrested, Echemendía waited quietly over to one side. Then Rosell ran over to say he was going to look for General Cantillo. "My chauffeur can drive you somewhere," he said, distracted. "As soon as I have some news, I'll call you up."

Climbing into the awaiting black Buick sedan, Echemendía asked the driver to take him to the FOCSA building in Vedado. That was the location of his safehouse apartment, which was supposed to be known to only a select few in the underground, but Echemendía was so dazed by the way events were turning and so tired after going nearly thirty-six hours without sleep that he no longer cared.

As the underground *comandante* went home, General Cantillo was sitting with two of his aides in rocking chairs on the lawn in front of his Camp Columbia house. On the parade ground, a few enlisted men were wandering toward the infantry barracks on the opposite side. He had just finished a large, American-style Christmas dinner, turkey with all the trimmings, and his full stomach had brought him a momentary contentment.

He had known for a day that Colonel Rosell was trying to reach him, and he had purposely told his aides to make excuses. Rumors were running wild in the camp, and one of the most prominent was that Rosell and General Del Río Chaviano were planning a coup d'etat, backed by the Tabernillas. Not only was Rosell a close friend of Brigadier General Silito Tabernilla, but Del Río Chaviano was related by marriage to Old Pancho. The whole idea of the Tabernillas plotting against Batista, their longtime benefactor, didn't make sense to him, but then nothing at Camp Columbia seemed to be making sense.

For the second straight time, Cantillo had returned from Santiago without Batista asking to see him for a personal report. It seemed as if Batista *had* to know about the meeting with Castro, but didn't want others to realize he knew. Or perhaps he didn't know and didn't care what was happening, which would explain why the Tabernillas were trying to do something. Cantillo, like the other high-ranking officers in the camp, had heard about the Aerovías Q planes sitting in a corner of the airfield, their pilots sleeping in them at night.

The more complex the game became, the more cautiously Cantillo played it. When he had told General Pancho Tabernilla about talking to the priest, he had asked that a helicopter be sent to Santiago. Then, on a map of Oriente Province, he had marked off a large rectangle. He told Pancho that the meeting with Castro would probably take place somewhere inside that area, but even when he found out exactly where, he was not going to tell the Estado Mayor. And if he saw any air force planes in that area, he was going to cancel the meeting.

That had protected him at least against a Tabernilla assassination plot, but he still didn't know what to do about Colonel Rosell. If Rosell were indeed planning a coup, he didn't want anything to do with it, and besides, he couldn't imagine someone like Rosell pulling it off. Yet with his personal balancing act, the general was reluctant to tell the colonel simply to go to hell.

Cantillo was still rocking and thinking when an olive-green army sedan pulled up at the curb. It was Rosell himself, looking wild-eyed and disheveled in his combat fatigues. One of Cantillo's aides stood up, and the colonel slumped into the vacant rocking chair.

"How are things going in Santa Clara?" Cantillo asked politely.

"Everything is lost there, unless something is done quickly," Rosell mumbled in a tired voice. He went on to describe some of the recent rebel victories and the dispirited troops on the armored train. When he was through, he complained that he had eaten nothing since breakfast.

Cantillo, flanked by his aides, led Rosell into the house and ordered his cook to prepare the leftover turkey and whatever else remained from dinner. They sat at the dining table as the colonel wolfed down the cold food. When he was finished, the aides went outside, leaving the two officers alone.

Quickly, Rosell gave a carefully edited version of what he had been up to. He did not mention the last two days he had spent with Comandante Echemendía, but he said that General Del Río Chaviano had opened negotiations with Ché Guevara, to reach some kind of settlement in Las Villas Province. Ché had turned him down flat. It seemed the rebels were only interested in a meeting between Cantillo and Castro. Rosell added that he had seen the message himself, directly from Fidel in Oriente.

Cantillo tried to keep his face blank. It was the first he had heard of the message from Castro. He replied simply that he had already talked to a priest in Santiago about setting up the meeting, but that didn't mean he was going to reach a settlement on his own. He was simply following the orders of Old Pancho and he had no plans whatsoever to do anything disloyal to the regime, especially to Batista himself.

The colonel stared at him curiously. He said it was absolutely essential that an agreement be reached with the 26th of July before the army collapsed completely. He himself had been in contact with Colonel Barquín and the other Puros at the Isle of Pines about forming a junta.

That was too much for Cantillo, who had helped arrest the Puros two years before. "You're crazy," he said firmly. "You are going to bring those people over here, and *they* are going to be *your* bosses. You are not going to be *their* boss."

Rosell, startled by Cantillo's sudden intensity, changed the subject, mumbling he was "afraid something will happen to me," that SIM officers might arrest him at any moment. Just before he had left Santa Clara, at the airfield, General Del Río Chaviano had wanted to take the C-47 for himself, so he could flee the country. Rosell had insisted he needed the plane to go to Havana, to make one last effort to see if he could pound some sense into the regime. He had won the argument, but the general was still anxious to go.

Suddenly, the colonel stood up and drew himself into a stiff military posture. In a grandiose voice, he announced it was time for the farce to end. He was going to see Batista and tell him *everything*, about the generals who didn't want to fight, of the unpopularity of the regime, of the need to stop the bloodshed. "If he does believe me, he can act to jail somebody. If he doesn't believe me, he can try to put *me* in jail. I'll try to flee. I'll leave. This is all lost."

Cantillo suddenly had to worry about what the colonel might say about him. With a burst of emotion, he said, "Rosell, I will be in the army as long as Batista is in Cuba. But on the day he leaves, I will resign, because I am sick and tired of this war against Cubans." He paused for effect, then continued: "And sick and tired of the behavior of Cuban officers like you, and some others I knew, who owe everything to Batista. If you go against Batista, nobody will trust you." As a final challenge, he added, "Of course, the best you can do is to tell *everything* to Batista."

Rosell left, looking tired and depressed. Cantillo went to the living-room window and watched him walk down the street bordering the parade ground toward Batista's two-story home a half block away. There, Cantillo knew, the president was meeting with the chiefs of the armed forces.

Cantillo paced for a while wondering what to do. Rosell's outburst could result in dozens of arrests, including his own, if Batista genuinely didn't know about his arranging a meeting with Castro. Furthermore, he had just heard Rosell confess to plotting for a junta to replace the regime, a fact which he should report immediately to the Estado Mayor. But the situation seemed too fluid for that, and he had the perfect excuse in that Rosell had told him he was about to confess everything. Cantillo, fighting down the growing pain in his stomach, decided it was best to wait.

31/DECEMBER 26: TIME FOR THE GREEN LIGHT

It was shortly after midnight when Colonel Rosell, not bothering to salute the guards, strode into Batista's military residence and bounded up the stairs. On the second floor, he found army officers and aides lounging in chairs in the large, screened-in Florida Room. Batista himself was behind a closed door, in a small room generally used by aides, conferring with his top commanders.

Rosell stormed up to his friend, Brigadier General Silito Tabernilla and demanded a message be given to the president. He needed to discuss with Batista immediately the situation in Santa Clara. Silito walked over, knocked on the door and peeked inside. Moments later, he came back. Batista didn't want to see him.

Rosell, more haggard than ever, paced the tile floor and ranted loudly about how the war was lost, the army crumbling.

Batista's eldest son, Rubén, was astounded. Here was the leader of the armored train, which was supposed to save the situation in Las Villas, and he was talking near treason. An officer leaned over and whispered to Rubén, "Someone should arrest that son of a bitch."

Yet no one made a move as Rosell kept pacing and bellowing. He announced he wasn't leaving until he had confronted the president, but the inner door did not open. At last, the colonel complained to Silito Tabernilla that he had gotten almost no rest the night before.

Silito led him into a small room, where there was a row of cots, usually used by the aides. Within moments, Rosell was asleep.

A short time later, Batista emerged. Trailed by his military commanders, he walked through the Florida Room, not even bothering to ask about Colonel Rosell and his urgent message.

As the black limousines of Batista and the officers left the house, General Cantillo stood watching them from a window in the Estado Mayor. Unable to stand the tension, he had decided to go to the military headquarters to see if he could get a whiff of what was happening. But the only high-ranking officer there was General Robaina, an elderly man whose chief distinction was that his daughter was married to Batista's eldest son. The general was watching television, and Cantillo looked at the late-night movie with him, waiting for something to explode.

But the limousines disappeared into the darkness. None of the military men were returning to the Estado Mayor, as they certainly would have done if there had been a bitter confrontation. Cantillo wondered if Rosell had lost his nerve.

At the besieged cuartel in Yaguajay, Alfredo Abón-Ly was slumped in his office chair, feet on top of the desk. For the second straight night, he was getting no sleep. It seemed that every time he started to doze, the rebels fired just enough shots to jar him awake.

The regiment in Santa Clara had continued promising help, including a plan to send a navy frigate to the north coast, a few miles away, where the army men could be evacuated. But Abón-Ly didn't have enough ammunition to attempt a break-out of the siege, and it was hard convincing the regimental commanders, because all messages had to be relayed through the Remedios cuartel, a few miles away.

About 2:00 A.M., Abón-Ly was again beginning to doze when the aged Magnavox shortwave emitted a loud squawk. His communications man zeroed in on the signal.

"It's all over here," announced a harried voice, which Abón-Ly recognized as belonging to the radioman in Remedios. "We're giving up. Take care of yourself. And good—" Then there was only static.

Abón-Ly's radioman tried to reach the cuartel. "Remedios. Calling Remedios. Calling Remedios. Calling Remedios. Calling Remedios."

After five minutes, he gave up. Abón-Ly's last link with the outside world was gone.

A short time after that in Remedios, Captain Rogelio Acevedo and his sixteen-year-old brother Enrique drove their jeep down the main street, where most of the twelve thousand residents were waving and cheering the victorious rebels. Ché Guevara had ordered the two boys and their platoon to maintain an ambush outside the city because he didn't want two of his officers fighting in their own hometown, but the brothers couldn't resist a brief visit.

When they reached their house, the lawn, living room and dining were crammed with dozens of people. Their parents, sister and younger brother smothered them with embraces. A cousin took a photograph of them by the white picket fence in front of their house. A year and a half before, they had simply been high-school students. Now they were conquering heroes. Acevedo felt triumphant, but he couldn't help thinking that not nearly as many "friends" had come to the house when his brother was arrested.

He stayed home only an hour before he went searching for his *comandante.* The two-story city hall was a smoldering ruins, its blackened interior gutted by a fire that the rebels had set to drive the Batistianos out. Nearby, the cuartel was surrounded by townspeople. They recognized Acevedo and grabbed him by the arms and shoulders as they shouted their complaints that criminals and informers were inside. They should be punished. Pushing his way through the crowd, he entered the cuartel. About two hundred army soldiers, policemen and Batista sympathizers were being held in the horse stables at the back.

The teenage rebel recognized many of them immediately. Staring at him glumly was an ugly fellow nicknamed Pig's Head, a notorious informer. Trying to hide in the shadows was the chauffeur of the army lieutenant who had testified against his brother at the trial. There were many more.

Acevedo marched into the cuartel commander's office, where he found Guevara behind a desk talking to aides. When the *comandante* saw him, his face turned grim. "What are you doing here?" he demanded.

"Well, this is my town. I wanted to come and look."

"Go back to your ambush site," Guevara said sternly.

Acevedo said he would, but first he wanted to see some of the prisoners punished. "I know three Batista henchmen here who have killed people. Have slapped and hit people." Guevara's face remained immobile. "Look," the teenager went on, exasperated, "these people are assassins and henchmen."

Guevara refused to do anything about it. He said one of the conditions of surrender was that all inside the cuartel would be freed, and the officers were even being allowed to keep their side arms. They were going to be transported to the northern coast, where boats could take them to Havana. Guevara said he couldn't go back on his word. If he did, the rebels could never convince another cuartel to surrender. They had taken the town, and that was the important thing. "Later," he promised, "revolutionary justice will take care of them."

Reluctantly, the young Acevedo agreed.

Early that morning, Comandante Echemendía was awakened from a sound sleep in his Havana luxury apartment. The telephone was ringing. Sleepily, he groped for it.

"Echemendía," Colonel Rosell shouted, his voice tinged with fear, "now the reports of my impending arrest are very serious. I'm afraid Cantillo has betrayed me. I want to see you immediately." He said he was sending a relative to pick Echemendía up. Then he hung up.

Barely awake, Echemendía struggled to get dressed, then took the elevator down to the lobby and waited outside the FOCSA building until finally Rosell's relative appeared in a green Volkswagen.

The sun was just rising behind them as they sped west, toward Rosell's waterfront home in the suburbs. When they arrived, the colonel was pacing in the living room. He seemed close to hysteria.

"I've just gotten a call from my brother-in-law," the colonel moaned. "He's in charge of the SIM radio room. He told me that Irenaldo García Baez has given the order for my arrest and that the squad cars are on their way over to pick me up. . . . I'm leaving for Miami in my yacht."

After days of spinning a web of contradictions and conspiracies, Rosell now tried to explain to the underground *comandante* why his promised coup d'etat had failed. Placing all the blame on Cantillo, the colonel said the general had backed down from his agreement to help stage the coup, that he was setting up a meeting with Castro on his own through a priest, but he was still claiming loyalty to Batista.

Rosell added he had heard rumors that Batista was planning to orchestrate a phony coup d'etat to relieve the pressures on his regime.

"Try to talk to Fidel," Rosell went on, still pacing. "Tell him I'll be leaving and returning to Las Villas, so I can lead an uprising from there. Try to make contact with the captain on board the train. Tell him to arrest the people who are going to replace General Del Río Chaviano. I'm told they're going to arrest Chaviano too. Everything has been discovered."

Rosell promised to explain more later; he could no longer delay leaving. Leaping over a sofa, he ran through a door and jumped on the yacht that was waiting at his backyard pier.

Echemendía, realizing that if a colonel was vulnerable, an underground *comandante* was doubly so, raced to the waiting Volkswagen. As the car sped away, he looked back to see the yacht pulling out to sea.

A few minutes later, Rosell's relative dropped him off in the Vedado area, and he ran to the house where the underground shortwave transmitter was located. Inside, he scribbled a quick note, not even bothering to use Castro's war name. "Comandante Fidel Castro: I returned from Las Villas but I will go back there immediately. Colonel Rosell tells me that Cantillo is trying to get in touch with you through a priest. The rumor persists that Batista will simulate a coup with people of his confidence. Upon my return I will explain further."

On the second floor of the SIM headquarters, Lieutenant Colonel García Baez erupted with an angry shout when the radio room announced that Colonel Rosell had fled in a boat. Summoning his department heads, he paced, his squat body bobbing up and down as he made his points, demanding to know what had gone wrong. For two days, SIM agents had been following Rosell and General Del Río Chaviano in Santa Clara, and they had confirmed that Rosell's "relative" was actually a 26th of July spy. García Baez hadn't dared arrest the two officers in Santa Clara—their support was too strong there—but he was planning to jail them as soon as they reentered Camp Columbia. Now, he wanted an explanation, not excuses.

Within an hour, most of Rosell's bodyguards and aides were at SIM headquarters, along with the agents in charge of the investigation. Saying he didn't want to use "wrong methods" to get them to talk,

García Baez was able to pry the story out of them easily. It seemed a captain had been assigned to guard Rosell while he was sleeping in Batista's house, but when the colonel woke up, he had persuaded the captain to take him down the block, to the home of Brigadier General Silito Tabernilla. Silito, Rosell's longtime friend, had ordered the captain to let Rosell go home by himself to change clothes and shave.

From Rosell's aides, the SIM chief learned the length, shape and color of the getaway boat. Its name was *Barlovento II*. With that information, García Baez raced in his Oldsmobile across the camp. He ran into the air force headquarters and barked orders for a pilot to track down Rosell at sea.

The SIM chief was just finishing his description of the yacht when Colonel Winsy Tabernilla, the chief of the air force, came in. Winsy was reluctant to send a plane after Rosell, but García Baez ranted that it was essential that Rosell be punished, as an example, if the regime were to survive. Winsy gave in. At 2:30 P.M., a B-26, piloted by Lieutenant José Crespo, took off to find the wayward colonel.

With that accomplished, García Baez raced downtown to the Presidential Palace, where he found Batista in his second-floor office. Hurriedly outlining the plot, he asked for permission to arrest General Del Río Chaviano. The general, he had learned, had sneaked back to Havana and was at the home of Pancho Tabernilla, the joint chief of staff.

Batista grimaced. "You can't arrest him there," he said simply.

In fact, it was just about that moment that the general was entering the residence of Ambassador Smith. General Del Río Chaviano, General Pancho Tabernilla and his son Colonel Winsy Tabernilla had asked for complete secrecy for their meeting, but they arrived in a convoy of olive-green army cars, accompanied by squads of bodyguards. As additional protection, an air force helicopter hovered overhead.

Old Pancho said he wanted to talk to Smith alone, and the two of them walked into the ambassador's spacious study. After Smith closed the door and the two men were seated, Tabernilla announced that the government was about to fall apart. The war was going very badly, and the army had suffered greatly because of the U.S. arms embargo. If Cuba were to be saved from chaos and Communism, he said, the United States would have to act quickly. He proposed a junta be formed, including General Cantillo. All the top military and political leaders, including Batista himself, would leave the country. He asked if the United States would support the junta.

Smith said all he could do was report the suggestion to Washington, but he was certain there would be no reply. "If we answer you directly, it would be undermining General Batista, and I can only do business with Batista because I am accredited to him."

The old general, looking confused and somewhat timid, asked for suggestions.

"Have you mentioned this visit to Batista?" Smith asked.

"No, I have not." There was a long pause. "I have not told him I was coming to see you, but I have discussed in general our future possibilities with Batista."

Smith asked what the president had said to him.

"He told me to come up with a plan."

Smith realized that the general was just groping for something that would extricate them from the mess they were in. He wanted to help, but he was shackled by Washington's reticence. Standing up to signal the end of the meeting, he suggested politely that Tabernilla talk again with Batista.

Within minutes after the three military officers left, the ambassador's home phone started ringing constantly. Dozens of neighbors had seen the helicopter and the army convoy, and rumors about the "secret meeting" were spreading throughout Havana. His wife's friends wanted to know what had happened. Some were saying that Smith and Tabernilla had agreed to stage a coup d'etat against Batista.

In the middle of the Florida Straits, Colonel Florentino Rosell was at the helm of his yacht, speeding along toward Miami, when he heard the drone of a plane in the distance. Squinting into the bright sunlight, he saw a Cuban air force B-26 heading straight toward him.

Diving for cover, the colonel waited for the American-made bombs to blow him out of the water. At the last moment, he looked up, just in time to see the silver plane swoop in, waggle its wings in a salute and fly on toward Florida.

On Mary Street, in the tree-studded Coconut Grove area of Miami, Justo Carrillo went to answer a knock at the front door. An American, an elderly man with a full head of gray hair, was standing on the porch.

Carrillo, leader of the small Montecristi Movement, led the man into his unpretentious living room and offered him a seat. The visit was not a surprise. A call from Washington the day before had said the man was coming.

Making no attempt at small talk, the visitor said he was quite interested in Carrillo's plan to free Colonel Barquín from the Isle of Pines. "I have followed this project very carefully, just in case. . . . We want the project completed. I have seen many mistakes committed. Many mistakes."

The main error, he said, was the schedule. Obviously, there was no time to construct a landing field in Mexico to launch a commando raid on the prison. The Batista regime was about to collapse. "But we could provide funds so that the warden might be bribed. He would allow Barquín to take over the prison. Then the planes could land, and the plan could go on as scheduled."

Carrillo leaned forward in his chair. For the first time, after months of pleading with State, the CIA and the Defense Department, there seemed a real possibility for action. He said he couldn't go to Cuba himself, because the police were certain to arrest him as soon as he stepped off the plane. He would have to find someone else, and then came the problem of how to get the money.

"We'd like to give you a satchel with cash," the American said calmly. He figured that between $100,000 and $200,000 would be needed to persuade the warden. "It can either be transported to Cuba if there is a safe way, or it can be kept in Miami for final payment after the deal is transacted."

"No, no," Carrillo responded quickly. "I can't accept responsibility for such a large amount of money. I don't want to touch a penny of it."

The visitor paused to consider. "Well, the funds will be available on short notice here in Miami. In fact, if it is necessary, they could be channeled to Havana. If that's the case, you should ask us, and we'd make the arrangements and tell you how to go about picking it up."

The discussion drifted into details. Both agreed the most important step was to contact the warden and see if he would accept a bribe. Later, they could arrange payment.

Feeling optimistic for the first time in months, Carrillo drove his visitor to the airport and waited until the man boarded his plane.

As he walked back to his car, a crowd of exiles was gathering in another part of the terminal, talking excitedly about the Cuban air force B-26 that had just landed. It seemed a young Batista pilot, Lieutenant

José Crespo, had announced he was tired of killing his fellow country-men. He wanted asylum.

That evening in Washington, three days after Eisenhower had read the Cuban memorandum, a second step was taken to help mold a "third force."

It was bitterly cold, with the temperature less than 20 degrees, and when William Wieland opened the door of his North Arlington home, he saw lobbyist Carlos Piad exhaling waves of steam.

Feeling unusually cheerful, the director of Caribbean affairs led the Cuban to his basement den. There, he served Piad a drink, then told him the good news. The CIA was willing to support the plan of Tony Varona, the former prime minister, to stage an uprising in Camagüey Province. "This is what we have been waiting for," he beamed.

Piad was to call Varona in Miami and tell him someone would contact him shortly. The visitor would give a code name, and Varona was to reply with a certain phrase. "Call your friend," Wieland said, "and tell him to trust his visitor one hundred percent."

Piad repeated the code words several times, until he was certain he had them memorized. Then he asked, "How is the other thing going?"

"What other thing?" Wieland was puzzled for a moment.

"The project with the Segundo Frente del Escambray. They're still waiting in Miami to take their weapons to the mountains."

Wieland shrugged. "I guess it's still cooking, but I haven't heard anything." He asked if Carlos Prio was still thinking of going on the flight.

Piad showed a small smile. President Prio had changed his mind. "Perhaps," he said, "he thought it was too dangerous."

As Wieland showed the lobbyist to the door, he felt a resurgence of hope. If the CIA was doing something with the Camagüey scheme, the agency might be involved in other "third force" operations he knew nothing about. But the plans would have to start moving very quickly. To judge from all the dispatches coming in from the Havana embassy, it was obvious that the Batista army was collapsing faster than anyone had imagined possible.

Late that night, Brigadier General Silito Tabernilla sat beside his father, Old Pancho, as they watched Batista pace the black-and-white tile floor in the office of the presidential residence at Camp Columbia. This time there was no looking at the photographs depicting his

Fidel Castro at the rebel stronghold in the Sierra Maestra mountains. June 1958.
(UPI)

The Presidential Palace, Havana. *(Fabricio)*

U.S. Ambassador Earl E. T. Smith (left) after presenting his credentials to Cuban President Fulgencio Batista. July 1957. *(Wide World Photos)*

Lieutenant General Francisco Tabernilla (left) promoted by Batista to General in Chief of Cuba's armed forces at a Camp Columbia ceremony. January 1958. (*Wide World Photos*)

The Copa Room at Havana's new Riviera Hotel. 1958. (*Wide World Photos*)

Right: Prime Minister Gonzalo Güell. April 1957. *(Wide World Photos)* *Below:* President-elect Andrés Rivero Agüero. November 1958. *(Wide World Photos)*

General Eulogio Cantillo (center). January 1959. (*Wide World Photos*)

Chow time at Castro's camp. 1958. *(UPI)*

A Radio Rebelde station. 1958. *(Yale University Library)*

Rebels in Oriente Province, a few hours before a hit-and-run attack on a local government patrol post. April 1958. *(UPI)*

Below left: Park Wollam (center), U.S. Consul in Santiago. 1958. *(Wide World Photos) Below right:* Celia Sánchez. *(Wide World Photos)*

Above left: Napoleón Bequer (with beard). *Above right:* Enrique Acevedo (left), sixteen, with Rogelio Acevedo, seventeen. Remedios. 1958.

Enrique Barroso (in glasses). January 1959.

Above left: Húber Matos. *(Wide World Photos) Above right:* Ramón Barquín. *(Wide World Photos)*

Rebels seize Fomento. December 1958. *(UPI)*

The park in Santa Clara from the roof of the Gran Hotel. *(Fabricio)*

Castro addresses a crowd in Santa Clara. January 1959, *(Wide World Photos)*

Entering Havana. January 1, 1959. *(Tannenbaum)*

Streetfighting in Havana. January 1, 1959. *(Wide World Photos)*

Rebels occupy the Presidential Palace. January 1959. (*Joe Scherschel, Life Magazine*
© *1959 Time, Inc.*)

Castro conferring with Guevera in Camagüey before his
triumphal entry into Havana. January 1959. (*Wide World
Photos*)

President Urrutia (center), flanked by rebel leaders Guevera (left) and Cienfuegos.
January 1959. (*Wide World Photos*)

Victorious Castro mobbed by followers. January 1959. *(Wide World Photos)*

Bank, police, and army men with some of the more than $3 million in cash and bonds found in a safety deposit box of Batista's. January 1959. (*Wide World Photos*)

Batista partisans leave Houston for Miami. From left: Rodolfo Masferrer, Alcides Perez, Raimundo Masferrer, Captain Julio Laurent, and Rolando Masferrer. January 1959. (*Wide World Photos*)

Castro's victory parade in Havana. January 1959. (*Joe Herschel, Life Magazine* © *1959 Time, Inc.*)

triumphs. Batista's face was emotionless, but his rapid pacing made it obvious that he was enraged. He was simply trying to control his emotions before he began.

Silito knew the conversation was going to be grim. The Presidential Palace was handing out a press release announcing changes in the army. Two thousand soldiers, the release stated, were being sent immediately to quell the uprising in Las Villas Province. That was an outright lie, but the rest of the report was true. General Del Río Chaviano had been replaced as commander of Las Villas Province by Colonel Joaquín Casillas Lumpuy, prison warden on the Isle of Pines. More surprisingly, General José Eleuterio Pedraza was being called out of retirement. Pedraza had been one of Batista's original co-conspirators in the 1933 coup, but he had been kicked out of the army in the 1940s for attempting a coup of his own. He was known as a hard-liner, and a bitter enemy of Silito's own Tabernilla family.

Even stranger was what had happened to the $15,000 Batista had given Silito for keeping the list of passengers. Silito had locked the envelope in the desk drawer in this very office, and the next morning the money was gone. Batista was the only other person with a key, but Silito felt he didn't dare ask why he had taken the money back.

Composed at last, Batista sat down behind his desk and stared straight at Pancho. With barely controlled anger, he said he had learned about the meeting with Ambassador Smith. To have one of his own military men go behind his back and talk to the American ambassador was the one action he could never tolerate. It was a complete betrayal.

"What you have done to me," he said evenly, "is a coup d'etat."

Silito saw his father's face turn pale. "Why, Chief?" the old man asked. "I haven't done anything. All I'm doing is obeying your orders and trying to find a solution to a situation that is completely lost."

Batista said he never meant a "solution" to include talking to the ambassador. That right belonged to him alone. Especially during times of crisis, a meeting with the American emissary was obviously a ploy to win approval for some kind of plot.

"Oh, Chief," Pancho mumbled with a saccharine humility, "you could not be the object of a coup d'etat because you are the idol of the armed forces, and we love you very much." He was only trying to find a solution "because the soldiers are tired and the officers do not want to fight. Nothing more can be done. . . . Rest assured that I hold you in the highest regard."

Batista didn't blink. "Nevertheless, there has been a coup attempted." He paused. "And I cannot replace all my commanders and reorganize their commands."

To Silito, that cryptic comment seemed to imply that he had considered firing all the Tabernillas but realized he couldn't without shattering what little stability remained in the camp. For Batista even to contemplate such an action was disturbing, but Silito didn't have time to contemplate its significance, because Batista swiveled in his chair and stared directly at him.

Speaking more calmly now, Batista said he had discovered that Silito had ordered the main entrance to Camp Columbia locked, its steel shutters closed even in daylight. SIM had reported a large number of troops around Silito's house, with a tank on the patio at night and a machine-gun nest in the shrubbery.

Such defense measures were absolutely idiotic, Batista said, his voice rising. All they did was make the people around the camp nervous because it appeared the army thought it was going to be attacked. It was like an open admission to the people of Havana that the regime was frightened.

Nervously, Silito tried to explain. The Columbia garrison, he said, was weakened by the men sent to fight in Las Villas Province. "We don't have enough troops, and the soldiers are tired," he complained. What's more, the rear of his house faced the Columbia airfield, where anyone, including terrorists, could come in and claim they were going to Aerovías Q airlines. The tank and the machine-gun nest were to protect against that.

Batista was not swayed. "No, no. Open the gates. Otherwise, all those people are going to keep talking about it."

Silito said he would obey, and he vowed to support his president until the end. But again he added that if the cause appeared lost, they should all leave, "the sooner, the better."

The meeting was over. Silito walked down the block toward his house, located on one corner of the parade ground. He still had the list of passengers in his pocket. When the time came, he was certain that they would be leaving together. To him the whole discussion had been nothing more than a family squabble, an attempt by Batista to keep the lid on for a few more days.

32/ DECEMBER 27: "STAY TUNED TO THE NETWORK OF LIBERTY"

That morning, almost all the Havana newspapers appeared on the streets with large headlines repeating the palace's report that the army was sending two thousand troops to Las Villas Province while denying that the rebels had gained anything more than a temporary foothold in a few small towns. In the English-language tabloid *Havana Post,* the report received a two-column, three-line headline, the largest the newspaper had given the civil war in weeks.

It wasn't that the editors believed the entire report, but it was at least an admission by the regime, the first, that something serious was happening in central Cuba. The people of Havana already knew that. It was impossible to get telephone calls through to the province, and all rail and bus traffic to inland towns had stopped. In the cheaper hotels of

Old Havana, harried families from Las Villas were appearing and paying for their rooms by the week.

General Cantillo had no time to read the newspapers that morning at Camp Columbia. He had arisen shortly after sunrise and, sitting in his living-room rocking chair, tried to figure out what to do. Within two hours, he was scheduled to leave for Santiago, where the priest probably would be waiting with information about the meeting with Castro. But events were moving so rapidly in Camp Columbia that he had no idea of where things were headed. A colonel fleeing in a yacht, a general replaced, secret late-night meetings—and still the president had not talked to him personally about what he should say to Castro. It seemed almost as if the officers were being allowed to drift, to fend for themselves, and that possibility made Cantillo, accustomed to the well-structured military life, highly uncomfortable.

What he needed, he decided, was for someone to protect his rear flank in Havana while he was in Oriente, and the only man he could trust for that job was Colonel José Martínez Suárez, the territorial inspector of the Fifth Military District, located just outside of Havana, and an old friend of both him and Batista. *

Avoiding the military microwave system, which the Estado Mayor might be monitoring, Cantillo used his regular telephone to call the colonel. After many rings, Martínez Suárez answered, his voice groggy with sleep. The general invited him to an "urgent breakfast."

A few minutes later, the colonel arrived, still sleepy-eyed. They had a light breakfast of *café con leche* and toasted Cuban bread. Cantillo waited until the cook had cleared away the dishes and disappeared into the kitchen. Then, as succinctly as possible, he told his old friend everything he knew about the Castro meeting.

Martínez Suárez frowned. He said the whole affair sounded bizarre and complicated. Something was obviously wrong.

Cantillo nodded. It would be some hours before Batista was awake, but when he was, Martínez Suárez had to find a way to see him. "You have to go tonight," he said, "to the palace or wherever Batista is. . . . Tell him what I am going to do. Sent by Tabernilla. And that I think it is Batista who is sending me. If he doesn't want me to tell Castro, send a

---

* Martínez Suárez was the officer who some weeks before had saved the life of Danilo Mesa, the high-fidelity store owner.

wire through the military channel and another through the civilian channel. If I get a wire, no matter what it says, I will not go to see Castro. You can say my wife is feeling better. Anything you want. If I get a wire, I won't go, but I don't want to get caught in the middle."

Martínez Suárez, his face ashen, said he would somehow find a way.

At a sidewalk café in Old Havana, Max Lesnik, dressed in his usual T-shirt and blue jeans, was lingering at a table as he tried to pick up the latest *bolas*. The underground leader of the Segundo Frente del Escambray had heard Florida radio stations were mentioning that a Colonel Rosell of the corps of engineers had entered Key West on a yacht and was heading toward Miami, where he was going to meet with former president Carlos Prio. It seemed everyone in the café had a different idea about what that meant, and *bolas* about conspiracies in the military were rampant, but to Lesnik it all meant only one thing—the Cuban army was falling apart before his little-known group could get into action.

As he listened and brooded, he felt a tug at his elbow. It was Jack Stewart, the "FBI man" from the American embassy, dressed in his usual light-colored suit. With uncustomary excitement, the American whispered to him, "Max, let's get in my car. I have news for you."

The two walked over to the American's 1958 green Chevrolet. Stewart eased the car into the congested traffic on the narrow street and drove about aimlessly, squeezing past the street vendors' pushcarts filled with tropical fruits and ice cream, as he talked about the planeload of weapons the Segundo Frente had waiting in Miami.

"The United States government," he said with a boastful bit of drama, "is giving you clearance. Your plane can take off from Miami on December thirty-first without any problems."

Lesnik felt a sudden exhilaration. At last, he thought, his group had a chance. Perhaps even now it was not too late to beat the 26th of July rebels in a race to Havana. And if they could reach the city first, then anything was possible.

Lesnik had no way of knowing, but the United States had just taken its third step toward promoting a "third force."

About 2:00 P.M. that afternoon, Comandante Echemendía approached Ché Guevara, his right arm still in a black sling. Since leaving Colonel Rosell's house, Echemendía had spent hours, first getting back to Las Villas, then in trying to find Guevara, who was moving constantly. The underground man had finally managed to bluff his way through the army lines with the help of a young auto mechanic, who had said they were going to a garage to fix their car.

Guevara was surrounded by about ten or fifteen rebel officers, and Echemendía had to wait until he was done giving orders before he could talk to him. Then, as quickly as he could, he described all he had seen during the past thirty-six hours, the location of the armored train and its weaponry, the changes in the regimental commands, the fortifications at the garrison and the tanks, jeeps and troops he had seen that morning moving through the streets of the city.

Guevara listened intently and asked him to dictate a complete report to his secretary, a bearded youth who was a member of the student Directorio.

That evening, about eight o'clock, Captain Rogelio Acevedo walked into the cuartel at Remedios, where Ché Guevara was sitting behind a desk. Seven or eight rebel captains were leaning against the wall.

In his usual calm, measured voice, Guevara told his seventeen-year-old officer that Column 8 was going to attack the city of Santa Clara. There was a large armored train there, tanks and a garrison of at least two thousand soldiers.

Acevedo's first reaction was that his *comandante* had gone mad. It was one thing to attack isolated cuartels and prepare ambushes for the reinforcements. But it seemed insanity for a force of less than five hundred rebels to try taking a city of more than a hundred thousand persons. He didn't see the logic in it, but he knew that Guevara wasn't interested in a teenager's opinions.

"What do I do?" he asked simply.

Guevara explained that most of the rebel platoons were scattered throughout the northern part of the province, some as far as forty-five miles from Santa Clara. Acevedo's group was closest, on the road that led north from the city. He was to move his men down the road to the University of Santa Clara, which was just beyond the city's northern limits. There was supposed to be an army detail there. His job was to drive them back to the city. Under no circumstances were the soldiers to be allowed to advance.

"Just wait for me," Guevara ordered. "I'll be there at daybreak."

Acevedo was startled. The rebels almost always attacked at night so that the army couldn't see them. "In the daytime?"

"Yes, at dawn."

Acevedo asked from which direction Ché would be coming. In preparing the latest ambush, his men had not only knocked out a bridge on the northern road but had also covered a two-mile stretch of pavement with palm trees and telephone poles. It was almost impassable.

"Don't worry," Guevara said simply. "We won't be going through there."

The *comandante* turned to the other captains, and Acevedo understood he was being dismissed. Rushing out the door to round up his platoon, he realized he and his thirty men, some of them not even as old as he, were being asked to contain two thousand soldiers.

With the headlights off as a security measure, Fidel Castro and his secretary Celia Sánchez bounced over a gravel road in the *comandante-en-jefe*'s green Land Rover. They were headed toward the Central Oriente sugar mill, to inspect the site where he was supposed to meet General Cantillo the next morning. He had wanted to get there earlier, but it had been an unexpectedly hectic day.

Before dawn, the last of the soldiers in Palma Soriano had surrendered, giving the rebels a total of 354 arms and 85,000 rounds of ammunition. Two hundred fifty-six soldiers had given up, and now the bulk of his troops, boosted by the volunteers carrying the newly captured arms, were only thirty miles away from Santiago itself. Only the bitter army holdouts in the Maffo coffee warehouses remained before he could launch an attack on the city. He had spent the day working on plans for the battle, but he still held out the hope General Cantillo might agree to stop the fighting, at least in Oriente. Havana, for the moment, was outside his reach. There were a disturbing number of rumors about military conspiracies coming from there, but he could do nothing about those, except to keep fighting regardless of what happened in Camp Columbia.

The Land Rover moved past the rusting, abandoned mill building and continued into the town, where a few families continued to live. Castro stopped in front of the house of a local 26th of July sympathizer, a pharmacist, and with Celia, walked up to the door.

The man's wife, Estrella Cabrerra, invited them in. A spry woman whose head barely reached Castro's chest, she looked up at the rebel leader as Celia explained they were looking for a house to hold an important meeting.

Estrella eagerly offered her own, but as Castro paced through the living room of the modest house, he decided it was too small. However, he added, it would be an enormous favor for the revolution if she had four white bed sheets that he could borrow.

The woman, confused but anxious to help, ran into her bedroom and emerged moments later with four of her best linen sheets. As she handed them up to the rebel leader, her puzzled expression showed she couldn't possibly imagine why anyone would need *four* bed sheets.

At the Moncada garrison in Santiago, General Cantillo sat rocking in his chair on the front porch. Nearby, on the parade ground, was the Sikorsky army helicopter that had been flown in from Havana. He had spent the afternoon in it, flying around the city, landing in the navy yard and other places, so that the soldiers would think nothing unusual was happening when he used it again in the morning. For a time, he had thought about flying it himself—he was a licensed helicopter pilot—but had decided against it. He had too many other things to worry about.

There had been no message of any kind from his friend Colonel Martínez Suárez, and now that he was six hundred miles away from Havana, he could look at things with better perspective. Whatever was really happening at Camp Columbia, whoever was really behind the orders for this meeting, it was obvious that the regime had only a few days left, at best.

As soon as he had arrived in Santiago, he had learned of the surrender of Palma Soriano, only thirty miles from the city. A rebel attack on Santiago could begin at any moment, and it seemed senseless to have a bloody fight on the city streets if the government were going to fall in any case.

In the distance, he saw the silhouette of his aide, bringing two officers across the parade ground. The one in the white naval uniform was Commodore Manuel Carnero, chief of the area's naval forces. Beside him was the squat figure of Colonel José Rego Rubido, the army's territorial inspector whose only real function was to be in charge of the garrison when Cantillo was not there.

The general had summoned them because he needed allies. Neither was a diehard Batista supporter. Carnero was a young professional military man who avoided politics. Colonel Rego was actually bitter about the regime, which had forced him into retirement for a while immediately following the 1952 coup because they suspected, correctly, that he was an avowed democrat. Both were likely to approve of a meeting with Castro that might stop the bloodshed, and both were innocent of any "war crimes," which meant they would be acceptable to the rebels.

The two officers saluted as they reached the porch. Cantillo, telling them to bring chairs, led them into his spartan bedroom and shut the door. When they were seated, he drew in a deep breath, realizing he was moving irrevocably toward something he hated to do.

"Tomorrow," he said as calmly as he could, "I'm going to see Fidel Castro. I am doing this under orders. I'm telling you this so that you do not misinterpret my actions and think I am acting on my own."

Colonel Rego's face flushed. "I would not question your actions, General," he stammered.

"No, no," Cantillo interjected quickly, "I want you to know because I may have to be away again, and then you will be in my shoes here. You should know in case you have to deal with the rebels."

Commodore Carnero nodded agreement, but the colonel was not so quick to agree. "General," he said with a touch of anger, "why is it that I, who have been out of power and command for so long, who was fired by the leaders of Batista's coup, who has not commanded a unit in eight years—why is it that I am put in this position?"

Cantillo knew the question was really a slap at him, because he had slipped so easily into the Batista regime, but he showed no hostility as he said, "Colonel, if you are going to be dealing with the rebels, it is actually *because* of your background. We can't have a man with a compromising past."

He explained that the priest had talked with him early that afternoon. The meeting was to be at the Central Oriente at 8:00 A.M. Except for the helicopter pilot, he was going to take no one with him, but the priest had agreed to attend as an impartial observer.

As the officers left, Cantillo could tell from their expressions that they were happy, or at least relieved. They sensed an end to the war.

A few blocks away, Connie Wollam lay on her bed listening to the late-night broadcast of 7RR, the main rebel radio station, which came booming out of her huge navy-surplus shortwave set.

"ATTENTION TO THE CUBAN PEOPLE!" the announcer shouted. "Rumors continue to circulate that foreign powers are trying to put together a military junta in Cuba to defeat Batista and to place in the government military men who are neither wanted nor accepted by the Cuban people. This constitutes a frank violation of the internal affairs of another country. If this happens, Cubans, if this news can be confirmed, you know what you should do. The campaign of Radio Rebelde, if such an act proves true, is a REVOLUTIONARY STRIKE IMMEDIATELY. All Cubans should support a strike the very moment that a military junta backed by foreign governments is established. Cuba is for the Cubans. No one has to intervene in our affairs.

"Stay tuned to the stations of the Network of Liberty . . ."

The announcer droned on about the victory at Palma Soriano, and Connie was getting sleepy. It had been an unusually peaceful evening. Her husband Park was gone on a trip, but this time the house was filled with life. Her daughters were still home, and so was Barbara's sailor-boyfriend. The two of them had spent most of the evening alone in the living room, listening to big band music on the hi-fi.

Just before midnight, the music stopped, then Barbara came in to say good night.

"Are you sure you turned off the record player?" Connie asked, knowing she was sounding like a typical mother. "Did you put the bar across the front door?"

"Yeah, yeah, Mother. Everything is OK." She said she was going to wash her hair before turning in.

Connie decided to double-check. Slipping on her white embroidered robe, she walked into the living room. Yes, the record player was turned off. The door was barred. She stopped to gaze through the sixteen-foot-high windows which faced the street. It was a beautiful moonlit night, and the two royal palms in the front yard looked majestic in the shadows.

Suddenly, she realized she was looking straight at a man standing beside one of the marble benches in the yard. He was wearing a white suit, with a flat, impassive face that looked half-Latin, half-Oriental and totally terrifying. He was staring directly at her.

She stepped quickly to one side and peeked back through the window.

For a second, he seemed to have disappeared. Then he looked out from behind a bush.

Running to the back of the house, she burst into the room of Phil Goodman, the navy lieutenant. "Phil," she shouted, "there's a man in the yard. Quick, there's a twenty-two pistol on top of my wardrobe."

The lieutenant grabbed the gun and, unbarring the door, ran into the front yard. He checked the front and side yards. When he came back he said he had noticed nothing except that the driver's door was open on their car.

"But that's very hard to open," Connie said. "It sticks. He must have done it."

"Well," the young lieutenant said, "he must have been sitting in the car and watching."

Connie looked around. Except for the baby, all the children were in the room. Barbara had a towel wrapped around her blond hair. For the first time, Connie realized that the navy man was wearing only his boxer shorts.

Again, Connie called the vice-consul, who hurried over with the police. She gave them an exact description, but the officers only mumbled a few pleasantries and left quickly.

As they drove away, Connie told her daughters, "I think they know who it is."

In Havana, the Copa Room of the Riviera Hotel was doing an unusually good business that evening, even for a Saturday night. About 350 persons jammed into the nightclub to watch the "internationally famous" Spanish dancer Roberto Iglesias and his Ballet Español. Some 270 persons had to be turned away at the door.

33/DECEMBER 28: "A TERRIBLE TREASON"

Just north of the Santa Clara city limits, Captain Rogelio Acevedo crouched behind a jeep with three of his men. In the ditch on the other side of the highway, four more rebels hid behind a second jeep. In front of them, the road was empty and silent, and distant streetlights revealed nothing but dark pavement. To his right were the barren, gently rolling Capiro Hills, topped by a CMQ radio-TV repeater antenna. To his left were some scattered concrete bungalows. Just above their roofs, like a vague crown, was the golden-tinged eastern sky. Dawn was not far away.

Acevedo cursed under his breath. The army was certain to discover them at any moment, and he did not even have the rest of his thirty-man platoon. Something had gone wrong, just when he was beginning to think that they had been terribly lucky. Their good fortune had begun when, shortly before 3:00 A.M., they had come upon a milkman near Camajuaní, and he had told them the only soldiers in the area were five aged watchmen at the University of Santa Clara, located a few miles north of the city. Acevedo had left most of his squad in two trucks to bring up the rear as he led the two jeeps in a race to the campus. The watchmen had given up quickly, even eagerly, handing over their Colt .38-caliber revolvers and thanking him for "liberating" the university. Acevedo had left one rebel at the campus entrance, to tell the trucks to come on ahead, but that had been more than two hours ago, and they had yet to appear. He couldn't imagine what had gone wrong.

Deciding he had to do something before it became completely light, he left two men in the roadside ditch and sped back to the campus. There, under a tree, he found the trucks and the rest of his men. They were lounging on the grass, drinking the milk that the milkman had left for the night watchmen.

The seventeen-year-old rebel captain exploded. "Didn't I tell you to send the platoon forward?" he demanded of the man he had left behind.

"Well, actually," the rebel replied, putting down his milk bottle, "I thought you said to stay here and wait for Ché."

Controlling his temper, Acevedo ordered the men to advance immediately. He jumped back in his jeep so angry that he forgot to take some of the milk for himself. There are always mistakes in wars, he thought, but no one ever makes the mistake of going forward when he isn't supposed to. The mistake always concerns staying where you are, or retreating.

When they reached their previous location, Acevedo ordered the men to dig trenches. The sun was beginning to rise above the bungalows, and still there was no sign of Guevara, who had promised to be there by "daybreak."

Acevedo was wondering what might have happened to him when suddenly he saw a blue-and-white police car coming down the highway. It swerved to a stop several hundred yards away and, just as the rebels opened fire, made a screeching U-turn. It sped back to the city untouched.

Now there was no doubt the Batistianos knew they were there. The next few minutes seemed like hours to the teenage captain as he waited for an army convoy to appear, but the road remained deserted. Finally, a rebel messenger ran up to him and said Ché had made it to the university. He wanted to see him.

When Acevedo reached the campus, he found the lawn near the entrance filled with rebels. They might not have been many compared to the army troops, but it was a relief to see at least some reinforcement for his small platoon.

Guevara was in a first-floor office, off an open-air corridor. "What's going on?" he asked as soon as he saw Acevedo.

"Nothing. Nothing's going on. Everything is quiet. But it's daylight, and we're in the middle of the road. We're right on top of Santa Clara."

"Fine," Guevara said, ignoring the fear in the teenager's voice, "that's the way we're going in."

"But aren't we going to wait for nightfall?"

"No, no, *no*," Guevara answered, a little testily. "We're going in now. We'll surprise them." He said he was sending a second platoon, of forty men, to join Acevedo's group.

By the time the teenager and the new platoon reached his men, the trenches were completed. The rebels crouched in them, their eyes fixed on the strip of pavement coming from the city. Several times within a few minutes, army patrol cars appeared, stopping just out of range. They looked at the rebel position and returned to the city. Acevedo felt a surge of confidence. Obviously, the army didn't want to fight. It was time to advance.

Leading his platoon along the right side of the road, they began walking slowly toward the city. The new squad advanced to their left. They were about six hundred yards from the city limits when they saw the top of a vehicle moving slowly over a slight incline.

"There's a tank. A tank!" several rebels shouted.

Their seventeen-year-old leader, bursting with his newfound confidence, didn't believe it. He knew telephone company cars were olive-green, like the vehicle they were seeing. "Don't be chicken," he yelled at his men. "It's not a tank; it's a telephone car."

Just then the vehicle came into complete view. It was a heavy armored car, with two machine guns mounted on the front. A round of gunfire splattered the pavement directly in front of them. Acevedo, with the rest of his men, dived into the ditch.

Cursing his own stupidity, he peeked out to see that a second rubber-wheeled armored car was following the first. To stay in the ditch was suicidal. Head down, he made a dash to a small bungalow. The front door was unlocked, and he fell inside. Seconds later, his sixteen-year-old brother Enrique jumped in after him.

Looking through the window, he saw the armored cars spraying the roadside ditches, where most of his men still remained. Acevedo aimed his Garand at the peephole of the lead vehicle. The odds were against him getting a shot through the narrow slit, but he guessed it would have a strong psychological impact on the men inside. He was right. After emptying two magazines at it, the armored car swiveled and retreated to the city, followed by its twin.

Acevedo's relief was only momentary. The battle was joined now, and it would be insane to advance any farther during daylight. Their only chance was to dig in, set up their .30-caliber machine gun and try to repel the infantry that would undoubtedly be coming.

A quick check of casualties showed that of the seventy men in the two platoons, four were dead and four injured. That was more than 10 percent of their force, and they still were not inside the city. As Acevedo contemplated that fact, B-26 bombers appeared overhead.

At the Central Oriente, Fidel Castro paced through the huge open room that had once been the main mill building. The air was heavy with the musty smell of rusty machinery, and gaping holes in the floor showed where the refining equipment had once been. A beam of sunlight shone in through a hole in the wall. It was a terribly dilapidated building, and, his secretary, Celia Sánchez, was trying to give it a bit of civility by arranging some folding chairs, borrowed from the pharmacist's wife, around a small table, on which rested a silver tray and delicate coffee cups decorated with colorful flowers.

Castro turned to Carlos Franqui, the director of Radio Rebelde, and talked about what he should say to Cantillo. He assumed, based on the messages from Comandante Echemendía in Havana, that Cantillo, like Colonel Rosell, was willing to work with the rebels to overthrow Batista. In that case, the general should be offered some position in their movement. But, he told Franqui, since he had structured the rebel army so that no one had a rank higher than major, he couldn't really offer an army position to a man who was already a major general. Someone suggested that Cantillo be made "minister of defense," but Castro did not respond. He was lost in thought.

The huge Sikorsky helicopter seemed to float above the landscape. To Cantillo's left was the brooding greenery of the Sierra Maestra. To the right was a winding ribbon of gray concrete, the Central Highway, littered with the charred skeletons of trucks and cars. In the scattered villages, he could see people walking toward the churches for Sunday-morning Mass.

Sitting in the copilot's seat, Cantillo's eyes occasionally drifted over to the instrument panel, but his mind, as he had suspected, was too preoccupied with what lay ahead to think about the joys of flying the Sikorsky. He had prepared carefully for the meeting, dressing himself in battle-fatigue trousers and a tight-fitting khaki shirt that had no insignia indicating his rank. He wanted the rebels to see immediately that he was carrying no weapon, and he saw no need to flaunt his position to a group of men who viewed even the title of "general" as a symbol of what they were fighting against.

His ulcerous stomach was beset with twinges of pain, but he kept telling himself that he was not afraid, because a good military man was never afraid. The problem with that, he thought, was that this wasn't a military operation. It was a political one, and nothing in his life, his straight A's at the military academy, his career as a professional soldier, had prepared him for what he was about to do. He was going into the meeting confused and uncertain, not knowing what the rebels would demand or what Camp Columbia was willing to accept. Everything seemed so vague that he decided it was best to let Castro do most of the talking. Then he could report back to Camp Columbia, and let Old Pancho and Batista decide.

The pilot spotted it first: four white bed sheets forming corners of a large square on the ground beside the abandoned mill's towering smokestack.

The Sikorsky churned a cloud of dust as it settled to the ground. When it cleared, Cantillo saw two or three rebels with guns standing off to one side. Beside the mill door, a cluster of people were waiting, Castro towering above his brother Raúl, secretary Celia Sánchez, Raúl's fiancée Vilma Espín and Father Guzmán. Cantillo was surprised so many rebel leaders were present. He felt outnumbered.

Ducking his head below the still-whirling propeller, the general climbed down. Castro walked forward to greet him, shaking his hand and showing a cautious smile. He made a remark about the general's unusual uniform.

"It was very hot in Santiago," Cantillo said, smiling. "And I don't like the formal uniform anyway." He apologized for not flying the helicopter himself, but he promised the pilot would remain on board while they talked.

Castro led the way inside. It was dark, and Cantillo had trouble adjusting his eyes, but he saw immediately the large holes in the floor. They would make perfect bomb shelters in case the air force attacked.

As soon as they were seated on the folding chairs, Celia Sánchez brought in a pot of steaming coffee and placed it on the silver tray.

When Cantillo saw it, he leaped up. "Oh—if you'll excuse me," he said, running out the door. A few seconds later, as the group watched nonplussed, he returned with a flask of Spanish brandy and an aluminum container filled with cigars. Castro took them politely and placed them on the table.

While Celia passed around cups of coffee and syrupy sweets on brown paper napkins, Castro talked about his respect for the general, the fairness with which he had treated rebel prisoners and his innocence of "war crimes."

Trying to collect his thoughts, Cantillo sipped at the rich, sweet coffee. Deciding it was best to be as vague as possible, he said simply there had already been too much bloodshed among Cubans. It was time to put an end to it. He had come to ask what Castro thought of establishing a civilian-military junta to replace the Batista regime and end the war.

Castro studied him carefully. He was not certain how much he could trust this general who, despite his clean record, had still been a defender of the dictatorship. Pulling a cigar from the aluminum case, he lit it with a wooden match. Then, shifting the cigar from side to side in his mouth, he stood and started pacing. He began by talking about Cuban history, about the long record of last-minute betrayals to revolutionary causes, about the tradition of corruption that had permeated the country since the time of the Spanish. For more than an hour he talked and paced, sometimes moving so close to Cantillo that their faces were only inches apart, trying, as he often did with strangers, to gain a quick intimacy, attempting to persuade with a force that was almost physical.

Uncomfortably, Cantillo sat and listened. For the first time, he realized how powerful Castro's personality was, how difficult it would be to make an agreement that was in any way equal.

The others simply watched their leader. After a while, Vilma Espín stood up and, hovering on the edge of the group, tried to take photographs by using the sliver of sunlight coming through the hole in the wall. Her black-and-white film had an ASA rating of 100, too slow to get good pictures in the murky darkness, but she snapped the shutter just the same.

A little later, Comandante Raúl Chibás, who specialized in talking to disenchanted army officers, and José Quevedo, the army major who had gone over to the rebels during the summer offensive, came in quietly. They leaned against the wall as Castro kept talking.

At last, the rebel leader came to Cantillo's mention of a junta. "We are totally opposed to a coup d'etat," he said firmly. Nor would he have anything to do with any plan suggested or supported by the American embassy. He had not spent two hard years in the Sierra Maestra just to see that happen. It was time to end such behind-the-scenes power plays. The military should be at the disposal of the people, not the other way around.

Still pacing, chewing on the end of the cigar which had long since gone out, he said Cantillo's mere presence there meant the army was admitting it had lost the war. Therefore, he saw no need to do any negotiating with such criminals as Batista and the Tabernilla clan. The only time he would talk to them was in a revolutionary court, which would deal with their barbaric habits of torture and murder, and the hundreds of millions of pesos they had stolen from the Cuban people.

But, he added, that didn't mean he was opposed to all the army officers. He knew there were many honorable men in the military, and there would be a place in the new Cuban army for decent officers like Cantillo.

With that statement, he at last stopped talking and looked at the general. Cantillo, his voice almost a whisper after an hour of silence, agreed that there were many excellent officers who could well serve the new Cuba, but he himself wanted only to retire when the war was over. He had been waiting for Castro to propose some names for a junta, to mention specifics such as President-designate Manuel Urrutia. From the way he was talking, it seemed he would want an all 26th of July group.

But Castro, ignoring politics, began talking about the military situation in Oriente. "Is this conversation being held with the knowledge of the Santiago garrison?" he asked.

Cantillo said it was. Colonel Rego Rubido and Commodore Carnero were both supporting him. Both were fine men with no record of criminal activities. Then he paused. From the way that Castro had talked about Batista and the Tabernillas, he saw it would be self-defeating to say the meeting had been suggested by Old Pancho himself. Instead, he decided to lie.

Clearing his throat, he told Castro that he also had the support of other officers scattered across the country, including some in Camp

Columbia and his brother Carlos, who was in charge of the Matanzas provincial garrison. All wanted to see an end to the war.

Castro paced and stared at the floor. When at last he spoke, he ignored the mention of Columbia and focused on the Oriente situation. While he was opposed to a coup d'etat, he would welcome the Moncada garrison if its leaders wanted to *join* the revolution. "The army has become very compromised with Batista, and it has lost some of its reputation as a result. It's necessary that there be some sort of gesture to the people, so the army can be vindicated of that great responsibility, of all the crimes it has committed during the war. . . . Carry out an uprising at the Santiago garrison, for the purpose of joining the revolution." If Batista did not give in immediately, then the combined revolutionary force, the rebels and the Moncada men, could march on Havana with all of the tanks and cannons the army had in Santiago. "Batista would be defeated."

He proposed the uprising take place in three days, at 3:00 P.M. Wednesday, December 31. Until then, he was willing to have an informal cease-fire with the Moncada garrison, though he would continue fighting in other Oriente towns.

Cantillo nodded numbly. With the rebels only thirty miles away from Santiago, a cease-fire could buy him at least a little time, and with the hierarchy crumbling in Camp Columbia, he couldn't just flatly turn down the proposal. What he needed was an out, an excuse, a way to continue his lifelong balancing act, even though Castro had already announced he would make no compromises with the regime. The best he could do, he decided, was to go back and report the whole conversation to Pancho Tabernilla, and see how quickly the Columbia leaders were willing to relinquish power.

When the general looked up, he saw that Castro and the others were staring at him; he must have been thinking a long time. In a soft voice, he said the plan sounded fine to him as a way of ending the bloodshed, but before it was carried out, he had to go back to Havana and consult with the officers who were supporting him, including his brother Carlos.

Comandante Raúl Chibás objected immediately. "If you go to Havana, this whole thing will be discovered. In Cuba, there are no secrets. You may be arrested." Raúl Castro was even more vehement. He implied that Cantillo might start double-dealing with the Columbia officers and betray the rebel cause if he weren't jailed.

The group had suddenly become tense, but Cantillo knew this was one point he had to insist on. It was his escape clause. With it, he figured, if the Columbia hierarchy turned down the proposal, the rebels couldn't accuse him of dealing in bad faith. "No, I don't think there will be any problem," he said smoothly. "I can travel without any risk of being arrested."

Castro supported his brother Raúl. Havana and Columbia were outside his immediate control, and he felt uncomfortable at the thought of Cantillo disappearing into their confines. But he mentioned only the danger of the arrest.

Cantillo remained adamant. "I have a number of officers who are loyal to me," he said, his voice growing stronger as he continued his deception. "They've told me, 'General, whatever you do, we are with you.' I can't let those men wonder what my intentions are. I must go back and talk to them. Otherwise, I'm going back on my word."

Reluctantly, Castro agreed. But, he added, he was worried that the "guilty ones," Batista and the Tabernillas, might flee if they found out about the plot. It wasn't a matter of vengeance, he said. The Cuban people had to regain the millions that had been stolen, and if the regime's leaders escaped into exile, their money probably would go with them.

"If Batista can escape," the rebel leader said, resuming his pacing, "so be it. But if we can prevent his getting away, we should stop him."

The general nodded numbly. All he wanted to do was leave. Standing up for the first time in four and a half hours, he promised he would get in touch as soon as he had talked to his "friends" in Havana.

Castro walked him back to the helicopter, putting an arm around the general's shoulder in a comradely embrace. Cantillo had always hated such intimate personal contact, but he continued smiling until he climbed into the helicopter.

As the Sikorsky's engine cranked up, the rebel leaders ran back to the mill to escape the swirl of dust. Briefly, they talked about Cantillo's attitude. Vilma Espín thought it showed how demoralized the army was, but she didn't trust the general at all. Comandante Raúl Chibás objected that the whole plan for a joining of forces was too vague to pull off in only three days. No details had been worked out at all. But Castro himself was confident. It was obvious to him that the army was about to collapse, and Cantillo would want to salvage what he could from the situation.

*   *   *

Shortly before 1:00 P.M., after a half-hour flight, the Sikorsky settled down on the Moncada parade ground. As the engine was turned off, General Cantillo climbed down to find Colonel Martínez Suárez, his friend from Havana, waiting, his hat in hand to protect it against the swirling propeller wind. The colonel looked agitated and sweaty, and Cantillo sensed immediately that something must have gone terribly wrong at Camp Columbia.

Colonel Rego Rubido and Commodore Carnero were also waiting for him, but Cantillo grabbed hold of Martínez Suárez's elbow as he led the way to his house. Ordering the two Santiago officers to wait on the porch, he took his friend into the bedroom and shut the door.

"What's happening, Martínez? What are you doing here?" Cantillo asked, trying to control his anxiety.

"Well, I have orders from the president." The colonel's hands were trembling.

Cantillo looked at him in amazement.

"I have orders from the president," Martínez Suárez repeated. "You are not to see Castro."

"What happened?" Cantillo exploded. "It's too late. I'm just coming from the Central Oriente, from seeing Castro."

Martínez Suárez slumped on the bed.

Cantillo asked why he hadn't sent the coded message.

Exhausted, the colonel said Batista didn't want him to send it, because it would have to go through the Estado Mayor, where the Tabernillas could see it. The civilian telegraph line had been cut. So the president had asked him to come in person. He hadn't realized the meeting was going to take place so quickly.

Cantillo said he hadn't either. The date had been set by Castro, and Father Guzmán had told him about it only when he returned from Havana. But that was past history. He wanted to know what Batista had said exactly.

Taking in a deep breath, Martínez Suárez started at the beginning. Not wanting to go through the usual army channels, he had contacted a friend, a doctor married to Batista's niece. The doctor found Rubén Batista, the eldest son, at the El Carmelo Restaurant, where he was having a late-afternoon lunch. Martínez Suárez, without explaining what the message was, convinced Rubén to get him in to see his father. About 3:00 or 4:00 P.M., he had walked into the president's office at the palace, and as soon as Batista heard the news, he erupted in anger, accusing Pancho of committing "treason" because "if Castro receives the chief commander of the war, he will assume the government has fallen." Batista had ranted about throwing Pancho in prison and expressed doubts about Cantillo's loyalty as well, but Martínez Suárez had convinced him Cantillo was "all right. He will fight if you want."

Cantillo collapsed on the bed beside the colonel. He had already lied a number of times to Castro, and now he would have to return to face a decidedly hostile audience in Havana. It seemed the straight-A student who was trying to please everyone was ending up pleasing no one.

His worries were interrupted by Martínez Suárez. That was not the end of the story, he said. About 2:00 A.M. this morning, he had gotten a call from an aide of Pancho Tabernilla. Pancho wanted to see him at the Estado Mayor immediately. Panicked, frightened that Pancho might arrest him, Martínez Suárez had called Batista, who told him, "Don't worry, Martínez. Go to the headquarters. There will be no trouble for you."

Cantillo frowned but before he could say anything, the colonel continued. At the Estado Mayor, he said, Pancho had told him, "Go to Santiago and tell Cantillo to delay the meeting if it is possible. Give it awhile. And tell him not to make it an official thing. Just a meeting. If it's easy for him, tell him to go ahead and do it, but it's no longer an order."

Cantillo began pacing. Still, none of it made any sense. He couldn't imagine Tabernilla going against Batista's orders, and he couldn't understand why, if he had, Batista hadn't thrown Tabernilla in jail. None of those people seemed to care anymore, and here he was, responsible for a regiment that might have dozens, perhaps hundreds, of casualties if they were asked to fight the rebels in the streets of Santiago. That seemed absolutely senseless.

"OK," Cantillo said, "go to Havana. Tell the president I have already attended the meeting because his message came too late. Go right now." He promised to fly back later in the day and explain everything.

He walked Martínez Suárez to the porch. As the colonel hurried across the parade ground, Cantillo fell in a rocking chair beside Colonel Rego Rubido and Commodore Carnero. The nearest soldiers were dozens of yards away, and there was no possibility they could overhear the conversation. But he wondered what he should say to the two officers. He had assured Castro that if any problem came up while he was in Havana, the rebel leader could contact Colonel Rego. Yet with the situation crumbling, he was no longer certain that Rego was trustworthy from his own viewpoint. The colonel was so bitter against the regime that he might start telling Castro more than he should. So, Cantillo decided, it was best to keep his Oriente and Havana problems separate. He would tell the officers only what he had discussed with Castro.

Keeping his voice low, he outlined the agreement with the rebels for an uprising at 3:00 P.M., December 31. It would end the bloodshed, and it was the only way to assure that the regular army would be allowed to make the transition to the new regime. That way, he said, the professional officers could serve as a bulwark against Castro's radical inclinations. He saw no other choice.

"I'm going to be here on the thirty-first," he said, looking directly at Rego, "but if for any reason I'm not, you will be in charge of doing this, of carrying out my orders."

Rego swallowed hard, and he complained about the burden of such an assignment. Both he and the navy man agreed they had no other choice if they were to end the fighting. Cantillo gave them some orders for troop movements, to bring more soldiers to Santiago from the outlying Oriente towns, and then dismissed them.

As the two officers walked away, Cantillo thought they seemed positively eager at the idea of joining the rebel cause. Certainly, they preferred it to dying for Batista. But he had not told them that he no longer had the backing of the Columbia hierarchy, just as he had not told Castro that it was Pancho Tabernilla who had ordered the meeting in the first place. What's more, he had not mentioned to Colonel Martínez Suárez about the tentative agreement to join with the rebels on New Year's Eve. It was as if his balancing act were now being performed on a tightrope at a height of thousands of feet, and certainly there was no net waiting to catch him if he fell.

In Santa Clara, Guillermo Domenech sat at the Gran Hotel switchboard as he unashamedly listened to the calls from the frantic guests to the regimental headquarters. It seemed the rebels had already taken the university, and the army infantry was holding back two 26th of July platoons on the northern road, just outside of the city limits. A battalion from the armored train was using .50-caliber machine guns to hold off another rebel group. And on the southern edge of the city, the student Directorio was besieging the 250 Rural Guardsmen at the Squadron 31 cuartel.

As the teenage Domenech tried to imagine what fighting would be like if it reached the hotel at the center of the city, two olive-green Oldsmobiles stopped in front. On their doors, in white lettering, were the words "Servicio de Inteligencia Militar"—the feared SIM. Domenech watched through the glass lobby doors while the intelligence men pulled rifles and machine guns from the trunks. Some were in uniform, others dressed only in khaki trousers and white shirts.

A fat sergeant led them into the lobby, their boots clacking against the green-and-black tile floor, and marched up to the hotel manager, who was almost as fat as the sergeant.

"You must move all the guests above the fifth floor for their own safety," he ordered, as if he were speaking to a boot-camp trainee. "There is going to be a lot of shooting in the city."

The manager sputtered a protest: "The higher floors would seem to be more dangerous."

The soldier's hand tightened on his rifle. "You do as I say and there will be no trouble. . . . And no one leaves. It's too dangerous to go anywhere else. You will all be safer here."

That thought panicked Domenech. Coming from behind the counter, he asked to go home, since he lived only four blocks away.

"*No one* can leave," the sergeant bellowed. To emphasize his determination, he walked over and ripped out the cable connecting the switchboard.

Feeling like a hostage, Domenech followed the hotel manager through the hotel floors as they knocked on doors and told the guests to move to higher rooms. None complained. It seemed as if they were waiting for someone to tell them what to do.

When all the guests had been moved, Domenech walked down to the fifth floor. There, he had to stop. Soldiers were throwing chairs, tables and mattresses down the narrow stairwell that led to the fourth floor. Occasionally, they leaped on the pile, pressing it into a tightly packed mass. They continued until the stairs were completely blocked, then shut down the elevator on the fifth floor.

They were trapped, but the forty-some guests and five hotel employees were relaxed as they stood in the corridor. The children, thinking it was a grand adventure, laughed and frolicked between their legs. The adults joked, and their mood grew even brighter when the manager announced that as long as the army occupied the hotel, no one would be charged for either food or lodging. That was worth a round of applause.

Climbing the stairs to the tenth-floor restaurant, Domenech found the SIM men, about eight of them altogether, spread around, looking through the windows with binoculars. Some had walkie-talkies. The young hotel clerk realized they had chosen the hotel because it had the best view in the entire city.

Back in the kitchen, the chef and manager were going over the supplies. They guessed they had food enough for five days. Much of it was canned goods, but there was some meat that would spoil quickly if the electricity went off, as seemed likely.

"Use the meat first," the manager said. He asked Domenech to count the stock of canned milk. That had to be reserved for the children.

As Domenech counted in the storeroom, he heard gunfire in the distance. Then came the unmistakable sound of heavy tanks clanking through the streets. To him, the noise was like "a thousand greaseless doors creaking at the same time."

Several thousand feet above Camagüey Province, former prime minister Tony Varona sat in a twin-engine Cessna, his face pressed against the glass. Below them was a string of mangrove keys and swamps that formed the province's northern coast. They had been flying over this featureless coastline for what seemed like an eternity without having spotted their landmark, the town of Nuevitas, which was at the base of a distinctive bay.

"We're lost," the pilot shouted back from the cockpit. "We must have overshot Nuevitas, and we're mixed up with all the island chains. We have to go back and look again."

Varona's men groaned as the plane swung sharply to the left. There were eight of them altogether: Varona, the two pilots and five associates, crammed in among the boxes of ammunition. Another ten men were waiting at the central Florida farm where they had taken off that morning; they were to come on a second trip.

The CIA man had never contacted him about his plan for staging an uprising in Camagüey,* and Varona had decided not to wait because, with all the 26th of July victories, time was becoming frighteningly short. They had taken off on a clear, sunny day, but then the pilot

---

* The CIA agent did show up in Miami, but he was late. He chatted for a while with Varona's brother, found there was nothing he could do and left. Even after Eisenhower's approval of a "third force," Washington was still moving far slower than events in Cuba.

complained his radio compass was malfunctioning. They had been wandering around the coastline hours after they should have been safely on the ground.

The Cessna flew west, but still they couldn't find the town. "I'd return to Miami," the pilot yelled above the roar of the engines, "except now we don't have gas to get back."

Varona was silent. The alternatives didn't look promising. They might crash and be killed. Or they could land at a regular airport, be captured, tortured and *then* killed. The minutes passed with agonizing slowness. The coastline of his beloved Cuba, which he had not seen in more than a year, seemed to have become a hideous trap.

"I know we're in the general area," the pilot announced, "but I can't say exactly where." He said he was heading inland, so at least they wouldn't have to land in the water.

"Look!" One of the passengers had spotted Nuevitas. Another yelled to the pilot that the landing strip was almost due south, a little to the west, just beyond the village of Santa Lucía, about halfway across the island.

The pilot said he would try to make it.

The minutes passed in silence, everyone's face pressed against the windows. The copilot saw it first: "It's down there. Look at the field."

The pilot swooped down, not bothering for a go-around to inspect the landing area. The Cessna touched down with a jolt and bounced to a halt. No one complained.

A truck and a few supporters were waiting for them. As the others handed down the ammunition, Varona conferred with the pilot. The plane no longer had enough gasoline to get back to Florida and pick up the other men. They might be able to find fuel in a nearby town, but it was already late in the day. It would have to wait until morning.

The men pushed the Cessna to the side of the airstrip and covered it with branches. Then, sensing the historical importance of the occasion, the former prime minister had a photograph taken of him and his men standing in front of the plane.

For Varona, who had gotten little sleep the night before, the rest of the day passed in a blur. His guide, Pepe Sosa, took the group in the truck to the ranch house of the enormous King Ranch, which was owned by Americans. "The Americans are on our side," Sosa explained, "and they have agreed to let us stay overnight."

At the ranch, the American manager told him, "Here, Mr. Varona, we have a guest room for you, and it's air-conditioned." Varona, with a newfound revolutionary fervor, said he would rather sleep in the barn with his men.

After sundown, he tried to contact the army captain who was supposed to join with him in the uprising. That proved impossible, and a short time later he suffered another setback when a local leader of the 26th of July appeared at the barn with a few badly armed men.

"We want your weapons," the rebel told him, his face grim.

"Well," Varona replied with what he hoped was a pleasant smile, "obviously you can't have them." He appealed for a show of anti-Batista unity, but the rebel only repeated his demand. Varona decided he didn't want to cause trouble on his first night back in Cuba. "Listen," he said, "we have plenty of weapons. We'll give you ten rifles and ammo. We remain friends, and you leave us alone."

The rebels took the guns and left.

On the first day of his mission, one of Washington's main hopes for creating a "third front" had managed to leave half his supporters in Florida, see his plane rendered useless and hand over weapons to the group against which he was trying to compete.

Falling exhausted onto a pile of straw in the barn, Varona decided that undoubtedly the next day would be better.

Early that evening, another of the CIA's hopes, Justo Carrillo, entered a room in a small Miami Beach hotel. Rafael ("Felo") Fernández, a thin man with brown hair and thick glasses, greeted him with an embrace.

Fernández was the owner of a small discount store in northern Las Villas Province and a member of Carrillo's small Montecristi Movement. He had flown in especially to detail the rebel advances in central Cuba.

Sitting in a chair as Fernández paced, Carrillo listened patiently to the shopkeeper list the towns that the 26th of July had taken. "I think that whatever you are working on," Fernández concluded, "you should go ahead and do it now. If you wait any longer, it will have been a waste of time. Fidel will have come in, and all the power will be his."

Carrillo nodded. Months before he had told Fernández vaguely about his hope of freeing Colonel Barquín and the Puros from the Isle of Pines, but nothing specific. Now, he peered at the shopkeeper as he considered the situation. Fernández was an eager member of the Movement, but he had no experience whatsoever in clandestine activities. That was not advantageous for what Carrillo needed to have done, but at least it meant that the man was not listed on police suspect lists. He could move in and out of the country without arousing any special interest.

After taking a deep breath, Carrillo described his hope of bribing the warden and the need for someone who could make the trip to the Isle of Pines.

Fernández seemed awed at the concept, but he said quickly, "Sure, I'll be glad to do anything."

Carrillo told him the warden was Colonel Joaquín Casillas Lumpuy. "I don't know if he will go for this. Some of the things I have heard about him tell me he could well be incorruptible. But in any case, I am sure he would not arrest you." He gave Fernández several names of friends he could contact in Havana if he needed help.

They agreed he should leave for Havana the next day.

About 9:00 P.M., General Cantillo's twin-engine C-47 landed at the Camp Columbia airfield. As the plane taxied toward the spotlights marking the air force headquarters, he felt exhausted, but he knew the most difficult task of the day still lay ahead.

When an aide opened the door, he saw a cluster of officers, including two of the Tabernilla sons, waiting for him. But after the ground crew wheeled the staircase into place, the first man who bounded up the stairs was Colonel Martínez Suárez, looking even more nervous and pale than he had that afternoon in Santiago. For the first time, Cantillo wondered if he were not going to be arrested after all.

"You can leave here," the colonel whispered, "only with four officers." He nodded to a group of Batista's personal bodyguards. "Batista needs to see you, and you can speak with no one else. Definitely not General Tabernilla."

Cantillo nodded grimly and followed Martínez Suárez through the crowd.

Colonel Winsy Tabernilla, chief of the air force, waved at him. "General, how are you? Would you like to see my father? He was asking about you."

"OK," Cantillo mumbled, telling yet another lie in a day that seemed to be the longest in his life. "But I need to change my clothes." Then he stepped into the waiting Oldsmobile.

The trip passed in a blur, and it seemed only seconds had gone by

before the car pulled up in front of the library wing of Batista's country
house at Kuquine. The agreement with Castro now seemed far away and
almost a dream. He guessed he was about to be accused of treason. As a
professional soldier, that would be the most bitter humiliation of all.

An aide opened the door and led him down the corridor, through the
main room with its busts of Lincoln and Martí, past the antique
biography of Napoleon, to the small inner office, where Batista was
sitting behind a simple wooden desk. The president didn't even say hello
as he motioned for him to sit in an upholstered leather chair.

"Cantillo," he began with a controlled fury, "how dared you speak
with Castro without letting me know."

Cantillo felt dizzy. "Mr. President, you *knew* I was going to see
Castro," he said in a voice that sounded more pleading than he
intended. "You had the power to stop me." He repeated the arrange-
ment of the telegram code and said he was only following the orders of
Pancho Tabernilla. *

Batista ignored the mention of the code, but his face reddened at the
sound of Tabernilla's name. He said Old Pancho had committed a
"terrible treason" by ordering the Castro meeting and by talking to the
American ambassador about forming a junta.

"If I stay," he announced, "I would have to imprison Tabernilla and
shoot him."

Cantillo, who had always disliked the Tabernillas anyway, grabbed at
the chance to show his loyalty to Batista. "Well, why don't we do that
right away? Give me the power, and we can do it tonight. We don't
have to show any reason for this, no matter what the American
ambassador might say. We're Cubans, not Americans."

Batista shook his head. "No, let's wait." He wanted to know first
what had happened during the Castro meeting.

Cantillo leaned back in his chair. It seemed that Batista was hinting
that he might stay and fight. In that case, maybe the war was not lost.

Cautiously, he described almost everything that Castro had told him
only twelve hours before: his refusal to accept a junta or even to suggest

* In fact, SIM chief García Baez had also told Batista that Tabernilla was
thinking that Cantillo should meet Castro. In his book *Cuba Betrayed*,
Batista wrote that even an aide had informed him about rumors of the
meeting. Altogether, he had been told three times, and either intentionally or out of indifference, he had been very slow to react. His
surprise and anger here are obviously theatrical.

candidates for a new government, his vow to fight on if there were a coup and his distrust of anything having to do with the American embassy.

Cantillo ended by telling Batista that a cease-fire had been arranged, but it was to end at 3:00 P.M., December 31, when the rebels were going to attack Santiago if the army continued to resist.

That was almost the truth, but Cantillo again had left out one crucial fact—his tentative agreement to join with the rebels in an uprising.

Batista leaned forward at the mention of New Year's Eve, but he switched the conversation back to the military commanders and the lack of loyalty within Camp Columbia. "Cantillo," he said in a low voice, "I am surrounded."

Cantillo thought to himself that it was Batista's own fault, that he had purposely surrounded himself with lackeys, men without professional military skills who could be counted on to be faithful only as long as the corruption money was flowing in; they panicked at the thought of actually fighting. But certainly he could not say that to the president. There was a long silence.

At last, his face still emotionless, Batista said simply, "I am thinking of leaving."

Cantillo tensed as the man who had ruled Cuba for a total of seventeen years started a rambling, vague speech about the bleak outlook for his regime. It was framed with the phrase "in case we have to go," but it seemed to be more than that. Batista confessed he had been considering a number of plans about how he and his closest followers could flee in a mass evacuation without arousing the suspicion that might instantly overthrow his government. One idea was to take his friends to the Isle of Pines and celebrate New Year's Eve there. The island had a large hotel and a good-sized airport that they could use to leave the country. "Perhaps," he said, "that would not attract attention." He asked Cantillo what he thought.

The general, still wondering if Batista were trying to lure him into a trap, was noncommittal. He suggested instead that the president go to Santiago, see the situation and lead the soldiers himself.

"Well, I've been thinking about it," Batista said, but he quickly steered the discussion back to the idea of escaping.

To Cantillo, it was obvious he was worried that he might not be able to use the Aerovías Q planes at Camp Columbia. They, of course, were controlled by the Tabernillas.

Casually, Cantillo mentioned that Playa de Baracoa, just west of Havana, had a landing strip. "It's a new airfield. It hasn't been used. It's only five minutes away from here. It's at sea level, which is ideal for planes. It has everything."

Batista bowed his head in contemplation. "Well, why don't you go look at it? Let me know what you think."

Cantillo agreed.

Then Batista, who had begun the conversation by chastising him, turned to compliments. He said Cantillo was the only man in Cuba who was respected by both the army and the rebels. Someone was going to have to face an enormous responsibility, to try to make the transition of governments a peaceful one. A thousand people had been killed by mobs following the overthrow of the Machado regime and, Batista added, the amount of bloodletting could be even worse this time, unless someone like Cantillo were in charge. Without any "war crimes," as the rebels called them, he could be accepted at least temporarily by the 26th of July, long enough to allow many persons who might otherwise be killed to leave the country.

Cantillo tried to keep his face a blank. Batista had not exactly offered him the leadership of the country, but he certainly was hinting at it. In the present situation, that was a dubious honor, and he felt so exhausted that retirement weighed on his mind more heavily than ever as his own way of escaping. But Batista was appealing to his sense of patriotism and his duty as a soldier to save lives—unless the president wanted to trick him into confessing political ambition. Confused and tired, Cantillo said simply that he had always been loyal to the president and would do whatever his duty was.

Batista nodded. Casually, he asked what Cantillo's travel plans were.

The general stopped to think. Probably, he said, he would return to Santiago the day after tomorrow, December 30. If Castro's threat to attack the city on New Year's Eve proved to be a bluff, as he thought it could be, he might make a quick trip back to Havana that evening, December 31, to celebrate his wedding anniversary with his wife.

Batista considered that for a long moment, then ordered Cantillo to see him on New Year's Eve for a progress report. He said he was no longer certain that the Tabernillas were providing him with honest information on the war; he wanted Cantillo to stop on his way to Santiago at the cities of Camagüey, Bayamo and Holguín, to get a firsthand report from the military commanders.

As Cantillo stood to leave, Batista stressed again the importance of reporting to him on New Year's Eve. And, he added, under no circumstances was Cantillo to talk about either the meeting they had just had or the meeting with Castro. Especially not to Pancho Tabernilla.

Cantillo walked grimly out to the waiting Oldsmobile. Incredibly, within a single day he first had tentatively agreed to a proposal by Fidel Castro and then to the suggestions of Fulgencio Batista. The general who had spent his career trying to please had encountered the two most forceful personalities in Cuba, and he had been swept away by both of them.

As the car sped toward the city, he tried to sort things out. Batista had stated nothing as being absolutely definite. Everything was based on "in case we have to leave." That was Batista's reputation, giving each of his associates a small piece of the puzzle while keeping the grand design to himself. To Cantillo, the president was "acting like a snake, never saying anything directly, but only slithering around the bush."

Still, all Batista's statements pointed to his leaving, and soon. Perhaps on New Year's Eve, when he could gather his closest followers together for a party without arousing undue suspicion. If that were true, Cantillo decided, he could maintain his balancing act, now escalated to an even higher level, for a few more days. He could pass word to Castro that his "friends" at Columbia supported the idea of a joint uprising but needed a few extra days to bring it off. That would give time for Batista and his followers to leave the country, and then the whole mess could be turned over to the politicians. For the army, the war would be over, the bloodshed ended.

Leaning back against the seat, he considered that a good possibility, a way to make everyone at least moderately happy. But if he had to make a choice between one side or the other, there was no doubt where his sympathies lay. His career of twenty-five years, his training, his entire life-style sided with the military men of Camp Columbia, not some bearded young ruffians from the Oriente mountains.

34/ DECEMBER 29: "IT'S A MONSTER!"

Shortly after midnight, Cantillo stepped out of the Oldsmobile and walked toward his Camp Columbia home. An aide of General Pancho Tabernilla was waiting in the shadows of the porch with a message. The joint chief of staff wanted to see him right away. Immeasurably weary from a day of stern confrontations, Cantillo did not want another one, especially with Old Pancho, but there was no way to refuse a request from the commander of the armed forces.

Walking across the darkened parade ground, he climbed the steps of the Estado Mayor. In his third-floor office, Tabernilla was staring at his electrified toy map. As soon as he saw Cantillo, he rushed over to shake his hand and, with uncustomary cordiality, offered him a seat. Cantillo lit a Chesterfield and watched the smoke curl toward the ceiling.

"Well," Tabernilla asked, "did you speak with Castro?"

"I'm sorry," Cantillo said more firmly than he had anything else that day, "but I've received orders from the president not to tell anybody. Including you."

Tabernilla's face soured. "But I am the one who ordered you."

"Yes, I know."

"What kind of ingratitude is this?" Tabernilla ranted about the rebels advancing everywhere, the government crumbling and now even one of his subordinates was refusing to speak with him about the most crucial event of the civil war.

Cantillo stood up, snapped to attention and repeated the order Batista had given him. Then he fell silent, ready for what further abuse Tabernilla wanted to heap upon him. After Castro and Batista, Old Pancho's anger seemed like nothing.

Tabernilla stared at him. His shoulders sagged in defeat. He told Cantillo he was dismissed.

Cantillo left thinking the old man was about to break down and cry. For the first time all day, he felt good.

About 2:00 A.M., workmen from the Narcisa sugar mill drove a yellow D-8 Caterpillar tractor, its exterior oddly modified, through the streets of Yaguajay in Las Villas Province. Its top, front and sides were protected by steel plating three-eighths of an inch thick. On the front were two .30-caliber machine guns and a flamethrower capable of five hundred pounds pressure. Sugar-mill workers had built the contraption, but Comandante Camilo Cienfuegos of Column 2 had given the machine its name: *Dragón Primero*—Dragon One.

The rebels at Yaguajay had become enraged at the bitter resistance Captain Alfredo Abón-Ly was putting up at the cuartel. By this time, they were supposed to have conquered the town and have joined Ché Guevara's forces for the attack on Santa Clara. Instead, Guevara's Column 8, with half the 26th of July forces in the province, was fighting in a city of a hundred thousand, while their half was still enmeshed in this town of six thousand.

Rejecting a frontal attack across the open fields as being suicidal, Column 2 had tried everything else, including all-night gunfire to keep the soldiers awake and constant propaganda speeches, via loudspeakers, most of which were addressed to "the Chinaman," meaning Abón-Ly. Relatives of the Rural Guardsmen had pleaded with their men to give themselves up, as had an army captain who had joined the rebels at Fomento. Local residents even told Captain William Gálvez that "the Chinaman's" mother lived in the town; others said she was a relative. She turned out only to be an acquaintance, but she too walked to the loudspeaker microphones and urged surrender. After that, the rebels had played the national anthem. None of it had done any good—and that's why they had decided to try the Dragón Primero, their version of a homemade tank.

Inside the cuartel, Captain Abón-Ly slouched half-asleep in his office chair. The building stank with the odors of stale sweat, death and feces. The stench of the corpses had become so bad that they had been buried in the central courtyard, but their smell lived on.

He had a few pain-killers left for the wounded, but no blood plasma. His men had eaten nothing except rice, black beans and potatoes for four days. Water was scarce: the well was at the back of the compound, reachable only by a thirty-yard dash across the open rear yard. Already, one soldier had died trying to bring back a bucket. Abón-Ly was certain most of his men preferred surrender to death, but none had argued with him when he stated adamantly that they had a duty to fight on until reinforced or ordered by the regimental headquarters to give up. There were no signs of mutiny, and gradually his men were adjusting to the tension, even learning to half-sleep during the nighttime gunfire.

Abón-Ly himself was drifting into sleep when a guard shouted that something was approaching. Instantly awake, the young army captain ran to the windows. He was ready for the assault he had been expecting for days.

From the distance came a rumbling that sounded like a truck engine. The moon was not out, and all he could see was a vague hulk coming down the road from town. His soldiers, rifles in hands, gathered behind him, trying to get a look.

Suddenly, a long tongue of fire spewed from the hulk.

"*Monstruo, monstruo,*" several teenage soldiers screamed. "It's a monster. The monster is coming."

"No, no." Abón-Ly tried to calm them. "It's a machine."

"A monster," one teenager repeated. Several nodded their heads in agreement.

"I don't believe in monsters," Abón-Ly said firmly. "It's just a machine. Listen to the engine." He ordered a soldier to get the cuartel's bazooka. There was only one shell left, and he figured this was the time to use it.

An enlisted man loaded the bazooka and slipped into a corner of the sheltered front porch. The *dragón* was creeping forward. It was so dark that only when flames spewed out could Abón-Ly see the steel plates covering the machine.

He ordered the gunner to wait until he gave the order to shoot. With only one projectile, they dared not waste it on a long shot.

At last, when the *dragón* was about thirty feet away, Abón-Ly drew himself up to attention, one hand behind his back as if he were directing a firing squad, and shouted as loud as he could, "Fire!"

Roaring out of the bazooka, the shell smashed against the front steel plating of the *dragón*, creating a two-foot crater about two feet from the right edge and six inches below the top. Then the shell clanked to the ground. It had not exploded.

Abón-Ly cursed. Once again, the ancient ammunition the army had given him proved worthless, but he could hear the men inside the tractor yelling frantically, "Retreat, retreat." In the trenches behind them, rebels shouted, "Come back, come back."

For a moment, Abón-Ly felt like a medieval knight who had killed a fire-breathing monster. His soldiers were even more enthusiastic as they let loose with a deafening volley of gunfire against the machine. It seemed unable to move.

"Let's pursue it," some of the younger soldiers shouted. "We can get it."

Abón-Ly considered that for only a moment. "No, that would be dangerous. You could be trapped out there. Maybe that's what they want."

In the rebel trench, Comandante Cienfuegos feared that the men in the Caterpillar had been wounded. Sliding out of his foxhole, he crawled through the barrage of bullets, but when he arrived at the machine, he found the men unhurt. They had simply panicked and stalled the engine. Within seconds, they restarted it, and the fiery *dragón*, dented but not slain, retreated to safety.

That morning in Washington, William Wieland sat in his office, staring at a two-page State Department report marked Security Classification: Secret. He had seen so many versions of the document that he was having a hard time concentrating.

Outside, a cold rain, driven steady wind from the north, was pounding the bare tree limbs on Virginia Avenue. Only two days before, the *Washington Post* had finally carried a front-page story about Cuba: "Cuban Rebels Claim Central Province." But over coffee breaks in the State cafeteria, more people were talking about what had happened yesterday: the first championship of the National Football League to go into overtime, settled finally by Alan ("The Horse") Ameche making a one-yard plunge to give the Baltimore Colts a victory over the New York Giants. Some were saying it was the greatest game in pro football history.

With difficulty, Wieland focused on the report. It was entitled "Opportunity to Present U.S. Policy Regarding Cuba to Fidel Castro." The idea had started two weeks before, when Father Bez Chabebe, a priest with close rebel connections, had suggested to Park Wollam, the Santiago consul, that an American emissary should go talk to Castro, to ease U.S.–rebel tensions. The priest had not made it clear whether the idea was only his, or the Rotary Club liberals', or Castro's.

The first draft of the State Department's response had been written by an assistant on the Cuban desk. It had been finished five days before, but then had come countless rewrites and revisions.

The director of Caribbean and Mexican affairs knew the final document was a convoluted exercise in bureaucratic muddling, but he thought it was the best that could be cleared through the hierarchy. In essence, the State Department was refusing to send an emissary to speak with Castro directly, but it wanted Wollam to communicate Washington's attitudes to the priest, so he could transmit them to Castro, *without* making it appear that State was trying to send a message to Castro. "Any statement which could be interpreted by Father Bez Chebebe as constituting recognition of his status as an emissary to Castro or that the United States is endeavoring to transmit a message to Castro should be strictly avoided."

As usual, State repeated its worries about Communism by stating it had "received many reports of communist influence and infiltration in the 26th of July Movement but has made no judgment that these reports are true; . . . they do, however, concern the United States as world experience has shown the communists to be adept at infiltrating revolutionary movements and in masking behind the spirit of nationalism."

Still, Washington was worried that "Castro, because of his isolation, and in part because of distorted and colored reports from his representatives in the United States, does not fully appreciate the fact that the United States has uncompromisingly followed a policy of non-intervention in Cuban political affairs and has never publically criticized Castro or his movement on political or personal grounds."

Wieland understood perfectly that the document was an exercise in double-talk. While it was true that Washington had not attacked Castro publicly, the dispatch, of course, failed to mention State's support of a "third force" to keep the rebel leader out of power. But that did not unduly bother Wieland's conscience. Not even Ambassador Smith had been told of the "third force" concept.

At the King Ranch, former prime minister Tony Varona had a quick breakfast of *café con leche* and bread, then decided to contact Captain Castellón, the army officer who was supposed to join with Varona's group and take over Camagüey Province, thus blocking Castro's way to Havana. Using the ranch-house telephone, he tried to reach the captain at the cuartel. He wasn't there. Varona made other calls; all ended in failure.

Desperate to get something accomplished on his first day back in Cuba, he telephoned a 26th of July man he knew in Camagüey City. He explained he was looking for Castellón, but didn't say why.

Immediately, the man became suspicious. He said he didn't know where the captain was, but he wondered why Varona wanted to find him. Varona tried to pass off some vague excuse, but the rebel sympathizer didn't believe it. It was odd, he said, that Varona would show up in Cuba after months in exile for no apparent reason.

"I suggest," the 26th of July man added, "that you join forces with Comandante Mora." He was the rebel leader in the province. "He's down in Santa Cruz del Sur. Between the two of you, you could establish a combined front."

Varona hesitated. That was really the last thing he wanted to do. "Well," he said cautiously, "I don't want to go all that way. I'll drive to Camagüey City and call you again."

In the living room of his Camp Columbia house, General Cantillo sat down in his rocking chair and motioned for Major Roberto Collado to take a seat facing him. Collado had been his devoted aide-de-camp for six years, even passing up promotions to stay with "the boss," and he was the only person Cantillo could trust for what he needed done.

Telling his aide as little as he could, he explained that Colonel Rego Rubido and Commodore Carnero in Santiago might be a little "nervous." Collado was to fly to Oriente and tell them that the plan they had talked about was being delayed a little. "Tell them to be careful," Cantillo ordered. "Tell them not to do anything until I get there." Rego was to pass the message along to the man who had conceived it in the first place.

The general added that it was important that Collado not use a military plane for the trip. There was a Cubana flight leaving from the international airport early that afternoon, and he should go on that. Absolutely *no one*, inside Columbia or out, was to be told about the message or the trip. Collado, knowing better than to ask any questions, simply nodded.

As he left, Cantillo called his wife into the living room. He apologized for having been so busy lately and suggested that, as a bit of family relaxation, they take their daughter for a ride.

Without explaining why, he led them to his personal car, a 1956 black Oldsmobile. The vehicle had less than four thousand miles on it, because he usually used his official army car, but this was one time he didn't want any military chauffeur seeing what he was doing.

Joking with his daughter, he drove the family through the western suburbs of Havana, ending with the village of Baracoa.

"Well, we're near that new airport," he said casually. "Let's take a look." Since he was a licensed pilot, he was sure his wife would not find that strange. There was no need, he decided, to involve her in his personal problems.

The airstrip was a long one, made of concrete. There were no buildings around, no watchmen. Large stones were scattered on the runway, probably placed there so that rebel gunrunners from Miami couldn't use it. They looked as though they could be easily removed.

Finding a straight line between the rocks, Cantillo drove down the runway while keeping an eye on the odometer. The strip was sufficiently long for a DC-4 to take off with plenty of room to spare.

Cantillo drove back to his house, where he summoned Colonel Martínez Suárez. He asked him to do two things: get a crew of enlisted men to remove the stones from the Baracoa airstrip and tell Batista that the runway looked fine to him.

Dressed in her olive-green uniform, Asela de los Santos paced on the linoleum floor of the Lyceo, a social club in Palma Soriano. The director of education for the rebels' Second Front watched as the last of the area's teachers filled up the folding chairs. She saw approvingly that a number of parents had decided to attend as well. For more than a day, the citizens of this city, only thirty miles from Santiago, had been celebrating their "liberation" by the rebels. It was her job to help restore normalcy.

Waiting till the group was quiet, she introduced herself. That brought a wild burst of applause, and she had to stop until again there was silence. Then she announced that classes were to resume as soon as possible, well before the end of the Christmas vacation.

De Los Santos stopped, expecting room-filling moans of complaint, but there were none.

The reason, she said, was that the rebels wanted to get the city back to normal as soon as possible, to make the area a genuine part of *territorio libre,* not simply a plot of land that had been conquered during a war.

Everyone agreed, and for more than an hour, she worked out the details with the teachers.

When the meeting was over, De Los Santos walked toward the center of town. Everywhere she looked, there was the atmosphere of a festival. On the crowded sidewalks, young bearded rebels chatted with admiring girls. Through the doorways of the houses, which opened directly onto the street, she could see other rebels, emaciated from months of mountain life, sitting at dinner tables staring in awe at the mounds of food that the women were bringing from the kitchens. Food here, as everywhere in Oriente, had become scarce, but the townspeople were finding all they could to feed the new victors.

At the town square, a small crowd had gathered, watching a white convertible go round and round the square. She spotted a familiar face in the passenger seat: Errol Flynn, the actor, whose deeply tanned face and pencil mustache made him look exactly the way he did in the movies. He was holding a bottle of liquor in one hand and waving to the people with the other. Some rebels, sitting in a sidewalk café, smiled at his obviously drunken antics.

From a passerby, De Los Santos learned that Flynn had been sailing his yacht through the Caribbean when he heard of the rebel victories and decided to join the celebration. She walked away, shaking her head, thinking that in movie-hungry Cuba, Flynn would ordinarily have drawn enormous crowds, but now, in the euphoria of triumph, he was only one small part of the merriment.

Thirty miles away, at the Moncada garrison, Colonel José Rego Rubido was slumped at the desk chair in his third-floor office overlooking the parade ground. He had felt a great sense of relief when Cantillo had told him about reaching an agreement with Castro, and because the war was ending, he wanted to make certain that no more blood was shed, that his own record as an anti-Batista man remained impeccable.

But that morning, he had awakened to find the four 75-millimeter howitzers missing from their usual spot on the parade ground. With a quick phone call, he learned that Lieutenant Colonel José Salas Cañizares, the chief of operations, had taken the cannons in an armored caravan to Santiago Bay's eastern shore, where the rebels were known to be hiding. He was planning to bomb the area around the Texaco refinery and drive the rebels out.

In an instant, Rego had imagined the Texaco tanks exploding, dozens of civilians and rebels being killed, and Castro, angered over breaking the truce, holding Rego himself responsible for "war crimes." Rego had managed to get Salas Cañizares to return to the Moncada only by threatening to throw him in jail if he refused. The man was a diehard Batistiano, one of the most effective, and brutal, commanders in the fight against the rebels.

Knowing he couldn't explain the secret agreement worked out with Castro, Rego was worrying what to tell the officer when he heard the convoy's trucks rumbling through the gates. Moments later, heavy footsteps echoed through the stairwell, and Salas Cañizares's tall, stout form appeared in the doorway. Sweating heavily in his battle fatigues, his face dark with anger, he marched over to the desk and slammed his fist down, sending papers flying.

"Listen, Rego," he bellowed, "you are giving me a hard time." He ranted how he had been about to launch a successful attack, and he could imagine no reason in the world why he shouldn't be allowed to fight the enemy.

Fearing this could be the start of an insurrection, Rego stood up and pulled out his .45-caliber automatic. He pointed it directly at the officer's head.

"Colonel Cañizares, come to attention. You are talking to the chief of the regiment."

Shocked, Salas Cañizares put his hands up. His face was ashen.

"Colonel Cañizares, this is not a posture of full attention, unless the military manual has changed since I last read it. Assume full attention, now."

The colonel dropped his hands and came to attention. For almost a minute, the two stood mute, facing each other, Rego still pointing his pistol at his subordinate's head. Thick drops of sweat ran down Salas Cañizares's face.

At last, Rego put his pistol back in his holster. "Colonel, you may leave. And be careful from now on to obey my orders any time I am in command here. If my command lasts five minutes, you will have to obey me during those five minutes."

"Yes, sir, Colonel." He started to leave, then turned back. "I want you to know, Colonel, that I will report to the chief of staff that you have held that gun to my head for over a minute."

"And," Rego shot back, "in the final paragraph of your report, you may tell the chief of staff that if you hadn't come to full attention, at this moment you'd be very dead." Then, lowering his voice, he added, "We are living through extremely difficult moments in the life of our country and of our army. You can't disobey me, and no one can disobey me. Is that clear?"

"Yes, sir."

"Then you may leave."

As Salas Cañizares walked out the door, Rego slumped back in his chair and wondered what kind of trouble the colonel could make for him at the Estado Mayor. He was still worrying when a telephone call came through. Major Collado, Cantillo's aide, had just arrived and wanted Rego to meet him at the airport.

Using the general's staff Oldsmobile, Rego picked up Commodore Carnero at the navy base and raced to the airport. Cantillo's aide was pacing on the concrete apron, about twenty feet from the one-story terminal.

Crisply, Collado repeated Cantillo's message about the delay and told them, "Don't be nervous."

But the message made the two Santiago officers very nervous indeed. They barraged the aide with questions. What had caused the delay? What was happening in Havana? How was Cantillo feeling? How long was the delay going to be?"

The aide simply repeated, "Cantillo wants you to know that you shouldn't worry." Before the officers could say anything more, a loudspeaker announced that the Cubana flight was returning to Havana. Collado waved a swift farewell and ran toward the plane.

Colonel Rego stood watching him in amazement. In one way, he felt relieved, because it meant he wouldn't have to be the one to hand over the historic Moncada garrison to the rebels. But still, it was he who was stuck in Santiago now, far from the safety of Havana, and it was he who might have to defend the city against the rebels.

Late that afternoon at Camp Columbia, Brigadier General Silito Tabernilla, still carrying the list of passengers in his pocket, walked into the living room of General Cantillo's home. He handed Cantillo a thick brown envelope, which he said Batista had just given him. Inside were 15,000 pesos, 5000 each for the regimental commanders at Camagüey, Holguín and Bayamo. Cantillo was to hand out the money to them the next day on his trip back to Santiago. It was being given "in case we have to leave."

Cantillo stared at the envelope. He realized Batista was making the payments to soothe his conscience because he was planning to abandon them, but the amount of money was small, considering that the commanders were risking their lives to defend his regime.

Feeling sad and rather philosophical, Cantillo placed the envelope on the table. "You know, Silito," he said, "every time I read a book about a great man, I skip the last few pages, because they always finish badly."

In Santa Clara, the fighting was raging block by block, rebels sneaking from one doorway to another as the Sherman M-8 light tanks rumbled through the streets. Sometimes when a tank appeared, a house door suddenly opened, and a resident motioned for the rebels to hide inside.

Column 8 had moved into the city overnight, following Ché Guevara's orders to go to the most populated parts of town, so that the tanks would have a hard time shooting the rebels without hitting civilians. Townspeople were helping, hurling Molotov cocktails at the tanks and blocking streets with overturned cars while air force B-26s and Sea Fury fighters bombed and strafed.

In the southern part of the city, near the bitter siege at the Squadron 31 cuartel, the rebels set up a hospital in a clinic. There, Leonardo Salmerón Hernández, a medical lab technician in his mid-forties, worked almost without stop, hopping from cot to cot to tend the wounded. A rebel lieutenant died before anyone could treat him, and when an army sergeant was brought in, he was put on a chair because it was all that was available. A few minutes later, a nurse passed the sergeant and saw he had slumped down in the chair. "He's dead," she said. "Let's move him out." Salmerón was about to agree when the sergeant lifted his head and said groggily, "No, I am only wounded." Before Salmerón had a chance to see to his wounds, a bleeding gray-haired woman carried in a bloody one-year-old boy. In tears, the woman described how she had been holding her grandson on her lap as she sat on a flat roof watching the air force bombardment. A fighter plane had swooped down, and a large-caliber bullet had ripped open his stomach. He was dead.

Gradually, as the day wore on, the army and police retreated to strongholds at the police station, provincial palace, justice building and the Leoncio Vidal regimental garrison. In early afternoon, the armored train tried to retreat into the city, but the rebels had used two Caterpillar tractors to rip out the tracks in the center of the town, where the rails crossed the gray-brick Camajuaní highway between a gas station and a coffee shop. The train did not slow down as it hit the twisted tracks, and several cars toppled over, a freight car jamming itself against the overturned locomotive. The rebels, led by a twenty-year-old captain, took over three cars and captured forty-one soldiers immediately. After a short truce, the train surrendered, and the rebels found themselves in possession of mind-boggling quantities of machine guns, antiaircraft guns and ammunition, much of it still in its original factory crates marked U.S. Army. For the first time in the two-year war, the rebels had more weapons than they could readily use.

Rogelio Acevedo, the seventeen-year-old rebel captain, was astounded when he heard how easily the train was captured, but he had problems of his own. At first, he and his thirty-man platoon had been assigned to besiege the police station, a large corner building overlooking a church and park, where about three hundred policemen were holding out. Acevedo managed to keep the policemen pinned down, but before long he was replaced by a cocky young captain who called himself El Vaquerito, the Little Cowboy, and his Suicide Squad, named after a Western movie.

Leading his platoon across town toward his next assignment at the courthouse, Acevedo discovered that unseen army snipers, apparently operating from considerable height, had a clear view of most intersections around the Central Park. At each corner, Acevedo's men had to stop. The teenager dashed across the open area first, his men following one by one. He thought he was being a courageous leader until he realized that it wasn't until the third or fourth man across that the snipers spotted them and made the shots close enough to be worrisome.

At one corner, Acevedo peeked around the edge of a building to see where the shots were coming from. It was the rooftop of the tallest building in town, the Gran Hotel.

On the sixth floor of the hotel, young Guillermo Domenech watched the chef cooking a stew on a portable gas burner. He was mixing in cans of soup, potatoes, cheese, vegetables and the last of the meat. Guests hovered around him, and some of the women gave advice as he sprinkled in the seasonings.

The SIM men had moved up to the rooftop apartment, above the tenth-floor restaurant, and ordered the guests to stay on floors six, seven and eight. The manager had pleaded with the fat sergeant to allow at least the women and children to leave, but he refused saying, "You are safer here." The guests weren't so certain of that, for the sound of bullets ricocheting off the building indicated that the rebels were firing back at the snipers. When the manager ordered mattresses propped against the windows, the hotel began to take on the look of a besieged garrison. There was no water on the upper floors, and the electricity had been off for almost twenty-four hours. Only the children still thought it was a game.

When it grew dark, the guests ate by candlelight on the corridor floors. No one objected to the makeshift stew, but afterward the salesmen bemoaned the lack of cigars for their poker game.

"Help yourselves," the manager said, pointing up to the tenth floor. He added that they were welcome to all the liquor they could carry back.

The men discussed it. Since the SIM soldiers were on the roof, there didn't seem to be much danger. Domenech, along with a dapper young salesman of Spanish sausage and two others, volunteered to form a raiding party.

Feeling their way up the dark stairwells, they found the restaurant lit only by the ghostly bluish glow of the moon. Quickly, they stuffed cigars into their pockets and picked up cases of Scotch, rum, wines, gin, vodka and soft drinks. Several cases of beer were left behind in the refrigerator. They were warm.

Their return was greeted with a round of applause. The men poured themselves stiff drinks, using water glasses from the bathrooms, and moved to one end of the corridor, where they set up their card game on the floor.

Domenech watched for a while, then walked into an empty room.

Peeling back a mattress, he saw through a window that rebels were attacking the stone-front provincial palace on the other side of the Central Park. Occasionally, there were bright flares, Molotov cocktails being tossed toward a window; they seemed to do little damage. As he watched, he wondered how long it would take the rebels to figure out a way to attack the SIM men on the rooftop. That led to another thought. Maybe the rebels didn't know civilians were in the hotel.

35/DECEMBER 30: "A REGRETTABLE ERROR"

That morning, telephones started ringing in Havana almost as soon as people woke up. Everyone had *bolas* to pass along. The more reputable talked about what they had heard on Florida radio stations concerning the civil war, especially the battle in Santa Clara. After a few intermediaries, reports of a hundred deaths escalated to a thousand and even to ten thousand. Others repeated the rumors they had received from "good ink," meaning journalists or any inside source. The wildest stories were always based on "good ink."

Bolas, plentiful even in normal times, had become an avalanche. Many knew that the island's leading businessmen, particularly the sugar-mill owners, were pleading for Batista to leave. Rumors of coups d'etat were so numerous that almost every army officer above the rank of major was considered a possible conspirator. The comings and goings at the U.S. embassy aroused special interest, and word spread quickly that high government officials were seen entering the consular section, obviously to get visas. Via radio, people heard that Florida bankers were receiving huge deposits in Cuban pesos.

Every traditional indication, based on decades of Latin-American history, pointed to the imminent downfall of the government, and knowledgeable Cubans searched everywhere for a sign, a telling detail that would reveal exactly when and how Batista was going to leave—or be overthrown.

But when the people of Havana turned to their newspapers that morning, they found no signs of any of this, except perhaps that the government propaganda seemed to be shriller than ever. *El Tiempo,* the newspaper of Senator Rolando Masferrer, had a banner headline proclaiming: "Rebels Suffer Violent Beating." The story boasted that "groups under the foreign Communist Ché Guevara have run away . . . The Fidel-Communists are now hiding in the caves of Escambray with few weapons and no ammunition."

That singular report was matched by one in Miami, where exiles opened their copies of *The Miami Herald* to find an article by Bert Collier, an editorial writer who had just returned from a brief visit to Havana:

"The famous Tropicana casino and nightclub had one of the largest crowds of its history Saturday night. The play was good at the Havana Hilton . . . It was good at the Capri, where George Raft personally greets the guests. They tell you at these places that most of the guests are Cuban—and Cubans wouldn't be out if they expected trouble."

Cubans were so hungry for tourist dollars, Collier wrote, that "you get the impression that even a battle might be postponed for a party of well-heeled American visitors."

In a small house near Maffo, Fidel Castro paced angrily across the living room, which had been serving as a rebel outpost to fire upon the army's fortified coffee warehouses. Occasionally, his black boots crunched some of the dozens of spent cartridges that littered the floor. It seemed to him inconceivable that after a siege of twenty days the soldiers were still holding out. Another truce had been called, and the army commander was expected at any moment. Castro was determined that this was going to be their last discussion.

As his brother Raúl and other *comandantes* listened, he raged that Maffo was "like a tumor," delaying his forces. It was the only army outpost left on the eighty-mile stretch of the Central Highway between the regiments in Bayamo and Santiago. He was still counting on General Cantillo to join the revolutionary cause, but that didn't mean he was waiting for the general to act. If the rebels were to fight on, he desperately needed the weapons of the Maffo soldiers.

If the soldiers didn't surrender that day, he said, he was going to "fry" them in their warehouses. His men had confiscated a fire department pump truck in Palma Soriano, and if all else failed, he was going to fill the truck with gasoline, have it driven as close to the warehouses as possible, spray the fortifications and throw in a torch.

Castro barely looked up when the army officer, his uniform dirty and sweat-soaked, entered the room.

"You know," the rebel leader said as the officer stood stiffly at attention, "we have pushed back all the reinforcements. We have taken all the positions around Santiago, which is under siege. And you have no water."

The officer showed a small grin. "I have plenty of water," he said firmly. "We opened a well."

Castro knew that was true. He stared at the army man for a moment, then decided to repeat what some prisoners had told him. "You only have food for three days, or two days. And most of that is bananas."

"No," the officer answered, "I have plenty of food."

Castro's temper was near the breaking point. "Well, we have turned back attempts to reinforce you. You're just a little island in a rebel sea. Let's say you have food for a week. When it runs out, what are you going to do?" He walked over to the man, peering into his eyes.

"Well, then I'll surrender." The man took a step backward.

"No!" Castro bellowed. "At that point you will commit suicide. Because if you know you are lost—let's say you have food for fifteen days, but you know you are lost. So by refusing to surrender now, you are making men lose their lives for no reason. Later, you will not be able to surrender. We won't give you a chance to surrender."

The officer's face turned ashen. He said he would have to discuss this ultimatum with his men.

As he walked out the door, an aide came in to tell Castro that two priests were waiting to see him.

Anticipating a message from Cantillo, he asked for them to be shown in immediately. He recognized Father Guzmán, who had brought the general's original message, but this time it was the other Jesuit, Father Félix Feliz who handed him the note. Feliz, blushing at his first contact with the rebel leader, said, "This is from General Cantillo. Everything is going fine."

Castro started to smile as he ripped open the envelope, but his face clouded when he read the message. "The agreement previously arranged is temporarily suspended. I will be in touch with you as soon as I can."

"That son of a bitch," Castro shouted. "That son of a bitch." He threw the note on the floor and stomped it with his boot. "He has betrayed me. I tell you, he has betrayed me." He raged and paced for several minutes. When he calmed down, he sat at a small table and pulled the notebook from his shirt pocket. After scribbling a brief message, he handed it to the priest.

"I tell you," he said to Father Feliz, who was now looking nervous and uncertain, "the only solution is unconditional surrender. Right away. Otherwise, we will march on Santiago."

The priests hurried away with the message. A short time later, the army men in the warehouses surrendered. One hundred seventeen soldiers walked out, hands above their heads. Inside were 129 weapons and 55,000 rounds of ammunition. Now, Castro was ready to launch an attack on Santiago.

That afternoon, in the American consulate in Santiago, Park Wollam sat in his black upholstered chair as he encoded a telegram to Washington. After days of agonizing about an evacuation of Americans, he had decided he had to act, no matter what Ambassador Smith thought. Rumors of an imminent rebel attack on the city were too persistent to ignore.

With the economy that comes from having to encode one's own words by hand, Wollam wrote: "Request put in effect warning phase emergency plans for Santiago in view possibility attack on city or its complete isolation. Americans could be endangered by military actions both sides. . . . Phase should include official warning by Department and embassy against all but most urgent travel this area until situation clarified. Request permission advise Americans they should prepare leave or face consequences. . . . Evacuation would be most difficult after any action begins. . . . Advise soonest."

At Yaguajay, Captain Alfredo Abón-Ly stood beside the window on the cuartel's front porch as he listened to the unending cacophony of rebels shouting over their loudspeakers, located several hundred yards away.

"Chinaman, give up."

"Chinaman, be a patriot. Do what is best for your country."

"Chinaman, do not hinder the revolution."

To Abón-Ly, the words had become a sea of noise, no different from the sporadic gunfire. Numbed by lack of sleep, his men now were reduced to one small meal a day. Ammunition was running low, and the possibility of reinforcements seemed almost nil. The rebels were boasting that they had frightened off a navy frigate sent to the north coast to rescue his soldiers, and he believed it, because he knew the army had worked out such a plan some days before. Worse, Radio Rebelde was claiming that the rebels were attacking the city of Santa Clara, and if that were true, it was highly unlikely that the regiment there would be able to send him any support. The only aid he had received had come from two Sea Fury fighter planes, which had strafed the rebel positions for a few minutes and then disappeared.

While he was trying to decide what to do, a guard shouted from the cuartel's rear yard. Running to investigate, he saw a bizarre sight: a long train of freight cars, camouflaged with branches and leaves, was coming down a set of tracks that ran directly into the rear wall of the cuartel. They were being pushed from behind by two sugar-mill locomotives.

Cursing, he ordered a squad to kneel behind the thigh-high wall and take aim at the lead cars. He had no idea why the tracks were even there; maybe some time long ago trains had supplied the cuartel directly.

Were the cars loaded with rebels? He couldn't tell, but as the train approached, he looked more carefully at the lead car, which had an open top. Underneath the branches were rocks and scattered among the rocks were clusters of dynamite sticks. A fuse was burning brightly near the top of the pile.

His soldiers saw it as soon as he did. "This is it," a teenager shouted, "it will blow us all up."

"No," Abón-Ly yelled back. "Start shooting." He pointed to the burning fuse, and his men fired off a desperate volley.

The train rumbled on. When the lead car was only a few yards away, Abón-Ly led a dash back to the protection of the cuartel.

The lead car banged against the wall with a crunching thud. The army captain, hands over his ears, waited for the explosion. Nothing happened. The silence was maddening.

Finally, after a wait that seemed like hours, he walked up to the car, which had partially collapsed the wall. The dynamite and rocks were intact. The fuse had gone out. It looked as though it had been severed. Apparently, Abón-Ly decided, a lucky bullet had snuffed out the fuse. *

* As incredible as this seems, the rebels' Captain William Gálvez believes it too. Of course, it is possible the fuse went out of its own accord.

He was still contemplating his good fortune when the rebels pulled the train back. Powerless, he watched the freight cars recede. A few minutes later, the train again rumbled toward the cuartel, its lead car this time filled with an enormous wood bonfire. The car crashed against the wall, sending more shards of concrete flying, but the fire burned fiercely only inside the car. It didn't spread to the cuartel.

Feeling a small satisfaction, Abón-Ly walked back to his office. While only the large regiments were still resisting elsewhere in the province, his tiny cuartel continued to hold out.

In Havana, shopkeeper Felo Fernández met at a relative's house with other members of the small Montecristi Movement. As soon as he outlined the plan to bribe the warden at the Isle of Pines, he learned what Justo Carrillo in Miami had not known: the warden had just been transferred to Santa Clara, where he was the new provincial army commander.

Not knowing who the new warden was or whether he would be amenable to a bribe, Fernández worried that he might be arrested as soon as he made the proposal. With no experience in clandestine activities, the whole plan seemed too tricky to carry any further.

Thus, Fernández abandoned the idea, and he didn't even bother to notify Carrillo because he feared that the phone lines to Miami might be wiretapped. Without ever really getting started, one of Washington's main hopes had collapsed.

In Camagüey Province, another of the State Department's dreams for a "third force," Tony Varona, spent a frustrating day trying to find the army captain who was supposed to join with him in an uprising. Perhaps, the former prime minister decided, the officer just didn't want to go through with the idea—another case of an army man being all talk and no action.

Varona was close to panic. The regime could collapse at any moment, and the 26th of July had become far more popular than he had imagined during his months of exile. Hoping to salvage something, he concluded his best chance was to see if he could form an alliance with the rebel *comandante* in the area.

By telephone, his 26th of July contact in Camagüey City told him, "Comandante Mora is expecting you at Central Francisco, near Santa Cruz del Sur."

Varona realized it was too late to leave that day. He would have to meet the commander on the last day of the year.

At 5:05 that afternoon, a National Airlines flight from Havana taxied to its arrival gate at Idlewild International Airport in New York City. On board were two of Batista's sons, Carlos Manuel, age eight, and Roberto Francisco, age ten. They were accompanied by one of their father's friends, governesses and bodyguards.

Somehow, word of their trip had reached New York even before they landed, and as they walked into the terminal, a crowd of Cuban exiles started chanting revolutionary slogans and waving placards saying LIBERTAD O MUERTE—Liberty or Death. Port Authority guards arrested four men and a fifteen-year-old boy for creating a disturbance.

After a family spokesman told reporters that the boys were simply in town for the holidays, the entourage left in two limousines for the Waldorf Towers, where the boys were put in a suite often used by the Duke and Duchess of Windsor.

Ché Guevara was pacing angrily over the tile floor of a Santa Clara clinic. In front of him on a hospital bed was the motionless body of Roberto Rodríguez, the cocky young captain who liked to call himself El Vaquerito, the Little Cowboy. A small trickle of blood had clotted directly below the bullet wound in his forehead. He had been shot leading his Suicide Squad over rooftops, trying to get closer to the police station.

Leaning over the body, Dr. Oscar Fernández Mell felt for a pulse. There was a faint one, but with a shot like that, the boy's brain was already technically dead.

"Well?" Guevara asked anxiously.

"He's still breathing," the doctor said, "but he will not recover."

Guevara cursed, then added, "They have killed me a hundred men."

Not far away, Captain Rogelio Acevedo, the seventeen-year-old who had been replaced by El Vaquerito at the police station, crouched below a schoolhouse window, only his eyes and forehead visible above the windowsill. On one side, his men had the courthouse under siege, on the other, the jail. But his attention was focused straight ahead, at an intersection blocked by two overturned buses. Several hundred yards beyond, a tank was rumbling down the street.

About a half block from the corner, it stopped and fired a shell into the first bus, apparently trying to demolish the barricade so that it could break through. The bus heaved, dust and bits of metal flying into the air, but it was still intact.

At that moment came the counterattack. Civilian supporters on the rooftops hurled down Molotov cocktails, which burst with a splash of flame on the tank's turret, charring the olive-green paint but nothing else. As the smoke drifted away, a rebel youth burst out of a door and tossed a recently acquired grenade under the tank. Nothing happened.

While Acevedo groaned, the tank swung its turret from side to side, like an angry rhino trying to find its tiny tormentors. Then it backed up and disappeared around a corner.

Acevedo ran outside to see what had happened to the grenade. He found it on the brick street, looking exactly as it had when it was pulled from a crate at the armored train. Apparently no one had told the youth that he had to pull the pin before throwing it.

A few blocks away, Guillermo Domenech prowled the sixth-floor corridor of the Gran Hotel with an open bottle of Scotch in his hand. Most of the guests, women as well as men, had started drinking in early afternoon, and they sat in the corridors, backs against the walls, in a quiet stupor. The only sounds were the occasional curses and triumphant shouts from the poker players at the end of the hall.

The constant sound of gunfire had made the tension almost unbearable. A gray-haired woman, the only occupant on the eighth floor, had been found screaming hysterically. Domenech helped move her to the floor below, where he discovered another isolated guest, a middle-aged man with thinning black hair who paced nervously through the corridor and wanted to talk to no one. When Domenech had the chance, he sneaked into the man's room and learned from papers in his luggage that the fellow was a customs inspector. Looking at his identification photo, Domenech mumbled, "You must have ripped off a lot of immigrants and tourists if you are afraid of revolutionary justice."

Domenech himself, like most of the guests, was more afraid of the immediate danger: fighting breaking out in the hotel. He knew that the hotel's electrician, a secret 26th of July supporter, was talking to the rebels over a telephone in a fifth-floor suite which had a direct outside line, bypassing the disabled switchboard in the lobby. The rebels were trying to find a way to get to the SIM snipers without endangering the civilians, but the electrician thought it impossible because the heaviest pieces of furniture in the stairwell were all on top, jammed so tightly together that they couldn't be budged.

Now, with his mind benumbed by liquor, Domenech had quit trying to imagine a way around the problem as he moved down the corridor to where a group of men were talking in low voices. Each was discussing his hopes and fears. The sausage salesman, who before had boasted only about his frequent sexual conquests, was speaking sentimentally about his fiancée in Camagüey Province: "She is so beautiful. A blonde. As pure as the Virgin Mary. Her skin is so white. . . . I think that after this I will want to get married and settle down."

The salesman turned to Domenech and asked him to tell his own story. Taking another swig of Scotch, the young hotel clerk described how he had decided to get into the hotel business, even though his late father had wanted him to go to work in the family's funeral parlor.

"Well, no wonder you're happy," the salesman kidded him. "Your family will get plenty of business with what's going on. You'll get rich."

The men were still laughing when the hotel electrician ran down the corridor and whispered to Domenech that he needed to see him alone. Slipping into a room and closing the door, the electrician told him that he had just talked to a 26th of July lieutenant. The rebels were now in the hotel lobby.

Three hundred miles away, at the Moncada garrison, General Cantillo wearily removed his black shoes and collapsed on the bed. His ulcer was acting up, and he had already had a long day, stopping at the three regimental headquarters on his way back from Havana to give their commanders 5000 pesos each. He had warned them that Batista was thinking of leaving, and they should make certain they had planes available, so that they themselves could flee at a moment's notice.

His mind swimming with details, Cantillo tried to doze, but almost as soon as his eyes were closed, there was a loud knock at the door.

It was Colonel Rego Rubido, followed by Commodore Carnero. Both of them looked angry and anxious. As Cantillo sat up, Rego thrust a small piece of lined notepaper into his hand. He said it was a note from Castro, which he had just picked up at the Jesuit high school.

Cantillo fumbled for a Chesterfield, lit it and put on his reading glasses. The handwriting was cramped, and he had to struggle to make it out.

"Colonel Rego Rubido: The content of the message is totally different from the agreements reached earlier. It is ambiguous and incomprehensible. It has made me lose confidence in the seriousness of the agreements. Hostilities will resume tomorrow at 3:00 P.M., which was the date and time agreed upon."

While Cantillo pondered that, Rego added that the priest who had brought the note to Santiago, Father Feliz, also passed along a verbal message from Castro: "Fidel is extremely disturbed. Not only that, he said he wanted a total and unconditional surrender of the army right away, because the agreement had been broken."

Cantillo's face reddened with anger. That was not the kind of demand, he said, almost shouting, that can be made of an honorable man.

"Look," Rego shot back, "this isn't what you told us. There was one plan, and now there is another plan. And now one of the priests says that at the sugar-mill meeting, Fidel really demanded surrender. That was not what you told us."

Cantillo tried to compose himself. With a tolerant smile, he said that the word "surrender" had never been mentioned at the meeting with Castro. He certainly had no intentions of surrendering the Moncada regiment, nor was he going to do anything to cause more bloodshed. There had been a change, but everything was going to work out for the best.

With that, he led the two officers into his small office, sat down at the typewriter and rolled a piece of blank white paper into the carriage. As Rego and the navy man watched over his shoulder, he rattled off a reply, using his two index fingers, occasionally x-ing out a word or striking over an incorrect letter. The keys were dirty, and the o's and e's were filled with the black ink of the ribbon.

"The solution found," he began, "is not a coup d'etat nor a military junta, and we believe it will best agree with Dr. Fidel Castro and his ideas, and that it would put the destiny of the country in his hands in 48 hours.

"It is not a local solution, but a national one, and any early indiscretion could compromise it, destroy it, creating chaos.

"We want you to have confidence in our effort, and you will have the solution before the 6th [of January].

"Concerning Santiago, owing to the note and the words of the messenger, one must change the plan AND MUST NOT ENTER. The words mentioned have caused a disturbance among the key personnel and never would arms be handed over without a fight. They are not surrendered to an ally, and they are not handed over without honor.

"If you do not have confidence in us, or if you attack Santiago, the agreements are considered broken and will paralyze the efforts of the offered solution, unbinding us formally from the agreement.

"We hope, owing to the time necessary to activate one form or another, that your answer arrives on time to be sent to Havana on the afternoon Viscount."

Cantillo pulled the paper out of the typewriter and handed it to Rego, telling him to get it to the priest as fast as possible.

Rego objected. There was no signature on the letter, and since the last note had been sent with his name on it, Castro would assume he had written this one as well. "General," he complained, "things are extremely confusing. This note, I don't understand it. It is another change. You should talk to Castro again, or you should authorize me to talk to him."

"No, no, no," Cantillo snapped. "I can't talk to him, and you can't talk to him. There is no time for that anymore. In fact, he can't know that I am back in Santiago, because he assumes I'm still in Havana."

The two officers left confused. That was understandable: Cantillo had said nothing to them of his meeting with Batista nor why he wanted a reply before the next day's Cubana flight to Havana. But in his own mind, the plan was becoming clearer. He was simply going to save as many lives as possible, both in Santiago and in Havana.

Late that evening, Father Feliz arrived in a Red Cross ambulance at El Cobre, a religious sanctuary in the hills above Santiago. Castro, his brother Raúl and a number of aides were in an office in the main sanctuary building when the priest walked in and handed the typewritten message to the rebel leader. The priest said nothing, and everyone sensed immediately that the news was bad.

Pacing, Castro read the note aloud. It was exactly as he had feared. A "national solution" was being worked out without his knowledge or approval, and that meant something was happening that could only tend to thwart the revolution. He attached no importance to the fact that the letter was unsigned; he assumed it had been written by Colonel Rego Rubido.

When he was done, he asked Father Feliz what exactly he had told the colonel. The priest explained. Castro turned to Father Guzmán, who had been present at the sugar-mill meeting, and repeated his understanding of what their agreement had been. Guzmán agreed. He said that was the way he remembered it, too.

Pulling out a cigar and chewing on it, Castro paced silently for a few moments. The idea of a "solution" without the rebels was of course absolutely unacceptable, and he could no longer postpone an attack on Santiago. But there was no need to insult Colonel Rego's personal integrity. He decided to make one more attempt to win Santiago with words, not bullets.

Castro ordered a young rebel to write down what he was about to say. Resuming his pacing, he began:

"Colonel: A regrettable error has been made during the delivery of my message to you. Perhaps it was due to the rush in which I answered your note and the rapidity of the conversation with the messenger. I did not tell him that one of our conditions in the agreements reached here was the surrender of the garrison at Santiago de Cuba to our forces. To have done so would have been a discourtesy, as well as an undignified offense to the military men who have frequently come close to us. The problem is something else."

He dictated what his understanding of the agreement with Cantillo had been, "a joint action taken by the military, the people and our forces," and what Cantillo had promised to do. Turning to Father Guzmán, he asked the priest what he thought of that. Guzmán suggested two or three small changes. Castro ordered the changes made and, picking the notepaper out of the transcriber's hands, reread the paragraph.

"Yes, Fidel," the priest said, "it was like that."

Handing the paper back to the stenographer, Castro launched into what he considered the betrayal, this odd "solution" which included Havana.

"Apparently," he said as he paced, "there were other plans, but I was not informed or told of the reasons behind them. . . . We were then dependent on General Cantillo and his frequent trips to Havana could become militarily disastrous for us. You must recognize that everything is quite confusing at this moment, and that Batista is a clever individual who knows how to maneuver well. The change could only be for the worse.

"We cannot be asked to renounce all the advantages that we have gained in the last weeks and patiently wait for events to unfold. I said quite clearly that there could be no unilateral action by the military. We did not fight for two horrible years to get just that. . . . It is not power itself which concerns us, but rather the fulfillment of the revolution. I am even worried that the military, due to an unjustified excess of scruples, will allow the guilty to escape and go overseas with their great fortunes in order to further harm the fatherland.

"I personally can add that power does not interest me nor do I plan to take any post. I will only be on guard so that the sacrifices of so many compatriots will not be in vain, regardless of what my destiny might be. . . .

"In our meeting with General Cantillo, the word 'surrender' was never mentioned, and what I said yesterday, I say again today: After 3:00 P.M., December 31, the agreed date, we will end the truce with Santiago de Cuba, even though it might injure the people. . . .

"What I told the messenger was not transmitted literally, which is clear from your message. I said the following: If hostilities break out because what we had agreed is not fulfilled, we would be forced to attack the garrison at Santiago. This is inevitable because we have directed our efforts toward this objective for the past several months. If that happens, we will demand the surrender of the troops defending Santiago. This does not mean that we think they will surrender without fighting because I know that, even without reason to fight, Cuban military men would defend their positions, and they have cost me many lives. . . .

"More than allies, I wish that honorable military men would be our *compañeros* in only one cause: the cause of Cuba. I wish above all that you, *compañero*, would not have a mistaken impression of my attitude, and would not believe I have not been strict in regard to the cease-fire in Santiago. In order to dispel any doubts, I certify that operations could begin at any time and that from today on, it should be known that an attack could take place at any moment. For no reason whatsoever shall we alter our plans again."

36/DAYTIME, DECEMBER 31: "TOMORROW IS SO NEAR"

As the sun rose over Cuba on the last day of 1958, vendors appeared on the streets hawking copies of *Diario de la Marina,* which featured an editorial cartoon showing Father Time, sickle in hand, watching an hourglass and saying, "Am I lucky." The editorial, somewhat more direct than usual, stated: "Tomorrow is so near already for us Cubans, who have lived through a period of turmoil for two years. . . . Tomorrow is a much-abused word in this land of *mañana,* but this time tomorrow may be more meaningful than ever. . . . We hope so."

Beyond the reach of Batista's censors, the comments were more direct. *The Miami Herald* estimated that three thousand were dead in the Santa Clara fighting, and *The New York Times* stated in an editorial: "The United States cannot act alone, due to the risks attending open intervention and because anti-American feeling is running high in

Cuba. The Organization of American States is the only hope. . . ."

In deference to the country's mood, the Havana country clubs had canceled their usual New Year's Eve celebrations, and most people in the city were planning to attend only small private parties in friends' homes. In other parts of Cuba, parties of any kind were not even being considered, and for some the beginning of a new year had only one significance—it seemed like the perfect time for the surprise attack.

In the village of San Miguel de los Baños, Vitalia Bequer received word that the small rebel group hiding nearby was planning to attack the small Rural Guard cuartel at seven the next morning. Her first thought was to leave town immediately with her son Napoleón, Jr., so that the boy's intestinal problems would not be intensified by the frightening sound of gunfire. But they seemed to have been running ever since they had to abandon their grocery store in Oriente Province. She could stand no more. "We have been fleeing for almost two years," she told her mother. "We left our home. We left Havana. We ended up in this little hole. Now, I'm not moving an inch. We are staying here. If we die here, well, maybe that is what the Lord wants."

In Santa Clara, Captain Rogelio Acevedo sat in the schoolhouse with his back pressed against the wall. Outside, B-26s and Sea Fury fighters were bombing and strafing the area where his rebel platoon was besieging the courthouse and the jail. Only minutes before, the jail warden had offered to surrender if his fifteen policemen could keep their weapons. Acevedo had been willing to let them go—without the weapons. Now, apparently, the air force was trying to rescue them.

Suddenly, a bomb exploded, so nearby that it rattled the school's windows. Acevedo risked a peek to see what had happened. Then he laughed. The bomb had hit the front of the jail.

"Do you surrender?" he shouted toward the jail.

"Yes," someone yelled back.

With one other rebel, Acevedo moved toward the jail, clinging to the sides of buildings to avoid not only the planes but also the twenty soldiers in the courthouse on the other side of the park.

As soon as he entered the jail, a fat sergeant handed him his rifle and a large metal ring containing dozens of keys, then he ran out the door. Before the teenage rebel knew what was happening, the other policemen threw their weapons on the tile floor and rushed after him.

From the cell area, he heard men shouting and banging on the bars.

Running toward the sound, he found 150 political prisoners, who erupted with a wild cheer when they saw him. It took minutes of fumbling with the keys to find the right ones, and then the doors swung open. Most of the men pleaded for a chance to fight. Acevedo directed them toward the Veterans' Center, two blocks away, where they could ask for weapons from the armored train.

Trying to devise a scheme to force the courthouse soldiers to capitulate, he returned to the schoolhouse headquarters, but before he could decide anything, he saw two rubber-wheeled M-8 light tanks moving down the street. Walking behind them were thirty soldiers.

Before Acevedo could even react, the two rebel machine guns on the roof opened fire. Two soldiers collapsed. A rebel gunner, carrying the platoon's newly acquired bazooka, ran to a school window and took careful aim. When Acevedo gave the command, he fired.

The shell ripped through an electricity pole, slammed through an overturned bus and crashed into a storefront. The shell had come nowhere near the tanks, but the explosion seemed to terrify the crews. The M-8s backed up, running over the two fallen soldiers, with the rest of the infantrymen hurrying after them.

As soon as they disappeared around a corner, Acevedo walked up to the two corpses. Their bodies had been crushed. Their rifles were bent and bloody. He wondered if they had been dead when the tanks hit them.

It was still early that morning when Ambassador Smith's limousine stopped in front of Prime Minister Güell's house in Miramar. Glumly, he walked across the patio. A servant showed him into the library, where Güell was waiting in an easy chair.

The meetings had become grim formalities, almost as if Smith were attending a deathwatch. In most cases, Washington was simply ignoring the proposals to have President-elect Rivero Agüero hold elections quickly if the United States renewed the arms shipments.

The prime minister, who had remained calm throughout the daily ordeals, waited until the ambassador was seated, then said President Batista had one last proposal to make. He was willing to turn over the presidency to Anselmo Alliegro, the president of the Senate. Alliegro would immediately pass power to a civilian-military junta. Batista would suggest names for the junta, or the United States could do so. In either case, Batista would leave the country immediately. Alliegro had to be used as an intermediary because if Batista himself talked to people about forming a junta, leaks would inevitably occur and weaken the army. That would cause "chaos and bloodshed." Again, as he had with all his proposals, he said the only condition was that the United States give full support to the junta, including arms.

Smith said he would recommend the plan without qualification, but he added that he didn't see much chance that Washington would give its approval.

Güell nodded, as if he had been expecting that. His tongue flicked against his upper teeth, a sign he was searching for exactly the right words in English. He began by saying that he was about to divulge something which had to be kept absolutely confidential. If the people of Havana found out about it, hundreds of lives would be lost.

Smith, as always, said he had to inform Washington of everything he learned, but he promised to tell no one in Cuba.

Güell paused. Speaking slowly, he said that no matter what Washington did, the end was near. The president and his family would be leaving the country "very soon." Most of the government and military leaders would be going with him.

Smith was not surprised. He knew that Batista had no other choice, that Washington had left him with none. Now, it was a matter of how many were going to die in the chaos that followed, and he understood that Güell, though he had had nothing to do with the sometimes brutal tactics of the Batista police, could easily become a victim of the mobs.

"I have one worry," Smith said. "You. The United States, of course, has never supported the right of asylum in its embassies, but I can say—I can offer for you to stay in my residence. You would be safe there."

Güell did not hesitate. "No. My place is with the president. Wherever he is, I will be with him." But he added that he was worried about his house. The mobs were likely to ransack the homes of government officials, as they had done in 1933, and he thought the only way to protect it was to rent it to an American. In that case, he was certain that no mob would harm it.

Smith said his secretary, Edith Elverson, was looking for a place to rent. He said he would send her over, to have a look.

The prime minister thanked him for that, then said that if he left with Batista, there would be no time to pack or space on the plane to carry anything. If it were possible, he would like to leave some valuables in one or two trunks with the ambassador.

Smith agreed. When the trunks were ready, he would send his chauffeur over.

As he stood up to leave, Güell mentioned that some members of Batista's family would probably fly to the United States. Was there any problem with that? Smith said he couldn't imagine any.

At the door, they shook hands, and Güell promised to call later in the day, when he knew exactly when they were leaving.

It was a cold, cloudy day in Washington, with the temperatures hovering in the mid-thirties. Most of the politicians had gone home for the holidays, but on Capitol Hill an emergency session was being held for the Latin-American subcommittee of the U.S. Senate Committee on Foreign Relations. It had been called by Senator Wayne Morse after he had heard a CBS radio report that the United States was contemplating military intervention in Cuba. The meeting was an executive session; a *New York Times* reporter was forced to wait outside the closed door.

Dick Rubottom, the assistant secretary of state for Latin America, was the subcommittee's only witness. Speaking in his distinctive Texas twang, he quickly dismissed the radio report as false and said that the State Department was concentrating its efforts on supporting a plan to have the Organization of American States mediate the crisis. He did not mention the secret plan for a Cuban "third force."

Senator Hubert Humphrey asked if there would be a "deterioration of our relations with Cuba" if Castro's movement came to power.

Rubottom said State had "not been able to show at this stage that it is a Communist-dominated revolt," but he was sure "there are certain Communists active in it." Regardless of the Marxist menace, "I think we would have a problem to deal with if the Castro Movement was to take over. . . . I would not be happy with Castro solely in command."

Then, revealing how much confidence he had in the hope for a "third force" without mentioning the plan itself, he said he doubted that the 26th of July Movement had enough clout to control a new government. If Batista fell, there would have to be a "political solution among the anti-Batista groups."

While Rubottom talked, Caribbean director William Wieland was examining the final draft of a three-page telegram that was to be sent to Smith that afternoon. It was a reiteration of everything he and

Rubottom had been telling the ambassador for months, but this time it was being signed by Robert Murphy, the deputy undersecretary. When a man at Murphy's level made a decision, all argument had to stop.

"In present circumstances," the cable stated, "any material increase in US military support of present GOC [Government of Cuba] would expose US Government to widespread charges within and without hemisphere of intervention in Cuba's internal dispute, expose US citizens and interests in Cuba to reprisals from opposition elements and damage long-range US position in Cuba by alienating many Cubans."

On the last day of 1958, Smith's plan to support the regime with arms had collapsed, completely and irreversibly.

Following his usual daily routine, Fulgencio Batista arose shortly before 11 A.M. Putting on a burgundy-colored bathrobe, he walked into the living room of the private quarters on the third floor of the Presidential Palace. There, sipping his customary watered-down coffee, he read *Diario de la Marina* and scanned the headlines of the other Havana newspapers.

A few minutes later, Batista summoned Major Cosme Varas, his thirty-four-year-old aide-de-camp. He said he wanted to invite the government leaders to a midnight gathering at his Camp Columbia home. It was to be a subdued affair—no dancing, no formal meal. Just a buffet and coffee, perhaps laced with brandy.

Going to the aides' room, Varas located most of the guests quickly with the help of the palace switchboard operators. No one refused or questioned the invitation. The Columbia party had become a New Year's Eve tradition. Only one person could not be located: Rafael Guas Inclán, the vice-president. He was said to be hunting deer somewhere in the hills. Varas told the operators to keep trying.

About 2:00 P.M., Batista ate a light lunch and disappeared into the bathroom, emerging minutes later in a light gray business suit. He talked briefly with Prime Minister Güell and the presidential secretary, Andrés Domingo Morales del Castillo, then announced to his aide that they were going to his country house at Kuquine.

Batista, his face as emotionless as ever, made the trip in complete silence. Sitting beside him in the backseat of the black Cadillac limousine with its license plate bearing the distinctive *1*, Major Varas scanned the buildings and intersections for snipers. Ahead and behind were two cars filled with machine-gun-carrying bodyguards, trailed by a second limousine with Güell and the presidential secretary.

When they reached the western suburb of Marianao, Varas remembered that one of Batista's major public works' projects had just been completed—the extension of Fifth Avenue toward the outlying villages. He had noticed it the day before.

"Look, it's finished," he said. "How about if we drive on the new road, and go through Punta Brava?" It was slightly longer, but Varas guessed Batista would like to see it.

"OK," the president nodded.

The limousine raced along the new concrete road, which the presidential press office had been boasting about for months. Batista just stared out the window and said nothing.

About 3:00 P.M., they arrived at Kuquine. Batista went immediately to his small private office off the main library room. He spent an hour alone, then began a long conference with his presidential secretary and Prime Minister Güell. Varas lounged in a chair and waited for orders.

Late that afternoon, in Las Villas Province at the Mayajigua airport, Captain William Gálvez of the rebels' Column 2 paced and stroked his blond goatee. After so many days of besieging the "Chinaman" at the town of Yaguajay, he and the other rebels had grown so bitter they were willing to pulverize the cuartel into dust to gain victory. Beside Gálvez was an undetonated air force bomb and several bottles of gasoline. He was waiting for the arrival of a rebel plane from Oriente; together he and the pilot were to bomb the cuartel. If that didn't work, the rebels had a mortar, given them by Ché Guevara.

Several miles away, Captain Abón-Ly sat inside the cuartel listening to the mortar shells explode in the fields nearby. Apparently, the rebels' gunner was inexperienced, but Abón-Ly knew it was only a matter of time before he found the target, for the rebels seemed to have a seemingly unlimited supply of shells.

His once-immaculate uniform was now stained with sweat and grime. For more than a week, his small group had held off half the 26th of July rebels in the province, and not once had his subordinates pleaded with him to surrender. Yet there was no denying the realities. They were almost out of food, ammunition and water. Already, they had suffered fifty or sixty casualties, including eight or ten dead. Most of the wounded had been evacuated by the Red Cross during truces, but twenty were still inside the cuartel, sprawled on cots in the dormitory. One night, he had sent out a messenger, who was to try to reach the regimental headquarters at Santa Clara. The man had not returned.

As the shells kept exploding in the field, Abón-Ly wandered back to the dormitory. The room smelled of excrement, and the wounded men stared at him with glassy eyes. Several had injuries which were an ugly blue. The medic, looking harassed and exhausted, told him that he had just used the last of the medicine.

Abón-Ly decided he had done all he could. It would be no shame to surrender. Calling the officers and noncoms into his office, he said simply, "I don't see how we can hold out any longer."

The men nodded. Abón-Ly knew they would be happy to see the fighting end.

They found two white bed sheets, attached them to poles with safety pins and waved them through the front windows.

"All right," a rebel shouted. "We won't shoot. Come out."

Without a cap, his back ramrod straight, his head held high, Abón-Ly walked through the cuartel door, followed by one subordinate. Comandante Camilo Cienfuegos was standing on the dusty road, about 250 yards away.

As he walked up to him, Abón-Ly decided to make one more try for a negotiated settlement. "I have men injured," he told Cienfuegos. "I will offer you a deal. If you allow me to take out my injured, I agree to leave the cuartel and go with my men to the coast."

Cienfuegos refused. He said the time for a deal had long since passed, and he was not going to accept any conditions whatsoever. Only total and unconditional surrender would stop him from destroying the cuartel and everyone in it.

Abón-Ly hesitated only a moment. "In that case, I wish all my soldiers to be given liberty and I will go with you as a prisoner." He said the men would give up their weapons.

Cienfuegos nodded.

"Should I give up my pistol?"

"Please."

Abón-Ly gave him his holster and weapon.

Cienfuegos ordered two men to take him to the city hall. As the rebels led him away, Abón-Ly looked back for a moment. His subordinate was leading several rebels toward the cuartel, where the white flags dangled from the windows. The place seemed so small now. After a week of the most bitter resistance the rebels had faced, the siege of Yaguajay was over.

37/TWILIGHT

The sun was beginning to set for the last time of the year as the British cruise ship *Mauretania* anchored just outside Havana harbor. Attorney Paul Tannenbaum was sitting with his family in the deck lounge as he studied the city's skyline. There was a light chop to the sea, and it seemed to make the buildings bob up and down.

After seven days at sea, Tannenbaum was sporting a deep tan and feeling only a little guilty about the quantities of food and drink he had consumed; after all, that's what vacations were for. At the tables around him, most passengers were getting a head start on the evening's drinking, but Tannenbaum was thinking only about his visit the next day to the city.

As he wondered what he would want to see first, the voice of Captain Alexander B. Fasting came over the loudspeaker. Because of the ship's size, he said, they were anchoring outside the port. Everyone was invited to the New Year's Eve ball that evening, and for those whose hangovers were not too severe, tenders should be ready to transport passengers to the city, starting early the next morning. "Meanwhile," the captain concluded, "have a Happy New Year."

Tannenbaum decided to go to bed early. He wanted to get his family on the first tender to leave.

On the western edge of Havana, Brigadier General Silito Tabernilla sat in a rocking chair on the porch of the Camp Columbia officers' club. As he chatted with friends while waiting for dinner, his restless eyes followed the enlisted men walking casually across the vast parade ground to the mess hall.

Each day, the list of passengers for the escape planes seemed to weigh more heavily in his pocket. He could not get out of his mind the stories he had been hearing since childhood about the thousand killed when the Machado regime crumbled in 1933. As he kept telling Batista, if they indeed were going to flee, "the sooner, the better."

An orderly interrupted his worries: there was a phone call. Walking into the club, he found a private office and lifted the receiver.

"Silito?" It was Batista himself. That was odd. Almost invariably, an aide placed the call.

"Yes, Mr. President."

"I want you to come to Kuquine. Bring my passport. And the list."

Not far away, in the penthouse of a high-rise building overlooking the Vedado Tennis Club and the Gulf of Mexico, Max Lesnik sat drinking a Canada Dry ginger ale. Dressed in his usual blue jeans and T-shirt, the Havana underground chief of the Segundo Frente del Escambray was listening to Jack Stewart, the CIA man, talk about reports of the fighting in Las Villas Province. Stewart had invited Lesnik's wife to have dinner with them, and Lesnik was hoping that the American would leave them alone for a while after they ate. He had not seen her in weeks.

As Stewart sipped an Old Kentucky bourbon and water, Lesnik wondered out loud whether the CIA's "green light" had succeeded in getting the Segundo Frente's planeload of weapons cleared out of Miami. If everything had gone all right, the plane should be about ready to land.

"Max," the CIA man said, "if it is going to do any good, it has to get down there in a hurry."

Lesnik detected a tone of despondency. He asked what rumors had been floating around the embassy.

"I'm sorry, Max," Stewart said, shaking his head, "I think the clearance came kind of late. The Batista regime can last only a few more days or weeks."

They lapsed into silence, and Lesnik's thoughts turned again toward the plane. He was convinced there was still a chance for his little-known group, if the weapons arrived.

At that moment, the old B-26 was flying low over the coast of southern Cuba. As with so many other gun-running trips, this plane was running out of gas as the pilots searched frantically for the small dirt strip where they were supposed to land.

Dr. Armando Fleites, the Segundo Frente captain, was squeezed between the two pilots; he too was looking, but he couldn't stop thinking about the terrible noise in back, the air roaring through an opening caused when the left cargo door had fallen off shortly after takeoff from Miami. Two crates of grenades had gone with it.

At last, the American pilot spotted the town of Trinidad and then the airstrip beyond. As the plane swooped down, Fleites heard gunfire. It took him a moment to realize that the Segundo Frente guerrillas were firing at them. They had mistaken the B-26 for an air force bomber.

"We're running out of gas," the pilot shouted above the noise. "Otherwise, I'd fly away and come back. We'll have to land under fire."

As they made their final approach, the pilot cursed that the field was too short for a B-26. The plane hit the dirt strip, bounced, came down again and bounced again, boxes of ammunition flying wildly in the rear hold. At the end of the runway, it crashed nose down into a ditch.

Fleites, groggy, peeked through the cargo hole. The guerrillas recognized him immediately. They ran to embrace him. On the last day of the year, the Segundo Frente finally had weapons.

To the north, teenage Captain Rogelio Acevedo stared down at five shoeshine boys, three white, two black, who had come to his headquarters in the Santa Clara schoolhouse. They wanted rifles so that they too could join the fighting.

Acevedo studied them intently, then looked out the window at the massive, two-story courthouse, where twenty army soldiers were still holding out. Since the jail had surrendered, Ché Guevara had visited him several times, demanding that he crush the courthouse resistance as quickly as possible. But there was a long flight of stairs leading up to the iron doors on the first full floor, where the soldiers were huddled. A frontal assault would be suicidal. There seemed to be only one alternative: By approaching from the sides, his men could get to the basement windows, beneath the fire of the soldiers. But the basement windows were barred.

Then he had an idea. Looking back to the shoeshine boys, he decided they seemed brave enough, and he certainly could not object to their youth when he himself was only seventeen. Deciding it was worth a try, he asked if each was willing to carry a five-gallon can of gasoline across the street and pour it into the basement windows. Without hesitation, the youths agreed.

As the rebels laid down a covering volley of gunfire, the boys, heads down, dashed to the building, dumped the gasoline and ran back. No one was hit. A rebel volunteer took a torch across the street and threw it inside.

Within seconds, flames leaped from the windows. Acevedo's confidence soared, but moments later it crashed. The flames were dying out. The fire had not spread to the soldiers' area.

High in the air above Las Villas Province, General Cantillo sat in his C-47, headed back to Havana. He was feeling a momentary surge of optimism. All day, he had waited at the Moncada garrison for Castro to attack, but the siege trenches around Santiago had been unusually quiet, and the 3:00 P.M. deadline had passed without a shot being fired.

That had given him renewed hope. The rebels had yet to take a single large city or to force a regimental garrison to surrender anywhere on the island. The commanders at Holguín, Bayamo and Camagüey City had told him they were in no immediate danger, and in fact only two of the country's six provinces were facing armed insurrection of any kind.

As he thought about what could be done, the pilot shouted back, pointing to their right. Cantillo looked out the window. In the distance, silhouetted against the golden sky, the new British Sea Fury fighters were using the last light of day for a final strafing run over Santa Clara. That disturbed him. He had no idea what the situation was there.

A few minutes later, the C-47 landed at Camp Columbia. The usual crowd of officers was waiting for him on the concrete apron, but he pushed through them, ignoring their questions, and entered the nearby air force headquarters, where he found General José Eleuterio Pedraza, the aging officer whom Batista had just reappointed to the army. Pedraza had made one quick trip to Las Villas Province, to get his family out, and then had stayed at Columbia, receiving by radio the reports of the fighting.

"How are things in Santa Clara?" Cantillo asked.

"Very bad," Pedraza said sadly. "They called me in too late."

Then, turning to a group behind him, Pedraza introduced Cantillo to some officers from the Dominican Republic. They had hoped to see Batista, to talk about shipments of arms and troops, but the president was avoiding them. One, dressed in civilian clothes, explained in English that he was from Taiwan, traveling on a West German passport. He was a munitions expert and Cantillo, forgetting momentarily about all his other problems, said it had long bothered him that the American-made napalm bombs were worthless, doing no damage when they exploded in wet treetops of the Sierra rain forest. The man said he would try to think of a solution.

As Cantillo walked back outside, he told his aide, Major Collado, that he could have New Year's Eve off to spend with his family. Then, climbing in his chauffeur-driven Oldsmobile, he went home. A small group of relatives and friends were already there, gathered in the living room, starting a quiet celebration of his wedding anniversary. Cantillo changed his clothes, putting on a casual *guayabera* shirt, and was just beginning to relax when the telephone rang.

He joked to a girl: "Now you are my aide-de-camp. Answer the telephone."

It was a presidential aide. Cantillo was ordered to be at Batista's country home of Kuquine at 10:00 P.M.

Early that evening at Kuquine, Prime Minister Güell called Ambassador Smith and said they would be leaving that night. He promised to call again, shortly before they left. As soon as he hung up, Güell phoned his wife and told her to bring to the midnight buffet the blank Republic of Cuba passports that he had left in his desk. She was to put them in a plain brown envelope. No one was to know.

A few minutes later, Brigadier General Silito Tabernilla arrived at the library to find the prime minister, his face pale, pacing in front of the busts of Lincoln, Martí and Bolívar.

Major Cosme Varas, the aide de camp, slipped next to Silito and whispered in heavily accented English, "What is happening?"

"Soon you will know," Silito replied, also in English.

Just then, the door to Batista's inner office opened, and secretary Morales del Castillo walked out. He too looked pale.

Silito hurried into the office and closed the door.

Batista was behind his desk. His face was bland. Over the past several days, there had been terrible accusations between the two, but now El Presidente said, "Do you have the list?"

Silito pulled it from his shirt pocket, along with three Batista passports, each marking a presidential visit to a different foreign country. The president took them and slid them into a suit pocket.

"Tonight we go," Batista said simply. "About one o'clock." He explained briefly what had to be done.

As soon as he was through, Silito burst through the door. He knew the next few hours would be the most critical of all—if anyone found out they were leaving, all their power would evaporate. People would fight for the right to boast to the rebels that they had helped arrest the leading Batistianos.

Summoning an aide, Silito told him to get together with Major Varas. Anyone on the list who hadn't been invited that morning to the Columbia midnight buffet was to be called now. No one was to be allowed to turn down the invitation.

Then, slipping into a small anteroom, he called his brother Winsy and asked if the Aerovías Q planes were ready. Yes, Winsy said, but not the pilots. He had given them the night off, to spend New Year's Eve with their families. He would have to locate them. Silito told him to hurry.

In the fashionable Biltmore section of Havana, Rosa Rivero stood studying herself in a full-length mirror. She was in her upstairs bedroom, trying on a new dress. It was strapless, with a rather revealing neckline. Was it too daring for a fifteen-year-old? Was red too bright a color?

A dress was a very important decision for a first date, and as she debated, she sat down at a small desk and picked up the blue-leather diary which Emilio had given her. On the first page, in a space for the last day of 1958, she wrote: "I am going out at 8 tonight and will have no time to write later. I have many plans for this last day of the year, but the atmosphere in my house is so tense that I don't know if my mother will let us leave. If she does, we will be very happy."

She put the diary in a drawer. Was she being too pessimistic? Since returning from New York, everything had been going well. There was the fascinating seventeen-year-old Emilio, an unending succession of parties and the realization that because her father was the president-elect, she was becoming very popular in social circles.

Just then, she heard the maid calling from downstairs. Her date had arrived. Now, there was no doubting the dress. She made one last check in the mirror, slipped into her high-heeled shoes, then picked up a short mink coat and a red leather purse.

As she descended the stairs, seeing Emilio standing in the living room, she thought how handsome and dignified he looked in his dark suit. Her heart quickened. Surely, she decided, this must be love.

38/THE NIGHT OF THE TWELVE GRAPES

New Year's Eve, like most customs in Cuba, had become an odd mixture of traditions. Some copied the Americans, donning funny hats held on with rubber bands, blowing through noisemakers and singing bleary renditions of "Auld Lang Syne." Most followed the native custom of celebrating at midnight by eating twelve grapes, one by one, followed by a glass of cider. Some even observed the old superstition of throwing a bucket of water out the door at midnight for good luck.

That night, as rumors reached the point of hysteria, many people simply chose to stay home. Reservations had poured into the Hotel Riviera's Copa Room, but in late afternoon, two hundred canceled. Some opted to watch television where the evening's prime fare was at 9:00 P.M. on Channel 7: *The New Adventures of Charlie Chan*.

For those who went out, there were plenty of attractions. The King American Circus was performing at the Sports Palace. The Tropicana Nightclub offered a spectacular show, *On the Way to Broadway*, which opened with an airport scene depicting Cubans hurrying to board a plane to New York. In Old Havana, the Alkazar Theater was showing for the last night *Around the World in 80 Days.* Workmen were already putting up the letters on the marquee for the next attraction: *Drácula.*

Still, an unmistakable somberness deadened the festivities that evening, and in the showroom of the Havana Hilton, Cuban men in business suits and their wives in lamé dresses and flashy jewelry showed no enthusiasm as Lilo, a French singer, performed her blend of American and Continental numbers. Her singing was as good as it had been in the Broadway version of *Can-Can,* but no one seemed to care. The audience was almost sullen.

Senator Rolando Masferrer was not one to let the tension spoil his evening. Sitting in his favorite rocking chair under a sprawling poinciana tree in his backyard, he took an occasional sip of *añejo* rum and played "Oh! Susannah" and "Red River Valley" on his harmonica.

Nearby, two pigs roasted in large pits, and the smell of pork permeated the terrace. Beside the bar were stacks of presents given by people trying to curry favor with him. There were crates of champagne, Scotch whiskey and Bacardí *añejo,* along with boxes of cigars, especially H. Upmann No. 1, his favorite.

While he waited for the food to be done, he called in his bodyguards and aides. Pointing to the presents, he said, "You better drink the liquor and smoke the cigars before Ché Guevara comes down from the hills and takes them for himself." The men laughed, but Masferrer was only half-joking.

Dressed in a tuxedo, Ambassador Smith had a drink in his hand as he stood glumly in the corner of a friend's living room, where he was attending a small party. He hadn't wanted to come, but he knew his absence would only fuel the rumors. And besides, there was one duty he had to fulfill. His friend, Porfirio Rubirosa was undoubtedly going to be in danger because, as the ambassador from the Dominican Republic, he was hated for helping his country supply weapons to Batista.

When he spotted Rubirosa across the room, Smith signaled for him to come over. Grabbing the Dominican by the elbow to draw him closer, he whispered that instead of coming with his wife to Smith's residence for lunch the next day, as they had planned, they should come for breakfast. A *long* breakfast. Smith said no more, but Rubirosa seemed to understand.

• • •

Shortly before 10:00 P.M., General Cantillo, trailed by his friend, Colonel Martínez Suárez, walked into the library room at Kuquine. He saw the pale faces of Prime Minister Güell and secretary Morales del Castillo. In a corner, Brigadier General Silito Tabernilla was talking nervously on a telephone. Instantly, Cantillo realized what was happening. He felt a sinking feeling in his stomach.

An aide showed him into Batista's inner office and closed the door. The man who had ruled Cuba for more than seventeen years sat behind his desk. He seemed absolutely calm.

"Well," he said slowly as Cantillo took a seat, "I have been thinking." He paused. "Any day is as good as any other day. The longer I stay, the more people will be killed. So I've decided to go, and I want you to stay."

Cantillo panicked. For three days, he had been living with this possibility, but now its reality suddenly seemed unimaginable. "But Mr. President, I have talked to the commanders at Holguín, Bayamo and Camagüey— they say they're not in any immediate danger. And at 3 P.M. today, which the rebels had said was their deadline for attacking, there was only silence. I don't think the danger is that great." His mind was spinning with hopeful possibilities.

Batista shook his head. His mind was made up. The departure was already being organized. Lives were at stake, he said, and only Cantillo, with his immaculate record with the opposition forces, had a chance to work something out and guarantee the lives of all those supporters who couldn't leave in the first three planes.

The general leaned back in his chair. For a long, awful moment, there was only silence. He knew that once Batista's mind was set, no one could change it. All Cantillo could do now, if he wanted to refuse his president's request, was to walk out of the room. Simply ignore the order; with the chaos all around him, he could probably get away with it. But as a professional soldier he had never turned down an order from a superior officer, especially not from the president of the republic. Twenty years of experience had been dedicated to obedience. To ignore an order now was to reject his entire career, to mock all the values he held dear.

Suddenly, Cantillo's mind was clear. After days of uncertainty and doubt, he understood it was his duty to help his chief. It was that simple.

Immediately, he turned to the logistics. If I'm going to stay and protect you, I have to have a command here in Havana. You would have to give me the Columbia infantry command. Otherwise, I would go there and say, 'Well, I am the chief here,' and somebody might think I was trying a coup d'etat."

Batista said that was no problem. Silito Tabernilla, the infantry commander, could hand over his position before he left. The political situation was more complicated. He said he had considered turning over the government directly to Cantillo or a military junta, but that would be a violation of the 1940 Constitution. Straight-faced, the man who had himself violated the constitution countless times in the past, said he wanted to leave behind, as a last gift to Cuba, a constitutional solution.

Batista said he and his presidential secretary had been working on that problem all afternoon. Guas Inclán, the vice-president, could not be found. That meant the presidency should pass to Anselmo Alliegro, the president of the Senate, but Alliegro was scheduled to go on one of the planes. Next in line was the justice who had the most seniority on the Supreme Court. That was the way the constitution dictated it.

"Who is he?" Cantillo asked.

"I don't know," Batista shrugged. He and his secretary had tried to learn who he was but failed. "You'll have to find out for yourself."

As one last favor, he asked the general to call the American ambassador after the planes had left and tell him that several of his children would be flying to the United States.

When Cantillo came out the door, he realized that everyone was watching him. He felt as if an enormous weight was bearing down on his shoulders, and his face probably showed it. Walking toward his staff Oldsmobile, he thought of the problems ahead. He had no charisma, no political contacts, no political experience. Batista had given him no advice about what to do after the planes left, and Cantillo didn't even know the questions to ask.

While a trio played cha-chas and boleros, Rosa Rivero and Emilio slipped away to a small terrace where they could be alone. They had eaten dinner and seen the first show at the Tropicana, accompanied by chaperones, before coming to this small party at the home of Luisito Pozo, the son of Havana's mayor. Most of the people there were government officials.

Staring at her with his dark eyes, Emilio said he was annoyed that she would soon be going back to school in New York. "Rosa, how can I stand to be so far away from you when I feel like I do about you, *mi corazón?*"

"I have to graduate." She was enthralled by his intensity. "My parents insist on it. We'll just have to wait a little, that's all."

"But you don't understand, Rosa. We have to get married. To see you like this, to dance with you, to sense you so close and then to know . . ."

They danced, there on the terrace, close together, Emilio's hands holding her tightly, becoming a little daring when he realized that the adults inside were not paying any attention to them, that the officials were huddling together, whispering, watching Mayor Justo Luis Pozo talk on the telephone with a forced smile.

At parties, in apartment building corridors, through the streets of the city and across telephone lines, *bolas* were starting to roll.

In a Vedado area home, Mrs. Ana María Salazar, who had relatives in the anti-Batista movement, received a call from one of her sons. He was at a party with some minor government officials, and he had heard that Batista was leaving. Mrs. Salazar made some phone calls. No, it couldn't possibly be true, she was told. Yes, it was. No. Yes. Maybe.

Not far away, Paul Bethel, the U.S. press attaché, was riding to a party when he passed the house of a Tabernilla son. Several olive-green SIM Oldsmobiles were in the driveway. Children, bundled in blankets, were being placed in the backseats as soldiers threw luggage into the trunks.

Elsewhere, at a small gathering attended mostly by government officials, Daniel Braddock, the U.S. deputy chief of mission, peered through his thick glasses at an upper-class Cuban woman. "Help us, help us," she pleaded. He didn't know what she meant.

At a safehouse near Vedado, the Havana underground risked a rare meeting of their top leaders to discuss the rumors. Julio Duarte, the man who had collected $450,000, listened as Carlos Lechuga, a well-known television newscaster, announced to the group, "I have heard *bolas* that Batista is leaving tonight."

Comandante Diego, the chief of Acción y Sabotaje, asked how good the rumors were.

"Quite good, but of course these days . . ." He didn't need to continue. Everyone understood about the avalanche of *bolas*.

Duarte asked if he could check it out. The journalist made telephone calls. Yes, many persons had heard the rumors. No, no one had anything definite. The group decided there was nothing they could do. The meeting broke up.

At the Isle of Pines, Colonel Ramón Barquín lay on his bunk in his third-tier cell. As always, lights had been turned out at 10:00 P.M. He tried Radio Caracas, to pick up uncensored news of the rebels, but the static was unusually bad, and he turned the dial to CMQ, the most powerful Havana station. It was reporting foreign news on the hour, but nothing about the war. The music was boleros and cha-chas, the traditional New Year's Eve fare that the station broadcast for those who wanted to stay home and dance. Just the sound of it made him even more depressed than he usually was.

In Miami, Justo Carrillo, the man who had been working for months to free Barquín from prison, was eating with friends at an Italian restaurant opposite the Gulfstream horse-race track. He was still hoping that his shopkeeper operative, Felo Fernández, had talked to the warden about the bribe, but he had heard nothing about it, and there was nothing he could do now. When the meal was finished, Carrillo and his friends lounged at the table for a long time as they speculated and argued about the political situation.

On the sixth floor of the Gran Hotel in Santa Clara, Guillermo Domenech huddled with the manager and the electrician. A rebel lieutenant had called a few minutes before from the lobby. He apologized for the inconvenience to the guests, but his men had to stop the SIM snipers. They were going to burn the furniture clogging the fifth-floor stairwell, and they wanted the guests to help him dislodge the larger pieces.

The manager said the building was poured concrete; it couldn't possibly burn down. The SIM men were holed up in the penthouse, and the guests hadn't seen them all day. It couldn't hurt to help the rebels.

The smell of smoke was already coming from the stairwell when they reached it. The men grunted, trying to pry loose the furniture, but it was stuck tight and the smoke was becoming thicker every moment. Choking, they left, closing the stairwell door behind them.

The manager moaned about what could happen if the rebels and soldiers started a gunfight in the hotel corridors. It could endanger everyone, especially if the SIM men wanted to use the guests as hostages.

The electrician had an idea. He led the way to one of the fifth-floor rooms and pointed through the window. About five feet away, directly across from them, was a window on the top floor of the Cloris Theater. He said that if one sat on the air-conditioning unit below the hotel window, the distance was only about three feet.

Before Domenech or the manager could object, the electrician opened the window, sat on the air conditioner and stretched his legs until his feet touched the theater window. He kicked. The glass clattered into the room opposite, and he slid across.

As Domenech watched, he leaned back toward the hotel with outstretched hands. He said the guests could sit, get their feet in the theater window, hold on to his hands and be pulled across without ever being in free flight. Domenech looked down. It was a fifty-foot drop to a concrete alley. Still, with the smoke billowing under the stairwell door and starting to fill the corridor, it seemed like their best chance.

Herding the guests down from the sixth floor, they decided women and children should go first. Bravely, each took the electrician's hands and moved across without a problem. The first real challenge was the manager's mother-in-law, an obese woman nearly six feet tall. As they helped her squeeze through the hotel window, Domenech whispered to the sausage salesman, "If the air conditioner can hold her, we have no problem with anyone."

Gently, they eased her down on the unit. It swayed slightly, then stopped. As she stretched out her long, flabby legs, the electrician grabbed them by the ankles. The manager placed both hands on her huge buttocks and shoved. She was across.

Next came the couple with the infant daughter. "Who is going to grab my baby?" the mother asked, running a hand through her short brown hair.

The manager said he didn't want the responsibility; he insisted the father do it. They wrapped the baby in a blanket and the father went across. The manager, holding the center of the bundle in one hand, stretched out as far as he could. The father took the end with one hand, then the full weight with the other. The baby was safe.

The rest went quickly. Domenech was one of the last to go, and as he slid into the theater, he saw that they were in the theater's projection room. A bearded rebel was standing there, smiling. It was the first rebel that Domenech had ever seen. Apparently, the guerrilla too had discovered that the window was the easiest way to get across. It would probably take the rebels a day or so to fight their way to the top of the hotel, where the SIM were, but their victory seemed assured. Suddenly, Domenech remembered it was New Year's Eve—a time to celebrate.

In southern Camagüey Province, Tony Varona wasn't even thinking of celebrating. With three associates, the former prime minister was tramping across the dark grasslands behind a fourteen-year-old boy. The youth had met them at the road and told Varona that he was to guide the group to the 26th of July rebel camp to meet the provincial commander. The four men were armed with heavy machine guns and automatic pistols, a protection against a possible trap, but on this fourth night of Varona's expedition, he was no farther ahead than when he had arrived, and he still had miles to go before he could meet the man whom he wanted to conspire against.

In war-torn Oriente Province, the evening passed like any other as the people stayed in their homes and listened to rebel radio stations. Ironically, on this last night of the Batista regime, the main rebel transmitter, 7RR, was off the air. The technicians were installing it in a new location, in Palma Soriano, to be closer to Santiago.

Still, there were other rebel stations. Supermarket owner Lily Ferreiro listened on his General Electric shortwave in his Santiago home. A few blocks away, Connie and Park Wollam were tuned to a station in the hills above the city. It was Connie's forty-first birthday, but she couldn't feel in the mood for a party knowing that the next day they might be facing a battle right in front of their house.

Thirty miles away, in Palma Soriano, Fidel Castro worked late, talking with his *comandantes* about the plans for attack on Santiago. Some time before midnight, he returned to his headquarters at the sugar-mill town of Central América. Exhausted from being up most of the previous night dictating the letter to Colonel Rego Rubido, he went straight to his room.

Rego himself was wide awake, pacing the tile floor in his small quarters in the Moncada barracks. He had just received Castro's letter, delivered by a priest. Considering the situation, he thought it was remarkably conciliatory. He read the letter again, then attached a short note and sealed it in an envelope. Ringing for an aide whom he trusted absolutely, he told him to rush the note to Cantillo in Havana.

Alone again, Rego sat down at his desk and tried to think. He too was irked at Cantillo for breaking the agreement with Castro and making vague hints about a "solution" which seemed to include Camp Columbia. As he saw it, there were two possibilities. Cantillo might stay in Havana and oppose Castro, which meant that Rego would have to face the rebels' wrath and bullets. Or Cantillo could carry through with his promise, in which case Castro would be Rego's new boss by January 6. Either way, he did not want to anger the 26th of July chief.

It was time, he decided, to send his own message to Castro. "I have just received your letter today," he began, "and I must say I am profoundly grateful for the clarification regarding the prior misunderstanding, for I have followed your behavior through the years and I have seen and been convinced that you are a man of principle." Rego promised he would do what he could to track down "war criminals" and hinder the escape of the "guilty ones." He wrote that he expected Castro to be in Havana before January 6.

As a final gesture of goodwill, he offered the rebel leader the use of the army helicopter so that he could enjoy a Sunday afternoon ride above the city.

Rego was still writing as midnight approached.

39/MIDNIGHT: "NEW YEAR, NEW LIFE"

At Batista's Camp Columbia home, the atmosphere was grim as the sixty or so guests milled around the buffet table in the upstairs living area. For years, this New Year's Eve ritual had been a festive occasion, a gathering of the most powerful people in the country, but now the guests seemed little more than mannequins, saying nothing to each other, standing stiffly in small groups, waiting to pay the required homage to their leader.

On one side of the room, President-elect Rivero Agüero, wearing a gray business suit with a blue-gray tie, stood quietly next to his wife Isabel amid a cluster of politicians. On the other side, near the screened-in Florida Room, the military men had gathered in their dress uniforms. Most of the wives were in formal gowns. In a corner by themselves, ignored, was the military delegation from the Dominican Republic, including the strange man from Taiwan.

Some, to break the tedium, drifted over to the buffet table, where military aides in crisp white uniforms served *arroz con pollo*—chicken with rice—on fine china. A few guests sipped champagne. Most drank coffee.

At 11:50 P.M., a convoy of cars stopped out front, brakes screeching. Moments later, Batista strode up the stairs flanked by aides and bodyguards. He was followed by Prime Minister Güell and secretary Morales del Castillo. Both men had large brown envelopes, which they clutched to their chests.

All guests' eyes were on Batista. He seemed to sense it, avoiding the Dominican delegation and going over to chat with some army officers.

Senator Jorge García Montes watched his leader's face closely. As always, it seemed without emotion.

"Don't you notice that Batista is nervous?" Justo Luis Pozo, the mayor of Havana, whispered to him.

García Montes shook his head. "No, I don't see that."

Seconds before midnight, an aide handed Batista a cup of coffee laced with brandy. As the clock struck, he raised it in the air and said, "*Felicidades.*"

"Happy New Year," his guests replied.

At that moment, Julio Duarte was parked in his two-tone 1956 Chevrolet just outside Columbia's main gate. After all the rumors he had heard at the underground meeting, he wanted to check them out for himself, but the place was absolutely quiet. The white-helmeted guards stood sternly at their posts with their awesome submachine guns. Heavy spotlights shone down on the street from the top of the light-yellow concrete walls.

Suddenly, from the distance came muted *pop-pop* sounds. Duarte tensed, then realized it was the traditional firecrackers going off in a nearby residential neighborhood. The camp itself was quiet. Duarte decided that the *bolas* had been no more reliable than usual.

At midnight, Ambassador Smith sat in an easy chair beside the telephone in his upstairs living room. Still dressed in his tuxedo, he was getting concerned that the prime minister hadn't yet called him from Columbia.

In the Miramar neighborhood, fifteen-year-old Rosa Rivero ate the twelve grapes, one by one. Spanish cider was passed around. The first toast was for Cuba, the second for peace, the third for Rosa's father, the president-elect. The last toast was for Batista. Then Emilio kissed her.

Aboard the *Mauretania*, the ship's captain led a toast as Paul

Tannenbaum and eight hundred guests clinked champagne glasses. The band played "Auld Lang Syne."

In Yaguajay, Captain Alfredo Abón-Ly sat alone on a cot in a small room in the city hall. The door was locked. In the next room, Captain William Gálvez and other rebel leaders sat in rocking chairs as they discussed how they should prepare Column 2 for the battle of Santa Clara.

In Santa Clara, Captain Rogelio Acevedo watched from the school as the besieged soldiers in the courthouse fired off a barrage of bullets at exactly midnight, a noisy frustrated protest against the war.

In the hills above Santiago, two dozen rebels ignored orders and fired their rifles in celebration. Captain Dunney Pérez Alamo was enraged when he heard the men wasting precious ammunition. He ordered the men disarmed and detained.

In the sugar-mill town of Ermita, at the administrator's house, Vilma Espín and Raúl Castro toasted with small glasses of Coca-Cola. Then they kissed.

At rebel headquarters at Central América, several youths celebrated by shooting their guns. Then the sugar-mill's chief engineer banged on doors to wake up the staff so that they could listen to the Women's Brigade and the Radio Rebelde announcers sing the 26th of July hymn, followed by "Silent Night." At the commander's house, secretary Celia Sánchez appeared in the doorway to thank them for the serenade, but Fidel Castro himself stayed inside. He was sleeping soundly.

40/JANUARY 1, 1959: "THE BURNING SPIKE"

At midnight in his living room, General Cantillo tried to hide his tension from the wedding anniversary guests as he toasted the new year with a cup of cider and ate, one by one, the twelve grapes. As soon as he had finished, he took his wife Yolanda by the elbow and led her into the bedroom. Behind the closed door, he told her what was happening.

"I don't know if I'm going to live another twenty-four hours," he said.

She cried. He hugged her for only a moment, then told her she had to be brave and entertain the guests as calmly as possible. As she walked out, he used the bedroom telephone to call the infantry division headquarters and told the duty officer that he was coming over shortly to take charge. The man was to round up all the officers he could.

"Yes, sir," the officer said slowly. Obviously, he wanted to know more, but Cantillo hung up.

Next, he called Colonel Martínez Suárez into the bedroom, described the situation and explained the order of succession to the presidency. "Martínez," he said in a whisper, "I need you to find out the name of the man who is going to be president." It had to be done with absolute secrecy.

"My God." Martínez paled. "How am I supposed to find out

something like that? You mean the chief justice of the Supreme Court?"

"No, no. The constitution says the most senior justice. Not the oldest. The one who has been on the Supreme Court the longest."

Cantillo paused to think. He remembered a man who had been in the army before becoming a government prosecutor for Cuba's highest court. The lawyer was a reliable fellow who could be trusted with a secret, at least until Batista stepped on the plane. Cantillo gave Martínez Suárez the prosecutor's name and told him that as soon as the new president was found, he was to be placed in a room at the Estado Mayor and allowed to talk to absolutely no one.

With that, Cantillo rushed out, jumped into his Oldsmobile and sped around the parade ground to the division headquarters. Brigadier General Silito Tabernilla was already in his office, surrounded by fifteen officers. The men looked tired and confused.

As Cantillo pushed his way through the group, Silito stood beside his desk, and announced in a quavering voice that the command was being transferred. The leaders of the regime were leaving.

At first, the news was greeted by absolute silence. Hurriedly, Silito produced a document from his pocket, a formal statement transferring command. He initialed it, then passed it to Cantillo, who added his own initials. The time was exactly 12:35 A.M.

Silito saw the soldiers look at each other with relieved smiles. He guessed they assumed the war was over. As he ran from the room, he realized the officers were thinking that "it was just like any other coup d'etat in Latin America, where the majors become colonels and the colonels become generals."

Cantillo, trying to be pleasant and low-key, invited the officers to stay and chat over coffee. It was a difficult moment. If Batista changed his mind and decided to stay, he didn't want to appear too eager to take over. But if the president did resign, he was going to need the complete confidence and support of these officers in the critical hours that lay ahead. The first threat against him might come from one of these men.

Casually, almost as if he were giving advice, Cantillo ordered the military police to go and protect the airfield. A tank commander was to send a squad of M-8 light tanks to the air force headquarters for additional support. Several officers volunteered to go to the airfield and say good-bye to their departing leader.

Surrounded by his military aides, Batista stood while he ate a plate of *arroz con pollo*. Everyone watched him carefully. The president-elect thought he saw Batista gag. Silito Tabernilla believed he was eating just a normal helping. Major Varas thought his president was only pecking at his food. Several started to approach, to make a comment, but Batista appeared to want solitude.

When at last he put down his plate, the minister of the lottery walked up to say good night. Batista welcomed him with an embrace and wished him a Happy New Year. The man left with his wife.

Turning to Major Varas, Batista whispered to have the military leaders meet with him in the downstairs office. He walked down the stairs, followed by Prime Minister Güell and secretary Morales del Castillo. As Varas spread the word, the military men joined the procession. Batista's wife Marta smiled and waved good-bye as she disappeared into a bedroom.

President-elect Rivero Agüero was confused. He wondered if this was supposed to be the end of the party. Many of the other politicians wondered too, and Havana Mayor Pozo and Senator Santiago Rey left with their wives.

As they walked down the staircase, an aide bounded back up. Anselmo Alliegro, the president of the Senate, was wanted downstairs immediately.

Alliegro turned to Rivero Agüero. "You are the president-elect," he said. "You should be in the meeting too."

Rivero Agüero's pride was wounded. No, he said. If he wasn't wanted, he wasn't going. Alliegro raced after the aide.

Downstairs, the men were gathering in Batista's office, across a covered walkway from the main house. Just outside the door, SIM chief García Baez found Silito Tabernilla and asked him what was happening. Silito showed him the list, with his name and that of his father, the chief of the national police.

"We need to leave tonight," he explained. "Bring your family to the airfield. Don't bring too much luggage. Only a few clothes, a small bag. We don't have much room." García Baez started to argue that they should stay and fight, but Silito cut him short. The SIM chief ran toward his car.

Silito walked into the office, where Batista was standing, studying the black-and-white framed photographs of his greatest feats. The military men watched him nervously. Moments later, General Cantillo and several aides marched in, and Batista signaled for the door to be closed.

The windows were shut and there were so many men in the room that the air was stifling, but Batista appeared absolutely calm as his secretary handed him a handwritten, two-page speech. It had been dictated that afternoon.

Without explanation, he began reading in a formal, distant voice: "In the city of Havana, on the first of January of 1959, gathered in the office of the president of the republic in Camp Columbia, the signatories of this document affirm the manifestation of Mr. President of the Republic, Fulgencio Batista y Zaldivar, who spontaneously expresses:

"That in the early morning of this day came to his residence the high military chiefs who have charge of the highest military commands, advising him of the impossibility of establishing order in the republic, considering that the situation is grave and, appealing to the patriotism of all those present and to the president's love for his people, saying that he should resign his office."

No one said a word. Not even a cough broke the silence. Cantillo knew that the statement was a lie, that Batista had never asked him for an assessment of the military situation and that in fact everything had been determined hours, perhaps days, before. He thought it typical of the man that even in this room crowded with his most intimate supporters, he was so rigidly formal that he would read a document which talked about himself in the third person.

Batista went on: "He expressed also that equally high-ranking members of the Church, of the sugar industry and of national industry and business have appealed to him. That taking into consideration the loss of life and material goods, and the obvious injury to the national life and to the economy of the republic, and praying to God that He may enlighten the Cubans so they can live in peace and harmony, he resigns his powers of the presidency of the republic, surrendering them to his constitutional successor.

"He begs the people to keep order and not to become victims of tumultuous passions which would be unfortunate for the Cuban family. In a like manner, he urges all members of the armed forces and the police agents to obey and cooperate with the new government and with the chiefs of the armed forces, which General Eulogio Cantillo y Porras has taken over."

Cantillo felt everyone's eyes turn toward him as Batista passed the document around the room and requested people to sign it below his own scribbled initials.

* * *

Upstairs, Rivero Agüero, García Montes and their wives were almost the only ones left. The other politicians had gone home because they assumed the party was over. As the president-elect, Rivero Agüero thought he should wait to say good night to Batista personally, but since no one had reappeared, he decided to leave.

"Let's go," he told his wife, "it's after two o'clock."

Isabel refused. She hadn't yet said good-bye to Marta, Batista's wife.

Just then, Marta appeared in the doorway. She was wearing a different dress. "Good night, Happy New Year," she said, smiling at them.

Rivero Agüero and García Montes, with their wives, waved back, then walked down the stairs. They were almost at the front door when Alliegro burst out of the office. "Batista's resigning," he shouted.

Rivero Agüero felt a sharp pain surge through his body. It didn't seem possible. Batista had told him nothing, not a hint, not a warning. All the plans he had, the dreams . . . He stared at García Montes for a moment, then the two of them ran to the office. Silito Tabernilla was reading off the list of who was going on which plane. The president-elect elbowed his way through the crowd until he was at Batista's side.

"Your government," Batista told him, "will not be able to take over. Castro will arrive in Havana, and your lives will be in great danger. I do not want the responsibility of having you face a firing squad."

Rivero Agüero, who had thought he was going to be president in fifty-four days, felt "a crumbling," as if a great weight had fallen on him. He didn't know what to say.

Senator García Montes asked to remain behind. "I have to call my relatives and friends. My daughter finding out that I deserted her . . . My friends . . ."

"Yoyo," Batista said, calling his canasta opponent by his nickname, "do what you want." But he added that seats were available for him and his wife.

Rivero Agüero, still trying to comprehend this cataclysmic change, remained silent, but his wife spoke for him.

"You have to go," she whispered to him. Then she turned toward Batista, her face reddening with rage. "So now you are leaving," she said derisively.

"Isabel, there are three hundred dead in Santa Clara." His voice was bland. "We have to stop this river of blood."

That made her even angrier. "I don't think this is the moment to think about those who died," she shouted. "What about those who are *going* to die because of what you are doing?"

Batista patted her on the shoulder. "There is a plane leaving later this morning," he said as if speaking to a child. "You and your children will be able to fly to Florida."

With that, he turned back to the group. Most were babbling nervously. "When we open the door here," he said loud enough to be heard by all, "grab your wives. Get in your cars. Don't tell your chauffeurs or bodyguards anything. Get in the planes. The engines are running. This is the most dangerous moment of all."

A military aide opened the door. He was almost crushed by the scramble of men, elbowing each other, shouldering, pushing on the backs of those in front of them, everyone trying at once to squeeze through the doorway, as if each feared there might not be room enough on the planes for all.

Silito Tabernilla was about to leave when Batista called him over. The leader's face was still stiff, his eyes dry, his mouth hard, even in this moment of his ultimate defeat. "Silito," he said, embracing him by the shoulders, "I will see you in Daytona in three months."

Looking around the room, Batista's eyes scanned the black-and-white photographs of his triumphs, his face smiling back at him from a span of twenty-five years: the 1933 coup, the 1940 election, the 1952 coup. "Take these pictures to my Daytona home," he ordered.

Silito nodded, but he was so anxious to get his family to the airport that he delegated the task to an aide. As an afterthought, he requested that his own personal files also be sent along. The aide promised to put everything on a plane the next day. *

As Silito ran from the office, he saw the frenzied exodus was getting underway. Men, pulling their wives by their wrists, were fighting to get through the main doors of Casa Columbia.

At the curb, where the long line of black limousines was waiting, startled bodyguards and chauffeurs stopped leaning against the fenders.

"To the airfield! To the airfield!" the politicians shouted. Aides

---

* Neither the photos nor files were sent. The files contained lists of how much various journalists and politicians had been bribed each month. Later, Castro appeared on television, waving and reading from the documents, an act which profoundly embarrassed many writers and editors.

scrambled, opening doors, jumping behind the wheels, automatically reaching for their guns.

Some women were crying, tripping over their long silken gowns, tearing skirts, losing their high-heeled shoes in the dewy early-morning grass.

As the first limousines screeched away, others dashed toward army jeeps or began running toward the airfield, which was a mile away. "Don't leave us behind," they shouted toward the vanishing cars as their women clutched at sequinned purses and struggled to keep up with the men.

All around them, military leaders were emerging from their own houses, carrying hastily packed luggage, which they tossed to aides waiting by khaki-green army cars.

At the back of Batista's own limousine, parked directly in front of the house, bodyguard Alfredo Sadulé was bent over the open trunk, pulling a Thompson submachine gun from its leather case. He wanted to take no chances during the next few minutes.

Looking up for a second, Sadulé saw the frantic rush of people who, until a few minutes before, had been the leaders of the country. Now they seemed like terrified animals. It was a "stampede, like a rush of cows in a Western movie."

On the other side of the camp, in his second-floor SIM office, Lieutenant Colonel García Baez was hurriedly removing the three-by-five-inch index cards from the secret "K" files, the lists of his top informers. Carrying the cards into the bathroom, he dumped them into the tub and doused them with alcohol. A match started a blaze that reached almost to the ceiling.

Running back to his desk, he pulled out his slender leather briefcase and stuffed into it dozens of small certificates which showed he had completed correspondence courses at two unknown schools, the National University of Jose Martí and the University of North Oriente. In another drawer, he found 2000 or 3000 pesos in cash, what was left of the $13,000 Batista gave him each month to pay informers. That too was jammed into the briefcase.

Then he went to a closet and pulled out his official army uniform, which was neatly pressed, on a hanger. Quickly, he removed the light-gray suit he usually wore. His overwhelming fear was that a group of young army officers might stage a coup d'etat, arrest the regime's leaders at the airfield and turn them over to the 26th of July, to show their support for the revolution. He knew he was going to need all the authority and prestige he could muster for the next few minutes, and the uniform could help a little.

As soon as he was dressed, he summoned an aide and rattled off the names of police and SIM officials, so that they could be notified immediately and told to get out of the country. Next, he called in his five bodyguards and said, "I want all of you to come with me. You are involved with 'problems' because of me. Cantillo is not the kind of guy who is going to keep power." Two wanted to go. Three said they would stay.

With that, García Baez ran from the room, hopping down the stairs, his briefcase banging against the railing, the bodyguards trailing behind.

On a darkened Havana street, an odd caravan of police cars was moving toward Camp Columbia. Colonel Orlando Piedra, chief of the Bureau of Investigations, was in the lead car. In the second was Lieutenant Colonel Esteban Ventura, chief of the Anti-Communist and Anti-Subversive Unit, the most feared and hated police official on the island. He was followed by a car with his top aides and, behind that, a vehicle carrying Colonel Conrado Carratalá, the police officer responsible for the beating of Danilo Mesa.

The police officials had always worked closely together, but this time Colonel Piedra had been unusually secretive, telling the others only that there were "a whole bunch of top revolutionaries" in a Miramar house and that each should bring only his closest aides. Ventura had been working when the call came, his only concession to New Year's Eve being the wearing of his formal uniform, navy blue with silver buttons.

The caravan moved west, under the Almendares River tunnel and down Fifth Avenue into Miramar. Ventura waited for the colonel to turn onto a side street, but he kept speeding straight ahead until they were beyond the suburb and heading into the Marianao Beach area, where the amusement parks were shuttered and dark. An aide said he "smelled something bad."

Ventura signaled out the window, and the colonel's car stopped. The two police leaders walked to the shadows of shrubbery, where Ventura demanded an explanation.

"The president," Piedra explained, "wants to have a frank exchange with you. But it has to be very private. We are going to Camp Columbia."

In Vedado, near Twenty-third Street, Lieutenant Colonel Martínez Suárez had found the house of the next president of Cuba. Trailed by the Supreme Court prosecutor and several aides, he walked up to the door and knocked. There was no answer. He knocked harder without success, then pounded on the wood with the butt of his pistol.

Just then a man appeared from a neighboring house. "We are looking for Carlos Piedra," the colonel shouted. "Maybe he isn't home. Is he at a party?"

"No, he's home. I saw him earlier."

Martínez Suárez realized that Piedra was probably frightened and confused, as most Cubans would be by a late-night appearance of army cars. He ran to the neighbor's house and used the telephone to call the magistrate.

"I have a very important mission," the colonel told him. "It is essential that you, as the most senior magistrate, go to Camp Columbia right away."

Piedra stammered that he would let them in.

As Martínez Suárez dashed back across the yard, the judge's wife, wearing a bathrobe, opened the door. Piedra, also in a robe, stood a short distance behind her, in the center of the living room. His teenage daughter was clinging to him.

For a long moment, the colonel stared at the judge. The fellow had a hangdog face, a long jaw and short gray-black hair. He was definitely frightened. Martínez Suárez decided he had to make the explanation convincing.

Suddenly, he snapped to attention and saluted. "Mr. President," he announced, "by order of General Cantillo, I am to take you to Camp Columbia."

The judge's face turned white. His features revealed, in sequence, bewilderment, shock and terror. The colonel knew he would never be able to forget those expressions and the way they moved across the man's face. Sometime in the future, he thought, this was going to be a very funny scene, but now it was only another problem.

"Why," Piedra stuttered, "do you call me the president?"

"Right now, you are president of Cuba. Batista is leaving."

Piedra said nothing, but he looked as if he were about to collapse. His wife cried. His daughter clung even tighter to his robe.

The prosecutor, trying to soothe them, stepped in and assured him that it was indeed true, according to Article 149 of the 1940 Constitution.

Reluctantly, Piedra agreed to go with them. He disappeared into a bedroom, where he took a long time getting dressed, so much time that Martínez Suárez feared he might have sneaked out a window. The man certainly was not pleased to discover that he was now the political leader of more than six million people.

When Piedra finally appeared, he was dressed in a light-colored business suit. The colonel started leading him toward the door, but the wife grabbed him by the arm.

"Colonel, please," she pleaded, "guard my husband well, I beg you. Don't let anything happen to him." Her eyes were wet with tears.

Shortly after 2:00 A.M., Senator García Montes and his wife drove up to the Rosita de Hornedo apartment hotel on the Miramar waterfront. They ran inside and pounded on the door of the Colombian ambassador until the man, sleepy-eyed, opened up.

García Montes hurriedly described the situation and ran to a telephone. Pulling his private phone book from his pocket, he began calling high-echelon officials and telling them to come to the apartment, where they would be safe in asylum.

At the Columbia airfield, General Cantillo stood under a sprawling bo tree beside the air force headquarters. He wanted to make certain that the planes could leave safely, but he wanted to remain inconspicuous, so that no one would think he was forcing Batista to go.

A few yards away, on the concrete apron, the scene was like a bizarre dream, lit by the stark brilliance of the floodlights atop the headquarters. Women in evening gowns were tugging at children. Husbands' faces were contorted in fear. All were hurrying toward the two Aerovías Q planes. Their engines were running.

Rubén Batista, the eldest son, was shepherding his wife and mother toward one of the stairways. In his arms was his eight-year-old daughter, clad in pajamas. As he moved up the steps, he looked down at the arriving olive-green Oldsmobiles of the military commanders. Aides were pulling luggage from the trunks.

Nearby, García Baez said a hurried good-bye to his SIM escort as he motioned his father, wife and children toward the plane. Silito Tabernilla, wearing a 9-millimeter Browning automatic, told his bodyguards, "You are in good hands," then rushed his wife and two young daughters to the stairway. Presidential secretary Morales del Castillo gave his bodyguard and chauffeur each a $100 bill and asked them to take care of his family.

Batista's black Cadillac limousine was the last to arrive. Ten persons climbed out of it, including his wife, teenage son Jorge, his brother-in-law, Prime Minister Güell, and three aides holding Thompson submachine guns.

"What should I do with the car keys?" the chauffeur asked Batista.

"Leave them here," he shrugged.

Someone pointed out that the Tabernilla clan was getting on the presidential plane. The passenger lists must have gotten mixed up.

"That's all right," Batista said. "We'll just use the other one." He turned to a delegation of army officers who had come to say farewell.

Prime Minister Güell, still clutching the brown envelope, walked over to Cantillo. Even now, his diplomatic dignity remained intact.

"General," he said slowly, "I'm leaving, but if you want me, I will come back."

Cantillo thanked him, and Güell hurried toward a plane.

A few feet away, Colonel Ventura, the hated police official, was arguing with General Pedraza. He had just been told the reason for his bizarre late-night trip, and he was enraged. "This is cowardice and betrayal," he bellowed. He refused to leave without his family. The planes would have to wait until his wife and children arrived.

Pedraza said that wasn't possible, but if Ventura left now, he would personally guarantee that his family would be put on a flight later that morning.

Ventura demanded that he be allowed at least to call his wife. The general said no, there wasn't time and no one could know about the escape until the planes had taken off.

Hearing that, the police official erupted. His hand reached for his .45-caliber, but he didn't pull it out. The motion itself was enough to make it absolutely clear that he was going to make the telephone call, no matter what anyone said. The general relented.

At the steps of the DC-4, Rivero Agüero paced in a daze. He had counted 215 pesos in his pocket, and he looked bitterly at the military men, whose homes were inside the camp, carrying luggage onto the planes. He imagined that there were considerable quantities of cash and jewelry inside those suitcases, enough to assure the officers of a prosperous exile.

Soldiers were shouting from somewhere in the darkness, perhaps from atop the air force headquarters.

"You should have left sooner."

"Viva Fidel!"

Rivero Agüero, who only minutes before had thought he was going to be leader of the country, was overwhelmed with shame. It is not, he thought, a good way to end something.

Suddenly, his leader grasped his left arm and led him up the stairs. At the top, Batista turned and waved to the soldiers below. His face was grim. Then, pushing Rivero Agüero ahead of him, he entered the plane and slipped into a seat beside his wife in the center of the compartment.

The passengers were silent, the engines running, but torturously long seconds passed without anything happening.

Rivero Agüero stared blankly through a window. His thoughts were interrupted by Batista's personal physician, sitting across the aisle. "What do you think of all this?" the doctor asked.

"It is the end of the world, don't you see?" Rivero Agüero mumbled, not thinking of what he was saying. He looked back at Batista. He thought he saw him chuckling and his wife smiling, but their faces turned serious when they realized he was watching.

Moments later, police chief Ventura marched onto the plane and sat down. Aide Cosme Varas closed the door.

The engines of the DC-4 revved as the plane pivoted and moved away from the apron, its Aerovías Q lettering disappearing into the darkness beyond the spotlights. The second plane followed, carrying the Tabernilla clan and others.

General Pedraza and Major Collado joined Cantillo under the bo tree. They watched in silence as the two planes moved toward the end of Runway 9. After more than six years of dictatorship and two years of civil war, after people being tortured by the police and officials assassinated by the underground, after the demands of the U.S. State Department and the plotting of army officers, it all came down to this.

At the end of the runway, facing northeast, engines droning, the

Batista plane paused for a moment, then picked up speed. At 2:40 A.M., it soared into the moonless night. The second plane took off a few seconds later.

"May God help us," Major Collado mumbled, thinking of the chaos the next few hours would inevitably bring.

"Well," said Pedraza, the old general who had seen more than one coup, "they have left you with a burning spike in your hand. I wish you luck."

Cantillo said nothing.

41/3:00 A.M.: "WELL, MR. PRESIDENT, WHAT DO WE DO NOW?"

As his Oldsmobile raced across the camp, General Cantillo had only one thought on his mind—end the bloodshed.

Entering the commander's office at the infantry division headquarters, he found Colonel Martínez Suárez waiting for him. The colonel said the new president was in the large conference room at the Estado Mayor, where an aide was making certain that the old man talked to no one. Then he described the magistrate's terror-stricken reaction to the news.

Cantillo scribbled down the justice's name. He ordered Martínez Suárez to keep the man quiet a while longer and make certain that the airfield was kept open, so that anyone who wanted to leave could do so.

As the colonel rushed out, Cantillo called Ambassador Smith. The two had never met, and the general introduced himself in his fluent English. He said that Batista was going to the Dominican Republic, but others would be flying to the United States and needed help in gaining admittance.

Smith said he would do what he could. He asked if everything was quiet at the camp. Cantillo replied it was, and he was going to make "peace efforts" with the Castro brothers. Then he hurriedly said good-bye.

Next, he called in an aide and dictated a telegram, to be sent to all army posts: "Batista, Guas Inclán and Alliegro resigned. The presidency has been assumed by the most senior magistrate who is Dr. Carlos M. Piedra y Piedra. All have left . . ." It was to be signed, "Chief of the Army, General Cantillo." Its priority was "Flash."

He followed that with a second message, intended only for Colonel Rego Rubido in Santiago: "Establish contact through persons you know and try to secure a cease-fire in the entire republic, in expectation that it will be officially requested by the Honorable President Carlos M. Piedra. This cease-fire is of the utmost importance to avoid useless loss of life."

That done, he began talking to his new subordinates and making appointments to replace the army officers who had fled. Someone suggested they move to the Estado Mayor, where there was more room. Cantillo had been reluctant to do that before, fearing he might look like a usurper, but there was no reason not to now. In a caravan of cars, they sped to the armed forces headquarters, where Cantillo took the stairs two at a time to the third-floor conference room. Nodding to an aide standing by the door, he went inside. Justice Piedra was sitting alone at the massive wooden table.

Cantillo handed him Batista's resignation notice. "Are you the senior magistrate?"

"Yes, I guess so," the old man said numbly.

"Are you the one who succeeds in case others are not available?"

"Yes." His voice did not sound certain.

"Well, then, you are the president."

Piedra looked down at the document and read it slowly. In spite of all that was happening, all the dangers he faced, Cantillo felt like laughing. He could imagine this man's simple New Year's Eve being interrupted by the news that he was being asked to lead a country torn by intrigue and fighting. There was no doubt in his mind that both of them, the general and the president, could be dead within hours if chaos erupted.

"Well, Mr. President," Cantillo said, trying to get the old man accustomed to his new title, "what do we do now?"

"Well, General, what *do* we do now?"

Cantillo sat down beside the old man. "Batista fled," he said in a tired voice. "We didn't put him out of office. The people did. And the people are represented by Fidel Castro, whether we like it or not." He wanted to call Castro and tell him to come to Havana, to help form a new government. That way, the army would still be intact, and compromises were possible.

Piedra said no. "I cannot talk to a man who is an outlaw."

Dismayed, Cantillo asked how they could negotiate a cease-fire if they didn't talk to Castro. He described the telegrams he had already sent and explained that a cease-fire was not the same as surrender. It was simply the beginning of negotiations to end the fighting. Piedra agreed there was nothing wrong with that, and Cantillo decided to send the order for a cease-fire to all army posts facing the rebels.

After he communicated the message to an aide, he turned back to the justice. "Mr. President, I am chief of the army by accident. You are chief of the government by accident. You don't know anything about government and neither do I. But we must do the best we can. . . . Do you think it would be wise to consult with people experienced in government?"

The justice agreed that would be wise. Each suggested names of politicians they had heard of. All were aged men and political conservatives. One was General Enrique Loynaz del Castillo, who had been a hero in the War for Independence sixty years before.

In her bedroom, Rosa Rivero unzipped the back of her dress. The fifteen-year-old girl was thinking about her date later that morning, when Emilio was to take her to a poolside barbecue party. She wondered if she should take her white swimsuit, the one with the low back.

Suddenly the front door banged open. Her mother ran up the stairs. She was crying, calling out the children's names. When she saw Rosa, she became hysterical.

"Is my father dead?"

Still hysterical, her mother did not answer. Rosa screamed. The two embraced and cried on each other's shoulders.

Rosa's grandmother rushed up with a glass of water, and Mrs. Rivero drank. It calmed her down enough to tell what had really happened. "Get a few things together. We have to go too. We don't know when we can come back."

Rosa ran to a telephone and called Emilio. He cried. "When will I see you?" he stammered. "Please call me as soon as possible. How can this be?"

Hanging up, she hurried to her room. Into a small blue suitcase, she threw a pair of blue leather shoes, an overcoat, a wool sweater, toothpaste and toothbrush, along with lingerie and her new diary. She wondered whether to take the mink coat. No, she decided. They would probably be gone only a week or two, until things quieted down. She left it lying on the bed.

Shortly after 4:00 A.M., the telephone rang at the home of Senator Rolando Masferrer. His wife answered on the bedside extension. He heard her mumble something about Batista leaving and grabbed the receiver.

It was one of his wife's female acquaintances, who he knew was in the 26th of July Movement. "*Comemierda,*" she screamed at him. "Shit-eater . . . Batista has left you and your Tigers holding the bag."

Masferrer knew it had to be true. No one would dare say that word to him otherwise.

After only a couple hours of sleep following his return from the underground meeting, Julio Duarte was awakened by the telephone.

"*¡Julio, se fue El Hombre!*" The Man left.

Duarte felt a chill run through his body. The caller was an associate editor of *Prensa Libre*, whose father had just been notified by Senator García Montes, calling from the Colombian ambassador's apartment.

Duarte knew the source was unimpeachable. He made several quick phone calls to other Movement leaders and suggested they meet immediately at a safehouse on Calle Ayesterán, near the Civic Plaza.

Racing over in his 1956 Chevrolet, Duarte was one of the first to arrive, and every time another person came in, the information had to be repeated. They were still debating what to do when someone saw cars stopping at a house on the corner. The drivers were carrying rifles.

"Tigers," someone whispered as they looked through the window. "That's the home of a Masferrerista."

The Movement people had only one or two pistols among them, and they didn't dare risk a confrontation. In the dark, they slipped out of the house and reconvened at a sympathizer's apartment on Eleventh Street, where they were joined by Comandante Diego, chief of Acción y Sabotaje in Havana.

Everyone shouted advice about what to do first. Duarte, who considered himself the Movement's political leader in Havana at that moment, made his own decision. He was going to call Camp Columbia. Grabbing a phone book, he found a separate listing for the Estado Mayor. It seemed ridiculously easy. As he dialed, a dozen persons huddled around trying to listen.

"Estado Mayor," a voice announced.

"I want to talk to General Cantillo. This is the 26th of July chief in Havana."

"Who's calling?"

"I won't tell you at this moment who I am, but I represent all the 26th of July people here, you can be sure of that."

"Just a moment." There was a long pause. Duarte was sweating as people whispered to him, "What's happening? What's happening?" Others gave advice.

At last, another voice came on the phone.

"Is this General Cantillo?" Duarte asked.

"No, he's tied up at the moment."

Someone whispered to Duarte that the phone call had gone on far too long. The Estado Mayor was obviously trying to trace it. Duarte agreed. "I'll call you back," he said abruptly, then hung up.

The group ran downstairs to another apartment. Trying to avoid chaos, Duarte allowed only one or two to enter with him. He decided that this time he was going to give his name. The next few hours could determine everything. There was no time for caution.

The same voice answered.

"This is Julio Duarte. I am the secretary-general of the Cuban Bar Association, secretary general of the Havana Bar Association and the political chief of the 26th of July in Havana." Now, he thought, there was no turning back.

"Ah," the army man said, as if he had been pleasantly surprised, "is Faustino there?"

"No." He didn't add that Faustino Pérez, onetime chief of the Movement in Havana, had fled to the Sierra months before.

The army officer gave his name. "You can ask Faustino who I am. He'll say you can trust me. Ask him how I treated him at the El Principe prison."

"Oh, yes," Duarte lied. He had never heard of the officer before. "I visited him at El Principe, and he spoke well of you."

"You see," the man said proudly.

Duarte told him what he knew. "Who is being designated president? Because I must tell you this—and this is the official word of the 26th of July: We will refuse to accept anyone, except President-designate Manuel Urrutia."

"Well, I don't know . . ."

"If you don't accept him, we will call all the people into the streets. The people will fight for what they believe."

The army man refused to make a commitment. He mumbled only that the situation was unclear.

Duarte could tolerate no more. "All right," he shouted, "at this moment, we are at war. We are going into the streets. We will fight with everything we have." He hung up.

42/DAWN: "A CARGO OF LIVE CORPSES"

As the first light of day tinted the Cuban countryside with a dark grayish hue, the Batista plane was flying at ten thousand feet over Oriente Province. Batista had shocked the passengers shortly after takeoff by announcing that they were going to the Dominican Republic, not the United States as most had expected. He gave no explanation.

Few passengers talked, but none slept. Presidential secretary Morales del Castillo considered the silence "funereal." Rivero Agüero thought that the DC-4 was "a huge casket carrying a cargo of live corpses."

Sitting in the back, aide Cosme Varas made out the passenger list, which would be needed for the customs and immigration inspectors in Santo Domingo. Forty-four persons were on board. Twenty seats were empty.

Rivero Agüero stared out the window. Below them, partially hidden in the early-morning fog, were the majestic heights of the Sierra Maestra, where the civil war had begun. "I wonder," he whispered to Senator Gastón Godoy, "what kind of welcome we would get from Fidel if we crashed."

• • •

In the second plane, the smallest children were sleeping. Rain was driving against the windows. The passengers had wanted to go to New Orleans, but the pilot told them they were on the edge of a massive cold front. Jacksonville, Florida, was a better choice. No one suggested Miami; there were too many angry exiles there.

In the rear of the plane, a group of officers talked quietly. "Now," Silito Tabernilla said, "we have to start conspiring again."

In Havana, groggy staff members were arriving at the U.S. embassy, where Ambassador Smith, still wearing his tuxedo, was there to greet them. He paced through the corridors, dismayed that his position, traditionally the second most powerful in Cuba, had been reduced to near impotence by the State Department. He had notified Washington and called his friend, Ambassador Porfirio Rubirosa, to invite him to his home for a "long breakfast," but there was nothing else he could do except watch developments and, if the mobs duplicated the violence of 1933, help protect American lives and property. That threat would begin when the people learned Batista had left. Until then, all he and the other staff members could do was wait.

On the fifth floor, political officer John Topping was listening to the radio in his office. Most stations were playing soft, early-morning music. On the twenty-four-hour news station, Radio Reloj, a tired announcer was reading news briefs from around the world, as a metronome ticked in the background. There was no mention of Batista.

Press attaché Paul Bethel listened at Topping's door for a moment, then walked down the hall and climbed the stairs to the penthouse conference room. There, through the broad windows, he had a perfect view of most of the city, which was covered by the glow of a golden dawn. Just a short distance away, two blue-and-white police cars stopped on the deserted six-lane Malecón, right beside the Maine Monument. The officers climbed out and conferred, gesturing wildly with their hands. Then they leaped back in and the cars sped off in different directions. From the east came a battered Ford, jammed with people, men standing on the running boards. One was waving the black-and-red flag of the 26th of July. They were laughing.

Quickly the news was spreading throughout the city, each telephone call producing a dozen more. "*¡Se fue!*"—he left—was usually all that was needed to tell the listener what was happening, and cause a shiver of excitement, or fear. For Cubans, it was the memorable moment in their lives, and no one would ever forget exactly where he was and what he was doing when he first heard the news.

As soon as they learned, Movement sympathizers rushed to meeting places and tried to determine what to do. Many youths sped to the long-closed campus of the University of Havana, where they gathered in the main plaza to celebrate and talk. One twenty-year-old, Manuel Granado Díaz, brought with him a .45-caliber pistol, a .38-caliber revolver and a hand grenade that he had obtained thirdhand. Most others also arrived with weapons, which had been carefully hidden away for just that moment.

While the opposition was organizing, the Batistianos hurried to Latin-American embassies or struggled to find a way off the island. The highest navy officials boarded the Batista yacht, *Marta III*, and raced toward Key West. Senator García Montes persuaded the Colombian ambassador to rent two apartments next to his, to house the dozen relatives and Batista officials who had come seeking refuge. Other embassies were filling up.

At the Camp Columbia airfield, Rosa Rivero and her family arrived about sunrise. Her two-year-old baby brother was sleeping, wrapped in a blanket. Her two older brothers were still in their tuxedos, and she herself felt rather foolish in her red evening dress.

For a long time, they sat in the plane. The door was shut, but the pilot refused to take off. At last, a military officer walked into the cockpit and argued with him. The pilot said he had no orders to leave. The officer drew his gun, and the pilot relented. As soon as the plane was airborne, Rosa rolled her coat into a pillow and went to sleep.

At that moment, Senator Rolando Masferrer, with about twenty of his bodyguards and Tigers, were arriving at Jaimanita Beach, where his old PT boat was at the docks. In his hand was a suitcase containing 20,000 pesos, all the cash he had in his house. As soon as he had learned that the new chief of the army was General Cantillo, the man who had forced him out of Oriente Province, he knew he had to leave.

They boarded the boat and waited briefly for other Tigers to arrive, but at 6:00 A.M., as it was getting light, Masferrer told his men, "We can't wait any longer. We're risking our own skins. For all I know,

Cantillo could well order the air force to bomb us in the middle of the ocean, just to ingratiate himself with Fidel." They tossed the lines on the docks and started the engines. Moments later the *Olo-Kun II* sped out to sea.

At 8:00 A.M., nursing a slight hangover, Paul Tannenbaum helped his wife, in-laws and two young sons from the tender onto the Havana docks. In his excitement to see the city, he had managed to get his family on board the first tender leaving the *Mauretania,* and now, with a floral-print shirt and a camera dangling from his neck, he was prepared for a full day of sight-seeing.

Some "rough-looking characters" were milling around the pier, and Tannenbaum quickly escorted the family past them to the street, where a dozen taxi drivers rushed toward them. Elbowing his way through the group, he chose a slender black man who had a black 1948 Mercury limousine with a sun roof. The man spoke little English, and they used sign language to haggle over the price. When that was agreed upon, the driver said the tourist shops would not be open until ten o'clock. Until then, they would drive around and see the sights.

The family piled into the limousine, the kids sitting on the jump seats, and the old Mercury started winding through the narrow streets of Old Havana. The place was nearly deserted. Tannenbaum assumed the Cubans were simply sleeping off their hangovers.

As the Tannenbaums examined the old Spanish stone buildings near the harbor, Havana radio and television stations were announcing cautiously that there were "transcendent developments in the country" and that the Estado Mayor was going to hold a midmorning press conference. CMQ, the flagship radio station of an islandwide network, was being even more careful. It simply canceled its regular programming and played Beethoven's Ninth Symphony.

In Miami, the exiles were learning the news quickly, from U.S. radio stations and phone calls from Havana. Justo Carrillo celebrated with a shot of Scotch and then, with a group of friends, rushed to the airport, where he hoped to get the first plane back to Havana. He knew that whoever arrived there first would have a good chance at forming a government.

Though Carrillo didn't know it, the exiles had one advantage. While they were making their plans, almost no one in Oriente Province yet knew that Batista had left. Telephone and civilian telegraph circuits there still weren't working.

43/8:00 A.M.:
"DR. CASTRO:
HAPPY NEW YEAR"

Colonel Rego Rubido paced nervously on the stage of the military theater at the Moncada garrison in Santiago as the last of the seventeen hundred soldiers tried to find places to stand in the aisles. He had decided to tell them exactly what was happening.

When the telegrams had arrived from Columbia, he read them with astonishment, assuming immediately that Cantillo had tricked both him and Castro in order to give Batista time to flee. The situation was exactly as Rego had feared. He was caught in the middle between the general and the rebel leader, the worst possible position to be in. Deciding he wasn't going to risk his own life for the remnants of a regime he despised, he had taken Cantillo's telegrams and attached a note to Castro: "I certify that this is a copy of the original. J. M. Rego MM, Cor. Insp. Terr. First Military District." As an afterthought, he added, "Dr. Castro: Happy New Year." A Jesuit priest was taking the message to the rebel headquarters.

Now, as the soldiers hushed, the last of them finding places along the wall, Rego stepped to the microphone. He cleared his throat to fight back his nervousness and said as firmly as he could:

"Well, gentlemen, once again it has happened. The chiefs and the main men responsible for commands have escaped. . . . You may already understand the gravity of the moment we are living through. . . . The situation is totally abnormal. If you trust me to command, tell me. For I am not particularly interested in command. But I want you to know that if I have your vote of confidence, in ten minutes I will expect you to carry out my orders fully. If I am in command, I am in command. Otherwise, I am not."

Most of the soldiers sat there, sullen, silent and fearful. A few shouted halfheartedly: "You have our support."

It was shortly after 8:00 A.M. when Fidel Castro sat down at the dining table at the Central América, where the rebel cook had prepared a breakfast of chicken with rice and *café con leche*. He had been awake since shortly after sunrise, dictating letters to Celia Sánchez and investigating the midnight gunfire, threatening to court-martial the rebels who had wasted precious ammunition simply to celebrate the coming of a new year.

He was just about to start eating when José Pardo Llada, a politician-journalist, ran in and shouted that the radio had announced there was important news about to come from Camp Columbia about "the chaotic conditions" in Cuba.

Castro, his face flushed, jumped to his feet. He started walking toward the door, then turned back and asked, "Where did you hear the news?"

"From Radio Progreso, from Havana."

Castro tugged at his beard. The more he thought, the angrier he became. "This is a betrayal," he bellowed. "A cowardly betrayal. They want to steal away our victory."

Pacing, he barked orders to his aides. "I'm going to Santiago. We have to take Santiago today." He wanted to see immediately the chief *comandantes* and the officers of the Santiago siege.

As he talked, a teenager who lived in the sugar-mill town burst into the room. He appeared excited, and Castro stopped to hear what he had to say. "An American station said that Batista and his family have left Cuba," the youth reported. Within seconds, others were running in with more news. One said that Cantillo was the new army chief and that a justice was the president.

Castro knew that somebody or something had been very persuasive to make Cantillo change his mind. He guessed it had been the American embassy, and that made him even more determined.

"We have to attack Santiago without delay," he announced, resuming his pacing. "If they are so naive to think they are going to stop the revolution with this coup, we are going to show them they are wrong."

"Comandante," an aide interjected, "I think you should wait at least fifteen minutes."

Castro ignored him. He gave orders for rebel units to move toward Santiago at once. The tank at Maffo was to be transferred to the edge of the city. "Tell Húber Matos to get his people ready to launch an artillery bombardment against the Moncada." Other troops were to move to El Cobre, near the city.

Outside the house, the ordinary rebel soldiers were shouting with jubilation as the news spread of the flight of Batista, the dictator they had fought so long. Juan Luis Céspedes, a barber from Guisa who had joined the rebels, was surprised to hear Castro raging inside. It seemed to him that all their problems were over.

That was exactly the attitude Castro was concerned about. As he paced the smooth concrete floor of the dining room, he worried aloud that all they had struggled for could be lost if the fight ended with the same military establishment controlling the country. But, with the Batista regime shattered, the symbol of dictatorship gone, that might be a difficult concept for the people to grasp. He decided that before he did anything else, he should speak on radio, to ask for the support of the people, to stop Cuba from once again being victimized by a late-night coup. Leaning against a chest of drawers, he pulled the bent, sweat-stained notebook from his pocket and began scribbling ideas for a speech.

As the top rebel leaders were trying to get together, the first contact between a rebel and army officers was taking place in the hills above Santiago. Captain Dunney Pérez Alamo, the officer whose troops had been at the edge of the country club golf course for weeks, was standing with twenty of his men and three jeeps about a hundred yards from the army machine-gun nests that protected the ancient Spanish fortress of El Viso. As soon as he had heard the news from a man in the Santiago underground, he had sent two women to talk to the soldiers. No orders had yet come down from his commanders, but he knew there was a standing policy to let nothing stand in the way of complete victory.

As he watched, two black sedans, carrying about a dozen soldiers, appeared from the fortress. The two women were in the backseat of the second car.

Just before they reached the rebels, the cars stopped, and an army officer jumped out. Dressed in crisp, olive-green fatigues and shiny black boots, the officer walked up to Pérez Alamo, saluted and introduced himself and his men with grave formality, as if it were an official military conference.

Pérez Alamo, suddenly conscious of his own grimy clothes, was impressed that he was meeting a "real gentleman." Not wanting to seem impolite, he introduced his own men, then asked, "You have heard the news?"

The officer said he had.

"Well," Pérez Alamo went on, lying, "I have orders from Comandante Húber Matos and Fidel Castro requesting your heavy weapons immediately, until further negotiations can begin between our superior officers."

The man said he had received no instructions about that, but he did not appear angered by the request. Taking the rebel captain by the elbow, he led him over to a spot where they could talk by themselves.

Regardless of what happened next, the army officer said, there was one thing that was bothering him: the foul language the rebels had shouted from their trenches. "If we have to meet on the battlefield again, let us not offend each other. I suggest that there be no further mention of our mothers, our manhood. This sort of thing isn't necessary to fight. It is demeaning, beneath ourselves."

Pérez Alamo blushed. He felt as if he had just been reprimanded by a priest.

A few miles away, in Santiago, Park Wollam was already sitting in his black-plastic upholstered chair at the U.S. consulate, where he had gone as soon as the Havana embassy notified him by radio. He was ready for a hectic day, and it began quickly, when a rebel officer called and stated politely that he was planning to attack the city that afternoon. He suggested that U.S. citizens stay inside their homes, because he didn't want any of them to be hurt.

At their home, Connie Wollam was worried about a more personal matter. From experience, she knew that any time turmoil erupted in a Latin country, it meant that the electricity would go out. There was only a pound of ground beef left, and she could use it that day, but she also had an uncooked turkey which could spoil quickly if the refrigerator wasn't working. Thus, her first response to the news that Batista had fled was to tell Azela the maid to bake the turkey immediately, complete with stuffing.

44/EARLY MORNING: "ENOUGH GAS IN THE TANK"

It was raining in Washington, a cold drizzle, as staff members entered the deserted State Department building and went to their offices in the Caribbean section on the fourth floor. Telegrams were streaming in from the Havana embassy, giving a running account of those who had left and those who were staying. Director William Wieland learned within three hours that Senator Masferrer had left, and he had a nearly complete list of those who had fled on the first two planes from Camp Columbia. It had been sent by U.S. military liaisons who were hanging around the Estado Mayor.

Several times, Wieland tried to telephone the embassy, but all circuits were busy. There was nothing else to do but wait, and he relaxed by telling his subordinates about his experiences in the 1933 Cuban revolution and what he had seen during his tour of duty in Brazil. When one regime collapsed, he said, the real struggle for power began. "Now, you have to understand Latin America. It all depends who has enough

gas in the tank to reach the headquarters first." He guessed it would take
several weeks before the "smoke starts to clear." The army probably
would attempt to contain Castro in Oriente, "and after that, we'll see
what happens. Maybe he can break out, or maybe somebody else will
have more gas in the tank."

As Wieland theorized, one of the State Department's main hopes for
a "third force" was tramping through the savanna grass of Camagüey
Province back toward the road. Former prime minister Tony Varona was
glum and tired. He had arrived at the rebel camp about 1:00 A.M., only
to find that the provincial commander wasn't there. Enraged that the
26th of July had tricked him, he and his men slept four hours, then
headed back to their car.

When they were about fifty yards from the highway, Varona spotted
his friend Sosa, who had stayed with the car. He shouted, and Sosa ran
though the field toward them. "Batista left," he yelled. "Batista left this
morning."

Varona cursed. Of all the places to be caught at that moment, he had
picked the worst. As a leader of the last democratically elected regime,
he should have been able to make a serious claim to power. But, he
complained to Sosa, "from here I can't manipulate. I can't call for a new
government. I can't even get to a radio station."

He decided his only chance was to find the army officer who had
offered to join with them in an uprising. "Let's go to the cuartel at
Guáimarco and see if that bastard Castellón is there. We still might
have time to control Camagüey if we hurry."

They jumped in the car. With Sosa behind the wheel, they sped off,
tires squealing, over the highway that ran through the flat, broad
grasslands. Varona watched as the speedometer reached the 160-
kilometer mark—almost 100 miles per hour.

Suddenly, there was a loud clank in the engine compartment. Smoke
billowed from the hood. Sosa stopped the car on the dirt shoulder.
Opening the hood, he peered inside for only a moment before he
announced what had happened: "The block is busted."

At the Isle of Pines, Colonel Ramón Barquín was in his cell after
breakfast when a shout rang out from somewhere down below. "Batista
has left. It's on the radio."

Barquín and the other political prisoners rushed to their hidden transistor radios. It was true. "Batista left. Batista left. Batista left." The circular courtyard of Building 4 reverberated with noise, men cheering, chanting, shouting, laughing, until the sound melded into an unintelligible howl.

When two guards appeared at the door, the shouting became even more frenzied. "Let us out. Let us out. Batista left. Let us out."

Barquín's voice joined the rest, for now he had only one thought: From this moment on, every hour he spent in jail diminished his chances of gaining power.

High in the sky above the Florida Keys, Justo Carrillo was in a plane filled with Cuban exiles, those fortunate enough to get on the first Cubana Airways flight of the day to Havana. Carrillo himself had booked the last fifteen seats for himself and his friends, and the passenger compartment was a cacophony of talk as everyone speculated about what was happening in Havana, who would be the first to make a bid for power and how each could take advantage of the situation.

Carrillo's own hope was that Colonel Barquín could be released quickly from the Isle of Pines. He was certain a free Barquín could easily organize the soldiers at Camp Columbia, and whoever controlled Columbia controlled all of Cuba. If Barquín were in charge, he would appoint Carrillo and the other Montecristi politicians to lead a provisional government.

As the plane flew over Key West, only ninety miles from Havana, Carrillo's dreams were interrupted by the pilot, who announced over the loudspeaker: "Ladies and gentlemen, I am sorry to inform you that we have just learned that the airport at Rancho Boyeros is closed, and we will not be allowed to land. We must return to Miami. Please keep in touch with the Cubana ticket counter."

The passengers groaned.

At the Havana airport, the terminal building was a scene of confusion and fear. Captain William Alexander, a pilot for Cubana Airways, had arrived about 8:00 A.M. to see men in tuxedos and women in long gowns running from the parking lot to the ticket counters. The first flights left on schedule, but then the Movement asked the airport to shut down. At 9:19 A.M., one last Cubana flight, its pilot forced into the cockpit at gunpoint, took off with ninety-one passengers, including a police major and the minister of transportation, bound for New York.

Moments later, 26th of July men arrived. One of them, a trumpet player, saw twenty cars blocking the airport driveway. The engines of some were still running. He chose a 1958 black Chrysler, drove it to a nearby parking lot and pocketed the keys. Then he helped drive trailer trucks to block the runways, and the airport was forced to close down. The Movement was starting its bid to control the city.

In Old Havana, the Tannenbaum family was in a tourist shop on the Prado, a broad street split by a walkway landscaped with trees and bronze lions. His wife was examining floral-print blouses, and his father-in-law was like a child at Christmas as he looked through the cigar section. Paul Tannenbaum himself was deciding that the prices weren't that high, especially since the driver was probably getting a commission, when he heard muted *pop-pop* sounds coming from outside.

His two sons ran up to him. "They're shooting," said Rich, the ten-year-old. Tannenbaum told them to calm down. They were probably hearing firecrackers set off by a New Year's merrymaker.

But when the shopping was finished, the family walked out to find the boys hiding behind store columns. Several men with revolvers and rifles were crouched nearby, firing at a rooftop across the street.

Racing to the old Mercury limousine, the Tannenbaums jumped inside and asked for the driver to take them to someplace more peaceful. Tannenbaum assumed he had just seen a skirmish in the ongoing struggle against Batista.

In Santa Clara, Captain Rogelio Acevedo was crouched in the front seat of an old four-door sedan with a shattered windshield. It was in an alley, directly across from the army snipers in the courthouse, but he was willing to run the risk because neighbors had told him that Batista had left and he wanted to check it out for himself.

Turning on the ignition, he tuned the radio until he found a station. It was playing hymns, interspersed with revolutionary slogans. The seventeen-year-old rebel officer decided perhaps the rumors were accurate.

Just then, a burst of machine-gun fire rattled the front of the car, and he changed his mind. It couldn't be true, because the army was still fighting.

Minutes later, after he had sneaked back to his headquarters at the schoolhouse, a messenger from Ché Guevara ran in to confirm the *bolas*.

He said that the cuartel of Squadron 31 had already given up, and Guevara was demanding that the courthouse be forced to surrender as quickly as possible.

As Acevedo pondered what to do, Guevara was meeting a few blocks away with Major Candido ("Cheo") Fernández, the chief of operations for the Leoncio Vidal garrison, where there were thirteen hundred soldiers, almost three times the number of rebels in the city.

Following General Cantillo's instructions, Fernández asked for a cease-fire, but Guevara immediately rejected the idea. He insisted on an unconditional surrender or the fighting would continue.

"At twelve thirty P.M.," he said, "I will give the order to all our units to renew the attack, and we will take the garrison at any price. You will be the responsible ones for all the bloodshed. Besides, you should know that there is a possibility that the government of the United States might intervene militarily in Cuba, and if this is the case, your crime will be even greater, because you will be supporting a foreign invader. For such an act, all I would have left to do is give you a pistol so that you could commit suicide, since knowing this fact you would be a party to high treason against Cuba."

Grim-faced, the army officer promised to relay the message to the regimental commander.

At the city hall in Yaguajay, a bearded youth opened the door to the small room where Captain Abón-Ly was being held prisoner. "Your chief has fled," the teenager said sarcastically. He left the door open so that the army officer could hear the radio. Abón-Ly couldn't understand how a small rebel group had defeated a forty-thousand-man army. He listened for only a few minutes before rolling over on his cot and trying to blot out the noise.

Still in her pajamas, Vitalia Bequer, the mother of the fear-ridden child, crouched underneath the window of a small house in San Miguel de los Baños. She and her schoolteacher friend were trying to talk the last of the cuartel's seven soldiers into surrendering.

They had learned of Batista's flight only minutes before the area's small rebel group opened fire on the army post. Two rebels were wounded before six of the soldiers gave up. The seventh had escaped to this house.

Hiding on the other side of the window, the soldier said he was holding out until reinforcements could arrive from Havana. The two women laughed at that and urged him to surrender.

"But they'll kill me."

"No," Vitalia said, "we can guarantee your safety."

"Are you sure?"

"Yes." There was a long pause, then the teacher said, "Give me your weapons."

A stubby hand appeared and slid a carbine through the window. The teacher passed it to Vitalia.

"Do you have a handgun?"

The hand produced a .45-caliber revolver.

"Do you have any bullets?"

One by one, the hand brought forth cartridges, each taken by the teacher and passed to Vitalia. She held the unwieldy load as best she could.

At last, the soldier came out. He was a fat man with straight black hair. His shirt and pants were soaked with sweat.

As the rebels led him away, Vitalia hurried home. Her ten-year-old son had heard the shooting, but he seemed more curious than frightened. She kneeled and gave him a big hug. Finally, she thought, it was all over. He would have nothing to be nervous about ever again.

45/MORNING, JANUARY 1: "¡REVOLUCION, SI!"

General Cantillo was getting tired of politicians. For hours, a group of aged men had sat in the third-floor conference room of the Estado Mayor. They drank coffee and small glasses of orange juice, and they seemed unable to agree on anything. To a professional military man, accustomed to receiving a direct order and carrying it out, the discussion was chaos.

Cantillo had made the introductory speech, emphasizing the seriousness of the moment, the danger of bloodshed in these first hours and days of transition. He said it was necessary that there be at least a symbolic government with constitutional authority, so that order could be maintained. There could not be a military junta or a coup d'etat, because Castro would not accept those solutions, but he believed the rebel leader would agree to a temporary government installed for only a short time. At the end he asked, "What is the best thing to do?"

Everyone started speaking at once. Some suggested that the government limit itself to three days. Others wanted it to be longer, and to Cantillo it seemed that a few were already jockeying for political positions, trying to gain seats in the new cabinet.

The tension increased when someone proposed that General Enrique Loynaz del Castillo, the aged veteran of the 1895 War for Independence, become the new minister of defense. The old man refused without hesitation. He called the Batista regime "the most bloody and cruel in the Americas," he had no trust for a regime "prefabricated in Camp Columbia" and he saw no need for a provisional government of any kind. The rebels had won the war, he said, and they had the right to consent to a government. If Cantillo agreed to that, history would record his deed "in golden letters." With that, the old man announced with cordial dignity that he was leaving. Cantillo, managing to smile, walked him to the door.

The others argued on. All were adamant that the cease-fire be maintained, because none had any desire to continue Batista's war, but Justice Piedra still refused to approve any contact with Castro.

As the politicians talked, Cantillo kept running between the conference room and the radio center, where reports and questions were flowing in from army posts throughout the country. Many already were facing 26th of July people at their gates, demanding surrender, and the army commanders wanted to know what to do. Cantillo told them to maintain the cease-fire, but not to surrender.

About 9:30 A.M., with nothing yet decided, Cantillo and Piedra met with the press to make a formal announcement. The general said little, but the justice read a short statement: "For the sake of constitutional respect, I appeal with all my heart to the leaders of the revolution to cooperate in these critical moments, so we can have stability and absolutely level-headed conduct. To these effects, I have ordered a cease-fire in the entire republic."

The newsmen immediately barraged him with questions about the new government, and Piedra's answers were halting and indecisive. He said he had called in some men "to exchange ideas with them. . . . The rest will be taken care of little by little. . . . I can't say anything else yet. Please, let me study and consider the events."

Castro was fording a river beside a demolished bridge near Contramaestre when he saw a large crowd gathering on the opposite bank.

Comandante Antonio E. Lussón of Column 17 was there, but a Santiago priest seemed to be the center of attention.

As he climbed up the riverbank, his pant legs wet with water, people shouted to him that the war was over, that the priest had a message from Colonel Rego Rubido.

Castro ripped open the envelope and read the Cantillo telegrams, along with Rego's New Year's greeting. He cursed, then shouted that this was not the end of the war, but only a coup d'etat trying to thwart the revolution. Leaving the crowd surprised and confused, he jumped into a jeep and ordered the driver to rush to the Radio Rebelde station in Palma Soriano.

About 11:00 A.M., he arrived at 201 General Quintín Banderas Street, a modest corner house with large French windows opening directly onto the sidewalk. The 7RR staff was working in a small, tile-floor bedroom, where they had set up the 120-watt Collins 32-V-2 transmitter on a long wooden table beside a tape recorder.

Castro was in a foul mood, muttering about Cantillo's betrayal, but he stopped when he heard one of the announcers, Miguel ("Microwave") Boffil, talking to a commercial radio station in Santiago. It was CMKC, which had been taken over by rebel sympathizers. They were rebroadcasting 7RR's messages.

Castro asked what was happening in the city. Boffil told him that many Movement people were patrolling the streets, but Batista's henchmen were still around. Others volunteered information. Francisco Verdejo Pupo, a local accountant and Movement worker, repeated what Havana stations were reporting about the new provisional government. Movement supporters in the capital were apparently taking over radio and television stations, but the situation there was still very uncertain.

Castro started to pace, then noticed that the room was so crammed with people that it was almost impossible to move. "Well," he said, "what are so many people doing here?"

His statement caused a stampede of supporters to leave through the French windows, until only the radio operator, Radio Rebelde director Carlos Franqui and the announcers were left. As Castro paced, he ordered Boffil to get the equipment ready to transmit and record simultaneously, so the speech could be rebroadcast later.

"Look, *Comandante*," the radioman said, "the problem is that we can't record and transmit at the same time."

"But don't you think it can be done?" Castro was in no mood to be told something was impossible.

Boffil made a quick test of the tape recorder, and when Castro heard the results, he nodded. "Good, it's OK. Let's record first." The recording would then be broadcast.

He moved into a corner, looked over the phrases scribbled in his warped notebook and added a few more. He understood well the "gas tank" mentality of Latin upheavals, and he wanted to make certain that it wouldn't happen now. Though he and the bulk of his troops were almost six hundred miles from the capital, he had two advantages which were beyond the experience of the old-fashioned *políticos:* he had an army willing to die and to kill to achieve victory, and he had the ability to ignore the military men and politicians because, via radio, he could appeal directly to the people, to gain throughout the country a mass support, the likes of which had never been seen before in Cuba.

When he signaled that he was ready to record, a staff member held up the microphone. Castro clutched the notes in his hand. He was sweating heavily, and a curl of wet hair dangled from beneath his khaki cap, pasted to the left side of his forehead.

"Whatever the news from the capital may be," he began, his voice almost cracking with rage, "our troops should not stop fighting at any time. Our forces should continue their operations against the enemy on all battlefronts. Parlays should be granted only to those garrisons that want to surrender. . . .

"It seems that there has been a coup d'etat in the capital. The conditions under which that coup took place are not known to the rebel army. The people should be on the alert and should follow only the instructions of our general headquarters. The dictatorship has collapsed as a consequence of the crushing defeats suffered in the last weeks, but that does not mean the revolution already has triumphed."

His booming voice carried through the French windows and far into the street, where several hundred persons listened, their packed mass stretching beyond the street corner. At the back of the crowd, two small boys sat atop a burro. Comandante Antonio Lussón heard the words with awe. President-designate Manuel Urrutia, who had learned about Batista's flight only minutes before, listened from an adjoining room.

Departing from his text, Castro shouted: "*¡Revolución, sí! ¡Golpe militar, no!*

"Military coup behind the backs of the people and of the revolution, no, because it would only serve to prolong the war!

"Snatching victory from the people, no, because it would only serve to prolong the war until the people obtain the total victory!

"After seven years of struggle, the democratic victory of the people has to be absolute, so that never again will there be in our country another tenth of March [coup].

"No one should be confused or deceived! To be on the alert is the order!" He asked the people to prepare for a general strike, to refuse to work until the revolution was in complete control. "Workers, this is the moment for you to assure the victory of the revolution. Cubans: For freedom, democracy and the triumph of the revolution, support the general revolutionary strike in all the areas that have not been liberated. . . .

"The people and the rebel army must be more united and more firm than ever in order not to let the victory that has cost so much blood be snatched from them."

Castro stopped. His shirt was soaked with sweat. The technicians tested the tape. It was fine. They immediately put it on the air and, using a separate receiver, heard two Santiago commercial stations rebroadcasting it simultaneously.

Working on other messages, Castro issued orders to all his principal commanders. Camilo Cienfuegos was to advance immediately from Las Villas to take over Camp Columbia. Ché Guevara was to go to La Cabaña fortress, on the edge of the Havana harbor. Raúl Castro was to force Guantánamo City to surrender. Victor Mora was to occupy all the garrisons in Camagüey Province.

Next, Castro gave an ultimatum to the army in Santiago: Surrender by 6:00 P.M. or be attacked. "Santiago de Cuba, the murderers who have assassinated so many of your children will not escape as Batista escaped. . . . Santiago de Cuba, you are not free yet. In your streets are those who have oppressed you for seven years. . . . The history of 1895 will not be repeated. Today, the revolutionaries will enter Santiago de Cuba."

With that done, Castro decided it was time to prepare the attack. As he walked into the street, he thrust a fist above his head and shouted, "We do not accept the coup d'etat. Revolution, yes!" The crowd cheered. He was absolutely certain at that moment that the revolution would triumph.

46/THE NEW EXILES

Andrés Rivero Agüero had a terrible headache. He was sprawled in a chair in the Cuban embassy, a two-story, semiclassical structure located at 25 Santiago Street in Santo Domingo. No one had slept during the flight, and most were keeping themselves awake by drinking cup after cup of coffee as they filled out the blank passports that Gonzalo Güell was handing them.

The Dominican government had not been expecting their arrival, and the plane had been forced to circle the city until the tower gave orders to land at the air force base shortly after 8:00 A.M. Ramfis Trujillo, the son of the dictator, bleary-eyed from a late-night party, had rushed to greet them.

Since then, everything seemed to pass in a dream. The men's suits and uniforms were wrinkled, their faces haggard. Only Batista seemed serene as he sat at the dining table talking to Rafael Herrera, editor of *El Caribe*, a prominent local newspaper.

When he said that he had left to "avoid great loss of life and destruction," the journalist stated politely that from his distant vantage point it was hard to understand how a small rebel group could have defeated the Cuban army. Batista replied that the army had no training in guerrilla tactics and added, in a preposterously inaccurate statement, that while the army had lacked certain weapons, the rebels were well equipped. He did not call the Castro Movement Communist, but he said, "When it becomes clear the magnitude and sources of these illicit weapons, it will be seen to what extent the international order has been broken."

After the interview was finished, Batista received a call from the Dominican dictator, Generalísimo Rafael Trujillo, who invited him to stay at the national palace, where he could have a colonel as an aide and a chauffeur-driven Chrysler. The leading politicians and military men could go to the Jaragua Hotel. The aides and police officials could get rooms at the more modest Hotel Paz.

Rivero Agüero hitched a ride with the journalist to the Jaragua. As he entered the lobby, he realized that he didn't even have an extra pair of underwear. But worse than that were his nerves. Going into the hotel's drugstore, he purchased a bottle of nonprescription tranquilizers, which cost $6.50. In Cuba, the same bottle was $1.05. For the first time, he felt homesick.

At Jacksonville, fifty-two Cubans were crowded into a small room at the rear of the airport terminal as a dreary rain pattered against the windows. They had been forced to wait in the plane for more than an hour before officials transferred them to the room. Then they were simply left alone. Babies were squealing for milk, the older children complaining of hunger and tempers of the sleepless adults were running short. Silito Tabernilla guessed that the State Department was deciding whether to admit them to the country. Irenaldo García Baez figured that the airport simply wasn't an international one, and the authorities had to find customs and immigration officials. But no one knew for sure what was happening.

Finally, after the complaints of his two young sons had become unbearable, García Baez had a long argument with two policemen at the door and persuaded them to accompany him to the cafeteria. The former SIM chief was so tired that he imagined the men's belts had small black-and-red insignias, the colors of the 26th of July.

As they reached the food line, he saw some anti-Batista Cubans sitting at a table. He thought there were hundreds, but there were less than a dozen. One was a man whom he had once questioned, and when the man saw García Baez in his wrinkled SIM uniform, he shouted,

"Torturer!" A gray-haired man sitting next to him picked up the chant. "You're a killer. A killer. And we're going to kill you."

"Why don't you keep your mouth shut," García Baez shouted back, adding that the only reason the man wasn't still in jail was that he had divulged the names of many other Movement people.

That made the group yell even louder. Protected by the policemen, García Baez hurried through the food line and returned to the room.

A few minutes later, U.S. officials began processing the passengers. Rubén Batista was one of the first cleared to leave, but as soon as he entered the parking lot, he got into a fight with the same two exiles who had been shouting at García Baez. The fight was quickly stopped by a state trooper, but it caused Batista's eldest son to decide to charter a two-engine plane, to take his wife, daughter, mother and two sisters to New Orleans.

The Tabernilla and García families, who just a few days before had been arguing bitterly with each other, chose now to stick together, rather than split up and risk being attacked by the exiles. Renting cars, they left the airport in a tight convoy. Deputy sheriffs escorted them to the county line. From there, they drove aimlessly toward the center of Florida until they guessed that they had left their tormentors far behind. At a deserted crossroads, they stopped and registered at the Bambi Motel.

While the Tabernillas settled in for their first day in exile, other Batistiano planes were landing at scattered airfields throughout the southeastern United States. Rosa Rivero was one of the forty-seven passengers, including a Batista brother and the lottery director, who landed at West Palm Beach, Florida. They cleared customs after a long wait and Rosa, her red evening dress badly wrinkled, went with her family to the Biltmore Hotel.

Two other planes touched down in New Orleans. One contained the two youngest Batista children, Fulgencio, age six, and Marta Marie, age four. Later, an Aerovías Q plane arrived with fifty-four men, most of them police and SIM officials. Customs officers confiscated fifty automatic handguns, a rifle, several hand grenades and a gold-plated pistol.

At Daytona Beach, Florida, where Batista had a mansion, two air force pilots landed a B-26 bomber. Four private planes went to the Florida Keys. Three charter planes carried away the leaders of the casino business: Meyer Lansky, head of the Cuban gambling syndicate; Santo Trafficante, operator of the Sans Souci Hotel and Casino; and Charles ("The Blade") Tourine. With their wives, girlfriends and cash, they landed at Jacksonville, where almost immediately Florida lawmen predicted that Batista's downfall would mean increased Mafia activity in the United States.

47/THE PALACE AND THE MOB

About noon, General Cantillo escorted Justice Piedra into the formal office on the second floor of the Presidential Palace. They had come so that Piedra could take the oath of office for the presidency, but first the photographers wanted to take some pictures. Arms folded across his chest, Cantillo stood against the wall, beside the bust of José Martí, as the justice sat down at the ornate desk and pretended to sign documents while the cameras clicked.

When that was finished, the justice disappeared into another room, and Cantillo was left alone to face an onslaught of visitors, politicians begging for government positions, relatives of political prisoners asking him to open the jails, and military aides who were running in every few seconds to report that almost everywhere the 26th of July forces were ignoring requests for a cease-fire. The garrison commanders were sounding increasingly nervous.

Cantillo tried to assure everyone that everything would be taken care of soon, but he was no longer certain of that himself. As he mulled over the possibilities, Ambassador Smith led a group into the room. Wearing a white suit and towering above the general, he stepped forward to shake his hand. "So you are General Cantillo."

"Yes." Exhausted, he wondered what new problems the ambassador was bringing.

"Well, you speak very good English," Smith said, relieved that he wouldn't have to use an interpreter. Then he introduced the rest of the group: the papal nuncio and the ambassadors from Spain, Argentina, Chile and Brazil. All, he said, were concerned about giving "safe conduct to all asylees as soon as possible."

Cantillo answered that it had already been done, and several planes were leaving each hour from the Columbia airfield. There was a long silence before Smith asked several vague questions, and Cantillo decided he had really come to find out what the situation was. But the ambassador did not offer American support, and the general did not request it. Cantillo ended the brief meeting by telling Smith simply that he wanted "to try to preserve law and order until the provisional government is ready to turn over authority to whomever should have it."

Shortly after the ambassadors left, an aide handed Cantillo the telephone. A Supreme Court justice was calling. The man said the court had just met and decided it was "not a normal moment in Cuban history." The revolution had triumphed, and it had more right to name a government than did laws left behind by a fleeing regime. Therefore, his fellow justices were refusing to give Piedra the oath of office. He said the man who should be president was Manuel Urrutia, who had been so designated by all the anti-Batista groups.

Cantillo hung up without replying. He knew that without constitutional backing, anything he did would be interpreted as a military takeover, which neither the rebels nor the people would tolerate. The general who had always followed orders no longer had any orders to follow. To him, the result could only be bloodshed.

Piedra walked in, looking tired and confused. He too had just heard the news. "I want to go home," he said simply.

Cantillo had not slept in thirty hours, and his nerves were almost at the breaking point. "Are you the senior magistrate?" he asked, his rage building.

"Yes, I am."

"Are you the one who, according to the constitution, has the right and the *duty* to become president in case others are not available?"

"Well . . ."

"Then you *are* the president." The oath was only a symbol; the constitution was still supreme.

"I know that," the old man said wearily, "but I don't want to be president."

Cantillo's benumbed mind was having a hard time functioning. All he could think of was that he had to find another senior magistrate. That meant killing Piedra. The constitution could work if Piedra died. He stared at the haggard-faced judge, and for a brief moment he contemplated killing him.

Then he realized how ridiculous his thoughts were. He was not the kind of man who would kill people to maintain power, and he didn't want to make himself president; he didn't believe he had the *right* to be president. Piedra could resign, so that there could be a new senior magistrate, but that would take time, and time was one commodity he didn't have. He disliked Castro, but as he stared at the frightened judge he thought, Cuba is like a girl in love with a very bad guy, and if you try to stop her, it's worse. She has to suffer through it, and then maybe she'll come home, after getting some experience.

As Cantillo was thinking, aide Major Collado kept tugging at his arm. He said he had been looking through a window. A mob was forming around the palace. "Listen, General, we have to move."

Cantillo said nothing. Collado persisted. "I don't know what's happening here, General. We should move right away to Columbia."

Jarred from his thoughts, Cantillo relented. Piedra asked if he could come too. Together, they rushed down the marble staircase to the side entrance, where three cars of bodyguards and the black presidential limousine were waiting. As soon as they climbed in, the small convoy sped off.

Slumped in the backseat, Cantillo saw the crowd singing, dancing and waving the black-and-red colors of the 26th of July. Some men were attacking parking meters with sledgehammers, and the general reflected that the meters had been one of Batista's worst mistakes. Cubans had been accustomed to parking for free, and they assumed the meters were merely another technique for lining the leaders' pockets.

The caravan sped down Malecón Boulevard without any trouble, but at Twenty-third and L streets in Vedado a large crowd blocked the street beside the CMQ broadcasting studios. The lead SIM car edged its way through, but when the mob saw the limousine with its *1* license plate, the people shouted and closed in. A stone shattered the right front window and sprayed glass on the bodyguard-sergeant's arm.

Several men had guns, but no one fired. Slowly, the limousine squeezed through the crowd and sped on toward Columbia. Major Collado, sitting on the jump seat, looked at the passengers. Justice Piedra was trembling. Cantillo was lost in thought, as if nothing had happened. *

People had taken to the streets spontaneously when they heard the news. At first there was only a trickle of demonstrators; the flood had come when Carlos Lechuga, the anchorman at Channel 2, had announced Batista's flight on television and launched into a vitriolic denunciation of the dictatorship. He labeled Batista "an assassin and a tyrant."

After that, there was no doubt that the rumors were true. The streets became a stage for celebration, a singing and chanting and waving of banners. It was like an enormous burden had been lifted from the populace. *Prensa Libre* managed to get out an early edition with a one-word headline that summed it all up: "YA"—Finally.

The blue-and-white police cars and the olive-green SIM vehicles disappeared from the streets quickly as most policemen simply abandoned their precinct stations and went home. Only on Calle Trocadero did the police make any attempt to maintain order when a crowd broke shop windows. There, five policemen, two with machine guns, opened fire. Six demonstrators were killed.

At the University of Havana, thousands of youths gathered on the central plaza. Many were supporters of the Directorio, but political distinctions meant little that day, and the statue of the alma mater was draped with Castro's red and black. The youths joined in singing the

---

* There was one last ironic twist to the saga of Justice Piedra, though neither Cantillo, Piedra nor the Supreme Court justices knew it at the time: Piedra was not even the most senior justice. The *Gaceta Oficial* of July 21, 1959, showed that Justice Carlos de la Torre had been appointed to the Supreme Court on June 4, 1935. Piedra was one of three tied for the second-most seniority; they became members on October 17, 1936. Gonzalo Güell and Jorge García Montes, both prime ministers under Batista, confirm these dates. At the time, the idea that presidential succession would ever go so low as a justice was so implausible that no one bothered to keep track of seniority. Justice Emilio Menéndez, who was at the Supreme Court meeting that morning, says the subject was never brought up. The constitution was no longer relevant.

national anthem, but their revolutionary enthusiasm was soon damp-
ened by the rumor that tanks from Camp Columbia were headed toward
the campus. Most fled in terror, not knowing that the crews of the four
tanks had abandoned them about halfway to the university and gone
home.

A hard core of students stayed on, determined to take over the most
repressive police stations and the prisons. For some, it became a game.
Manuel Granado Díaz, a young Directorio, helped four friends "occupy"
a blue Ford Consul in the name of the revolution, and every time they
heard a rumor of Masferrer's Tigers being engaged in a gun battle, they
sped off to investigate. They found no skirmishes that day, but they
enjoyed the excitement.

Julio Fernández León, the youth who had once spent months at El
Principe prison, was twenty-two years old that day, but his birthday was
forgotten as he organized a group of teenagers to help take over the
town. He raced first to El Principe to free his friends, but when he
arrived he found all the prisoners, common criminals as well as the
political inmates, already gone. One of them, a 26th of July man named
Aldo Vera, had led a group to the Great Taxi Stand, where they had
"liberated" about twenty taxis to form a mobile squad. After chatting
with Vera, Fernández León hurried to the Ninth Precinct Station,
where the notorious Colonel Ventura had worked over his prisoners. A
young Directorio was sitting in Ventura's chair. He put a pair of
colonel's insignia on his shoulders as everyone laughed. After that,
Fernández León decided he needed a headquarters of his own. Near the
university he found a showroom of jeeps and used cars, which he
believed was owned by a Batistiano. He declared it "liberated territory."

A few blocks away, Max Lesnik took over a clinic across the street
from Vedado High School to serve as the headquarters for the Segundo
Frente del Escambray. He had realized immediately that Batista had left
at the wrong time, that his little-known group could not possibly
counteract the enormous publicity Castro had built up. He spoke at a
few television stations and, later, talked with Jack Stewart, his CIA
friend. Stewart wanted a way to contact the rebels. Lesnik couldn't help
him with that, but he gave the American thirty stickers reading,
"Permission to Travel, Segundo Frente del Escambray."

Meanwhile, the Communists moved into second-floor offices overlooking the Central Park and hung out a banner announcing their
location. An assistant to photographer Eduardo ("Guayo") Hernández

filmed a crowd on San Lazaro Street, where a youth was carrying a large red flag depicting the hammer and sickle, but there were far more red-and-black banners of the 26th of July.

Most of those who took to the streets had no formal affiliation with any anti-Batista group. They started off in small groups merely celebrating, but as their numbers grew, their mood became uglier, and they started reacting with rage to the hated symbols of the Batista regime or, at least in some cases, joining in for the thrill of vandalism which they knew no policeman was going to stop. Starting about noon, these people became mobs, roaming the streets without leaders.

They were usually selective in their targets. They sacked the offices of Masferrer's *El Tiempo* newspaper and burned a government-owned paper. The plant of *Alerta,* owned by Batista's minister of communications, was taken over. Shell gas stations were a favorite target because the president of Cuban Shell was believed to have helped negotiate the sale of British tanks and planes to Batista.

Most of the casinos, symbols of Batista's corrupt connection with American organized crime, were attacked, and mobs rampaged through the gaming rooms at the Deauville, El Morocco, Capri, Plaza and St. John's hotels. In Old Havana, slot machines and crap tables were dragged into the street, where they were thrown into massive bonfires.

In the residential neighborhoods, crowds stampeded through the houses of those who were close to the regime. The home of Batista's mother-in-law was sacked, as was that of his daughter, Mirta Batista de Pons Domenech. Colonel Ventura's home was looted. On Third Street in Vedado, an angry group burst into the home of Batista labor leader Eusebio Mujal and pushed out the air conditioners. One man left carrying two bottles of champagne and a blue curtain. At the home of Major Cosme Varas, the aide who had accompanied Batista to Santo Domingo, his wife Elena cowered, holding her month-old son, her five-year-old clinging to her neck, as a gang of twelve youths raced through the house and took what they wanted.

Near the El Principe prison, one Batista supporter was hung from a lamppost, but that was the only case of vigilante vengeance. Most leaders of the old regime had already fled the country or were safely inside foreign embassies. Compared to the thousand who had been killed during the 1933 revolution, the New Year's demonstrations were practically bloodless. On that first day in Havana, according to the Associated Press, only thirteen persons died.

Nor did the mobs even approach the American embassy, where five Marines sat in the lobby. All they could do was hand out the flag decals to U.S. citizens who came to get them for their houses and cars. Except for the casinos, the decals worked exactly as intended: American property was left alone. But there was at least one incidence of anti-American feeling.

In the backseat of the 1948 Mercury limousine, Paul Tannenbaum was standing up, his head and shoulders jutting through the open sun roof, as he took photographs of a jubilant crowd, dancing in the streets, climbing over cars, honking horns. "They sure are enthusiastic about their New Year's," he remarked to his wife.

The Tannenbaums still didn't know Batista had left, but they understood at least that something unusual was happening. Militiamen with armbands and rifles were directing traffic at intersections. Several policemen had trudged by, heads down, their caps gone, the shields missing from their uniforms. It all seemed a bit much for ordinary tourists, and Tannenbaum had ordered the driver to take them back to the docks. He was trying, but everywhere he turned, the narrow streets of Old Havana were so filled with people that the car could barely move.

At last, at one street corner, the limousine had to come to a complete stop, its path blocked by a gang of chanting youths. They yelled something at Tannenbaum in Spanish, which he couldn't understand. His father-in-law, who had been sitting quietly smoking a large cigar, waved his left arm out the window. "Good luck," he said, smiling. "Congratulations. Happy New Year."

Those words in English changed the mood of the youths, and they began shouting angrily. To Tannenbaum, they seemed to be saying, "Yankee, Yankee, Yankee, go home, go home. Imperialists. Imperialists."

Some youths grabbed his father-in-law's arm and tried to pull him from the car. Tannenbaum tugged back. They let go, and the lawyer moved quickly to close the sun roof as the others rolled up the windows.

They sat inside the car for what seemed like an hour as the crowd banged on the roof and fenders, and shouted, "Viva Fidel! Viva Fidel!"

At last, the crowd dispersed enough for the driver to move on. "But," he said, "there's no hope of getting back to the ship now. I'm going to head out of the city. Why don't we go see the rum factory?"

At the CMQ broadcasting center in Vedado, Emilio Guede was

running back and forth between the television studios and the front offices, where dozens of Movement workers were making frenzied reports over the telephone. The propaganda chief of the Civic Resistance seemed to have a hundred things to do at once, and there were countless self-styled "advisers" telling him what the main priorities were.

The 26th of July and the Civic Resistance were working hard to get the city under control, but it was not easy. Despite Julio Duarte's pre-dawn threat to the Estado Mayor, the Movement had no real organization for such a large action. It had always consisted of merely small groups of friends, each of which had only tenuous connections with other groups.

In trying to overcome the Movement's deficiencies, Comandante Diego had occupied the CMQ studios, across the street from the Havana Hilton. There, radio and television could be used to reach into almost every living room in Havana. It was a weapon far more powerful than the news releases or press conferences from the Estado Mayor.

The key problem was to get the mobs under control, so that they could help the 26th of July take over the city. While chaos reigned, the situation remained fluid enough for anyone to inspire the crowds and grab power. And if the bloodshed became too great, the people might welcome the return of military authority.

Thus, via television, the Movement prohibited the sale of alcoholic beverages. Rebel sympathizers were asked to stop the destruction and avoid violence. Batistianos were to be detained but not harmed. Castro's speech calling for the general strike was tape-recorded and rebroadcast. Volunteers were sent to protect the tourists and casinos at the Riviera, Nacional and Hilton, three of the largest hotels. Others, often boy scouts, manned roadblocks and directed traffic. Each order from CMQ was preceded by "Comandante Diego says . . ." "Comandante Diego requests . . ." "Comandante Diego demands . . ."

Emilio Guede was pressed into duty as one of the announcers. After years of hiding his connections with the underground, it was a shock to be speaking for the Movement to hundreds of thousands of people, and it took him awhile to understand the power of television.

Once, in giving a news bulletin, he reported that Batistianos had been spotted in an ambulance in Miramar. Almost immediately hospitals called to complain that people everywhere were stopping ambulances and beating up the drivers. Guede rushed back to the microphone.

"People, people," he shouted, "in your patriotic fervor, you have been stopping ambulances. We must cease that right now. All ambulances must be left alone. It is better that a car full of Batistianos escapes than one innocent victim dies."

Between such announcements, people appeared on camera to give personal testimony of the horrors of the Batista regime. Some, sensing sudden fame, exaggerated their stories outrageously, but others gave specific and accurate accounts of their experiences in Batista jails. As Guede watched, one emaciated man unbuttoned his olive-green shirt in front of the cameras. His back and chest were covered with blue-black bruises and cigarette burns.

Throughout Havana, people watched their television sets with fascination as this unrehearsed show of a revolution in progress unfolded in front of them. Before long, hundreds jammed the streets outside the studios, forming themselves into ad hoc militias. The biggest group was led by a little-known Movement worker who dubbed himself "Comandante One Star." Within a short while, he had promoted himself to "Comandante Two Stars."

48/"THE REPUBLIC IS HEADLESS"

Standing beside his broken-down car on the deserted Camagüey highway, Tony Varona scanned the flat grassland horizon for some kind of movement. Suddenly, there it was, a black 1955 Ford. "We'll commandeer that car in the name of the revolution," he shouted to his associates as he ran into the center of the road and waved his Thompson submachine gun.

The Ford stopped, and a leather-faced farmer poked his head out the window. "What's going on?" he asked, as if he thought he were seeing a mirage.

"Your car," the former prime minister announced, "is needed for official business."

His four associates pointed their guns directly at the driver. The old man screamed obscenities, but they simply pulled him from the car, jumped in and sped off.

A few minutes later, they arrived in the town of Guáimaro. The streets were filled with people, running, laughing, chanting, "Viva Fidel!" Varona cursed under his breath as the Ford eased through the crowd and went on to the cuartel. Its doors were locked. Varona sent one of his men inside to find out what was happening.

The fellow returned quickly. Captain Castellón, the officer who was supposed to join them in an uprising, had fled, and no one knew where he was. The soldiers inside were terrified, and they were planning to go in a convoy to the regimental garrison in Camagüey City.

Varona slumped back against the car seat. After five days of nothing but failure, he was facing yet another setback. Then his face brightened. Great men, he decided, become greater in the face of adversity.

"Listen," he told his men, "we'll follow them, and when we get to Camagüey, it may just seem like they are coming with us. *They* are *our* convoy."

In western Havana Province, Enrique Barroso was mobbed as he walked down the main street of Güines. The former media director had only a month-old beard and the only action his twenty rebels had seen was the disastrous attack at the bridge, but the townspeople treated him as if he were a hardened veteran of the Sierra. They slapped him on the back, hugged him and offered food and drink.

Already, the day had been a dizzy success. His men had conned the cuartel in the village of Aguacate into surrendering before the army commander realized how few rebels there actually were, and Güines, only an hour's drive from Havana, was proving to be almost the same. A sergeant was haranguing the soldiers not to surrender, because a junta was forming at Camp Columbia, but it was obvious that no one wanted to fight.

As Barroso was working his way through the crowd, he saw the familiar gray-and-white Buick Century, its engine coughing as usual. Lizzy jumped out and ran to embrace him. When he took her in his arms, she cried, overwhelmed by the victory they had struggled so hard for. Then, wiping the tears away, she said she had been trying to find him ever since she had heard the news, going first to their mountain camp, then Aguacate, before hearing that the group had moved on to Güines.

Putting his arm around her shoulder, he led her to the El Congo Restaurant, a rustic place with wooden benches, where the management was serving the rebels free helpings of the house specialty, spiced sausages. The owner of a nearby winery was carting in cases of papaya wine and brandy.

Swept along with the delirium, Barroso and Lizzy drank heavily. When they had first met, he considered her too skinny, and she thought the revolution was her substitute for insensitive men, but a month of contact in the Madruga Hills had changed all that.

After a while, they moved to a corner. Oblivious to the crowd, they put their arms around each other and began kissing. They knew they were going to be seeing each other for a long time to come.

In Santa Clara, Captain Rogelio Acevedo watched as the last of the army prisoners was led away from the courthouse. The twenty besieged soldiers had decided to surrender even though the regimental garrison was still holding out. When they disappeared around a corner, the teenager sat down on the courthouse steps and began listening to a portable radio that was blaring revolutionary denunciations of the fallen dictatorship.

Everywhere he looked, people were celebrating in the streets. A few blocks away, hundreds were gathering at the rebel headquarters, in the two-story Public Works Building, where they shouted demands that the Batista criminals and henchmen be executed immediately. Movement supporters were handing out mimeographed forms, on which the people could name the criminals and list specific instances of brutality or murder.

Down in the Central Park, Guillermo Domenech stood in the crowd looking at the front entrance of the Gran Hotel, where he had just spent four harrowing days. At last, more than twelve hours after the guests had escaped, the SIM men had surrendered. Rebels were leading them, arms tied behind their backs, out of the lobby entrance. As the new prisoners were placed in jeeps, the crowd jeered and spit on them. One man grabbed a soldier's ear with such force that he almost yanked him out of the jeep.

At the Leoncio Vidal army barracks, a team of negotiators sent by Ché Guevera was walking in to talk to the soldiers. As soon as they saw them, army men dropped their rifles and embraced the bearded men as if they were long-lost brothers. The regimental commander, Colonel Joaquín Casillas Lumpuy, fled in civilian clothes while Major Fernández, the second in command, tried desperately to reach General Cantillo.

But the Estado Mayor kept telling him that he was in a car coming back from the Presidential Palace.

Tired and confused, Cantillo returned to the third-floor office that only twenty-four hours before had belonged to Pancho Tabernilla. Sweating officers were crowded around the desk, shouting at each other and screaming into telephones. Everywhere, it seemed, cuartels were surrendering to 26th of July groups. At least, Cantillo thought, someone had had the decency to pull the plug on Pancho's toy map. The lights of the garrisons were no longer lit.

As he walked to his desk, Colonel Martínez Suárez grabbed him by the elbow. Cheo Fernández at Santa Clara needed to talk to him immediately on the microwave hookup. Picking up the red telephone receiver, Cantillo heard the officer's shaky voice say that the soldiers didn't want to fight.

Cantillo was just about to say something when a rebel's voice suddenly came on the line. He berated Cantillo for the corruption of the Batista regime, its murders and tortures and the evils of businessmen. The man ranted on and on until finally Cantillo slammed down the receiver in disgust. Santa Clara was lost.

The general slumped into the chair behind the desk. In front of him was a report from Colonel Tomás Arias Cruz, the director of personnel. It stated that the army had about 7300 soldiers in Havana: 5000 at Camp Columbia, 1100 at La Cabaña fortress beside the harbor and another 1200 at the San Antonio base just outside the city. But other reports showed that soldiers were fleeing the camps, and Cantillo himself had seen no sign of the city's 10,000 policemen on his way back from the palace. Armed force was no longer the point.

As he considered what to do, officers gathered around his desk. All were shouting advice, and it bombarded his skull like the sound of an artillery barrage, so much noise that it was hard to think. No one was urging the army to fight on and everyone seemed to be making some small point so that he could claim to the 26th of July that he had helped the Movement's cause. They sensed what was happening, and obviously they wanted to move over to the winning side. Cantillo didn't blame them. But none of their ideas seemed to make any sense.

While the shouting continued, a group of young officers elbowed their way through the crowd. Captain Carlos Carrillo, saying that he was speaking for the group, pleaded that Cantillo release Colonel Barquín from the Isle of Pines. As a professional soldier and a well-known anti-Batista man, Barquín could gain the respect of both the rebels and the army.

Cantillo sat up straight. He and Barquín had always been bitter rivals. He had helped arrest Barquín two years before, and just a few days ago he had berated Colonel Rosell for aligning himself with the imprisoned officer. But now there seemed no other possibility for saving the army, for keeping it intact and serving as a counterbalance to Castro's growing political power.

After only a few moments' thought, Cantillo told the young officer to fly to the prison in an air force C-47. "Explain the situation to Barquín and tell him to bring back whomever he wants."

As the captain ran from the room, the general dictated a telegram to the Fifth Military District, regimental headquarters for the Rural Guard detachment at the prison: Captain Carrillo was to be given any help he needed. At 2:25 P.M., the district passed the message along to the Isle of Pines.

There was nothing to do now except wait to hand over command to Barquín. Cantillo was exhausted. The last twelve hours, he thought, had been a time when "the minutes seemed like hours, and the hours seemed like minutes."

As he lit a crumpled Chesterfield, General Pedraza, the elderly officer who had warned him he was being left with a "burning spike," came in to say good-bye. He was going to use a military plane to flee to the Dominican Republic.

Cantillo thought about going with him. "I don't know what is the best thing to do," he told his second-in-command, Colonel Martínez Mora. "I can't just leave this thing to you." His subordinate agreed wholeheartedly with that; he didn't want to be left in charge, even for a few hours. Cantillo decided to remain in the camp. It would be unprofessional to abandon his men.

With that, he lapsed into thought. One problem was still plaguing him. Though it was obvious the rebels were ignoring the cease-fire, he had yet to hear from Castro personally, and he did not know what was happening in Oriente, especially at the Moncada garrison. Still, something had to be done about the presidency. As long as the government was without a leader, the mob violence in the streets could only get worse. He himself had seen the Havana crowds waving the 26th of July colors, and even the Supreme Court, made up of old, tradition-bound judges, had said that the Movement should be allowed to name the new president.

In his tired mind, Cantillo might have had some notion that with Manuel Urrutia leading the government and Barquín the military, some kind of moderation could be guaranteed. Or it could have been that he too was now trying to score a point with Castro, to fulfill part of the agreement he had made at the dilapidated sugar mill. Or he could have been simply opening the gates, allowing anyone to try whatever he wanted. Cantillo was so weary that his thinking was not clear, but he knew he had to do something.

At 3:45 P.M., thirteen hours and five minutes after Batista fled, he ordered a telegram sent in code to Colonel Rego Rubido in Santiago: "Inform Dr. Castro that the Republic is headless and we [are] awaiting the person he designates to give him possession of the presidency."

On the edge of the city, Paul Tannenbaum and his family were being led through the grounds of the rum factory by a lone guide who seemed bewildered to have any customers on such a day. The place was an oasis of tranquillity, and since the guide had nothing better to do, he gave them a lengthy tour of the place, including a small zoo housing monkeys and tropical birds. When they were done, he provided the adults with extra servings of free rum.

49/"CAN I TRUST YOU, COLONEL?"

Under a zinc roof covering the patio beside a general store in the Santiago hills, Fidel Castro was pacing and talking in front of a group of army officers. He was giving his usual lecture, one he knew almost by heart, about how the rebels had only been fighting the dictatorship and had nothing against the soldiers themselves. Castro had no idea what was happening in Havana or Santa Clara, and at that moment he didn't care. His one concern was taking Santiago; everything else had to wait. He was optimistic, especially after a Baptist minister had arrived with a letter from Colonel Rego Rubido, written the night before, in which the colonel offered him a helicopter ride. Castro was hoping to take the city without a battle, but he was willing to do whatever he had to in order to achieve victory.

The soldiers he was talking to were from the El Viso fortress, the ones that Captain Pérez Alamo had made contact with early that morning. After sharing cans of fruit cocktail inside their garrison, he persuaded them to come up to his headquarters at Villalón. The usually sleepy hamlet, which for weeks had housed only a couple of dozen Column 9 rebels, was now inundated with people. Parked beside the gravel road was an old municipal bus, filled with forty police officers from Santiago. All were wearing black-and-red armbands, and anytime a rebel approached, they shouted, *"¡Viva la revolución!"* Their leader was Haza, a short, fat man who was the Santiago police chief and whose stolen patrol car was parked only a short distance away. One of Pérez Alamo's men jokingly asked if the chief had come to pick up his car, but the chief, grim-faced, said that he only wanted to help the rebels take over the city.

Vilma Espín, in her usual black beret, stood nearby, watching the police chief with undisguised hostility. She and Raúl Castro had arrived a few minutes before, and she couldn't believe that the man had the audacity to come there. She had heard that in recent days he had made contact with the rebels through a relative in the Civic Resistance, but seeing him in a black-and-red armband was intolerable, for she was certain he was responsible for many of the bodies found in the city's gutters.

When she saw that Fidel had momentarily stopped talking, she drew him and Raúl aside. Pointing to Haza, she said, "If the mothers of the martyrs could see this, they would die."

"Don't worry about him," Fidel told her. "We first have to consolidate power."

A short time later, Colonel Rego Rubido came bouncing up the road in a jeep. About a hundred yards from the general store, he ordered his driver to stop, and he walked the rest of the way. Rebels gawked at him, and he realized they probably had never seen a full colonel before. For hours, he had been trying desperately to reach Castro, first flying in the Sikorsky helicopter to the radio station in Palma Soriano, only to find that the rebel leader had left minutes before, then returning to the Moncada garrison for a jeep, because the Santiago hills were too treacherous for a helicopter landing. He had seen the telegrams about what was happening in Havana and Santa Clara, and that made him even more determined to do what he could for himself.

When he arrived, he found Castro and Comandante Húber Matos talking to the El Viso soldiers beside some shrubs. Rego introduced himself, then said, "I am bringing an urgent message from Cantillo." He handed Castro the coded version.

Castro looked down at the colonel, whose head barely came to his shoulder, and tried to see what kind of man he was. The officer seemed to have an open, friendly face; he was obviously nervous.

The message looked like gobbledygook. "MSQ XATGH STSHS XWUWU RHKHD KHUJS QZUKH RXTSS SQYDD JHFJG NDGU ICUJI JCVSZ PVGZQ ITGWG SWYFY NEFUT MRCFT NEISH XWUFU WXBBB. STOP. Reply urgent."

As Castro puzzled over the telegram, Rego gave him the decoded version, which stated that the republic was headless and that he should designate the president.

Castro's facial muscles tightened. "Cantillo is a traitor," he shouted. "A double-crosser. He made certain agreements with me, and then he betrayed me." The general had gone back on his word once, and he was never to be trusted again. Certainly, he bellowed, he had always made clear his opposition to making any deals with Camp Columbia.

Rego, a little frightened at Castro's outburst, slipped the message from the rebel leader's hand and turned it upside down. "Look, Dr. Castro," he said humbly, handing it back, "this will remain for history. Write what you want to Cantillo on the other side."

Pulling a fountain pen from his pocket, Castro scribbled in black ink: "The present chaotic state is a consequence of the nonfulfillment of the given word. Of that, you are the only one responsible. Between you and me there can no longer be any possible agreement."

As soon as Rego read that, he said quickly that he too felt betrayed by Cantillo, that he had disliked the Batista regime and that he would do what he could to stop the bloodshed.

They talked awhile more, and both agreed that Raúl Castro and a small group of rebels should go back with Rego to the Moncada and explain the situation to the officers there.

As Castro walked Rego to his jeep, Raúl told Vilma he was going. She begged to be taken along. To be among the first rebels to enter the garrison, the symbol of the repression she had fought against for years, would be an experience she would never forget.

Raúl said no. He was taking only a few men because he didn't want to give the impression they were launching an attack, and it could be dangerous. "You stay here with Fidel. I'm coming right back." With that, he ran toward his jeep.

Nearby, Castro was pacing beside Rego, who was already seated and ready to go. He kept staring at him, trying to decide if this army officer would try to trick him as Cantillo had done.

Rego sensed his thoughts. "*Comandante*," he said, "be at ease. The man who is going to solve your problems is here." He tapped his own chest.

Castro leaned over until his face was only a few inches from the colonel's. "Can I trust you, Colonel?"

"Yes, I believe you can."

Raúl gave the signal that his men were ready, and the caravan, spraying clouds of dust, sped down the road.

Castro walked back to Vilma, who was still miffed at Raúl's gesture of male protectiveness, at his "little trick" of having her stay behind. "What am I doing here?" she asked.

Castro shrugged. "Why didn't you go with the others?"

That made her even angrier, and she walked away. Because she was a woman, she had been deprived of witnessing a momentous event. She was "really burned up."

Though Castro did not know it, rebels had been wandering into Santiago since noon. They came spontaneously, without orders, as soon as they heard that Batista had fled. All assumed the war was over.

Townspeople rushed to greet them, police officers surrendered their stations and the underground secured the radio stations and whatever else they could. Claudia Roses Monte de Oca, the young housewife whose family had been getting a steady diet of spaghetti, passed out her long-hidden armbands as she and her friends took to the streets.

At the U.S. consulate, Park Wollam collected reports on what was happening and radioed the information to Havana. Some local sympathizers, unaccustomed to the war, were firing indiscriminately, but the rebels themselves were well behaved. Two cafés owned by Batistianos were sacked, but there was none of the widespread destruction that was going on in Havana.

At the Wollam home, Connie and her nine-year-old daughter Janet watched from their front patio as the rebels walked down Mandulay Avenue and waved cheerfully to the onlookers. Connie was shocked at how young the rebels were, many of them teenagers without beards, scrawny youths in ragged, dirty clothes who obviously had not been eating well for months. Her daughter, seeing what the other children were doing, ran back into the house and moments later rushed back wearing a black-and-red dress.

A block away, Lily Ferreiro went into the storeroom of his supermarket and carried out hams, cheeses, five-pound cans of Keebler crackers and Coca-Cola—all the food he had left. He told an employee to give the rebels all they wanted to eat and drink.

As the youths began to wolf down the food, Ferreiro rushed to El Rancho Motel on the edge of town, where his brother, who had been with the rebels for a few weeks, was said to have been seen. Two blocks from the motel, a police car was parked beside the road, but the patrolmen were doing nothing.

He found his brother on the motel's thatched-roof dance floor, and they embraced. As Ferreiro listened to tales of what life was like in the hills with the rebels, he saw Errol Flynn, cameras dangling from his neck, moving through the crowd. The movie actor was drinking Scotch, chased by beer, and boasting about how much he had helped the rebel cause.

50/"IT WOULD HAVE CHANGED THE COURSE OF HISTORY"

In some low-lying hills near the edge of Camagüey City, Tony Varona and his men were following the two-truck army convoy when suddenly, rounding a curve, he saw about a hundred unarmed men blocking the road. The former prime minister's first thought was that the soldiers would massacre the mob, but instead they simply came to a halt. The crowd demanded their weapons and the soldiers immediately began handing them over.

Varona groaned. The army men had no idea he was following them, but he had been hoping to use them, somehow, as a bargaining chip when they reached the regimental garrison in the city. Now, unless he did something quickly, that hope was lost.

Jumping out of the car, he ran to the first truck.

"Listen, people," he shouted. "I'm Tony Varona. I have come here from exile to join with these valiant men of the army in an uprising against the dictatorship. These are revolutionary soldiers, and you should not disarm them because they are in fact guarding me and my men in a most important mission to liberate the garrison."

Some in the crowd recognized him, a few applauded and most started giving back the weapons. Varona walked over to the army truck driver, who looked bewildered at the news that he was a "revolutionary soldier."

"Soldier," Varona whispered to him, "I have been following you since Guáimaro. Now all I want is that *you* follow *us* in your trucks. When we get to the garrison, we'll just drive in ahead of you."

With the mob still surrounding the trucks, the driver realized he was practically Varona's prisoner. He nodded numbly.

As Varona chuckled about his "Trojan horse" plan, the convoy moved on, the battered Ford this time in the lead. On the eastern edge of the city, they sped past the small Monteagudo cuartel, which seemed to be in complete confusion. Soldiers were walking around in a daze.

At the regimental garrison, the Ford and two trucks moved through the gates without any problem and stopped in front of the headquarters building. Varona bounded into the commander's office, where most of the officers recognized him instantly. "I've come to take control of the garrison," he announced grandly, "and declare Camagüey a liberated province."

The officers readily agreed that it was a good idea and that they would like to join him, but one added, "Just an hour ago, we agreed to surrender to the 26th of July, and we don't know how they would interpret it if we surrendered to you."

Varona sagged, but he was still not ready to give up. Running back to the Ford, he shouted at his men, "Let's go back to the Monteagudo cuartel and take over that one." At least that would give him a base of operations.

Racing back over the highway they had just traveled, the Ford squealed to a stop in front of the cuartel's front door. Just minutes before they had seen it engulfed by confusion, but now, as Varona stepped inside, Comandante Mora, the provincial commander of the 26th of July, was standing in the office, talking on a telephone. He was demanding that cuartels all over the province surrender to the rebels immediately, and only to the rebels.

Varona collapsed into a chair. The man who had been one of the CIA's main hopes had failed completely. Imbued as he was with the traditional Cuban political philosophy, the concept that "enough gas in the tank" could determine a new government, he thought back to all the things that might have been. If only the army captain had joined with him in the uprising, if the 26th of July had not led him astray in the wilds of southern Camagüey, if Batista had waited two more days before fleeing and, especially, if his car had not broken down, "it would have changed the course of history." He decided to go to his mother's house.

In Yaguajay, the rebels of Column 2 were running around frantically. They had just learned of Castro's order for them to take Camp Columbia, and they were trying to get organized. After days of battling 250 soldiers, they were being asked to confront a garrison manned by five thousand men. In midafternoon, Comandante Camilo Cienfuegos decided to move out to confer with Ché Guevara in Santa Clara, but so many roads and bridges had been destroyed that the sixty-mile trip was going to take hours. Captain William Gálvez was left behind to organize the rest of the column and follow as soon as he could. Félix Torres, the leader of the small band of Communist PSP guerrillas, would remain to control the town.

In Santa Clara, Ché Guevara decided to make the city secure before he left for Havana. One of his first actions was to order part of the rebels' newfound surplus of weapons taken to the hills and hidden. He still feared American intervention, and if all else failed, he wanted rifles available so that the struggle could continue.

At the Plaza-Athénée Hotel in Paris, lawyer Rolando Amador paced the floor in his room. He had been waiting hours, it seemed, to get a call through to his bride in Havana. The business trip had gone well, the negotiations for the casino cruise ships had proceeded without problem, but everything had been shattered by the news of Batista's flight.

When the telephone rang, he raced to it. The operator told him she had finally gotten a line to Cuba, and seconds later Carmen said hello. She sounded sad.

He told her that he was going to New York for a few days to await developments. He was worried that his business connections with the regime might cause him trouble with the new government.

"What do I do with the apartment?" she asked, exasperated. "The furniture is in. All the things I bought for your return are there. The apartment is ready to be moved into."

Amador, overwhelmed by depression, wondered if he would ever see the first home of their marriage. "I don't know what is going to happen," he said. "I'll call you from New York, and we'll decide then."

Late that afternoon, Senator José González Puente and his wife Carmelina arrived at the Miami airport, where the terminal was overflowing with anti-Batista exiles, arguing and begging the airlines to get them on the first flight to Havana.

González Puente checked with the National Airlines ticket counter, found out that no one knew when the Havana airport would reopen and then slumped against a column to think. He was a diehard Batistiano, a politician who had hoped to be appointed minister of agriculture in the cabinet of Rivero Agüero. He had heard the news while visiting his youngest daughter in Canada, and his first instinct was to rush back to Cuba. But now, with the airport closed and all these anti-Batista people clamoring to return, he realized it had been a quixotic idea.

Finding a Yellow Cab, he took his wife on a meandering ride, until they reached Seventy-ninth Street, where he ordered the driver to turn into the driveway of a small, unpretentious apartment building because its name was in Spanish: Las Villas. He paid a week's rent.

Though it is impossible to know for certain, it is probable that González Puente and his wife were the first exiles of the Castro regime to arrive in Miami's Dade County, becoming the first members of a group that would eventually grow to 450,000 persons.

While the Batista senator bitterly assessed his future, most of Miami was celebrating. At the Orange Bowl, seventy-five thousand spectators watched the University of Oklahoma defeat Syracuse, 21-6. A few blocks away, downtown, cars filled with Cubans were parading up Flagler Street and Biscayne Boulevard as the men waved red-and-black banners and chanted revolutionary slogans.

But the most important *políticos*, such as Justo Carrillo, remained at the airport. Their only pastime was trying to find out what was happening in the Cuban capital. They tried placing phone calls, but the circuits were busy. Radio stations were preoccupied with music or New Year's bowl games. Newspapers were no help. The morning edition of *The Miami Herald* was still on the newsstands with its Associated Press story written the night before: "The rebels are out-numbered up to 10 to 1 in the Las Villas Province offensive. . . . Batista remained in the

Presidential Palace amid reports he hoped to announce a sweeping victory over Castro's insurgents soon."

As each hour passed, Carrillo's frustrations deepened. He and the others tried guessing what the army was doing, what the underground would do to combat it and who was really in charge in Havana at that moment.

The answer was that no one was in charge. The Movement could plead with the people from the CMQ studios, but its power was severely limited. Street corners were manned by gangs of unaffiliated youths, many little taller than the rifles they held so somberly. They demanded passwords before they let people through, and each of the hundreds of checkpoints had a different password, known only to those who manned it. Julio Fernández León, traveling around the city with his teenagers in their "liberated" jeeps, caught on quickly. "Well, what *is* the password," he asked the checkpoint guards. They told him, he repeated it, and they allowed his jeeps through.

Many of these new militiamen wore 26th of July armbands, but that meant little, as journalist Luis Aguilar found out when he was stopped near the edge of the city by a man he recognized as a lower-echelon Batista official. When the man demanded, "Password, *señor*," Aguilar asked what he was doing there. "Shssh," the man said, putting a finger to his lips, "no one knows who I am."

In another area, Ted Scott, the New Zealand journalist, was astounded to see the cousin of a wealthy American who owned a sugar mill manning a barricade. A little farther on, he recognized a raven-haired seventeen-year-old named Marta, well known around the Sevilla Biltmore Hotel for "fun and games" as long as she was given a fine meal or a piece of jewelry. She was holding a Thompson submachine gun and a hand grenade.

In late afternoon, Paul Tannenbaum and his family huddled together on the floor of the old Mercury limousine. There was the occasional sound of gunfire in the distance, and they had just passed the El Morocco Club, where a mob was dumping slot machines on the streets.

When the driver shouted that he had at last found a way to the docks, Tannenbaum peeked above the window for one last photograph: a dozen people crouched behind black limousines. He wondered how Cubans' nerves managed to hold up if every day of the Batista regime were like this.

As soon as the limousine stopped, Tannenbaum paid the driver and hustled the family to the pier, where a dozen ship's officers were waiting for them. They were wearing sidearms and holding rifles.

The family jumped in the tender, and the boat sped off. "We've been looking for you all day," one of the officers said, a puzzled look on his face.

Tannenbaum confessed that they had witnessed considerable excitement, even for New Year's.

"Haven't you heard?" the officer asked, unbelieving. "The Batista government has been overthrown."

The lawyer looked at his family in amazement. Then he saw something even more startling: his father-in-law was holding a twenty-four-inch machete. "What's that?" he asked.

"It was on the floor of the backseat," the elderly dentist answered. "Someone must have thrown it through the sun roof while they were pounding on the car."

Most tourists were not reacting nearly as calmly as the Tannenbaums. At the Hilton, an elevator crammed with people went up and down, stopping at every floor. No one got out. The passengers kept arguing about which floor was safest. At the Hotel Nacional, women sobbed in the lobby or hid in corridors. One American woman told a reporter that when a hotel window broke, the tourists dived for cover. "You never saw so much mink hit the deck so fast," she said.

As the general strike took hold, maids and kitchen help abandoned the hotels. Beds were left unmade. Guests had to line up for hot dogs in the hotel coffee shops. That brought more grumbling from the tourists, and many called the embassy to complain. One enraged visitor reached Edith Elverson, Ambassador Smith's secretary, and demanded, "When are you going to send in the Marines to help?"

On the embassy's fifth floor, political officer John Topping was trying to help the tourists by getting the airport reopened, but when he contacted the Movement people at the CMQ studios, he learned that they had no idea who was controlling the airport and, therefore, no influence over them. Besides, Comandante Diego didn't want to be responsible for Americans moving in the streets, where they might be hit by Batistiano sniper fire in an attempt to discredit the revolution.

Topping's work was interrupted by taunting calls from Latin American diplomats who said, with obvious sarcasm, "I thought you people didn't give asylum." At first, Topping hadn't believed that Smith would have given refuge to a man as hated by the Cubans as was the Dominican ambassador, and when he learned it was true, he muttered to an assistant, "That's the last thing we need for our image right now. . . . What's the new government going to think of that?"

Down the hall, Smith was pacing in his office and bellowing about the stupidity in Washington. The State Department had learned of his trip to see Cantillo at the Presidential Palace and was accusing him of interfering with Cuban politics, of trying to find a "solution." Washington wanted absolute neutrality. Smith felt unjustly accused. He knew the situation was well beyond his control.

But resting on his desk was one glimmer of hope, one with which even Topping could agree. It was a report from a U.S. military liaison officer at the Estado Mayor: Colonel Ramón Barquín, well-known as a pro-American, anti-Batista moderate, was going to be freed from the Isle of Pines. The embassy had learned of the order only thirty minutes after it was transmitted to the prison—several hours before Barquín himself found out.

51/"LIONS WITHOUT TEETH"

Dusk was settling over the Isle of Pines when a guard unlocked the door to the circular courtyard of Building 4 and Captain Carlos Carrillo walked in, shouting that he was there to take Colonel Barquín and the other imprisoned Puros back to Camp Columbia.

Elated, Barquín elbowed his way through the crowd of prisoners, while the 26th of July men howled that the plan sounded like a coup d'etat intended to thwart the revolution.

"This is a stab in the back," shouted Armando Hart, a boyish-faced man with a black crew cut who was leader of the 26th of July prisoners. He threatened that if his group was kept in prison while the military men were freed, Barquín and the others would be branded counter-revolutionaries.

Not wanting to waste time arguing, Barquín relented. Two men from the Movement could go on the plane. Jesús Montané, the man who had been imprisoned for both the Moncada attack and the *Granma* landing, would be made governor of the island.

With that, five military prisoners and three Movement men ran into the prison compound and then through the open gates in the barbed-wire fences. A crowd of relatives were standing just outside the main gate and shouting for the officials to release all the political prisoners. Major Enrique Borbonnet saw his wife and daughters; he embraced them for only a moment before hopping into a new SIM Chevrolet with the other prisoners. Lieutenant "Gallego" Fernández rode on the hood.

They drove a short way down the road, then made a sharp left into the island's cuartel. Jumping out of the car, the men yelled, "¡Atención! ¡Atención!" They were still dressed in their prison uniforms, but the soldiers fell into formation without question. Captain Carrillo, the man who had come to rescue them, explained what was happening and said they were taking over the cuartel. None of the soldiers objected. Lieutenant Fernández was left in charge, to free the rest of the political prisoners.

It was almost dark by the time the Chevrolet reached the airfield. As soon as the men jumped into the twin-engine C-47, a crewman shut the door and the plane took off. The military officers sat near the cockpit, the 26th of July men by themselves in the rear. In a soft voice, Barquín whispered to Colonel Manuel Varela: "Let's see how we can save the army. . . . We have to be identified as being outside the dictatorship, closer to the revolution. . . . And we must be able to have a dialogue with the revolution." Then he began wondering aloud which officers he could trust enough to appoint to his new army comandancia. After more than two years in jail, he was worried that he had lost touch with what was happening at Columbia, but he knew that he had only hours to make his plan work.

When the C-47 landed at the Columbia airfield, he looked through the window to see a crowd of officers bathed by the same spotlights that had lit Batista's departure. Still wearing his blue-denim prison shirt with the large white *P* on the back, Barquín stepped to the door.

"Viva Barquín!" the officers roared. His two brothers, both doctors, waited at the bottom of the steps. He ran down and embraced them. Colonel Varela's wife was there, and Varela gave her a quick kiss before he told her to go home immediately, because he thought they could be killed at any moment.

Barquín wasted no time enjoying his moment of triumph. "What is the radio saying?" he shouted to the crowd. "Where is Fidel?"

No one seemed to know, but one officer mumbled, "We are faced with chaos."

As the crowd surrounded him, Barquín spotted faces he knew well, men in uniforms who had been secretly anti-Batista or officers in civilian clothes who had been kicked out of the army by the old regime. In a near frenzy, he began shouting appointments, naming officers to command the police, the ports, the airport and various garrisons around the island. He worked so fast that several times he appointed more than one man to the same position.

That done, Barquín leaped into a jeep with the other Puros and, skirting the Estado Mayor, raced around the parade ground to the infantry division headquarters. There, the officer in charge snapped to attention so quickly that Major Borbonnet almost laughed at how much respect their prison uniforms were suddenly able to command. Barquín told the major to take charge of the infantry, while Colonel Varela went to take over La Cabaña fortress.

Rushing back across the parade ground, Barquín saw ten Comet tanks lined up in front of the Estado Mayor, the grass around them chewed up by their treads. A young officer told him that the tanks had arrived just a few days ago from Great Britain. They were "lions without teeth"—their cannons had not yet been set up.

In the third-floor office, General Cantillo was waiting, half-asleep in a chair. He had gone to the airfield to welcome Barquín, but when he saw the emotion and confusion, he decided to wait for him at the Estado Mayor. To him, it seemed as if Barquín were trying to carry out a coup d'etat when all Cantillo wanted to do was hand over command as quickly as possible.

On the desk was a telegram from Colonel Rego Rubido, sent from Santiago at 7:40 P.M. It repeated Castro's warning that Cantillo was "the only one responsible," and Rego had added: "You should know Fidel Castro very concerned and does not designate anyone for presidency."

To Cantillo, Castro's anger meant nothing at all. Everything now seemed to be happening in a nightmarish fog. As he waited, Colonel Arias Cruz walked in to find out what was happening, and Cantillo showed him the telegram.

"What are you going to do?" the colonel asked.

"I am going home," Cantillo said simply.

A few moments later, Barquín rushed through the door. Cantillo, managing a tired smile for this once-bitter rival, stood to shake his hand. Then, as best he could, he described the military situation. Almost all the cuartels in Havana, Matanzas and Pinar del Río provinces were still in the hands of the army. Las Villas and Camagüey were completely controlled by the rebels, as was most of Oriente. The Guantánamo City garrison was talking to the rebels but had not surrendered. It was not clear what Colonel Rego Rubido was doing in Santiago. Cantillo did not mention his telegram asking Castro to name a president, nor did he say anything about the rebel leader's angry reply.

After that, Cantillo showed him around the Estado Mayor, introduced him to other officers and ordered a document drawn up formally transferring command of the army to Barquín. Then they posed for a *Bohemia* photographer, who took a picture of Cantillo, smiling, pointing with his glasses to a piece of paper, which Barquín pretended to study intently.

It is not clear what happened next. Barquín says he told Cantillo to go to his house and stay there "because I do not know how responsible you are for what happened here." Cantillo and his friend, Colonel Martínez Suárez, maintain that Barquín offered the general a plane, so he could flee the country, but that Cantillo refused, saying he would suffer the same fate as his men.

Whatever the two men said, Cantillo walked out the door, down the long concrete staircase of the Estado Mayor, and cut across a corner of the parade ground to his house. Exhausted from going without sleep for forty hours, he gave his wife a kiss and collapsed on his bed. He fell asleep immediately.

Within seconds after Cantillo left, Barquín was barking orders to his new subordinates. Though he did not know it, his plan was almost identical to Cantillo's: army posts were to maintain the cease-fire, but not surrender. It was his rationale that was new, for he was saying that the army was now being led by revolutionary soldiers, who were part of the anti-Batista cause. Therefore, there was no need for one ally to surrender to another.

After that, he made another decision, again copying Cantillo, to contact Castro and tell him that President-designate Manuel Urrutia could come to Havana and form a government, under the protection of the new "revolutionary" army. He called the Moncada garrison, but the officers there would tell him nothing. Then he sent telegrams. They were not answered. At last, a crisp message arrived stating simply that Castro was not at the Moncada.

Barquín had little time to think about what that meant, for his office was filling up with politicians and army officers, each with a different idea of what should be done. Shouting to make themselves heard above the din, some wanted an immediate capitulation to the 26th of July. Others maintained that Barquín should ignore Castro completely, that Columbia was still the center of power in Cuba. Andrés Suárez, a member of the pro-Barquín Montecristi Movement, did so much yelling that he suffered the worst fate that could befall a Cuban politician at that moment—he lost his voice.

Amid the confusion, two young members of the student Directorio fought their way through the crowd and demanded that Barquín give them weapons, so that they could arm their members in the streets. Barquín refused. He said it would be too dangerous to have civilians running around with guns.

Then, ignoring the clamor, Barquín ordered an aide to have the Columbia airfield closed. No more army men or civilians were to be allowed to leave Cuba until the "criminals" had been caught.

After that, he wasn't certain what else could be done. He kept mumbling, "Where is Justo? Where is Justo?" He was certain that Justo Carrillo, leader of the Montecristi Movement and a close ally of the Puros, would be able to give him the kind of advice he needed. Andrés Suárez promised to locate him by telephone in Miami, but someone else would have to do the talking. Suárez could only whisper.

A short time later, Julio Duarte, the Movement leader who had made the pre-dawn call to the Estado Mayor, arrived to find the third floor in near chaos. In an anteroom, he encountered an old friend, Armando Hart, the 26th of July leader from the Isle of Pines, talking on the telephone.

"Yes, yes," Hart said crisply, "so the 26th of July is at the gates of your cuartel? Well, of course, you should give in. Give them your weapons. The war is over. The revolution has won."

Hart put down the receiver with a boyish smirk. "All the cuartels are calling," he told Duarte, "asking what to do. So I'm telling them." They were only a few feet away from where Barquín was talking to the politicians.

Duarte asked if he had been able to reach Castro. Hart said no, it was impossible to get a call through to Santiago. Something big had to be happening there.

At 9:00 P.M., Ambassador Smith, who himself had gone without sleep for almost two days, sent a dispatch to Washington about Barquín's idea to invite Urrutia to Havana. At the end, he commented: "This is an encouraging development, increasing possibility of early accord between armed forces and rebel movements. Also strengthens position of military vis-à-vis rebels." But Smith also did not know what was happening in Santiago.

At 10:11 P.M., the U.S. Navy, following a prescribed plan on what to do if chaos in Cuba threatened American lives or property, sent an order: "Sail 3 or 4 DE types and 2 AS from Navbase KWest ASAP without fanfare. Proceed to vicinity Havana Cuba. Do not enter Cuban waters, lie off Havana just over horizon. Make no public announcement."

A few minutes later, the Key West Navy Base dispatched three destroyer escorts, the *Jack W. Wilke,* the *F. M. Robinson* and the *Peterson.* Each had three-inch guns and 220 men. Two submarine tenders, the *Gilmore* and the *Bushnell,* with five-inch guns, were to follow as soon as possible.

52/"THE REVOLUTION IS NOW BEGINNING"

Castro's headquarters had moved a mile down the road, to the village of Escandel, a scattering of thatched-roof *bohíos,* a general store and a large white house on a hill which had been abandoned by a Batistiano. Fourteen Santiago municipal buses lined the side of the road; Colonel Rego had brought almost all the army and navy officers in Santiago up to meet the rebel leader.

At the bottom of the hill, *campesinos* stood looking up at the white house, trying to get a glimpse of Castro through the large glassless windows. Victoriano Rivera, an aged peasant who had an eighteen-year-old son fighting with the rebels, saw him briefly; he cried with joy.

Inside the house, politicians, military men and rebels mingled happily on the red-and-gray tile floor, their faces accented by the harsh light that came from bare light bulbs dangling on cords from the fourteen-foot ceiling. Carlos Rafael Rodríguez, the Communist PSP leader, was there, chatting with rebel officers. Nearby, in his ever-present sunglasses, President-designate Manuel Urrutia stood beside his wife and teenage son. Urrutia was feeling more presidential every minute, and he was surprised to see Castro so concerned when it was obvious they had won. Comandante Raúl Chibás thought Castro was the only one not swept away by the euphoria. It was as if "his brain was far ahead of everyone else's."

In the rear, standing on a table, Castro was talking to the Moncada officers. Carefully, he was explaining his position, his "betrayal" by Cantillo, his admiration for Colonel Rego Rubido because he was "an honorable man who supported the agreements we reached." He said he was not afraid to talk in front of such a large group of soldiers because he knew he had been right in opposing the corrupt dictatorship and had nothing to fear.

As he talked, Castro was studying the faces of the men in front of him. He still had no idea what was happening in the other large garrisons of Oriente—Holguín, Bayamo, Guantánamo City—and after that would come the problem of Havana. His forces were still small, and there was always the danger that these smiling army officers might quickly betray him. He wanted to win their confidence completely, to assure himself of a base of support, before he went any farther. He was thinking not only of the moment, but what lay ahead.

Raúl Castro, as if sensing his brother's thoughts, whispered to Captain Napoleón Bequer, "Fidel is not being careful at all. There are so many armed Batistianos here who could kill him. Guard his back." Bequer and Comandante Juan Almeida climbed onto the table and stood behind Castro, their hands on their pistols.

But the soldiers did not stir, and when Castro ended by talking about the unity of the revolution, about it being fought so that all Cubans could be brothers, soldiers and rebels alike, the army men responded with a loud ovation.

Before the cheering died, Castro leaped from the table and pulled Rego Rubido aside. He told the colonel that Oriente Province was now the center of revolutionary Cuba, that they should ignore what was happening in Camp Columbia. What the military needed now, he said, was an enlightened, honest leader, and he wanted Rego to become chief of staff of the new combined rebel-army forces.

Rego, who had started the day simply trying to save his own life, was overwhelmed by the offer. He eagerly agreed.

A short time later, the ragtag caravan of vehicles began moving slowly down the gravel road toward Santiago. With all its buses, jeeps and trucks, the line was almost two miles long. Castro and Rego rode together in one of the lead jeeps.

Beyond the village of El Caney, the crowds began. Five-and-a-half years before, Castro had moved toward this same city, an unknown youth preparing to mount a pitiful attack on the Moncada garrison. For the past two years, he had been fighting from the wild solitude of the mountains, starting with a dozen starving men and slowly building his forces. There had been hunger, hopelessness and the threat of annihilation countless times. Only in his own dreams had this moment of triumph always seemed clear.

Along the road, people stood waving and cheering among the trees which formed a covered archway above the pavement. For them, what had once been only a magical voice of Radio Rebelde was now flesh and blood. Spectators shoved and pushed each other, some falling into the road as they tried to touch their new leader. The caravan slowed to a crawl. Castro, oblivious to the danger, stood in his jeep; he waved and shook the hands outstretched to greet him.

As the caravan reached the city, rebels saw people hanging from balconies. The crowd packed the streets so tightly that sometimes the caravan came to a complete halt.

"¡Viva Fidel!"

"¡Viva la revolución!"

"Viva! Viva! Viva! Viva! Viva!"

The shouts became a thunder of noise, a delirium of sound. For those who had risked their lives to achieve this moment, for those who had begun by hiding in underground safehouses and ramshackle mountain camps, the motion was almost indescribable. The once-tiny band was being greeted as the conqueror of all Cuba, and the triumphant journey continued to the center of the city in an atmosphere approaching ecstacy. Manuel Urrutia, the new president, considered it "the most impressive sight I had ever seen. . . . The country was being reborn." Captain José Machado Ventura, the health director for the Second Front, thought of it as a moment Cubans had been waiting sixty-five years for, a moment when the heirs of those who had fought in 1898 were at last entering the city they had fought for. Captain Napoleón Bequer, who had seen his own son become ill because of his activities, thought it was "like a messiah arriving. We were walking on a cloud."

At last, sometime after midnight, Castro's jeep squeezed through the crowd and arrived at Céspedes Park, where ten thousand people were jammed between the twin-towered church and the red-tile-roofed city hall. Vilma Espín saw women in hairnets and men in pajamas crying with happiness.

Castro, his telescopic rifle slung over his right shoulder, bounded into the city hall. He moved through a crowd gathered on the red-and-yellow tile floor and climbed a wooden staircase to a large, second-floor conference room. There, under a wood-beamed ceiling, many of Santiago's civic leaders, the Rotarians and Lions who had supported the rebels, sat on wicker-back chairs around a large mahogany table. Castro shook their hands quickly and moved to the small wooden balcony overlooking the park.

The crowd roared as soon as it saw him. He stood there for a long moment, hands upraised, basking in the adulation, then introduced President Urrutia, Police Chief Haza and Colonel Rego Rubido. Rego, with a newfound egotism, thought that he received more applause than even Urrutia.

As the Santiago bishop stepped forward to give a prayer of thanksgiving, Castro went back inside, where an army aide was waiting for the colonel with a message. Rego read it first, then passed it to the rebel leader: Barquín was now in charge of Camp Columbia and wanted to talk to Castro.

Castro threw the message down and banged his fist on the mahogany table. He knew instinctively that putting an Isle of Pines prisoner in charge of the camp was a ploy to hinder the revolution, "a maneuver to preserve the status quo, to save the old institutions." He did not even need to hear what Barquín had to say. He had already ordered Column 2 to take Columbia, and he would settle for nothing else.

"Tell them at Camp Columbia," he shouted at the colonel, "I will only talk to Camilo Cienfuegos, when he is in charge of the camp."

Rego ordered the aide to send the message to Havana, then he and Castro talked about military tactics. The rebel leader wanted to go to Havana by land, not by air, and he wished to take all the Moncada tanks with him so that he could move up the Central Highway and overwhelm by force any garrison which continued to resist. Even if Guevara and Cienfuegos succeeded in taking the Havana military installations, they had only a few hundred men; they would need all the support they could get. Rego nodded and promised to hand over all fourteen tanks at the Santiago garrison.

At last, about 2:15 A.M., after a series of short speeches by labor and civic leaders, Castro returned to the balcony. He was worried about the military situation in Havana, but that was a tactical problem. His mind was already rushing far ahead, and he decided that he didn't want this moment to be wasted by merely gloating in the defeat of the Batista dictatorship or warning about the problems in Columbia. It was important the people realized all the work, all the Cuban history that had led up to this moment. And he wanted too for everyone to know that his plans stretched far into the future. This was not to be just another change of governments.

Speaking without notes, he declared that he was making Santiago the capital of Cuba, that the rebels had accomplished the task of those who had fought against Spain in 1898, "when the Americans intervened at the last minute and prevented Calixto García [the independence leader] from being present at the fall of Santiago." His Movement had not simply freed the Cuban people from Batista, but from all the tyrannies since the Spanish had settled the island. Cuba was going to be truly free for "the first time in four centuries."

But, he warned, the country was not yet rid of the Batista menace. "The great guilty ones have escaped. From abroad, they will spend their millions to fight against us. To harm our country." He estimated that Batista had gotten away with between $300 million and $400 million.*

"The most important thing is to consolidate power," he shouted to the crowd in a voice that was almost hoarse after a long day of speeches. "This foremost before anything else. Later, we can gather commissions of army and rebel officers and adjudicate guilt and responsibility. . . . When we were twelve men, we never lost faith. Now that we have twelve tanks, you can imagine how we feel. . . ."

He announced that as soon as Urrutia's government was formed, civil rights and freedom of the press would be restored, and he promised not to forget the Sierra *campesinos* who had helped the rebels so much. For

---

* How much Batista profited from his years in power is still a matter of conjecture. The Associated Press on January 2, 1959, estimated that it was $200 million. Several days later, Rolando Masferrer gave U.S. customs officials in Key West a letter with the same estimate. Suárez Núñez, Batista's press secretary, guesses that Batista was worth $300 million in 1958. The exact figure will never be known, but it was certainly considerable.

them, the new government would build a school "for twenty thousand peasant boys. . . .

"The revolution is now beginning. The revolution will not be an easy task . . . but in this initial stage, especially, full of danger." After an hour and a half, he stopped, but the crowd demanded more. He relented and started speaking again.

Connie Wollam was hearing the speech only dimly as it blared from a small radio in a faraway corner of the stucco house owned by Lily Ferreiro's mother; it was directly behind the Ferreiro Supermarket. She had come because Ferreiro told her that after his speech Castro was planning to stop by for a late-night dinner with the family he had known since his elementary-school days, and like the hundred other persons crowded into the house, Connie wanted to see the rebel leader close up. As she and the others chatted excitedly and waited, another group was oblivious to the commotion. Some bearded, sweat-stained rebels, their stomachs filled with the supermarket handouts, were lounging on the concrete floor separating the living and dining areas. Many were sleeping.

For Connie, the day had passed in a whirlwind of activity. The electricity had not gone out, but her turkey, baked that morning, was being put to use. As soon as she had entered the Ferreiro house, Lily had groaned that the rebels had nearly cleaned out his store and he had nothing to serve their leader. "Lily," Connie had whispered to him, "if you promise never to tell anyone, you can have a cooked turkey I have at home." Ferreiro promised, and the turkey was now sitting in his refrigerator.

It was a long wait, but finally, about 5:00 A.M., Castro marched in, followed by his secretary and several aides. With Connie following, Ferreiro led him across the patio to the dining table, where Castro said he was starved; he hadn't eaten all day. And, he added, there was one food he had been yearning for ever since he had gone to the Sierra: fresh fish.

Ferreiro blanched. There was no fish, he said, but he had a fine turkey and plenty of sandwich materials.

Castro shrugged his approval and, sitting down, turned to an army officer, who was dressed in battle fatigues and wearing a Movement armband. Connie, standing in a corner, quickly realized the officer was the commander of the Moncada tanks, for Castro was discussing with him how the tanks should be organized for the trip to Havana. She was amazed how crisp and energetic his ideas were, even after almost two days without sleep.

When Ferreiro brought the food, Castro was so hungry that he tore off a drumstick and chomped into it. The turkey was followed by a sandwich of ham, Holland cheese and salami, topped with strawberry preserves. Then he had a piece of cake and a small glass of Spanish brandy. All the while, he barraged the army officer with questions about the capabilities of the tanks.

Connie listened with fascination, but as the meal came to an end, she felt a little like a spy, eavesdropping on such a crucial conversation when none of the rebels had even been told that she was the wife of an American diplomat.

Retreating across the patio, she walked to the corner of the living room farthest from the front door and stood beside Vice-Consul Bernie Femminella and his wife Ginny. There, she relaxed for only a moment before she saw Ferreiro pointing her out to Castro.

As the rebel leader elbowed his way through the crowd, she froze. He loomed above her by more than a foot, which was a little frightening, but he bent down to shake her hand courteously and thank her for the turkey. Then he said, in words that became etched in her mind forever, *"Ya los americanos no van a tener dificultades ningunas."* Now the Americans are not going to have any difficulties.

"Ojalá," she replied—let it be so.

With that, he turned around and marched out of the house. Moments later, Connie left too, running down Mandulay Avenue to her home, where she found her husband slumped in a living-room chair. He had just returned from sending a telegram to Washington about Castro's speech. Though he was exhausted, he jumped when Connie burst out with the news about her conversation with Castro. At first he was angry he hadn't been there himself; then he became excited, making her repeat the words again and again. Was she sure those were the exact words? Yes, she was sure.

Bone-tired, Wollam sped back to the consulate, where the vice-consul was waiting for him with the same information. At his Danish modern desk, he scribbled down Cable Number 46, marked it Official Use Only and encoded it by hand: "At unexpected encounter with

member staff early this morning Fidel Castro commented he had
instructed full respect foreigners and their property and Americans
would have no more problems."

In Washington, the telegram was passed along to sixteen groups
within the Department of State, plus the U.S. Information Agency, the
CIA and all three branches of the military. Because of Connie Wollam's
turkey, the United States had made its first contact with Castro.

Dawn was coming when Castro and his entourage arrived at El Cobre,
where they were to sleep for a few hours. The fact that the revolutionary
leader was staying at the sanctuary for the Virgin of Charity, the
national shrine for Cuba's patron saint, was quickly noted by press and
radio.

In one of the longest days in his life, Castro had appealed successfully
to the people of Cuba to start a general strike and had won the loyalty of
the army in Santiago, while rejecting all the offers of "support" from
Camp Columbia. Then in two short hours, after going without sleep for
almost two days, he managed to get a reassuring message to the
Americans and placate any fears that religious Cubans might have had.
As with all supreme politicians, it was not a matter of truth or lies, but
doing what was necessary in that moment: in his case, taking the edge
off his radical image. He had accomplished much; he had given away
nothing, except a hollow title to Colonel Rego Rubido.

53/JANUARY 2: "ROBINSON CRUSOE" ENTERS HAVANA

At Camp Columbia, Colonel Ramón Barquín sat idly in the third-floor office that within the past forty-eight hours had belonged to first General Pancho Tabernilla, then General Cantillo. Now it was his, but it was certainly a hollow honor, as empty of meaning as the unlit electric map on the wall. Most of the politicians had gone home, and the army officers had stopped giving advice. On the parade ground, soldiers were wearing black-and-red armbands and refusing to follow orders. Barquín knew they weren't revolutionaries, simply men trying to salvage what they could for themselves.

He knew his ploy was failing. If he could not talk to Castro, if President Urrutia did not accept his invitation to come to Havana, he had nothing, except a threat to continue the war, and that idea seemed absurd.

More cuartels were surrendering each hour, and many of those that hadn't were leaning toward it. The most bitter blow was a telegram lying on his desk. It was from Colonel Rego Rubido in Santiago, announcing his appointment as chief of staff and demanding that every army garrison in Cuba acknowledge his command. Barquín, thinking of the years he had languished in jail while Rego was enjoying an army salary, crumpled up the message and threw it at a wastepaper basket.

Idly, he inspected the desk that was still filled with the belongings of Old Pancho Tabernilla. About twenty pornographic photographs were in the top drawer, along with sex booklets, magazines, and a deck of obscene playing cards. There was also a small plastic doll dressed as a priest. Barquín lifted its cassock and a tiny penis rose up.

"No wonder they are lost," Barquín muttered.

In the early hours of the morning, still before sunrise, Barquín received a telephone call from Comandante Camilo Cienfuegos, who said he was on the road between Santa Clara and Havana.

"I have orders," the young rebel said. "I have been designated military chief of the province of Havana. I have orders to come in and take command."

A short time before, when he was spinning dreams of glory in his cell at the Isle of Pines, Barquín couldn't have imagined even listening to such a statement by a man who had only a few hundred rebels, compared to the five thousand soldiers at Camp Columbia. But now, facing the political realities, he said simply, "Well, if you have your orders, then come on in."

When Barquín hung up the phone, he sent out for coffee and cigars. Someone brought him a Cuban sandwich. After his stomach was filled, his thoughts turned to more personal matters. He had about $6000 in debts. Perhaps it was time to retire from the army and start a military school.

About dawn, Justo Carrillo and some twenty other politicians from Miami arrived in an air force plane which Barquín had sent to pick them up. After years of working and waiting for this moment, he finally had a military ally in charge of Camp Columbia, and Carrillo was bursting with enthusiasm as he sped to the Estado Mayor in an army car.

But as soon as he entered the third-floor office, Carrillo could tell from Barquín's dejected face that something was wrong. The colonel embraced him and, without speaking, led him into a private bathroom, where Carrillo sat on the toilet lid as Barquín described all that had happened and named the major garrisons that had surrendered. "What do you think we should do?" he asked the veteran politician.

Carrillo grimaced. In one awful moment, he realized that all his labors had been useless. "There is absolutely nothing you can do," he said.

When political officer John Topping learned of Barquín's reply to Comandante Cienfuegos, he forgot about his problems with the tourists and walked into the next-door office of Jim Noel, the CIA station chief. "That's incredible," Topping said. "It makes no sense, the weakest possible posture. Barquín and the army are giving away all their bargaining power."

Like the others at the embassy, Topping had been hoping that Barquín could do something to moderate the 26th of July's influence, but the U.S. government was not actively assisting him. Ambassador Smith's only contact with the colonel had come when he telephoned to ask that those in embassy asylum be allowed to leave the country. Barquín had replied that Cienfuegos would have to make that decision because he, Barquín, had been left with a "dead army."

As Topping sat and chatted with Noel, the CIA chief told him that Barquín had used even stronger language with an agent that had been sent to the camp: "What can I do?" Barquín asked the CIA man rhetorically. "All they left me with is shit." But, Noel added, information had come from Santiago that Castro too was puzzled by Barquín's concession.

Topping asked if that meant it could be a trap.

"It's just crazy," the CIA man answered.

The rebels' Column 2 was also wondering about Barquín's decision. The group had stopped in the town of Colón, almost exactly halfway between Havana and Santa Clara, to wait for ammunition, a truckload of cartridges that was being sent by Ché Guevara. But more than an hour had gone by, and the truck had not appeared.

Captain William Gálvez, who had arranged for the truck, stood helplessly as he watched Comandante Cienfuegos pace angrily in front of his jeep and curse. The column had not quite five hundred men, and even that number included some Directorio volunteers who had joined them in Santa Clara. If there were any fighting in Havana, they could use up their small supply of ammunition within minutes. Perhaps,

Cienfuegos suggested, the truck had been attacked by a squad of Batistiano *esbirros*.

Gálvez rushed to the rear of the convoy, but the truck was nowhere in sight. When he reported that to his *comandante*, Cienfuegos lost his temper. "Damn it," he shouted, "you better find that truck."

Jumping into a jeep, Gálvez sped back toward Santa Clara. Just west of the town of Santo Domingo, he found the truck parked at the side of the road. The driver was sleeping.

The rebel captain slammed on the brakes, marched over to the driver's window and yelled as loud as he could. The man awoke with a start and mumbled an apology. He had not slept in a week.

Not interested in excuses, Gálvez ran to the center of the road and commandeered two motorcycles that happened to pass by. With the motorcycles leading the way, the truck horn blaring, they sped down the highway, racing to catch up with the main group so they too could participate in the conquest of Havana.

Shortly after sunrise, the last major army post in Oriente surrendered when Comandante Efigenio Ameijeiras and the men of Column 6, after several tense hours, simply walked into the garrison at Guantánamo City and disarmed the soldiers.

Worried that the army might counterattack in Santiago, or that the Marines at the U.S. Naval Base might launch an invasion, Ameijeiras ordered Captain Manuel Fajardo and eight of his men to take three hundred of the newly captured rifles and ammunition to the mountains, where they could be hidden. It required four trucks to make the trip. Like Ché Guevara in Santa Clara and Camilo Cienfuegos on the road to Havana, the rebels in Oriente were not at all certain the war was over.

While other rebel leaders were still worrying, Captain Rogelio Acevedo in Santa Clara was celebrating as he thought any seventeen-year-old would. He decided that since the revolutionary forces had won, they were entitled to the spoils of victory, and when he spotted a 1958 Chrysler with the keys in the ignition, he did not hesitate to take it. With some of his men, he went on a glorious joyride around the city in the car that seemed to have everything—large tail fins, automatic transmission and radio—but when he drove up to the regimental barracks, Ché Guevara saw him and frowned.

"What are you doing in that car?" the *comandante* demanded.

"Well," Acevedo answered, not feeling at all guilty, "I need a car to move around, to go to Havana in."

Guevara didn't smile. "Well, if you need a vehicle, use a jeep. Don't take that big car."

Acevedo went back to look for his old jeep.

Like Acevedo, most people in Santa Clara were trying to celebrate, but the joy of witnessing the end of the war was tempered by the destruction and death the battle had produced. Guillermo Domenech, the young hotel clerk, saw much of it himself when he visited his family's funeral home: eight caskets were laid out in the visitation room. His uncle told him that was just part of it because most families, following the Cuban tradition, were holding wakes in their own living rooms. He said the city's two funeral homes had split the corpses between them, to avoid accusations of body snatching. Altogether, sixty persons had died during the four and a half days of fighting: eleven rebels, eleven soldiers and thirty-eight civilians. *

In Havana, on the first regular day of business following the New Year's holiday, Castro's call for a general strike proved to be a complete success. All commercial establishments were closed; no food or liquor was available, and even cigarettes were impossible to find. For the new militiamen, olive-green became the fashion of the day. El Zorro, a tailor shop that had been secretly supplying uniforms to the Segundo Frente del Escambray, opened its doors and handed out the rest of its stock to anyone who wanted to look like a rebel. By noon, the line was a block long. Most of the men had day-old beards.

At the CMQ studios, reports of Batistiano snipers still poured in with

---

* Oscar Fernández Mell, the chief doctor with Guevara's troops, says that sixty deaths sounds accurate to him. Salmerón Hernández, a medical technician with the rebels, says he saw the corpses of twelve civilians and guesses that about another twenty-six persons died altogether. Whatever the exact figure, the number of dead was low considering the amount of shooting. The figure of three thousand dead in Santa Clara, which found its way into some American newspapers, and Batista's farewell talk about the "river of blood" were both gross exaggerations. In fact, the entire six-year struggle against Batista was not a particularly deadly one. In late 1958, a former Cuban president, Grau San Martín, said that twenty thousand had died, and that figure has been the one most repeated through the years, though it is undoubtedly an overstatement. Hugh Thomas, in *Cuba: The Pursuit of Freedom*, concluded that about fifteen hundred to two thousand died, including peasants in Oriente.

alarming frequency, and in Old Havana there was a bitter gunfight with four of Masferrer's Tigers, who were holed up in a five-story department store, the Manzana de Gómez. When the Tigers ran out of ammunition, a crowd charged the building. Three of Masferrer's men died. The fourth was led away as the crowd howled for his execution.

Soon, however, Emilio Guede and the other Movement announcers at CMQ realized that most of the reports of sniper fire were simply youths shooting at shadows. Guede himself saw one gunfight, on M Street alongside the broadcasting studios, in which twenty militiamen opened fire on an olive-green SIM car. As the car's four passengers collapsed in a splash of red, one of them moaned weakly, "Don't shoot. We are comrades." They had taken the SIM car for a joyride. All four died. The oldest was sixteen.

Guede ran back to the studio and stepped in front of the cameras: "We plead with all those who have weapons to please use them in a peaceful way, to be patriotic about the weapons that the revolution has liberated. . . ."

About noon, General Cantillo's wife came into the bedroom to wake him. There was an army lieutenant in the living room who demanded to see him. He seemed very angry.

Sleepily, Cantillo dressed. He did not try to anticipate what this was about. After the past week, nothing would surprise him.

When he walked into the living room, he saw that the officer, standing grim-faced and rigid in the center of the room, was Lieutenant "Gallego" Fernández, one of the Puros from the Isle of Pines. Cantillo's friend, Colonel Martínez Suárez, sat on the sofa; he looked worried.

Cantillo walked forward and embraced the crew-cut lieutenant. "It's been a long time since I've seen you," he said.

Fernández's expression didn't change. "General, it's only because you didn't want to."

Cantillo studied him carefully. He had, after all, ordered Fernández and the other Puros freed from the Isle of Pines, but he could tell that meant nothing now.

His face still grim, Fernández said he had heard about Castro's speech in Santiago, in which Cantillo had been denounced as a traitor to the revolution because he had broken an agreement with Castro and tried a coup d'etat. Because of that, Cantillo was now under arrest.

Cantillo started to say that he hadn't pulled off a coup at all, but he saw it was useless to argue and followed Fernández quietly out the door. Several men in civilian clothes and 26th of July armbands were standing about a hundred yards away. They watched but said nothing.

By car, Cantillo was taken to the post's jail, beside the old officers' club. There, he was put in a cell that held about sixty other officers, more than twice the number the room was intended for. A few minutes later, Colonel Martínez Suárez arrived and was pushed inside the cell. Cantillo managed a weak joke: "Ah, Martínez, what happened? You're here too." But his mind was not on humor. Cantillo had forgotten to bring his ulcer medicine, and his stomach was feeling decidedly queasy. In his own mind, he thought that he had maintained his delicate balancing act, allowing the Batista people to flee and then inviting Castro to designate the president. But Castro himself did not see it that way, and so he had failed.

As Cantillo became accustomed to his crowded cell, the first large group of rebels was entering the outskirts of Havana. They were the men of the Segundo Frente del Escambray, armed with the weapons Dr. Fleites had flown in from Miami, and their theory had been proved right. They *could* beat the 26th of July guerrillas to the capital. But it was only because Cienfuegos' Column 2 had stopped at Matanzas to demand the surrender of the garrison there from a Barquín appointee.

The Segundo Frente leaders had already decided not to make a bid for power. They knew they were disliked by Castro and they had no large personal following of their own; their only plan was to set up camp at the inconspicuous Vedado High School campus, where they could await developments.

For Roger Redondo, it was the first time in his twenty-four years that he had seen the Cuban capital, and he gawked at the tall buildings on the horizon. As he drove through the suburban streets in the Segundo Frente convoy, people cheered, and Redondo realized the crowd saw no difference between the rebel groups.

Along the way, women and children reached out and tried to touch the rebels' beards. Redondo was ashamed he didn't have one of his own, but all he could grow were chin whiskers and since he thought goatees looked foolish, he was clean-shaven.

They were still in the outskirts when a young brunette in her mid-twenties jumped on the right fender of Redondo's jeep. "Get off," he shouted at her. "You may be thrown off." She simply smiled at him.

We're in a hurry. We're in a war." She kept smiling. Exasperated, Redondo stepped on the gas. The girl clung to the hood. He jammed on the brakes. She kept smiling.

At last, he got the message. Ordering one of his men to climb into the backseat, he invited the woman to sit beside him. She did so, quietly, all the way through Havana. After he dropped his men off at the high school, she directed him through the streets to Regla, a lower-class neighborhood. They stopped at a small white house on a narrow brick street which ran down to the bay. As the woman led him into the house, she confessed she had been fantasizing about the rebels for months. She was somewhat disappointed that he didn't have a beard, but he was still a rebel. Redondo stayed for three days.

While the rest of Havana was seeming to settle down, the American tourists were still clamoring to get out. Many of the hotels had run out of food, and tourists flocked to the U.S. embassy, where they ate turkeys that had been cooked at the ambassador's residence or took stale sandwiches from the snack bar. The first floor was littered with paper coffee cups and cigarette butts.

Embassy staffers were doing what they could. Ambassador Smith called a friend of his, the president of the company which operated the *City of Havana* car ferry and gained an assurance that the boat would land as soon as the port was declared open. For a brief time, some Movement leaders said they would allow the airport and port to resume operations, but other leaders countermanded the order.

In Washington, complaints poured in to the State Department, and Assistant Secretary Rubottom, in exasperation, told the Havana embassy that unless the Movement did something it "would be a black strike" against them. As a more tangible threat, the White House released the information that five navy ships were hovering just out of sight of land, and the navy, in a classified document, estimated that it could take out two thousand tourists on the two submarine tenders that had the "capability [to] commence airlift Marine battalion on two hours' notice."

To keep the tourists calm, embassy staffers went to the major hotels. Wayne Smith, a young vice-consul in his first overseas post, was assigned to the Nacional, where he developed an ingenious plan to quiet the impatient and hostile guests—he signed up everyone on lists. There was a "Lightning Flash" list, a "Star" list and others, all with names chosen to sound like each was the premier group. Smith had no idea which list would have priority if it came to a decision, but the lists seemed to placate everyone.

In late afternoon, the airport and port were finally reopened. Using the cars of staffers and resident American businessmen, the embassy formed three car pools of eighteen cars each.

The rush to the *City of Havana* was especially hectic. Tourists crouched in backseats of cars, as if World War II was about to break out. At the docks, Wayne Smith struggled to control the crowd, but the tourists, refusing to form lines, charged toward the boat as if they were at Dunkirk. A crippled man was knocked down. About five hundred were on board when the boat left the dock.

In New York, on the first day of stock trading since Batista's flight, Wall Street greeted the end of the civil war with enthusiasm because it meant an end to the destruction of American property and promised an unhindered *zafra*, which was scheduled to start in a few days. West Indies Sugar was up 3¼ to 56¼. International Nickel closed up ¾, to 89. Companies with oil and utility interests in Cuba also showed good gains, and an executive of the American-owned electric company announced that he expected no problems with the new government.

Shortly after 5:00 P.M., the first rebels of Column 2 reached the gates of Camp Columbia. They circled the huge military garrison in jeeps, battered cars, old pickup trucks and all the other vehicles they had confiscated in their wild rush to Havana.

Their victorious ride through the city had been slowed by the crunch of people who greeted them, and they had to wait outside the camp so that their leader, Camilo Cienfuegos, could catch up, for he had become an instant hero: a veteran of *Granma*, a close associate of Castro's and, not to be discounted, a man with an appealing appearance. To some, his long dark hair and full beard made him almost "Christlike." Others saw his easy grin, cowboy hat and cartridge belts slung from his hips; they thought of him as a Western movie star. A reporter from *Bohemia* said he looked like Robinson Crusoe.

At exactly 6:00 P.M., the first rebels entered the camp, and army soldiers rushed to greet them. Major Enrique Borbonnet welcomed Cienfuegos' aides and then, at 6:30 P.M., Cienfuegos himself entered the camp in a jeep and sped to the Estado Mayor. Colonel Barquín walked down the steps to meet him. They embraced and walked together back to the third-floor office.

Barquín, who only hours before had tried to keep the rebel army out, laughed and smiled. Cienfuegos joked along, but he made one serious point: he was worried how to disarm the five thousand soldiers inside the camp. Major Borbonnet said the concern was understandable, but the troops were so demoralized and frightened it didn't matter. Still, Cienfuegos asked Barquín and Borbonnet to stay on and help run the camp. They agreed.

There were no great crowds at four the next morning when the three hundred men of Ché Guevara's column moved into Havana. The streets were deserted, and only a handful of militiamen were waiting for them outside the gates of La Cabaña fortress. Captain Rogelio Acevedo, who was once again in his old jeep, had been told to be cautious, that there were eleven hundred army men inside and the rebels were still technically at war.

It was only a technicality. The tanks facing the main gate were unarmed. The camp commander was Colonel Manuel Varela, one of Barquín's fellow Puros. He had been so worried that Batistiano army men might try to kill him by poisoning his water that he had drunk nothing for twenty-four hours. He relinquished command quickly.

54/SANDBAGS AT THE SPORTS PALACE

Even after the arrival of the rebels, the city of Havana stayed on edge. There were still more than seventeen thousand policemen and soldiers, most of them armed. Opposing them, including the guerrillas of the Segundo Frente del Escambray and the Directorio, were less than fifteen hundred rebels. A coup seemed possible at any moment, and the Movement ordered the general strike to continue. Businesses stayed closed, and most of the cars that appeared on the streets displayed the 26th of July colors. Trash piled up. Bread, milk, coffee, eggs and potatoes were almost impossible to get. A cigarette was a treasure.

To control the city, the Movement had shifted its base of operations to the futuristic Sports Palace, a circular building which from the distance looked like a white-topped flying saucer. Sympathizers helped fortify it with sandbags and barricades. Manuel Ray, the leader of the Civic Resistance in Havana, arrived to find newly armed militiamen rushing in to say they had "liberated" such places as the National Theater and the Department of Mines, locations which never had been defended by the Batistianos. Ray understood that everyone was seeking a slice of the glory, but he worried about so many weapons being loose on the streets. An order to confiscate them would never work among the individualistic Cubans, but he and Comandante Cienfuegos worked out a plan so that all at least would be registered.

Ismael Suárez de la Paz, who for the first time in months no longer had to use his war name of Comandante Echemendía, returned from Santa Clara and began taking charge of those accused of "war crimes." Most were minor government officials and policemen, though some enthusiasts even dragged in neighbors whom they accused merely of being Batista sympathizers. Suárez de la Paz knew that at least some of them were unjustly suspected, but at that moment the paramount concern was gaining control of the city. Injustices could be sorted out later. He registered the new prisoners' names in a book and ordered them held in the Sports Palace locker rooms. Even with such a grim task, the hours spun by in a state of near ecstasy. It seemed almost unbelievable to him that they had toppled the Batista regime and that he had lived to see it. This is the beginning of my new life, he thought.

But the men in charge of the Sports Palace were not well known to Castro or to Ché Guevara or Camilo Cienfuegos. It was Guevara's first time in Havana, and he felt especially uneasy about dealing with so many people who claimed to be rebel sympathizers, people he had never heard of. Because of that, Castro ordered Comandante Efigenio Ameijeiras, the *Granma* veteran who had lost three brothers in the struggle, to rush to Havana with two planeloads of troops and establish himself as the new chief of the national police. Ameijeiras knew Guevara well, but by the time he arrived, a new problem was facing the revolution: the first open conflict between anti-Batista groups.

The rift had started when President Manuel Urrutia, still in Santiago, named the first members of his cabinet, which was to be headed by José Miró Cardona, the president of the Havana Bar Association, with the title of prime minister. The new cabinet men were not veterans of the traditional political system, but they were generally older and more moderate than the rebel army leaders. And, most importantly, all were members of the Civic Resistance or the 26th of July Movement, the two organizations that directly recognized Castro as their leader. No members of the Auténtico party, the democratic regime Batista had overthrown, or the student Directorio were included.

Some anti-Batista, non-Castro politicians grumbled privately that it was exactly as they had feared, that the "unity" of all the anti-Batista groups was merely a hollow promise. But only the Directorio objected vigorously and publicly. Rolando Cubela, the group's military leader, issued a statement demanding "the participation of all the revolutionary organizations which have overthrown the dictatorship." Unless Urrutia agreed, the Directorio men threatened to stop him from occupying the Presidential Palace, which had been handed over to them by one of Barquín's men.

On the morning of January 5, the day Urrutia was scheduled to fly to Havana, tension had increased so much that Comandante Cienfuegos declared martial law in the city. Most people stayed inside their homes; only rebels moved on the streets. Two hundred members of the Segundo Frente del Escambray, wishing to avoid the conflict between two fellow revolutionary groups, moved out of the Hotel Nacional, where Directorio guerrillas had also been staying.

The Directorio members gathered at the University of Havana, where the organization had five hundred new rifles and machine guns that had been obtained from the arsenal at the San Antonio de los Baños air base, just outside Havana. Near the campus, Emilio Guede looked out the windows of the CMQ broadcasting building to see a Directorio jeep with a mounted .50-caliber machine gun and five bearded guerrillas patrol up and down the street. The studio's ragtag militia, led by a man who was now describing himself as "Comandante Five Stars," crouched on the sidewalk with guns ready to fire. The confrontation lasted five minutes before the jeep squealed onto a side street and disappeared toward Malecón Boulevard.

Faure Chomón, the group's political leader, directed the Directorio troops from the massive wooden chair in the rector's office at the university. Dr. Tony Lima, who had just returned from Miami, where he had been treasurer of the exile Directorios, listened as a stream of visitors came to plead with Chomón to stop the intrarevolutionary rivalry. Politicians, businessmen and industrial leaders all asked for the Directorio to turn over the palace. Telegrams poured in, accusing the Directorio of being "anti-unity." Chomón appeared more depressed each time a visitor arrived; he kept repeating that all he wanted was that the 26th of July honor the Pact of Caracas, made the summer before, which had promised that all anti-Batista groups would share in the new government.

But outside his office, in the campus plaza, few Directorio students were in a mood to fight. Most were like Manuel Granado Díaz, the

twenty-year-old who had been milling around the campus ever since
Batista had fled. He had close friends in the 26th of July, some of them
former Directorios, and he couldn't imagine a gunfight breaking out
between people who had worked so long together.

At 4:00 P.M., Urrutia's plane arrived at the Rancho Boyeros airport
on the edge of Havana. As the C-47 taxied toward the terminal, the
new president looked out the window and saw only rebel soldiers and a
few relatives waiting to greet him. He had understood that there would
be a crowd of thousands, that a massive reception had been arranged for
him.

But he was hours late in getting to the capital. That morning, shortly
after he left Santiago, the pilot had received a call from Castro asking
Urrutia to meet him at the Camagüey City airport. They had met inside
the plane, where they discussed the Directorio threat and the new
cabinet. There were still several positions open, but Castro did not
recommend naming any Directorio members. Instead, he suggested that
Armando Hart, the 26th of July leader recently released from prison, be
minister of education. Urrutia agreed.

Now, as the new president stepped from the plane in Havana, he
peered through his ever-present sunglasses and waved at the few who
had come to see him. Relatives ran up, and he asked about the crowd.
"Oh, yes," one said, "thousands of people were here, but the loudspeakers said you were meeting with Fidel." It had been announced his
flight was being delayed indefinitely.

For a moment, he wondered bitterly if Castro had intentionally
arranged the lengthy conference just to spoil his Havana reception, but
he didn't have long to dwell on it, for just then Julio Duarte and Manuel
Ray, two leaders of the Movement in Havana, rushed up to explain the
latest developments with the Directorio men.

Urrutia listened. He agreed the two should go talk to the group's
leaders at the palace while he waited at Camp Columbia. Duarte and
Ray sped downtown in Duarte's 1956 Chevrolet. At the iron gate at the
rear of the palace, they showed identification, and a squad of machine-
gun-carrying guerrillas let them into the inner courtyard. The palace's
first floor, its enormous lobby, seemed untouched, but the second floor
was a shambles, with rebels sprawled over the furniture in all the formal
meeting rooms. In Batista's private office, a rebel officer sat in the
presidential chair, his muddy combat boots atop the highly polished

desk. A servant in a white coat hovered nervously, holding a wooden box of cigars.

In the private quarters on the third floor, it was even more chaotic, servants standing around uncertainly, the tile floors and Persian carpets caked with mud. Ashes and cigar butts and coffee cups were everywhere. Some guerrillas, oblivious to the noise around them, were sleeping on the floor, their rifles by their sides.

Piles of Batista's suits and his wife's dresses were on the floor near the bedrooms. A large oil portrait of Marta was nearby, lying in a corridor; there was a large muddy boot mark right across her face. Dr. Tony Lima, the Miami treasurer for the Directorio, had gone through the private quarters, room by room, drawer by drawer. He had found a few pesos, some letters and documents—but nothing like the fortune of cash some people had expected.

Picking their way through the men and trash, Duarte and Ray found the Directorio's military leader in one of the bedrooms, sprawled across a broad bed, its silken bedspread on the floor, the sheets soiled with mud and cigar ashes. Cubela's arm was in a sling, the result of a minor wound.

The two Movement men had expected a lengthy argument, but Cubela had already decided to give up. He said the Directorio merely wanted to be asked to relinquish the palace. That was all. After a few moments, Duarte was given a large ring of keys, and he hurried back to the first floor. There, as photographers clicked their shutters, he fumbled with the keys until he found the proper one to unlock the large, ceremonial doors at the front of the building.

A short time later, about 7:00 P.M., Urrutia and his wife Esperanza arrived in a limousine. The Directorio rebels, who had cleaned themselves up a little, presented their rifles at formal attention, forming an honor guard to welcome him at the main door.

Urrutia shook hands and chatted briefly with the Directorio leaders, then led his cabinet ministers to the second-floor Hall of Mirrors for a press conference. His voice cracking with emotion, he said, "This is the moment of so many dreams, so many conversations, of plans, from so many nights in the Sierra." Armando Hart, the new minister of education, cried.

As Cuban and American journalists scribbled in notebooks, Urrutia decreed that the civil rights of the 1940 Constitution were once again in effect. Elections would be held within eighteen months. Gambling was to be outlawed, and "only decent Americans will live in Cuba."

After a few more statements, he decided it was time to organize a cabinet meeting, but he became lost in the maze of rooms around the palace's central courtyard. He ran across the Hall of Mirrors, only to find a corridor with no exit. Someone had to direct him to his new office and from there someone else led him to the cabinet room.

As the new political leaders settled into their chairs around the broad table, Ambassador Smith and a diplomatic delegation entered the room. The sight of Smith, so closely identified with Batista, brought murmurs from the journalists and new politicians. Urrutia, an obvious look of displeasure on his face, offered the ambassador only the tips of his fingers as Smith tried to shake his hand.

Once again, Smith's only concern was for the Batistianos. He announced he wanted to make certain that the right of asylum in embassies was guaranteed. Urrutia replied coldly that the traditional laws would be followed. The delegation left quickly.

After that, the new politicians settled down to talk about the *zafra* and how to return the economy to normal. Captain José Machado Ventura, the health director from the Second Front, sat against the wall in his old rebel uniform; a machine gun was across his lap. Raúl Castro had sent him to watch Urrutia, and as he listened, he couldn't believe how much time the politicians wasted talking; they seemed to have a hard time agreeing on anything.

While the talk droned on, Urrutia's wife Esperanza inspected the third-floor private quarters. She was beginning to think like a First Lady. The only clothes they had, outside of their olive-green uniforms, had been borrowed from friends in Santiago and brought in old, frayed luggage. If they were going to look like a presidential couple, she would have to get one of the new aides to make a trip to El Encanto department store.

As soon as she saw the rooms, she was horrified. But she insisted on tramping through the mess, followed by several servants displaying forced smiles. The Directorio rebels had left; their trash remained behind. "We need to repair and put new drapes all over," she told an anxious servant who only days before had catered to the Batista family. "This French furniture needs to be reupholstered and repainted . . ."

When the Cunard Line's *Mauretania* docked in New York, newspapermen rushed to interview the passengers who had been eyewitnesses to the Cuban revolution. Paul Tannenbaum thought that New Year's Day was "the most exciting moment in my life," but his ten-year-old son Rich gained all the attention when he showed reporters his diary. In three lines, he had written, "Left the *Mauretania*, saw the revolution, came back."

With Urrutia's arrival, the general strike in Havana ended. Office workers who hadn't seen each other in six days traded anecdotes. Buses were operating again. Sanitation workers started to haul away the mounds of garbage. Stores reopened and housewives flocked to them for groceries. The Nacional movie house offered *Song of the Mockingbird;* the America showed *The Reluctant Debutante.* The Tropicana Nightclub reopened with its old show, *On the Way to Broadway,* but it dropped the first scene, which had depicted Cubans hurrying to get a plane to New York. Musicians rushed to record new songs to catch the popularity of the moment: "Sierra Maestra," "Just Like Martí Dreamed It" and "Wings of Liberty." Two humorists announced plans to write two plays: *The General Flew at Midnight* and *The Legacy of the Animal.*

The Association of Cuban Landholders announced its support for the new government, as did the Odd Fellow lodges. Even the usually conservative *Diario de la Marina* was swept along with the euphoria. Amid advertisements thanking Castro and Urrutia, the newspaper's editorial writer stated, "We believe in the rebirth of the country. . . ." A columnist wrote that the nation had been "the victim of the worst tyranny of the Americas." Cartoonists, freed at last from censorship, poked gentle fun at the new heroes. One showed a man asking a shopkeeper, who was counting a stack of money, "No one is doing any business. How come your sales are so good?" The shopowner replied: "I'm selling razor blades." Another had a man, a dark stubble on his face, being asked, "And you, sir, how long have you been with the rebels?" "About twenty-four hours," the man answered.

Daily, rumors swept the city that Castro was expected soon, but his military caravan was being forced to stop by the cheering crowds in almost every small town along the Central Highway; they wanted to hear him speak, and he almost always obliged. By radio, he apologized to the people of Havana, but his arrival date kept getting postponed.

As the people waited, the government slowly began to function again. Justo Carrillo, who had worked so hard to get Barquín into power and keep Castro out, accepted a post as president of the Agricultural and

Industrial Development Bank. Emilio Guede, the propaganda chief, became a director of *Revolución*, the new daily newspaper of the 26th of July. Dr. Raúl Trillo, the rebel doctor with Castro's Column 1, became chief of the Columbia military hospital. Comandante Raúl Chibás was selected as minister of the treasury, but he declined because he wanted to help reorganize the army. Manuel Ray, the engineer who had been chief of the Havana Civic Resistance, became minister of public works.

The appointees arrived at their new government offices to find the civil servants nervous and cooperative. Antonio Jorge, an exile from Miami, went to his new position at the National Planning office, where an assistant administrator told him that he and the other employees were members of a secret 26th of July cell. Jorge wisecracked that perhaps everybody in the building, with the exception of the old Batista minister, had supported the rebels. The assistant nodded eagerly.

As President Urrutia became accustomed to the palace, he began enjoying his new prerogatives. When he realized he needed a haircut, he wondered what his barber in New York was doing. "What the heck," he decided, "I'll just get him down here as the presidential barber." He issued an order to that effect.

At Camp Columbia and La Cabaña, rebels gradually took the weapons away from the soldiers and padlocked the arsenals. The soldiers were eager to comply. Denio Machado, a 26th of July man who had joined Guevara's column in Santa Clara, was shocked to see colonels and majors approach him and ask how they could be of service. The officers saluted anyone with a beard, and often the rebels, who had no knowledge of such military formality, ignored them; they simply didn't know what was expected. One army man stood at attention for half an hour, sweating, shaking, waiting for a rebel to return his salute.

New prisoners streamed in. All SIM officers were arrested, and the two cells at the Camp Columbia jail, intended to hold sixty men, had almost six hundred squeezed into them before many were transferred to La Cabaña. The president of the national bank under Batista was arrested, as was Carlos Márquez Sterling, the conservative politician who had run against Batista's candidate in the November election. Castro, on the way to Havana, felt sufficiently in control to issue an order demanding summary courts-martial for all "war criminals" accused of killing or torturing civilians or rebels. The guilty were to be executed by firing squad.

For Colonel José Martínez Suárez, that was not a comforting thought. Cantillo's friend was in the Columbia military hospital, where he had been transferred after complaining of intestinal trouble. As he lay in his bed, he tried to imagine what he could be charged with. The worst incident had been several weeks before, when the body of a Movement worker had been dumped in the Fifth Military District, where he had been territorial inspector. To him, it was obviously the work of the Havana police, but he wasn't certain the rebels would believe him. And he wasn't at all sure how political the trials would be. It was not good that he was the one who had located the justice who was Batista's constitutional successor. He could only hope that someone would remember that he had helped rebel sympathizers, like Danilo Mesa, to get out of the clutches of the police.

One morning, about three o'clock, Martínez Suárez was awakened by the *klop-klop* of military boots coming down the walkway between the hospital beds. He opened one eye to see five or six men spread around the foot of his bed. Most were bearded rebels, and one of them was shining a flashlight in his face. Oh, my God, he thought, they have come to take me to the firing squad.

"How do you feel, Colonel?" a man asked. He was a small fellow without a beard, but Martínez Suárez couldn't see his face in the glare of the lights.

"Pretty bad," Martínez Suárez said, not having to lie.

"Do you remember me?"

"No . . . I don't remember anything."

The man introduced himself. He was Danilo Mesa, and he had just assured Comandante Cienfuegos that Martínez Suárez was guilty of no crimes. The colonel was being released into Mesa's custody. Suddenly, Martínez Suárez felt much better.

Martínez Suárez was an exception, for most prisoners stayed locked behind bars as *bolas* of impending executions spread through the city. Late one night, Ambassador Smith received a call from one of his military attachés. General Cantillo's wife had just told him her husband was going to be shot at dawn.

Smith knew that had nothing to do with official embassy business, and already Washington was moaning about one "unofficial" escapade, in which Bob Clark, Jr., the naval attaché, and the U.S. Navy mission chief had slipped the son of Batista's admiral out of the country. They had taken the youth, a midshipman at the U.S. Naval Academy in Havana for the holidays, out of a Latin American embassy and driven him right into rebel-controlled Columbia. The rebels were so ill-organized that they didn't even notice when Clark loaded him on the navy mission's two-engine Beechcraft and flew him to the United States.

Such a blatantly partisan act had riled political officer John Topping and Washington, and Smith knew he already had one mark against him personally for harboring the Dominican ambassador. Still, he was not going to let the rules of diplomacy stand in the way of a humanitarian act.

Accompanied by the Brazilian ambassador, Vasco de Cunha, Smith went to Camp Columbia for a late-night meeting with Camilo Cienfuegos. They met in a small room, where the comandante was surrounded by rebel friends.

Smith looked at the group and thought of photographs of the old Dillinger gang—dirty, unshaven, shoeless and well armed. Comandante Raúl Chibás looked at Smith, who was dressed in a white suit, and thought, How unpleasant he is. A Batista friend, trying to anchor the tyranny in power and to plan our defeat, and yet he has the nerve to come here.

The Brazilian ambassador, who had been friendly with the rebel movement, did most of the talking. He said that not only the United States, but all of Latin America would frown on the execution of a general so well known for not having committed war crimes. Smith added: "The 26th of July would lose face with the rest of the world if Cantillo is executed without a trial."

Cienfuegos said he could not rescind the order without Castro's approval, but he would delay the execution until he could pass along the ambassador's message.

Cantillo knew about neither the dawn execution nor the ambassador's visit, but a navy officer, a good friend who had served under him in Oriente, rushed back to Havana to tell him that Castro was going to have him shot.

By that time, Cantillo too had been transferred to the military hospital, because his ulcer had become progressively worse in the jail and he had been able to eat nothing. Conditions in the hospital were much better, but the mood was morose. Officers, crying, told him they were certain they were destined for the firing squad, and such whining made Cantillo angry. He thought they should face their fate like men.

Cantillo himself was careful not to complain, he had done his best and he had failed, but he was relieved when a newspaperwoman visited him. She said the archbishop of Santiago had talked to Castro and said, "Cantillo has already been judged by the people of Santiago, and they don't want him shot." The woman said Castro had denied any plans to execute the general.

While the prisoners brooded, rebels were enjoying their status as the new celebrities. Girls followed them everywhere, and children begged for bullets as souvenirs. Most rebels obliged.

Captain Rogelio Acevedo was trying to have his fun too. After a shoot-out with a suspected police agent in Havana, the seventeen-year-old confiscated the man's Ford Fairlane 500. He declared the car "recovered misappropriated property" and drove it back to La Cabaña, where he paraded it around the large grounds of the fortress until Guevara saw him. Then he was ordered back to his jeep.

That was just one of the ways in which Guevara set a tone of spartan morality for his soldiers at the fortress. He himself used an old Studebaker rather than the two new Oldsmobiles that had belonged to Batista's brother-in-law. At night, when he found five or six rebels sprawled asleep on the king-size bed in the old Batista commander's house, he simply shrugged and went to sleep in the car.

Almost always, he had been frank about his Marxist leanings, but in his first days in Havana, he felt compelled to sidestep the issue of his political ideas and talk only about party membership when he told Herbert Matthews of *The New York Times:* "I have never been a Communist. Dictators always say their enemies are Communists, and it gave me a pain to be called an international Communist all the time. When a thing is said often enough, people begin to doubt and believe, as I think your State Department did."

But beyond the sight of journalists, Communists were coming into La Cabaña. On the morning of January 4, acting on the orders of Guevara, Captain Antonio Núñez Jiménez, a professor of geography at Santa

Clara University and a longtime Communist who had joined the rebel forces in late December, took four trucks to the headquarters of BRAC, the Anti-Communism Repression Bureau. He carted all the bureau's documents back to La Cabaña, where they were placed in a garage behind the commander's house.

Captain Oscar Fernández Mell, the doctor for Guevara's column, looked at some of the papers, which showed clearly that BRAC had worked closely with the CIA. Many of those who had been investigated and detained were not Communists at all, merely anti-Batista people. To him, it was obvious that BRAC worked simply to keep Batista in power because "there was no Communist danger whatsoever. There were Communists in Cuba, but they did not at that time present any threat."

The documents were examined by a special group, led by Núñez Jiménez. No one talked about their activities, but one afternoon, Denio Machado, the 26th of July man who had joined the rebels at Santa Clara, saw six men unlocking the new padlocks on the overhead sliding doors of the garage. Machado, who worked in the audiovisual department of the university, knew the six by sight. They were all Communists who had done little until the rebels started taking towns in Las Villas Province. When the men left, Machado peered through a garage window and saw the BRAC files stacked against the wall, beside a desk and a typewriter. He asked a rebel commander about the files, but he was told that no one in the rebel army, regardless of rank, could be admitted to the garages. Machado wondered what that had to do with the Cuban revolution, but he asked nothing else.

Indeed, freed from the prohibitions imposed by the Batista regime, the Communist PSP was moving into action. They seized the headquarters of the barbers' union, the musicians' union and a number of other labor offices. A spokesman for the 26th of July told reporters that they would not be ousted immediately, but the Movement did ask them to leave a magazine office that had been owned by Batista.

The day after Urrutia arrived in Havana, the Communist newspaper *Hoy* made its first appearance on the streets. It supported, in essence, the program Castro had outlined after his arrest in 1953, and an editorial called the 26th of July's Agrarian Reform Law "the first important step" although it was "insufficient." The party gave its approval to improved education, an end to racial discrimination and freedom for labor unions, while decrying "the antipatriotic complex in which our fatal geographical situation forces us to accept anything that is said or decided by the American State Department." The editorial suggested the nationalization of public services—telephone, electricity, railways and aviation—while calling for the beginning of a process leading to the restoration of the 1940 Constitution "after the changes or adjustments deemed necessary by the people."

As the city awaited Castro's arrival, *Hoy* ran an editorial by party leader Juan Marinello: "The triumphant revolution has not been the work of one party, nor of one class, nor of one group. If it has triumphed, it has been because it has brought into its fold men and women of all ideologies and beliefs, and because of the much blood shed together by Communists, Auténticos, militants of the 26th of July and the Directorio and other organizations and sectors. The people have gained the victory." But it went on to mention especially the "victory of the rebel army."

Few Cubans paid any attention to the Communist pronouncements in those first days, but the American embassy staff, driven by the staunch anti-Communism of Smith and the Eisenhower administration, compiled reports on any signs of Communism they could find and sent them up to Washington, which was trying to decide whether to recognize the new regime.

Ambassador Smith thought the State Department was rushing far too quickly toward recognition. Even before the tourists were evacuated, he had been asked to fly up for consultations, but he refused to leave until the last tourist was out. Then the brief Directorio crisis at the palace postponed his departure yet again.

When he did leave, Daniel Braddock, his deputy chief of mission, gathered the information. He reported that eight workers, including two Communists, had made "sweeping demands" of an official at the American-owned Cuban Electric Company, and the company's general manager had gone into hiding because of threats against his life. The embassy learned, also, that the Communists had become one of the five groups in the United Workers Front, which was taking control of the country's unions. Commented Braddock: "While embassy not surprised by participation of Communists . . . many sympathizers of July 26th Movement, who were repeatedly assured by leaders of July 26th that PSP was being kept out, were surprised and apparently nonplussed."

But these scattered indications of Communism were almost lost in the inundation of pleas from Cubans and American businessmen that the new government be recognized quickly. One conservative politician, Guillermo Belt, who had only weeks before warned of widespread bloodshed unless the United States stepped in, called the lack of violence "one of the miracles of the Americas." Smith's committee of U.S. businessmen was "unanimously of the view that present government was better than they dared hope for. . . . One previously strong Batista supporter said this was most popular government he had seen in Cuba in his sojourn of more than 30 years." A staff memorandum, prepared by Braddock, political officer Topping and CIA chief Noel pointed to Guevara's statement that he wasn't a Communist and Urrutia's announcement that he was opposed to Communism as examples that "present indications are favorable."

In Santiago, Consul Park Wollam was also looking for signs of Marxism, but as he reported to Washington, "So far there has been no overt evidence of Communist activities. There is an unconfirmed rumor that the PSP attempted to open an office here, but was refused permission by Húber Matos," the *comandante* of Column 9 who had become military chief of the city. "It may be expected that the PSP will have a freer hand with propaganda with the lifting of censorship. . . . The general run of Santiago citizens seemed to go out of their way, however, to tell Americans that the 26th of July is not in any way Communist."

In Washington, William Wieland received all these reports, along with messages complaining about Smith. A 26th of July spokesman in the United States demanded Smith's recall because he was "openly showing his hostility to Dr. Fidel Castro, the national hero of the Cuban people." Representative Adam Clayton Powell, the black congressman from New York, also wanted Smith's removal, accompanied by $200 million in aid to the new government.

When Smith reached Washington, he was shown immediately into Assistant Secretary Rubottom's office on the fourth floor.

"How do you stand with the new government?" Rubottom asked him. Smith answered that his position "on the Castros" was well known, and he wasn't about to change it. The two went up to the fifth-floor office of Christian Herter, where the undersecretary informed them that the new regime was going to be recognized immediately and that Smith was being recalled. After Rubottom left, Herter told Smith that President Eisenhower wanted to offer him another ambassadorial post, but Smith declined. He had had enough of being an ambassador.

On the afternoon of January 7, Smith returned to Havana and hurried to the new foreign minister's office, where he formally presented the note of recognition expressing the United States's trust that the new government would "comply with the international obligations and agreements of Cuba."

Smith was despondent when he returned to the embassy. He strode grim-faced past his longtime secretary without even saying hello; it was the most upset she had seen him since he had come to Cuba. Smith sat brooding in his office. He was convinced he had just handed Cuba over to the Communists.

In its slow, methodic way, the State Department machinery was still grinding along, and it was one day in early January when the diplomatic pouch arrived at the Santiago consulate. Park Wollam opened it and found inside Washington's tortured, double-speak memo about getting a message to Castro without appearing that it was sending a message. It seemed so bizarre that Wollam wondered how he would have managed to carry out the instructions.

The city was undergoing some odd changes. At first, a feeling of *continuismo* pervaded the town. Policemen still walked the streets, and Lily Ferreiro had to endure seeing the policemen who had once helped beat him come into his supermarket wearing armbands and greeting him with a friendly, "Hey, Lily, how are you?"

Townspeople became so bitter that Vilma Espín led a delegation of Santiago mothers to see her fiancé, Raúl Castro. The women told him how frustrating it was to see the murderers of their sons still walking around so calmly. Raúl asked them to be patient, that they had to wait until Fidel reached Havana. "Keep trusting us," he said. "We will not disappoint you."

In fact, even before Castro's arrival, rebels in Santiago started to jail the most notorious policemen and Masferrer henchmen. Their disappearance from public view helped raise the spirits of the townspeople, and on the Epiphany, the city had its first real celebration in months, with three bearded rebels leading the Three Kings parade through the streets. Women appeared in olive-green uniforms and some rebels took their first bath in weeks. When Comandante Matos was the guest speaker at the first post-victory meeting of the Rotary Club, he received a standing ovation.

Not everyone was so happy. Colonel Rego Rubido at the Moncada garrison was being completely ignored by the rebels. After he had sent out a few telegrams to other army posts and cosigned several decrees with Raúl Castro, he was simply left alone in his office. Gradually, he realized that being "chief of staff of the Cuban army" was a hollow honor.

For Americans, the concern was getting back to work. Daymond Elmore, the assistant manager of the Ermita sugar mill who had been forced to flee on foot some weeks before, returned to Cuba on a ship from Baltimore that carried the navy base's weekly supply of bread. He found his house still pockmarked by the dozen or so bullet holes that had been there when he left, but there was no new damage. Now, he told himself, he could get back to business as usual.

Connie Wollam was, in those early days of January, still bitter about the terror caused by the mysterious visitor to her house. With a Cuban woman friend, she marched down to the Santiago prison, a large, gray-stone building where the rebels were putting the Masferreristas and Batista henchmen. At the gate, she showed her passport to a teenager with a submachine gun, and the youth let them in.

They walked into a concrete courtyard, surrounded by two tiers of cells. A few prisoners, sullen and frightened, stood near a brick horse trough. On the balcony was another boy with a submachine gun, and since he seemed to be the warden, the two women climbed the stairs to explain what they were looking for. The boy led them from cell to cell. Connie peered into each and saw men sitting in silent terror. It was so depressing that, about two-thirds of the way around, she whispered to her friend, "I feel very uncomfortable. You can feel the hate and fear here." They left. *

As Cubans turned their attention to "war crimes," people throughout the island began pointing out unmarked mass graves, shallow holes where bodies were dumped. They looked more like the work of gangsters than a recognized government.

* Some days later, a Santiago newspaper ran photographs of about seventy men who had been lined up in front of a trench, executed by machine guns and covered with dirt by a bulldozer. One photo was of a half-Oriental, half-Latin man. He was listed as a Masferrerista guilty of numerous war crimes. Connie Wollam was certain he was her intruder. She never learned why he had bothered her, but it is known that Masferrer's men suspected the American consul and his wife of being rebel sympathizers.

Park Wollam saw some of it himself. When taking a tour of Oriente Province to survey the war damage, townspeople led him to a ridge above the mining town of Charco Redondo. Thirty-seven badly decomposed bodies lay in a narrow trench amid old shoes and ragged bits of clothing. A horse carcass was there too. Wollam stared down at the stinking mess, unable to take his eyes off a leg bone with a steel pin in it.

The villagers said they didn't know who the bodies were, but they assumed army soldiers were the killers because if the corpses were those of soldiers, all the belt buckles would be the same. Wollam looked. There were different kinds of buckles.

Near Havana, Enrique Barroso tried to find out what had happened to Joseito, a peasant who had helped him in the Madruga Hills before disappearing in late December. By piecing together army intelligence reports and bits of information yielded by frightened army officers, he found the corpse at the town of Güines. It had been put in a burlap bag and set on fire in the cemetery. An autopsy revealed that the peasant's leg had been badly mangled by a bullet, but he must have been still alive when a railway spike was driven through his skull.

In Pinar del Río Province, Father Amando Llorente, director of Agrupación Católica and Castro's high-school adviser, spent several days looking for the bodies of four Catholic students who had gone to the province in late December to deliver medicines and armbands to the underground.

He found a number of mass graves, but none contained the boys he was looking for. Then, by getting a terrified army chauffeur to talk, he was led to a steep ravine beyond the mountain of Pan de Guajaibón. The bodies were in a grave covered only by an inch or two of dirt; a vulture had been eating the flesh of a hand poking through the soil. The corpses were clad only in underwear. A rope was still tied around the wrists of one of them. It appeared they had been hung.

As more and more bodies were uncovered, people began howling for vengeance, and nowhere did the cries come faster and more emphatic than in the city of Santa Clara, where some of the first rebel executions were carried out. None of the prisoners there were tried under the laws of the 1940 Constitution, which both Urrutia and Castro had promised to uphold. No one seemed to complain. If Cubans supported a rule of law, based on a constitution, they certainly did not reveal it now. Residents had simply gone to the rebel headquarters at the Public Works

Building, filled out complaints and, if there were no one to stand up and defend a prisoner, the 26th of July immediately approved the death sentence.

Guillermo Domenech, the young hotel clerk, saw the first executions at a target practice field just outside of town. The atmosphere resembled that of a party. Men walked around renting folding chairs. Vendors in trucks sold ice cream and *pirulis,* a pointed candy on a stick.

The police and SIM men were brought in a truck. The first two were led to a tree and shot. Then came a third. As his body slumped to the ground, the crowd cheered.

Angered, the rebel commander confronted his audience. "Ladies and gentlemen, this is not a circus. We can't carry out justice with you turning this proceeding into one." As the crowd shuffled and stared at the ground, the rebels led the remaining prisoners to the truck and returned to the regimental garrison.

There, the executions continued in front of a smaller audience. The SIM men who had taken over the Gran Hotel were executed one by one. Then Alejandro García Olayón, a captain of navy police accused of killing an underground worker, refused a dark handkerchief as a blindfold, but when the squad leader gave the order to aim, the policeman suddenly put up his hands as if to cushion the impact. The marksmen fired. The body collapsed. The commander delivered the coup de grace with a .45-caliber pistol shot behind the left ear.

Colonel Cornelio Rojas, the Santa Clara police chief and uncle of Rolando Masferrer, also refused the blindfold. Grim-faced, wearing a broad-brimmed hat, he stood in front of the concrete wall without revealing a hint of fear. As journalist Eduardo ("Guayo") Hernández snapped photos, the colonel said, "All I have to say is, now that you have your revolution, don't lose it."

The squad of eight marksmen fired. Some aimed directly at his face. His hat flew off. His head was split in two. Brains and blood covered the wall and his face looked like a rubbery mask with nothing behind it. The rebel commander, seeing the condition of the head, fired the coup de grace into the ground.

Later, when Castañeda was riding with Castro in a car headed toward Camagüey City, the radio announced President Urrutia's first choices for the cabinet posts. Castro had never heard of several of the men, and he had to ask the journalist who they were.

As the caravan moved into Las Villas Province, the rebels were exhausted. Some joked, "We haven't slept since 1958," and their tempers occasionally flared when they saw men with three-day-old beards wearing their black-and-red colors. Several times, they forced the new converts to take off their armbands.

In each city, Castro was speaking for two or three hours, pausing only for an occasional sip of water. He was hoarse and his eyes bleary from lack of sleep, but the response of the people seemed to renew his energy. At Santa Clara, he gave a lengthy talk and then moved south, trying to skirt the town of Sancti Spíritus, but a crowd spotted him and he was forced to stop and make a speech.

At Cienfuegos, Castro had dinner at El Covadonga Restaurant with the Segundo Frente del Escambray leaders who had taken over the city. That night, he started speaking at 11:30 from the back of a flatbed truck, and he became so carried away with his own rhetoric that it seemed he was about to fall off. Father Francisco Guzmán, sitting behind him, several times leaned forward and grabbed Castro by the back of his belt to help him keep his balance. Castro, oblivious to the gesture, talked until 3:00 A.M.

Everywhere, Castro tried to reassure the people. To a reporter from *Diario de la Marina*, which was closely connected with the Catholic Church, he said, "Without religion, we can't have a well educated citizen, and so I feel the public schools should teach religion for those who want it." He said he did not plan to commence diplomatic relations with the Soviet Union or other Communist countries. Elections would be held in eighteen months, although they might have to be postponed until two years.

The night before entering Havana, Castro visited an orphanage run by nuns in the city of Matanzas and gave them cash to buy a television set. At 10:00 P.M., he began speaking at the central plaza as searchlights swept over the crowd. He stopped talking at 1:30 A.M. so that he could hurry to the provincial palace, where Ed Sullivan was waiting to film an interview for his Sunday-night television show.

Early the next morning, January 8, after two hours' sleep, he visited the parents of a Directorio hero who had been killed trying to assassinate Batista. Then he went to the man's gravesite as thousands lined the streets. That sudden side trip put him behind schedule. All of Havana, he was told, was waiting for him. Businesses were closing at noon. Mobile television cameras were scattered along the route.

Castro rushed ahead. He was supposed to have lunch at the Hatuey brewery, but as he reached the workers' welcome sign on the factory fence, a messenger said that his nine-year-old son was waiting for him at a nearby Shell gas station.

"Let's go," Castro shouted, and his jeep raced past the factory. He found the boy, Fidelito, dressed in a new olive-green uniform. Rebels helped lift him into the jeep.

On the edge of Havana, at El Cotorro, it became almost impossible to move. Including the army men from Bayamo and Santiago, there were between five thousand and six thousand men in the victory column, and the streets were jammed with trucks, buses, old cars, tanks on the back of flatbeds—all filled with sleepless men waving at the delirious crowd that had come to greet them. Men made a V sign with their fingers; women and children reached out to touch the rebels. Many cried with joy.

Captain Reinaldo Blanco of the Bayamo army garrison lost his temper for the last time in the heated traffic. Still constipated and depressed after a week in the "new army," he shouted at his driver: "I don't care what the orders are. I can't stand to drive through Havana with these people." They pulled out; no one noticed.

Castro's jeep weaved between the stalled trucks, the driver urging people to step back on the sidewalks. When they reached an open field beside a church, Castro leaped into the helicopter, which carried him to an area south of Havana harbor. Another jeep took him up Avenida del Puerto, past the old Atarés fortress, along the edge of the bay. The sides of the street were a waving sea of placards and banners. People sang, cheered and shouted slogans. They threw confetti and black-and-red rolls of crepe paper as army planes circled overhead.

As they neared the pier area, Castro spotted the *Granma*, the aging American yacht which had brought him and eighty-one others to the shores of Oriente two years before. Its white paint was peeling, but a new Cuban flag fluttered from its stern. Castro, ordering his driver to stop, dashed over to the boat. "That boat," he announced to the crowd, "is like a piece of my life."

He stared at it with mixed emotions, for he had "the sensation of a person changing jobs. From the role of a warrior, which was what I had been, to the role of a public man. . . . Something that was very difficult had been accomplished. But there is a feeling that everything you know, everything that you have been doing in a certain job, to which you have dedicated many years, is no longer relevant." To him, there had been something simple and pure about the war, a struggle of honest, altruistic men whose best qualities had been brought out by the hardships of the Sierra.

He knew Havana was going to be much more complicated, and he was certain that even some who were cheering him at that moment were going to be a threat to his revolution, that the Byzantine ways of traditional Cuban politics would try to take over, to twist the victory back into the usual channels of corruption, compromise and factionalism. He had a "profound concern" about the Directorio's bid for a slice of power. They had given up the palace, but they still retained the weapons they had taken from the army arsenal.

Running back to his jeep, he and the caravan moved on to the Presidential Palace. Castro, shouldering his telescopic rifle, walked across the plaza. President Urrutia was at the palace door to greet him. They went into the Hall of Mirrors, where Castro drank two glasses of Coca-Cola and, still holding the rifle, posed for pictures with the president. The rebel leader looked tired, his face drawn, but Urrutia thought he appeared happier than he had ever seen him.

When the two walked to the balcony, Urrutia introduced the rebel in glowing terms: "He is without any doubt the most selfless fighting leader in history."

After the applause subsided, Castro said, smiling, "This building . . . I never liked this building, and I don't think anyone liked it. The closest I came was there, to that wall, when I was a student. Do you want to know what is the emotion, the feeling that the leader of the Sierra has when he enters the palace? I will confess my emotion: I feel just as I would feel entering any other building of the republic. . . . If it were a matter of feeling, of love, the place for which I have the most feeling, the place where I would like to live, would be Turquino Peak [the highest mountain in the Sierra]."

He invited everyone to follow him to Camp Columbia because "now Columbia belongs to the people. And [that] the tanks, now belonging to the people, should go in front, opening the way. Nobody is going to keep you out. We'll meet you there."

Then, in a moment that those who were there or saw on television would never forget, he asked the crowd to make way for him so that he could walk across the plaza to his jeep. His advisers had told him he would need a large escort to get through the packed crowd, "but the people must take care of the revolutionaries. So once again, I will prove that I know the people. Without a single soldier walking ahead of me, I will walk through a line with the president of the republic. He and I will walk together so that, compatriots, we can show the entire world, to the journalists here today, just how disciplined and civilized we are in Cuba."

As Castro walked toward the crowd, the people made way for him. To one journalist, it was like seeing Moses part the Red Sea. Political officer John Topping saw the scene on an embassy television set and mumbled, "That guy knows how to press the button."

Castro reached the jeep without problem and, with his son beside him, led the caravan toward Camp Columbia. It was twilight. Thousands had been waiting hours for one glimpse of the man who had overthrown the dictatorship. They were packed on balconies, clinging to rooftops, hanging from trees. In Vedado, the caravan was showered with confetti tossed from the windows of the Havana Hilton. A CBS correspondent said, "It looks like Ike and MacArthur coming home."

A little before 9:00 P.M., Castro entered Columbia and moved through a sea of people to the grandstand facing the parade ground. His eyes were glassy with exhaustion. The house from which Batista had fled was just a few yards away. In front of him were television cameras, carrying the speech to all of Cuba.

Taking the microphone in his right hand, he shouted to the restless crowd, "Compatriots, I ask you to keep the greatest silence possible. Are not those who are here revolutionaries?"

"Yes, yes," people shouted.

"Then here one has to have discipline, and everyone has to keep quiet so that people are able to hear."

Starting slowly, building his own enthusiasm and that of the audience, he promised an end to the cult of personality and corruption. "We must ask ourselves if we carried out this revolution thinking that, just as soon as the forces of the tyranny were defeated, we were going to get in a 'duck tail' [Cuban nickname for a Cadillac] and were going to a place somewhere and from now on in life were going to have a [free] ride. . . ."

He turned to Comandante Cienfuegos, standing to his right, and asked, "Am I doing well, Camilo?"

"Yes, you are doing well, Fidel," Cienfuegos answered, beaming.

Castro then turned to the subject of peace. ". . . I swear before my compatriots that if any of our *compañeros*, or if our Movement, or if I should be an obstacle to peace, from this very moment the people can decide about us, and tell us what to do. I am a man who knows when to leave. . . ."

As he talked two white doves fluttered down on the podium. A third landed on his right shoulder. He was hardly conscious of the dove being there, it was so light, and he did not even pause.

After a week of euphoria, the doves converted that already giddy moment into a transcendent experience. The audience watched in awed silence. Batista soldiers removed their caps and placed their right hands over their hearts. Some civilians fell to their knees in prayer. Believers in the Afro-Cuban *santería* cults stroked their red-and-white beads.

In the offices of *Diario de la Marina*, an editorial writer watched the doves land and was inspired to start an editorial for the front page: "We interpret the incident of the dove . . . to be more than simply coincidence. We believe it is a sign from the Lord who is sending us the universal symbol of the peace which we all desire." *

The dove stayed on his shoulder as he continued: "We cannot ever become dictators. Those who do not have the people with them must resort to being dictators. We have the love of the people, and because of that love . . . we will never turn away from our principles."

Then he launched into what had been bothering him: the Directorio's bid for power. It was a signal, the first tangible one he had given, that the revolution was not over, that it would now turn to the enemies within, that it would accept nothing other than a complete revolution-ary unity, a unanimity like that which had moved the crowd at the palace.

". . . The greatest crime that can be committed in Cuba today—the greatest crime, I repeat—is a crime against the peace. No one would forgive it. All those who endanger peace and tranquillity and the happiness of millions of mothers are criminals and traitors."

Without naming the organization or its leaders, he described the

---

* No one knows exactly how the doves got there. One popular and cynical theory is that the birds had either clipped wings or stomachs loaded with lead pellets, and when someone released them nearby, they simply alighted on the closest subject. Certainly, Castro himself does not attribute the doves to any supernatural entity: "I don't even know who sent the pigeons," he said during the interview for this book.

seizure of the weapons. "*¿Armas para que?* Arms, for what? To fight against whom? *¿Armas para que?* To blackmail the president of the republic? To threaten the government? Are they going to use them against us? *¿Armas para que?* Do they want to return to the times of the gang wars? If the answers are no, then we wonder why they need all those weapons."

The crowd picked up the chant: "*¿Armas para que? ¿Armas para que?*"

Castro stepped back from the podium and smiled. He, the leader of the rebel army, had won over the people gathered in the camp of the old military might. It was all over. Yet it had only just begun.

EPILOGUE

As the euphoria of victory subsided, most Cubans returned to their daily routines assuming that the revolutionary leadership would slip into the usual habits of Cuban governments, with idealistic rhetoric giving way to materialistic comforts. But, as Castro himself said later, his was one revolution that was going to do more than it had promised, not less.

That was true right from the start. As soon as Castro arrived in Havana, rebels began pursuing their enemies with a vengeance. In mid-January, some seventy Batista officials were placed in front of a bulldozed trench near Santiago de Cuba and executed by machine gun; one of them was Police Chief Haza, whom Castro had embraced on January 1. It was the same elsewhere, from the eastern- to the westernmost provinces: dozens upon dozens of police and army "enforcers" were shot after brief courts-martial. Most were lower-echelon figures; their bosses were safe in exile. The most sensational cases were reserved for the Havana Sports Palace, where crowds jeered and shouted late into the night as witnesses gave emotional, but unsubstantiated, testimony against army officers. Several American journalists sympathetic to the new regime thought the proceedings were "circuses."

As an afterthought, the government ordered changes in the 1940

Constitution, legalizing the death penalty and empowering the cabinet to make laws at will. Though elections were still promised for the following year, the constitution the rebels had vowed to uphold was slipping away. On February 11, Prime Minister José Miró Cardona resigned in disgust. Castro replaced him.

In the following months, the rebel leader maneuvered brilliantly to gain more control, each step preceded by emotional speeches to the public, each time winning increased support for himself and hostility for any who dared oppose him. In March, the government ordered all rents cut by 30 to 50 percent and took over the telephone company "temporarily." On May 17, a new Agrarian Reform Law was promulgated, breaking up the large estates and announcing that all sugar companies would have to be owned by Cubans within a year. On June 11, the United States sent a formal note expressing "concern." The next day, Castro forced six moderate cabinet ministers to resign. On July 17, President Manuel Urrutia, who had been giving outspoken speeches against Communism, was pressured to step down; he fled to asylum in a Latin embassy.

Castro was still maintaining his revolution wasn't Communist, saying it was green as the Cuban palms, not red, but an increasing number of party members were being brought into the government by his brother Raúl and by Ché Guevara. In October, Comandante Húber Matos resigned his military position because he feared Communists had infiltrated the Movement. Nineteen of his officers quit too. All were arrested and charged with conspiring against the government. One of these was Captain Napoleón Bequer, the father of the ill boy who had been assured a few months before that he would never have to worry again. Bequer eventually escaped by scaling the wall at La Cabaña prison.

As many middle-class Cubans began to panic, old-time labor leaders were expelled from their unions, and the land of a few U.S. corporations was seized. In February 1960, Foreign Minister Anastas Mikoyan of the Soviet Union visited Havana and arranged a trade agreement. In late March, almost all radio and television stations came under government control. In April, a law required all employees looking for work to go through the ministry of labor. In May, the last of the major daily newspapers was taken over. The Church also was attacked.

As rumors spread that the United States was organizing an invasion of anti-Castro exiles, the Havana Hilton and Hotel Nacional were seized.

When Washington threatened to remove the subsidies for Cuban sugar, the U.S. oil refineries were nationalized. When Eisenhower banned almost all exports to Cuba on October 13, the Cubans responded by taking over 382 large businesses. All rental property was to be given to the state. Private schools were taken over.

With that, the revolution was completely Communist, and it was inexorably split. Many who had once supported Castro, especially the middle-class leaders in the Havana clandestine movement, were fleeing into exile. Enrique and Lizzy Barroso, the couple who fell in love in a broken-down Buick; Danilo Mesa, who had been beaten by Batista police; Havana propaganda chief Emilio Guede; Julio Duarte, who had collected hundreds of thousands of dollars for the Movement—all left the country in disgust and fear. To them, the revolution for which they had struggled so hard had been betrayed. Many joined the emerging anti-Castro forces in Florida or Central America.

Yet the split was not exactly along the economic-class lines. Some peasants and factory workers opposed the new regime; some middle- and even upper-class youths remained loyal to the revolution. Families split, brother opposed brother, and those who stayed behind felt betrayed too—betrayed by their countrymen who seemed to be committing the ultimate treason of appealing for help to the United States, Cuba's perennial master.

That help, of course, turned out to be less than overwhelming, and when the Bay of Pigs invasion failed in April 1961, the status and stability of the revolution were assured. It is worth noting that most of the State Department personnel and several of the Cubans involved were the same ones who took part in the "third force" plan of December 1958. Both Justo Carrillo, who had the plan to bribe the warden at the Isle of Pines, and Tony Varona, who schemed to block Castro's way through Camagüey Province, were at various times among the political leaders of the invasion brigade. Washington's hesitant policies, the Cubans' persistence in waiting for Washington and their own inept blunders—all of it was repeated in the disaster of the Bay of Pigs.

When the invasion failed, U.S. conservatives, led by former ambassadors Earl E. T. Smith and William Pawley, began looking for scapegoats in Washington. William Wieland, the director of Caribbean and Mexican affairs, and John Topping, the Havana embassy's chief political officer, were subjected to extensive loyalty examinations. Wieland's investigation dragged on for years and filled volumes of U.S.

Senate subcommittee testimony in a style reminiscent of the McCarthy hearings of a decade before. Eventually, both men were cleared, but they had difficulties getting promoted for the rest of their careers.

The more pervasive drama, of course, was what happened to the Cubans. Between five thousand and fifteen thousand were executed, most of them during the early years of the Communist regime. Shortly after the Bay of Pigs, as many as a hundred thousand may have been detained, but a more typical number of political prisoners (according to Castro himself) was fifteen thousand—approximately three times as many as were imprisoned under the Batista regime. About one thousand are still in jail.

Many opponents chose exile rather than resistance, and an estimated 750,000 left the country. Unlike some of the early Batista supporters, many had to flee with little or no money. For years, they struggled in new lands, but as a group they have proved to be enormously successful economically. By the mid-1970s, the Cubans in Miami had a larger per-family income than did their non-Latin neighbors.

Batista himself, however, never made it to the United States; he was always refused the U.S. visa he cherished. On August 6, 1973, still an exceedingly wealthy man, he died of a heart attack at a villa in southern Spain.

Here is what happened to some of the others who lived through the Cuban drama:

Abascal, Gerardo—Rum company president, rebel supporter in Santiago de Cuba. Now rum company president, Miami.

Abón-Ly, Alfredo—Army captain who held back rebels for eleven days at Yaguajay. Six years in prison. Now garment-factory worker, Union City, New Jersey.

Acevedo, Rogelio—Seventeen-year-old rebel captain. Now general of division, vice minister of defense, member of Central Committee of the Communist Party.

Aguilar, Luis—Havana journalist. Now professor, Georgetown University, Washington, D.C.

Almeida, Juan—Rebel *comandante*. Now member of elite Politburo.

Amador, Rolando—Havana lawyer who married in December. Now school principal and lawyer, Miami.

Ameijeiras, Efigenio—Rebel *comandante*, hero at Bay of Pigs, later demoted for "sectarianism." Now construction-site supervisor, Havana.

Armada, Humberto—Pilot for Urrutia's plane. Now liquor store manager, Miami.

Barquín, Ramón—Imprisoned army colonel. Was asked to leave Cuba in spring, 1959. Now owner of American Military Academy, Puerto Rico.

Barroso, Enrique and Lizzy—Underground couple who fell in love. Married 1959. Now a television producer, housewife, Puerto Rico.

Batista, Rubén—President's eldest son. Investor, Miami.

Bequer, Napoleón—Rebel captain with seriously ill son. Imprisoned October 1959 after denouncing Communism. Escaped. Now owns hospital-supply company, Tampa, Florida. Son is a doctor in Philadelphia.

Bethel, Paul—U.S. press attaché. Later, publisher in Miami. Died May 1979.

Blanco, Reinaldo—Army captain, Guisa. Now real-estate salesman, Miami.

Borbonnet, Enrique—Imprisoned army major. Now vice minister of education.

Braddock, Daniel—U.S. deputy chief of mission. Now retired, Maryland.

Cabrerra, Estrella—Housewife, Palma Soriano. Still lives in Oriente Province.

Cantillo, Eulogio—Army general, nominal head of Cuba for fifteen hours after Batista left. Later served eight years, three months, nineteen days in prison. Then partner in a small paving company, Miami. Died 1978.

Carratalá, Conrado—Police colonel who arrested Danilo Mesa. Now pizza-parlor cook, Puerto Rico.

Carrillo, Justo—Chief of Montecristi Movement. For a time was a political leader of Bay of Pigs invasion forces. Now retired, Miami.

Castañeda, Carlos—*Bohemia* magazine reporter. Now editor-publisher, Puerto Rico.

Castro, Fidel—Rebel leader. Now president of the Council of State, chairman of the Central Committee, commander in chief of the armed forces.

Castro, Raúl—Rebel *comandante*. Now vice minister of the council of state, member of Politburo, minister of defense, commander of the armed forces.

Chibás, Raúl—Rebel *comandante*. Now high-school Spanish teacher, Great Neck, New York.

Chomón, Faure—A leader of student Directorio. Now a provincial official of the Communist party.

Cienfuegos, Camilo—First rebel *comandante* to enter Camp Columbia. Disappeared in light plane, October 1959.

Collado, Roberto—Army major, aide to General Cantillo. Released from jail, May 1959. Bay of Pigs invasion force, imprisoned and released. Owner of a jeans boutique, Hialeah, Florida.

Cubela, Rolando—A leader of student Directorio. Later conspired with CIA to kill Castro. Sentenced to thirty years in prison, 1966. Released 1979.

Del Aguilar, Ismael—Aide of Masferrer. Now security chief, jai-alai fronton, Miami.

De Los Santos, Asela—Rebel education coordinator. Now vice minister of education, married to José Ramón Fernández.

Del Río Chaviano, Alberto—Army general. Died 1978, Miami.

Díaz Tamayo, Martín—Army general linked to Borrachos conspiracy. Now Buick salesman, Miami.

Domenech, Guillermo—Hotel clerk, Santa Clara. Now owns a print shop, Miami.

Dorticós, Osvaldo—Head of Cuban Bar Association, arrested briefly in December 1958. Now member of Politburo.

Duarte, Julio—Movement money collector, secretary of Cuban Bar. Now professor of Spanish literature, Georgia State University, Atlanta.

Echemendía, Comandante—See Suárez de la Paz, Ismael.

Elmore, Daymond—Assistant manager, Ermita sugar mill. Now retired, Miami.

Elverson, Edith—Secretary to U.S. ambassador. Still works for Smith, New York.

Espín, Vilma—Rebel coordinator, Second Front. Now married to Raúl Castro, mother of four, president of Cuban Federation of Women.

Fajardo, Manuel—Rebel captain. Hero at Bay of Pigs. Now administrator of a state cattle farm, Pinar del Río Province.

Femminella, Bernard—U.S. vice-consul, Santiago. Still in foreign service, Washington.

Fernández, José Ramón ("Gallego")—Imprisoned army lieutenant, arrested General Cantillo. Hero at Bay of Pigs. Now vice minister of state, married to Asela de los Santos, vice minister of education.

Fernández, Rafael ("Felo")—Montecristi Movement courier who was unable to bribe warden. Died 1973, in exile.

Fernández Leon, Julio—Havana underground. Now a bookstore manager, Union City, New Jersey.

Fernández Mell, Oscar—Rebel captain with Ché Guevara. Now president, provincial Popular Power Assembly of Havana.

Ferreiro, Edelberto ("Lily")—Pro-rebel supermarket owner, Santiago. Now fiberglass repairman, Walt Disney World, Florida.

Fleites, Armando—Segundo Frente del Escambray man in Miami trying to get weapons. Now doctor, medical clinic, Miami.

Galíndez, Ignacio—Retired army general, helped brother-in-law Danilo Mesa get out of jail. Now real-estate salesman, Puerto Rico.

Galíndez, Nelia—Sister of Danilo Mesa. Lives with her brother in Gainesville, Florida.

Gálvez, William—Rebel captain, Column 2. Now a colonel in the Cuban army.

García Baez, Irenaldo—Lieutenant Colonel, chief of Batista's feared SIM. Now a school principal, Florida.

García Montes, Jorge—Senator, former Batista prime minister, three months in asylum before allowed to leave. Now retired, Miami.

González Puente, José—Batista senator, first exile to arrive in Miami. Now retired.

Granado Díaz, Manuel—Directorio youth who went to University of Havana campus on January 1. Now major, U.S. Army.

Guede, Emilio—Propaganda chief of the Civic Resistance, Havana. Now owns a film company, Puerto Rico.

Güell, Gonzalo—Batista's last prime minister and foreign minister. Retired, lives in a modest duplex, Miami.

Guevara, Ernesto ("Ché")—*Comandante*, Column 8. Later treasury minister, guerrilla fighter in Africa. Killed by CIA-trained forces, 1967, Bolivia.

Gutiérrez Menoyo, Eloy—Chief, Segundo Frente del Escambray. Captured as an anti-Communist guerrilla chief, 1965. Sentenced to sixty years in prison.

Guzmán, Father Francisco—Jesuit priest who was courier between Castro and Cantillo. Now runs a religious commune for peasants, Dominican Republic.

Hart, Armando—Leader of 26th of July prisoners, Isle of Pines. Now minister of culture, member of Politburo.

Hernández, Eduardo ("Guayo")—Pro-26th of July photographer. Died Miami, 1978.

Lemus, Miguel—Santiago Lions Club member who assisted rebels. Now fiberglass worker, Orlando, Florida.

Lesnik, Max—Havana underground man, Segundo Frente del Escambray. Now publisher of *Replica* magazine, Miami.

Lima, Dr. Tony—Miami treasurer for student Directorio. Now a psychiatrist, Maryland.

Llorente, Father Amando—Jesuit priest who discovered students' bodies. Now director of Catholic University Association, Miami.

López-Fresquet, Rufo—Member of Civic Resistance, Havana, friend of political officer Topping, first treasurer for the revolutionary regime. Now college professor, California.

Lussón, Antonio Enrique—Rebel *comandante*, Second Front. Now minister of transportation.

Machado, Denio—Santa Clara 26th of July worker. Now supermarket co-owner, Union City, New Jersey.

Machado Ventura, José Ramón—Rebel director of health, Second Front. Now member of Politburo.

Martínez Suárez, José—Army colonel, located "President" Piedra on January 1. Bay of Pigs invasion force, captured and released. Retired, Miami.

Masferrer, Rolando—Senator with private army. Arrested several times in United States for mercenary activities. Assassinated by car bomb, October 31, 1975, Miami.

Matos, Húber—Rebel *comandante*, Column 9. Arrested October 1959 after denouncing Communism. Sentenced to twenty years. Released 1979. Exile.

Mesa, Danilo—Havana 26th of July clandestine worker, beaten by Batista police. Now bookstore employee, Gainesville, Florida. Wife Rosa is chief of Latin-American Department of University of Florida library.

Miró Cardona, José—First prime minister of revolutionary government. Later in civilian junta, Bay of Pigs invasion forces. Law professor, University of Puerto Rico. Died 1975.

Montejo, Cachita—Rebel supporter, Guisa. Now a housewife in Guisa.

Monte de Oca, Claudia—Housewife, Santiago. Now party member, Santiago.

Morales del Castillo, Andrés Domingo—Batista's presidential secretary. Exile in Miami. Died 1979.

Morgan, William—U.S. captain of Segundo Frente del Escambray. Later arrested for conspiring against Castro regime. Executed March 1961.

Murphy, Robert—U.S. deputy undersecretary of state. Died 1978.

Noel, James—CIA station chief, Havana. Retired.

Paneque, Victor—As Comandante Diego, he was action and sabotage chief, 26th of July, Havana. Now in exile in United States.

Pawley, William D.—CIA emissary to Batista. Committed suicide, 1977, Miami.

Pérez Alamo, Dunney—Rebel officer stationed near Santiago country club. Arrested for conspiracy October 1959, found not guilty. Fled by boat July 1961. Now a mechanic, Miami.

Piad, Carlos—Anti-Batista lobbyist in Washington supporting "third front." Active with invasion group's political wing for Bay of Pigs. Now retired, Washington.

Piñeiro, Manuel—Second Front rebel captain. Later became chief of G-2, tracing counterrevolutionary groups. Now heads Americas Section of Central Committee.

Prio, Carlos—The president whom Batista overthrew. Committed suicide, April 5, 1977, Miami.

Quevedo, José—Army captain who joined rebels during summer offensive. Now Cuban military attaché to the Soviet Union.

Ray, Manuel—Chief of Civic Resistance, Havana. Now a construction-company owner, Puerto Rico.

Redondo, Roger—Rebel, Segundo Frente del Escambray. Now a bodyguard, Miami.

Rego Rubido, José—Army colonel who handed Santiago de Cuba to the rebels on January 1. After ten days as "chief of the army," he was named military attaché to Brazil. Exile 1960. Died 1978, Puerto Rico.

Rivera, Victoriano—Peasant, still lives in same house near Escandel, Oriente Province.

Rivero Agüero, Andrés—Batista's president-elect. Retired in a modest stucco home, Miami.

Rivero, Rosa—Daughter of the president-elect. Now a mother of two, lives with her parents, Miami. Since her last night in Cuba, she has never heard from her boyfriend, Emilio, again.

Rodríguez, Carlos Rafael—Leader of Communist PSP who went to the mountains in late 1958. Now member of the Politburo, vice minister of state.

Rosales, Elias—Santiago clandestine worker for 26th of July. Now party member, Santiago.

Rosell, Florentino—Army colonel who commanded armored train, negotiated with rebels. Now owner of construction companies in Miami and the Dominican Republic.

Rubirosa, Porfirio—Dominican Republic ambassador to Cuba. Died in sports-car accident, 1965.

Rubottom, Richard—Assistant secretary of state for Latin American Affairs. Now political science professor, Southern Methodist University.

Sadulé, Alfredo—Police captain, Batista aide. Now operates a public-relations firm, Puerto Rico.

Salmerón Hernández, Leonardo—Medical assistant for rebels, Santa Clara. Still a medical assistant in the same city.

Sánchez, Celia—Castro's secretary. Now secretary of the Council of State, member of the Central Committee.

Sanjenís, Sergio—Clandestine 26th of July person in Havana. Now Cadillac salesman, Miami.

Santamaría, Haydee—Chief of 26th of July group in Miami. Now head of Casa de las Americas, the state-operated publishing company.

Scott, Ted—New Zealand journalist in Havana with NBC radio news. Now retired, Cocoa Beach, Florida.

Silva, Luis—Pilot of rebel aircraft. During Bay of Pigs, he was shot down and killed by the invasion forces.

Smith, Earl E. T.—U.S. ambassador. Later mayor of Palm Beach, Florida. Now retired, Palm Beach.

Stewart, Jack—CIA man in contact with opposition group, Havana. Now retired.

Suárez, Andrés—Member of Montecristi Movement, Havana. Now professor, University of Florida.

Suárez de la Paz, Ismael—As Comandante Echemendía, he negotiated with army concerning armored train. Later became personal assistant to Celia Sánchez, Castro's secretary. Defected 1971, debriefed by CIA in Florida safehouse for forty days. Now owns an interior-decorating boutique, Puerto Rico.

Tabernilla, Carlos ("Winsy")—Colonel, chief of Batista air force. Now a cropduster, West Palm Beach, Florida.

Tabernilla, Francisco ("Pancho")—General chief of Batista's armed forces. Died Palm Beach, Florida, 1972.

Tabernilla, Francisco ("Silito")—Brigadier general, Batista's military liaison. Now office manager of a construction company and owner of a plush house, Palm Beach, Flordia.

Tannenbaum, Paul—New York lawyer who was tourist on January 1. Still has law practice in Great Neck, Long Island.

Tasi Martínez, Luis—Rebel at Guisa. Now worker in Cuban forestry department, Guisa.

Topping, John—U.S. chief political officer, Havana embassy. Now retired, Washington.

Trillo, Raúl—Rebel captain, doctor with Castro's Column 1 at Guisa. Now surgeon, New York City.

Urrutia, Manuel—President-designate of anti-Batista groups. Resigned 1959, asylum for two years in Havana embassies. Later Spanish teacher at Queens College. Now retired, Queens, New York.

Varandela, Raúl—Rebel with Column 9, Santiago siege. Arrested October, 1959. Escaped from La Cabaña fortress. Now door-to-door cosmetics salesman, Puerto Rico.

Varas, Cosme—Army major, Batista aide. Now a sales representative for oil company, Miami.

Varela, Manuel—Imprisoned army colonel who took over La Cabaña, January 1. Now manager, Las Americas social club, Miami.

Varona, Tony—Former prime minister who was conspiring to form a "third force" in Camagüey Province. Later became political leader of Bay of Pigs invasion forces. Former owner of print shop, Quens, New York. Now retired, Miami.

Wieland, William—U.S. director of Caribbean and Mexican affairs. Now retired, Maryland.

Wollam, Park and Connie—U.S. consul at Santiago. Now retired on the Florida Gulf Coast.

APPENDIX

There remains one unanswerable puzzle about the Cuban revolution: the contents of Fidel Castro's mind during those last weeks of 1958. Was he indeed a Communist then? Or did his conversion take place later?

The problem, of course, is that only Castro himself can provide an accurate answer, and like most politicians, he has made varying, sometimes conflicting statements over the years. For the first year or two after his triumph, he continued to separate himself from the Communists. Then, on December 2, 1961, seven months after the Bay of Pigs, he made a dramatic, late-night speech in Havana: "Do I believe absolutely in Marxism? I believe absolutely in Marxism! Did I believe on the first of January [1959]? I believed on the first of January! Did I believe it on the 26th of July [1953]? I believed on the 26th of July! Did I understand it as I understand it today, after almost ten years of struggle? No, I did not understand it as I understand it today. . . . Could I call myself a full-fledged revolutionary on the first of January? I could not call myself almost a full-fledged revolutionary."

When Castro said this, his relations with the United States and most other Western Hemisphere countries had been irrevocably broken. He was, in effect, confirming publicly that Cuba's future lay in an alliance with the Soviet Union. Some historians argue that, at such a moment, he could have done nothing but state that he had been a Marxist all along, that he had to show longstanding Communist credentials to justify his continued leadership of the Cuban revolution at a time when the old-line PSP Marxists were starting to come to the fore.

Some, especially those who were close Castro supporters in 1958 but who later fled the country, continue to believe that Castro was not a Marxist before the triumph of the revolution. President-designate Urrutia, Comandante Raúl Chibás and Manuel Ray, among others, maintain that they saw no indications of Communism at rebel headquarters or in Castro's private discussions with them. Carlos Rafael Rodríguez, the PSP leader, was living at the main camp in late 1958, but Castro paid as little attention to him as he did to the other politicians. To moderates such as Urrutia, Rodríguez's presence seemed to indicate what Castro had been saying all along: he favored a united effort against Batista, and he was willing to accept support from anyone, from any political group.

Ray, the Havana leader of the Civic Resistance who later became one of the main chiefs of the anti-Communist struggle, feared that Castro's own political ideas were so formless that he might have shifted as easily to the right as to the left. Certainly, there was plenty of precedent for such erratic political changes in Cuba, where idealistic students had become corrupt administrators, where a onetime Communist, Rolando Masferrer, could change into a right-wing gangster with his own private army. In fact, Masferrer had more Communism in his background than did Castro, and the two had once fought on the same side, during the planned invasion of the Dominican Republic in the late 1940s. Ray and others thought Castro's totalitarian tendencies would have to be watched closely after the revolution triumphed, but they assumed that since the rebel army was so small, the urban moderates would have no problem in controlling the new government.

In the sixties, Ray became one of the main proponents of the "betrayed revolution" theory, that Castro had promised one revolution and delivered another, but what he and others overlooked was the *style* of the revolution, which was radical indeed. In almost every way, Castro in 1958 was rejecting the styles of the past, the wheeling and dealing of *políticos*, the compromises made with opponents, the recognition of Camp Columbia's pre-eminence. Instead, he was emphasizing the raw power of the gun, the guerrilla force of the mountains far removed from the *políticos'* smoky rooms, an attitude that considered the Oriente peasants as important as the Havana middle class. And in his speeches, though there was nary a trace of Marxism, he continually hammered on the point that his revolution was going to be radical, that it would sweep away the sad vestiges of past politics, that it would herald in a new (though unspecified) era of idealism.

In the interview for this book, Castro said that when he entered Havana on January 8, 1959, he did not know how far this idealism was going to take him, that he had no specific program in mind at that moment. Even those who later felt "betrayed" agree with him on that: the revolution was so shapeless at that moment, so chaotic, that for the first few weeks, the government was run on the cash that secretary Celia Sánchez carried around in a metal box. Whenever Castro decided a project was worthwhile, Celia dipped into the box. With such disorganization, with such a small band of rebels to run a country of 6.5 million, the "scientific framework" of Marxism could have offered an attractive means of governing the country.

That consideration was perhaps less important than the threat of American intervention. As Oscar Fernández Mell, now a Central Committee member puts it: "We did not realize then [1958] that you couldn't go only part way." Cuba had always been threatened by America's "big stick," and if Castro began turning the great American landholdings over to the peasants, the danger of Washington's anger was even greater. Certainly, the revolution had a desire to achieve true independence from the United States—a desire that intensified over the decades every time it was thwarted—and to do so, the Cubans decided, they had to align themselves with a power large enough to stand up to the United States, a power such as the Soviet Union.

One other factor: Cubans had rarely known moderating influences in their political history. One can listen to Vilma Espín, Fernández Mell and José Ramón Machado Ventura—liberal progressives in 1958, Communist leaders today—and hear no great distinction between their attitudes then and now: they were opposed to poverty, racial prejudice, economic injustice; they are still opposed to them, and they are mystified by the attitude of the American liberal, who announces his concern about the disadvantaged while insisting that civil liberties be maintained. Revolutionary leaders say freedom from hunger is more important than, say, the freedom of the ballot box, but the differences to them seem slight. Consider Fernández Mell's statement, about the outrage he felt toward the CIA-backed Anti-Communist Repression Bureau because "there was no Communist danger whatsoever." Fernández Mell, then a progressive, now a member of the Central Committee of the Communist Party, does not see the bizarre irony in his own statement because, in his own mind, he himself has not changed.

Castro, as leader of the revolution, does not indulge in such complexities. For years, following his dramatic 1961 speech about Marxism, he has maintained the same basic interpretation with only minor variations, but the interview for this book, on the eve of his twentieth anniversary in power and with his leadership of Cuba virtually unthreatened, he modified his opinion considerably, saying that in 1958, he had only "an essence of Marxist mentality."

Some of his foreign sympathizers have claimed he concealed his most radical thoughts because he feared American intervention, but Castro himself has a different explanation: The Cuban people themselves were so imbued with anti-Communist prejudices that they would have refused to accept his proposals.

"When I finished at the university, I had an essence of Marxist mentality. But this was in a country where Marxist-Leninist ideas were still in a minority. We were heavily influenced by the anti-Communist campaign. . . .

"We were not proposing a socialist program [in 1958]. We were carrying out the program we had proposed at the Moncada, when the proposal of *History Will Absolve Me* was our plan. Not because I was not more advanced in my thinking, because I had much more advanced ideas. Had had them since I was a student.

"But our people could not understand a larger plan. . . . It was a matter of evolution, of the evolution of a revolutionary idea. We supported at that time a program that was within the reach of the people, that was within the reach of the political culture of the people. . . .

"A revolution goes as far as it can get, but in certain moments, it establishes certain objectives. . . . My own ideas were more advanced, but I certainly could not be preaching them publicly to everybody . . . because that would not have had a practical result."

NOTES ON SOURCES

In the past twenty years, scores of books have been written about Cuba. The most exhaustive work in English is Hugh Thomas's *Cuba: The Pursuit of Freedom*. Its 1696 pages, covering from 1762 to the early 1970s, has no rival, and remains an indispensable starting point. Another excellent study, covering the Batista years, 1952 to 1959, is Bonachea-San Martin's *Cuban Insurrection*.

Ambassador Smith's book, *The Fourth Floor*, is an important first-person account of the American side, but it leaves out certain information that doesn't support his point of view. Batista's own *Cuba Betrayed* has some interesting footnotes, especially on military conspiracies, but it is so completely self-serving as to be practically useless. Even some of Batista's former associates now admit that the book is filled with lies.

Among the Spanish-language sources, the most important are the recounts of the rebel battles that have been appearing in the Cuban revolutionary army magazine, *Verde Olivo*, over the past fifteen years. These articles, along with the Castro regime's publication of two war books, *Días de combate* and *Diciembre del '58*, form a nearly complete history of the battles. They are remarkably accurate, with one exception: some names are omitted, especially those who fought on the rebel side and later decided to oppose the revolution.

Because of censorship, Cuban publications of the time had little information on the war, but *Diario de la Marina,* a prestigious, conservative Havana daily has plenty of details describing the flavor of pre-Communist Cuba. After Batista left, the first three issues of the national magazine *Bohemia,* called the Editions of Liberty, form a fascinating word-and-photo portrayal of the Batista regime and the rebel triumph.

What follows is a list of the most important print sources for our research, and then a chapter-by-chapter explanation of our sources. The "Senate Testimony" mentioned several times refers to the hearings called "Communist Threat to the United States Through the Caribbean," held by the Senate Internal Security Subcommittee.

SELECTED BIBLIOGRAPHY

Alvarez Díaz, José R., ed. *A Study on Cuba*. Prepared by the Cuban Economic Research Project. Miami: University of Miami Press, 1965.

Barquín, Ramón M. *Las luchas guerrillas en Cuba*. Tomo 2. Madrid: Playor, S.A., 1975.

Batista, Fulgencio. *Cuba Betrayed*. New York: Vantage Press, 1962.

Bethel, Paul. *The Losers*. New Rochelle, New York: Arlington House, 1969.

Bonachea, Ramón L., and San Martin, Marta. *The Cuban Insurrection, 1952–1959*. New Brunswick, N.J.: Transaction Books, 1974.

Bonachea, Rolando E., and Nelson P. Valdés, eds. *Revolutionary Struggle, 1947–1958. Vol. 1 of the Selected Works of Fidel Castro*. Cambridge, Mass.: MIT Press, 1972.

Castro, Fidel. *History Will Absolve Me*. Havana: Guairas Book Institute, 1967.

Communist Threat to the United States Through the Caribbean, Senate Internal Security Subcommittee. Washington: U.S. Government Printing Office, 1959–1971. 25 Parts.

Cuba: Ideal Vacation Land, Tourist Guide, 1954–55. Havana: Instituto Cubano del Turismo, 1954.

Días de combate. Havana: Instituto del Libro, 1970.

Diciembre del '58. Havana: Editorial de Ciencias Sociales, 1977.

Dubois, Jules. *Fidel Castro: Rebel—Liberator or Dictator?* Indianapolis, Ind.: New Bobbs-Merrill Co., 1959.

Eisenhower, Dwight D. *Waging Peace, 1956–61.* Garden City, N.Y.: Doubleday, 1965.

Franqui, Carlos. *Diario de la revolución cubana.* Paris: Ruedo iberico, 1976.

———. *The Twelve.* New York: Lyle Stuart, 1968.

Gálvez, William. *¡Vamos Bien!* Supplement to *Granma*, December 31, 1974.

Guevara, Ernesto Ché. *Reminiscences of the Cuban Revolutionary War.* New York: Monthly Review Press, 1968.

Kirkpatrick, Lyman B., Jr. *The Real CIA.* New York: Macmillan, 1968.

Lazo, Mario. *Updated—American Policy Failures in Cuba, Dagger in the Heart!* New York: Twin Circle Publishing, 1968.

Lisagor, Peter, and Higgins, Marguerite. *Overtime in Heaven.* New York: Doubleday, 1964.

Lockwood, Lee. *Castro's Cuba, Cuba's Fidel.* New York: Vintage Books, 1969.

López-Fresquet, Rufo. *My 14 Months with Castro.* Cleveland: World Publishing, 1966.

Macaulay, Neill. "The Cuban Rebel Army: A Numerical Survey." *Hispanic American Historical Review*, May 1978.

———. *A Rebel in Castro: An American's Memoir.* Chicago: Quadrangle Press, 1970.

Mankiewicz, Frank, and Jones, Kirby. *With Fidel: A Portrait of Castro and Cuba.* Chicago: Playboy Press, 1975.

Martínez Victores, Ricardo. *7RR: La Historia de Radio Rebelde.* Havana: Editorial de Ciencias Sociales, 1978.

Matthews, Herbert L. *The Cuban Story.* New York: George Braziller, 1961.

———. *Fidel Castro.* New York: Simon and Schuster, 1969.

———. *Revolution in Cuba.* New York: Scribner's, 1975.

Núñez Jiménez, Antonio, ed. *Atlas Nacional de Cuba.* Havana, 1970.

———. *El Segundo Frente Oriental "Frank Pais."* Lima: Industrial grafica, 1974.

———. *Geografía de Cuba.* Havana: Editorial lex, 1959.

Osanka, Franklin Mark, ed. *Modern Guerrilla Warfare.* New York: Free Press of Glencoe, 1962.

Pardo Llada, José. *Memorias de la Sierra Maestra.* Havana: Editorial Tierra Nueva, 1960.

Pérez, Louis A., Jr. *Army Politics in Cuba, 1898–1958.* Pittsburgh: University of Pittsburgh Press, 1976.

Phillips, David Atlee, *The Night Watch.* New York: Atheneum, 1977.

Phillips, R. Hart, *Cuba, Island of Paradox.* New York: McDowell, Obolensky, n.d.

————. *The Cuban Dilemma.* New York: I. Obolensky, 1962.

Proenza, Eliades. *La Batalla de Guisa: Eslabón de Oro de la Victoria del Pueblo.* Guisa: November 20, 1977.

Rosell, Florentino, *La Verdad.* Miami: 1960.

Smith, Earl E. T. *The Fourth Floor.* New York: Random House, 1962.

Suárez, Andrés. *Cuba: Castroism and ·Communism, 1959–1966.* Cambridge, Mass.: MIT Press, 1967.

Suárez, Núñez, José. *El Gran Culpable.* Caracas: 1963.

Suchliki, Jaime. *Cuba: From Columbus to Castro.* New York: Charles Scribner's Sons, 1974.

Taber, Robert. *M-26: Biography of a Revolution.* New York: Lyle Stuart, 1961.

Urrutia Lleo, Manuel. *Fidel Castro & Company.* New York: Praeger, 1964.

The William Wieland Case. Testimony before the U.S. Senate Internal Security Subcommittee, U.S. Government Printing Office.

Articles of special importance in *Verde Olivo,* the magazine of the Cuban army:

Casañas, José. "Escenarios de Lucha," December 5, 1971.

"Los Días Que Precedieron Al Desembarco del Granma," December 4, 1966.

Drake, Victor. "La Toma del Escuadrón 31," January 5, 1969.

Fernández Mell, Oscar. "La Batalla de Santa Clara," January 28, 1968.

Isidrón, Aldo. "El Pelotón Suicida," June 19, 1966.

Pavón, Luis. "El Ataque de La Maya," December 8, 1963.

"La Revolución Llega a la Capital," January 2, 1972.

Reyes, Alfredo, "El Ejércitio de la Tiranía," November 13, 20, 27, 1966.

————. "La Toma de La Maya," #49, 1973.

Yasells, Eduardo. "La Fuerza Aérea Rebelde en el Segundo Frente Oriental "Frank País," April 4, 1966.

SOURCES

PROLOGUE—OLD HAVANA AT TWILIGHT

The main Havana mood comes from interviews with dozens of residents, plus *Diario de la Marina, El Mundo, Havana Post* and *Bohemia*. An interview with Ted Scott and *Diario de la Marina* form the basis for the prostitute scene, and Rolando Amador re-created his own activities. The estimate of the eight-thousand-man police force is from Colonel Ventura. The list of mobsters and casinos can be found in several places: the main source for ours is a January 2, 1959, story from the Associated Press. The *Zig Zag* anecdote comes from Cuban humorist George Childs. Specific information on times and frequencies of Radio Rebelde comes from 7RR. The underground scene is from interviews with Enrique and Lizzy Barroso, Sanjenís and Ray.

Other contributors to Havana mood: Macaulay book, *Miami Herald*, Jaime Suchliki interview (on university closing), *Havana Arrivals* (a tourist book), Castañeda interview, Phillips's *Cuba, Island of Paradox*, Dubois's book, Bethel's book.

CHAPTER 1—THE REBEL

The rebel scene in the clearing comes from interviews with Castro, Trillo and Tasi Martínez, with some details substantiated by Pardo

Llada's *Memorias de la Sierra Maestra*. *Cuban Insurrection* has a discussion of the rebels' *santería* beads. Castro background comes from Castro interview, Franqui's *Diario* and *The Twelve*, *History Will Absolve Me*, Llorente interview, Matthews's *Castro* and *The Cuban Story*, Bonachea's *Revolutionary Struggle*, Lockwood's book. Background on fifties is largely from Thomas and *Cuban Insurrection*. The number of army troops sent to the Sierra comes from General Pancho Tabernilla's letter of May, 1959, quoted in *El Gran Culpable*; others give a figure of ten thousand, twice as much, but they had no firsthand information. The Chibás death comes from Trillo, Raúl Chibás interviews. Mood of rebel camp comes from *7RR*, Taber, Bethel, *Días de combate*, Castro interview, *Diciembre del '58*, Chibás interview, Senate testimony and interviews with several dozen rebels. Wollam's Santiago weekly reports help fill in about Oriente conditions, as does a December 1 *Time* article. Also: Matthews and others discuss Celia Sánchez's background; Manuel Ray helped explain the failure of the general strike; the 85 percent figure on the weapons comes from Castro himself; Chapelle and other guerrilla experts have tended to agree, though exile and urban supporters have long insisted they provided a more significant percentage of the weapons.

CHAPTER 2—A BATTLE BEGINS

Besides interviews with Blanco, Castro, Tasi Martínez, and Dr. Trillo, the material is substantiated by many other sources, including: *Días de combate*, *Verde Olivo*, Franqui's *Diario*, Pardo Llada's book, *Batalla de Guisa*, Manuel Prado interview, Cachita Montejo interview, Juan Luis Céspedes interview, *Revolutionary Struggle*, *La Sierra y El Llano*, Taber. Castro once told Matthews that he felt hurt that this battle, of so much importance in Oriente, had never achieved the same prominence that Ché Guevara's campaigns had in Las Villas Province.

CHAPTER 3—THE AMBASSADOR

The party scene is re-created from interviews with Smith and García Montes, substantiated by *Life* and *Diario de la Marina*, which had the most complete account. Rosa Rivero tells her own story. The Washington conference is based on a lengthy November 22 memorandum, plus interviews with Smith, Rubottom, Leonhardy, Little and other State Department officials, with Piad giving confirming support of the third force idea. The Kirkpatrick book helps explain the Smith–CIA–Washington rift. Wollam in Santiago, among others, watched the voting places. *El Gran Culpable* has the most detailed report of the voting fraud.

CHAPTER 4—THE DICTATOR

Information of the military conspiracy comes from interviews with García Baez, Silito Tabernilla, Topping, along with several U.S. embassy reports and a confirming letter from Castro Rojas, one of the conspirators. The Batista background is substantiated by Thomas's book and interviews with son Rubén Batista, García Baez, García Montes, Santiago Rey, Cantillo, aide Cosme Varas, Rivero Agüero, Silito Tabernilla (who saw the handing over of the 100-peso note), Sadulé (who received the $2500 Christmas bonus). *El Gran Culpable*, written by Batista's former press secretary, has the best information on how corruption worked, with Silito giving details about his role at Camp Columbia, as well as Batista's Esso map. The stroke was confirmed by Cantillo, García Montes and Varas. Batista's odd eating habits are discussed by Rey, Rubén Batista, Rivero Agüero and Varas. Smith interview, substantiated by *Fourth Floor*, Senate testimony and Lazo's *Dagger in the Heart* contribute to the Thanksgiving scene at the Havana Yacht Club. Topping, Smith interviews form the text for their confrontation; Güell gives sidelights.

CHAPTER 5—THE GENERAL

Cantillo himself is the main source. Supplemental information comes from Collado, his longtime aide, with Martínez Suárez, Silito Tabernilla, Colonel Rego Rubido, Ramón Barquín, Father Guzmán, Wollam (with Ferreiro and others, who confirm that Cantillo tried to end Santiago violence). More information on the El Cristo skirmish is in *Verde Olivo*. Some military men (including Rego) claimed that Cantillo had been one of Batista's co-conspirators with prior knowledge of the 1952 coup, but Martínez Suárez and García Baez (who always disliked Cantillo) agree that Cantillo coyly avoided a decision for the first few hours on March 10, 1952.

CHAPTER 6—"WE CAUGHT A TIGER!"

All sources for this chapter are the same as those in Chapter 2, which described the beginning of the battle.

CHAPTER 7—A CITY OF TERROR AND TRANQUILIZERS

Most of the mood of Santiago comes from interviews with those who lived there: Lily Ferreiro, Park and Connie Wollam, Miguel Lemus, Rolando Masferrer, Claudia Roses Monte de Oca, Gerardo Abascal, Elias Rosales, Vice-Consul Femminella. *Time* and Wollam's dispatches help substantiate details. The information on Ocho Chicos Malos comes from interviews with Bequer, Pérez Alamo and Varandela (rebels with Column 9, which originated the broadcasts). Masferrer is the main source concerning his leaving of Santiago (confirmed by his aide, Ismael Del Aguilar); his information is supported by Cantillo, but the general (like many others) was reluctant to talk too much about the former gang leader.

CHAPTER 8—THE APPLAUSE OF LEPERS

This information is based almost entirely on the testimony of the participants: Varandela, Pérez Alamo, Napoleón and Vitalia Bequer. Because of what happened later, these rebels of Column 9 have been ignored by both Cuban Communist historians and American writers. Elmore tells his own story.

CHAPTER 9—A NEW PRESIDENT IN SUNGLASSES

Interviews: Manuel Urrutia and his wife Esperanza, along with pilot Humberto Armada. Also substantiated by Urrutia's book.

CHAPTER 10—MISSION A-001

Interviews with participants: Manuel Fajardo, Vilma Espín, Efigenio Ameijeiras, Asela de los Santos, Manuel Piñeiro, José Ramón Machado Ventura, Antonio Lussón. The most complete account of Raúl Castro's group is found in book, *El Segundo Frente Oriental "Frank País,"* published in Lima, Peru, but there are many other accounts in *Verde Olivo*, *Días de combate* and *Bohemia*. The best articles on the La Maya battle are in *Verde Olivo* and *Diciembre del '58*.

CHAPTER 11—REVOLUTIONARIES IN A BUICK

Based primarily on interviews with Enrique and Lizzy Barroso, with secondary information from Sergio Sanjenís.

CHAPTER 12—WHEN A DICTATOR SAYS "MAYBE . . ."

García Baez gives the main account, with supplemental information from U.S. dispatches. Silito Tabernilla says he too urged Batista to take steps on General Díaz Tamayo. The general has always steadfastly denied any participation in any conspiracy, but SIM, his fellow conspirators and the U.S. embassy believed otherwise. Rivero Agüero and his family tell their own stories. Tannenbaum (substantiated by *The New York Times*) is his own source.

CHAPTER 13—LIFE INSURANCE FOR THE UNDERGROUND

The tourist description comes from *Cuba: Ideal Vacation Land;* an interview with Fernández León provides the bulk of the prison information. Lengthy descriptions of the underground's contribution (or lack of it) can be found in Thomas and *Cuban Insurrection*. Duarte gives the estimate of 400; Ramón Bonachea suggests the figure of 2000. Interviews: Guede, Suárez de la Paz, Duarte (Emilio Caballero provides confirming information about the arrest of Dorticós). Danilo Mesa, wife Rosa and sister Nelia provide the bulk of their information. The story of Mesa's arrest is confirmed by interviews with Martínez Suárez, Rubén Batista, John Topping. The Gómez death is from *Bohemia*. Lesnik tells his own story (the broad outline of which is confirmed by State Department and CIA sources).

CHAPTER 14—AN EMBASSY DIVIDED

Interviews: Smith, Braddock, Topping, Bethel, Kail, Noel provide the bulk of the information, with substantiation of morning staff confrontation from Bethel's book. Lyman Kirkpatrick's *The Real CIA*, has some interesting insights on the CIA's relationship with Smith. Other sources: *confirming The Fourth Floor*, Senate testimony, Andrés Suárez interview, Gonzalo Güell interview, Edith Elverson interview, *Biographic Register* (1959, U.S. Department of State), *ABC Directory* (a fascinating telephone book of the foreign community in Havana, in possession of Ted Scott), and an anonymous CIA source. The economic statistics come from *The New York Times* (January 2, 1959), on the value of U.S. investment in Cuba, Taber book, López-Fresquet's book (on *barrios* and lack of upper classes paying taxes), with the bulk of the material coming from *A Study of Cuba*, prepared by a research team at the University of Miami in 1965; much of their material is found in the 1953 Cuban census, the annual Sugar Yearbooks and annual reports of the National Bank. Lists of new business development in late 1958 comes from dispatches of the commercial attaché at the U.S. embassy, including Emtels 667, 632, 591, 587, and many others. No. 626, a report on November, dated December 16, has an excellent summary of the economic problems the civil war had caused the country. The Smith dispatch on his meeting with the businessmen is numbered No. 572. Rubottom, State Department sources and Smith provide the bulk of the Washington scenes.

CHAPTER 15—A MESSAGE FOR BATISTA

The Havana mood is mainly from *Diario de la Marina*. Pawley's Senate testimony and Noel interview form the bulk of Pawley scenes, with Güell giving some crucial information about Pawley actually lying on his first meeting with the prime minister. Aide Cosme Varas and Brigadier General Silito Tabernilla offer reports on Batista's reaction. For the Braddock-Güell meeting, the information comes from the two participants, plus Dispatch 608, a lengthy report of the conversation. Cantillo and Guzmán interviews make up the general's scene.

CHAPTER 16—EXILES ON FLAGLER STREET

The Miami Herald and the *Miami News* help give the mood, along with interviews with Dr. Fleites, Justo Carrillo (with confirmation from CIA and State sources), Antonio de Varona, Dr. Tony Lima (Directorio treasurer), plus Guayo Hernández, Senate testimony, Captain Gabino Rodríguez Villaverde (an exiled Puro), Charlie Hormel (a pilot for the Directorio).

CHAPTER 17—CONSPIRACY OF "THE PURE ONES"

Interviews: Barquín, Varela, Borbonnet, Gallego Fernández, Montané, with confirmation from Colonel Rosell.

CHAPTER 18—LAS VILLAS: WAITING FOR DISASTER

Domenech interview (with details from *Verde Olivo*) forms the Gran Hotel segment. Gálvez (backed by his article in *Granma* and *Verde Olivo*) and Abón-Ly interviews create the scene in eastern Las Villas.

The Segundo Frente del Escambray material comes from interviews with Roger Redondo, Lazaro Asencio and Max Lesnik, all of whom were members of the group.

CHAPTER 19—CHÉ GUEVARA AND HIS TEENAGERS

Interviews with Fernández Mell and Acevedo give the intimate details of life with Guevara, along with Guevara's own *Reminiscences, Días de combate, Diciembre del '58* and *Verde Olivo.* Matthews's *Cuba in Revolution* has an extensive biography of Guevara. *Cuban Insurrection* contains important details about the Directorio's attitude toward the Pact of Pedrero.

CHAPTER 20—A MEETING AT KUQUINE

The main account comes from interviews with Smith and Güell, substantiated by *The Fourth Floor, Cuba Betrayed* and Senate testimony. Also: García Montes interview, *Diario de la Marina* (on the storm), *Havana Post.* The bridge incident is from the Barroso interview.

CHAPTER 21—FIDEL ORGANIZES

The main account is Castro's. Also Vilma Espín interview. Matos's quote is confirmed by Wollam Dispatch 71, based on a January speech by Matos to Santiago Rotary Club. A photo shows Matos meeting with Fidel. Others: Pérez Alamo (on El Viso), *Días de combate, Diciembre del '58,* Franqui's *Diario* (for the Radio Rebelde speech).

CHAPTER 22—THE REBELS PUSH ON

The Mayajigua incident is based on interviews with Abón-Ly and Gálvez, *Verde Olivo, Granma.* Fomento information comes from Acevedo interview, *Diciembre del '58, Días de combate,* 7RR, Fernández Mell interview. The Gutiérrez Menoyo material comes from Redondo interview confirmed by Bethel book. The Sagua incident is based on

Lussón interview, with confirmation from *Segundo Frente, Diciembre del '58, Días de combate.*

CHAPTER 23—A BATTALION GIVES UP

The basic information comes from General Cantillo and Colonel Rego Rubido. The telegram appears in *Diciembre del '58.*

CHAPTER 24—CONNIE'S VISITOR

Interviews with Park and Connie Wollam, plus a number of Santiago consul dispatches, plus confirming interview with Vice-Consul Femminella. The Miami plot is based on Varona, Piad interviews, with confirmation from State Department sources. The personal material is based on interviews with the participants: Lizzy and Enrique Barroso, Vitalia Bequer, Amador, Danilo and Rosa Mesa, and Rosa Rivero.

CHAPTER 25—"LIFE IS A RISK"

Interviews with Smith, Güell, Rivero Agüero, substantiated by *The Fourth Floor.* Description of the palace comes from personal observation and interview with Batista aide Cosme Varas. The Batista meeting with his generals is recounted by Silito Tabernilla, and confirmed by Batista's book.

CHAPTER 26—THE ARMY PANICS

The main account comes from the Cantillo interviews, parts of which are confirmed by Batista book, *Cuban Insurrection* and Silito Tabernilla. The train conspiracy is based on interviews with the two principals, Echemendía and Rosell, plus *La Verdad. La Verdad* was written in 1960 by Rosell, when Cantillo was in a Cuban jail and unable to reply. After Cantillo arrived in Miami in the late sixties, Rosell began admitting (as he did in our interview) that he had lied both to the rebels and in *La Verdad* about Cantillo's involvement. Also: Echemendía's telegram is in Franqui. Batista making out the passenger list is based on Silito interview, confirmed by *El Gran Culpable*. The late-night conspiracy meeting is based on interviews with three participants: García Baez, Silito and Rosell. The discussion is substantiated in both Batista's book and *La Verdad*. The Cantillo meeting with Father Guzmán is based on interviews with the two men. Castro explains his own scene; background material is from Echemendía; the text of Castro's telegram can be found in Castro's personal files and in Franqui's *Diario*.

CHAPTER 27—THE $450,000 BRIEFCASE

Rosita Ferrer tells about seeing the rebels; Duarte talks about collecting the money.

CHAPTER 28—WAGING SEMIPEACE

Interviews with State Department officials, plus the *Washington Post* and Eisenhower's *Waging Peace*. The text of this crucial summary of the "third force" idea comes from the State Department files.

CHAPTER 29—DECEMBER 24: CHRISTMAS EVE

Varona tells his segment, with confirmation from Piad and State sources in Washington. Tannenbaum's account is supplemented by later interview with *The New York Times*. Braddock interview, *Diario de la Marina*, *Havana Post*, *Bohemia* and State dispatches help form mood for the city. Guede tells the bizarre story of 03C, wih confirmation from appropriate *Diario* issues. The jingle is quoted in *7RR*. García Baez, with confirmation from Silito Tabernilla, recounts the planes incident. García Montes interview is basis for this scene. Masferrer interview. Fajardo tells his own story, Pavon's version is confirmed by Comandante Ameijeiras, Barrel's Maffo anecdote is backed by *Verde Olivo* material, part of Varandela's interview on the antenna siege is backed by *Diciembre del '58* (which, however, does not mention his name). Lussón, *Días de combate* and *Verde Olivo* stories recount the Sagua surrender. Acevedo and Fernández Mell interviews are confirmed by

Verde Olivo and Guevara's book. Gálvez and Abón-Ly interviews on Yaguajay are aided by articles in *Granma, Verdo Olivo, Dias de combate*. Echemendía of the rebels and Colonel Rosell of the army recount the story of the armored train scenes, plus *La Verdad*. Minor scenes come from interviews with hotel clerk Domenech and Barquín on remaining in prison (with supplements from interviews with prisoners Gallego Fernández, Varela, Borbonnet and Montané). The Batista uniform scene is told basically by Sadulé; confirmation from García Baez, Cosme Varas and Senator García Montes. Rivero tells about his own evening, as does Urrutia and Vilma Espín. Castro scene is based on interviews with him and Celia Sánchez, plus Dubois book.

CHAPTER 30—DECEMBER 25: TOY CARS AND CONSPIRACIES

Castro scene: Interviews with Castro, Celia Sánchez, Father Guzmán. Wollams's story told by Park and Connie, with Vice-Consul Femminella. Smith party comes from Smith interview, *Havana Post* and several dispatches on Güell trip. Armored train: Echemendía, Rosell interviews; *La Verdad*. Cantillo and Rosell interviews re-create their conversation, with supporting material from Cantillo aides Martínez Suárez and Collado. Rosell now denies a different version, which appeared in *La Verdad*.

CHAPTER 31—DECEMBER 26: TIME FOR THE GREEN LIGHT

Rosell's visit to Batista's home is recounted by himself, Silito Tabernilla, Rubén Batista. Abón-Ly tells about his own plight, supported by *Verde Olivo* material. Remedios: Acevedo interview, *Días de combate, Verde Olivo, Diciembre del '58*. Rosell flight: Interviews with Rosell, Echemendía, García Baez; the telegram is in Franqui's *Diario*; plus *La Verdad*. Ambassador's scene: Smith interview, confirmed by *The Fourth Floor*, from Silito Tabernilla and Batista's book. Miami CIA contact: Justo Carrillo interview is confirmed by several State and CIA sources. Pilot Crespo's defection was reported in *The Miami Herald*.

Piad, Varona and State sources confirm the Washington section. Batista scene: Silito interview, *El Gran Culpable*, plus Batista book.

CHAPTER 32—DECEMBER 27: "STAY TUNED TO THE NETWORK OF LIBERTY"

The mood of Havana comes from *Diario de la Marina* and the *Havana Post*. Cantillo scene is based on Cantillo and Martínez Suárez interviews. Underground CIA contact comes from Lesnik interview, backed by CIA and State sources. Echemendía and Acevedo interviews explain their meetings with Guevara. Castro scene: Interviews with Castro and housewife Estrella Cabrerra; Palma Soriano material is found in *Verde Olivo*, *Dias de combate* and *Diciembre del '58*. Interviews with Cantillo and Rego form their scene. Connie and Barbara Wollam, plus Bernie Femminella tell their story; the text from Radio Rebelde comes from 7RR. *Diario* reported the nightclub scene.

CHAPTER 33—DECEMBER 28: "A TERRIBLE TREASON"

Santa Clara: Acevedo interview, with details from *Verde Olivo*. Castro: Castro interview and Franqui's *Diario*. The main meeting scene: Interviews with Cantillo, Castro, Raúl Chibás, Vilma Espín, Celia Sánchez and Father Guzmán. *Bohemia*, *Revolución* and *Diario* all had accounts of Castro speeches in early January in which he recounted his version of the discussion. Almost all other versions are secondhand, and many (including Matthews) wrote erroneously that the meeting took place on December 24. The quotation from Castro—"If Batista can escape, so be it. But if we can prevent him from getting away, we should stop him"—is as Castro remembers it. Father Guzmán agrees with Castro's version. Cantillo recalls a slightly different statement, with a subtle shift in meaning: "I can't accept, or approve, of Batista leaving the country," he thinks Castro told him. "But I don't have the power to prevent it. If Batista leaves the country, it's a *fait accompli.*" The Moncada barracks scene comes from interviews with Cantillo, Colonel Martínez Suárez and Colonel Rego Rubido. Gran Hotel: Domenech interview, *Verde Olivo* adds details. Varona tells his own story; Carlos

Piad and State sources confirm the CIA agent was late. Carrillo tells about meeting with his new messenger. Cantillo-Batista conversation: Cantillo and Martínez Suárez interviews form the bulk. Batista's book gives a self-serving version which is obviously wrong. *Cuban Insurrection* confirms some details.

CHAPTER 34—DECEMBER 29: "IT'S A MONSTER!"

Generals' scene: Cantillo interview, confirmed by Silito Tabernilla. Yaguajay: Abón-Ly, Gálvez interviews; *Verde Olivo*, *Dias de combate*, *Diciembre del '58* and *Granma* all have lengthy articles about the Dragon, which is now accorded a place of honor alongside the Presidential Palace in Havana. The measurements of where the bazooka shell hit come from personal observation. Washington: Interview with State sources, *Washington Post*, and State document No. CA-5512. Smith in interview said he had never heard of third-force concept and would have opposed it if he had known about it. Varona interview supplies the Camagüey material. Cantillo material: Interviews with Cantillo and Collado, confirmed by Martínez Suárez, who was ordered to get rocks cleaned up. Asela de los Santos interview is basis for her segment. Colonel Rego and Major Collado each described their segment, and both Silito Tabernilla and Cantillo gave interviews about their encounter. Santa Clara: *Verde Olivo*, *Días de combate* and *Diciembre del '58* give the background, plus interviews with Salmerón, Acevedo, Fernández Mell and hotel clerk Domenech.

CHAPTER 35—DECEMBER 30: "A REGRETTABLE ERROR"

Havana mood comes from *Diario de la Marina*, *Havana Post*, *El Tiempo*, Masferrer interview, and *The Miami Herald*. Castro scene: Interviews with Castro and Guzmán, with *Verde Olivo*, *Días de combate*, *Diciembre del '58* and Barrel providing background on Maffo battle. Santiago scene: Wollam interview and Emtel 645. Yaguajay: Abón-Ly, Gálvez interviews and the usual battle written sources. The Felo Fernández anecdote is told by Carrillo and Andrés Suárez, another

Montecristi member. Varona tells his own story. Information for the Batista children scene comes from *The New York Times* plus *Life* magazine. Ché scene: Fernández Mell interview, *Verde Olivo*, plus Acevedo interview and hotel clerk Domenech. Santiago army confrontation comes from interviews with Cantillo and Rego. Cantillo's letter appears in the private collection of Castro; we copied it by hand during our interview, Cantillo confirmed. Until we told him, Castro maintained the impression that Rego had written the letter, though both Rego and Cantillo say Cantillo did it. Castro and Guzmán recount their scene. His letter appears a number of places, including Franqui's *Diario* and Bonachea-Valdés's *Revolutionary Struggle*.

CHAPTER 36—DAYTIME, DECEMBER 31: "TOMORROW IS SO NEAR"

Diario de la Marina, *The New York Times*, *Miami Herald* provide the mood. Vitalia Bequer tells her own story. Acevedo, plus *Verde Olivo*, etc., describe Santa Clara battle. Güell and Smith interviews, confirmed by *The Fourth Floor*, give the facts for their scene. Secretary Elverson confirms her role. Washington scene: Rubottom interview, *The New York Times*, plus the Senate transcription, which has been declassified. Also State Department sources and documents. Batista scene is based primarily on interview with aide Cosme Varas. Yaguajay: Abón-Ly, Gálvez interviews, plus *Granma* and many other written sources.

CHAPTER 37—TWILIGHT

Tannenbaum interview (plus *Times* account); Silito interview (details from Major Varas); Lesnik interview with CIA confirmations; Fleites interview; Acevedo interview; Cantillo interview (with details from aide Collado); plus interviews with Smith, Güell, Rosa Rivero, Rivero Agüero.

CHAPTER 38—THE NIGHT OF THE TWELVE GRAPES

Mood comes from *Diario de la Marina, Bohemia, Havana Post.* Interviews: Masferrer (and his aide Del Aguilar), Smith (confirmed by *The Fourth Floor*), Cantillo, Martínez Suárez, Varas, Silito Tabernilla, Morales del Castillo, Rosa Rivero, Mrs. Ana María Salazar, Paul Bethel (confirmed by his book), Julio Duarte, Barquín, Carrillo, Domenech (*Verde Olivo* confirms the story), Varona, Ferreiro, Park and Connie Wollam, Castro (details from Pardo Llada's account in *Bohemia*), Rego. Batista's book version of these hours—the last twelve hours before the flight—are such a distortion as to be almost worthless.

CHAPTER 39—MIDNIGHT: "NEW YEAR, NEW LIFE"

Interviews: Rivero Agüero and his wife, aide Major Varas, Morales del Castillo, García Montes all report on Batista's midnight scene. Also: Duarte, Rosa Rivero, Tannenbaum, Carrillo, Varona, Abón-Ly, Acevedo, Pérez Alamo, Vilma Espín, *Bohemia* account for Castro.

CHAPTER 40—JANUARY 1, 1959: "THE BURNING SPIKE"

Interviews: Cantillo, Martínez Suárez, Silito Tabernilla (he has a copy of the document changing commands), Major Varas, Morales del Castillo, García Montes, Rivero Agüero and his wife, García Baez, Major Collado, aide Captain Sadulé, Colonel Ventura (confirmed by *El Gran Culpable*), Rubén Batista. Batista's resignation can be found in Dubois and *Revolución*. Almost all written versions of Batista's departure are secondhand and unreliable. Rumors that Batista took a large amount of luggage with him are untrue.

CHAPTER 41—3:00 A.M.: "WELL, MR. PRESIDENT, WHAT DO WE DO NOW?"

Interviews: Cantillo, Smith, Martínez Suárez, Rego (who provided copies of the telegrams), *Bohemia*, Rosa and Isabel Rivero, Masferrer (with aide Del Aguilar and embassy dispatches about his flight) and Duarte.

CHAPTER 42—DAWN: "A CARGO OF LIVE CORPSES"

Interviews: Aide Varas, Rivero Agüero, Morales del Castillo, Silito Tabernilla, Rubén Batista, Smith (confirmed by *The Fourth Floor*), Topping, Bethel (confirmed by his book), Rosa and Isabel Rivero, Masferrer (and aide Del Aguilar), Tannenbaums (with *The New York Times* account) and Carrillo. Also: *Bohemia*, *The New York Times*, *Revolución*, *Cuban Insurrection*, *Time*, *Life*.

CHAPTER 43—8:00 A.M.: "DR. CASTRO: HAPPY NEW YEAR"

Interviews: Rego (with telegram in his possession), Castro (combined with Pardo Llada's account in *Bohemia*, which mentions the order to Matos), Juan Luis Céspedes, Vilma Espín, Pérez Alamo, Park and Connie Wollam.

CHAPTER 44—EARLY MORNING: "ENOUGH GAS IN THE TANK"

Interviews: Ed Little, Rubottom and other State Department sources, Varona, Barquín (plus prisoners Montané, Varela, Borbonnet, Fernández), Carrillo, William Alexander, Tannenbaums, Acevedo, Fernández Mell (with *Dias de combate*, *Verde Olivo*), Denio Machado, Abón-Ly, Varela, Vitalia Bequer.

CHAPTER 45—MORNING, JANUARY 1: "¡REVOLUCÍON SÍ!"

Interviews: Cantillo (supported by a lengthy account in *Bohemia* and interview with journalist Abel Mestre), Castro, Lussón, Verdejo Pupo (*7RR* has a detailed account of the speech at the makeshift radio station). The radio speeches have been reprinted in several places. Our version is based on Bonachea-Valdés's *Revolutionary Struggle* and the Dubois book. It was during the interview with Castro that an aide discovered that he must have departed from his scribbled text when he said, "*¡Revolución, sí! ¡Golpe militar, no!*" It was not in the text, though it became the best-remembered phrase of this crucial speech.

CHAPTER 46—THE NEW EXILES

Interviews: Rivero Agüero, Rafael Herrera (with the January 2 edition of *El Caribe*), aide Varas (*El Gran Culpable* adds details of Batista's arrival), Silito Tabernilla, Rubén Batista, García Baez in Jacksonville, Rosa and Isabel Rivero. *The New York Times, Miami Herald, Miami News* all provided news of the various arrivals. The mobsters' flight comes from the *Herald.*

CHAPTER 47—THE PALACE AND THE MOB

Interviews with Cantillo, aide Collado and Smith provide the main palace account, supplemented by photos and text in *Bohemia.* Justice Menéndez gave supporting material. *New York Times* correspondent Herbert Matthews, waiting outside on palace steps, thought Smith was inside conspiring to set up new pro–U.S. government; he repeated his accusations in a number of his writings. Both Cantillo and Smith have denied that; their versions, given independently, support each other almost exactly, as does an embassy telegram. Also: Manuel Granado Díaz, Fernández León, Lesnik, Guayo Hernández (who showed us the film of the Communist flag waving), Ruby Hart Phillips (plus her books), Cosme and Elena Varas, Tannenbaums (with *Times* account), Guede. Among the many written accounts of the mob action: *Bohemia, Diario de la Marina, The New York Times, Miami Herald, Miami News, Time, Life, Newsweek, Revolución.*

CHAPTER 48—"THE REPUBLIC IS HEADLESS"

Interviews: Varona, Lizzy and Enrique Barroso (with confirming material from Sergio Sanjenís), Acevedo, Domenech, Fernández Mell (with *Verde Olivo, Días de combate, Diciembre del '58* descriptions of Santa Clara surrender); Cantillo, Collado, Martínez Suárez with Arias Cruz (backed by *Bohemia* accounts among many others; a copy of the telegram to Isle of Pines was given to us by Rego Rubido). The astounding telegram that the "Republic is headless" was in the possession of Rego, and confirmed by Cantillo. It has rarely, if ever, been printed. Also: Tannenbaums.

CHAPTER 49—"CAN I TRUST YOU, COLONEL?"

Castro scene at Villalón is created from interviews with those there: Castro, Rego, Pérez Alamo, Bequer, Vilma Espín (and her account of the "sexist" incident was confirmed in Franqui's *The Twelve*). The telegram is from Rego's collection. Santiago scene is based on interviews with the Wollams, Monte de Oca, Ferreiro, Lemus and several Wollam dispatches.

CHAPTER 50—"IT WOULD HAVE CHANGED THE COURSE OF HISTORY"

Interviews: Varona, Gálvez (plus *Granma* account), Fernández Mell (and numerous written accounts of Santa Clara, especially *Verde Olivo*). Guevara had always been Cienfuegos's superior in Las Villas, but Castro apparently wanted a Cuban to take over the prestigious Columbia, and so Guevara's role was downplayed in the hour of triumph. Also: Amador, Gonzáles Puente, *Miami Herald* (on Orange Bowl game), Carrillo, Aguilar, Fernández León (many others tell similar "password" incidents), Ted Scott, Tannenbaums (with *Times* account), Topping, Smith (confirmed by *The Fourth Floor*, Senate testimony). The Barquín telex is from a Navy message, c-4-59, 011650Z. *Bohemia*, the Phillips's books, *New York Times*, Matthews's books all give accounts of the mood on Havana streets, and *Bohemia*'s photographs give an excellent flavor.

CHAPTER 51—"LIONS WITHOUT TEETH"

Isle of Pines' accounts include interviews with prisoners Barquín, Varela, Borbonnet, Fernández, Montané. Columbia scene includes prisoners' accounts, plus Cantillo, Martínez Suárez (telegram text is from Rego's collection), plus *Bohemia*. Arias Cruz saw Cantillo and Barquín greet each other with smiles. Andrés Suárez, Luis Botifoll and others give accounts of hectic mood in Barquín's first hours, as does Duarte. Unnumbered Navy message is identified by time: 020211Z.

CHAPTER 52—"THE REVOLUTION IS NOW BEGINNING"

Castro caravan scene is told by participants: Castro, Rego, Raúl Chibás, Urrutia, Vilma Espín, Victoriano Rivera, Bequer, Pérez Alamo, Machado Ventura, Gerardo Abascal (Santiago resident who mentions how Rotarians were hoping to spend more time talking to Castro). Wollam dispatch has a version of the Castro speech, as do many others, though the best account remains *Revolución*. A copy of the Masferrer letter is in the collection of Gordon Winslow. Suárez Núñez estimate is in *El Gran Culpable*. The Castro dinner scene comes from interviews with Lemus, Ferreiros, Femminellas, Connie Wollam, all of whom were there, plus Park Wollam and the dispatch.

CHAPTER 53—JANUARY 2: "ROBINSON CRUSOE" ENTERS HAVANA

Interviews: Barquín, Duarte (with *Bohemia*), Carrillo. Barquín claims that Cienfuegos told him, "I have signed orders in triplicate," from Castro and Urrutia, but it seems impossible for such orders to have been sent all the way from Santiago; Cienfuegos's aide, Gálvez, never heard of such signed orders, though he certainly had them verbally. Also: Topping, Noel, Gálvez (with *Granma*). The Thomas book, along with State officials, place a severe amount of blame on Barquín for his quick capitulation to Castro, but none of these sources knew of the "Republic is headless" telegram; certainly neither Columbia nor Moncada soldiers wanted to fight at that moment.

Other sources: Ameijeiras, Fajardo (plus *The Twelve, Dias de combate*), Acevedo, Domenech interviews. The El Zorro incident comes from the Lesnik interview, among others. Also interviews: Guede, Cantillo, Collado, Martínez Suárez, Fleites, Redondo. Tourist incidents told by dispatches and interviews with Braddock, Wayne Smith, Topping, Elverson, Ambassador Smith, Rubottom, other State officials, substantiated by *The Fourth Floor. The New York Times* had stock-market analysis, along with several stories on Havana mood. R. H. Phillips and her books have a good description of arrival, as does journalist Jay Mallin, *Miami News* and *Time*. Barquín and Borbonnet give the army's side. Acevedo, Fernández Mell and Denio Machado all describe the arrival of La Cabaña, as does Colonel Varela of the army. *Bohemia, Life* and many others have photos and text of rebels' arrival in city.

CHAPTER 54—SANDBAGS AT THE SPORTS PALACE

City mood comes from *Bohemia, Revolución, Diario de la Marina, The New York Times, Time,* and others. Interviews at Sports Palace: Ray, Echemendía, Sanjenís, Barrosos, Duarte, Ameijeiras. Also Urrutia interview (confirmed by his book). Dr. Tony Lima and *Cuban Insurrection* give accounts of the Directorio's dissatisfaction. Guede gives a hilarious account of the continuing self-promotion of Comandante Five

Stars, as does Echemendía. Urrutia, Ray, Duarte, Machado Ventura account the new president's arrival in Havana, backed by a lengthy *Bohemia* version. Smith does not recall seeing Urrutia, but Topping, *Bohemia* reporter and Urrutia all agree that he did. Castro and Celia Sánchez provided the information about appointing Hart, backed partially by Matthews's *Times* story from Camagüey. Mrs. Urrutia is descriptive about the first look at her new "home." Carrillo, Trillo, Chibás, Guede, Ray, Antonio Jorge talk about their new jobs. Urrutia tells the barber story on himself. Denio Machado, Fernández Mell, Martínez Suárez, Mesa, Smith (substantiated by *The Fourth Floor*), Raúl Chibás, Bob Clark, Jr., Cantillo (supported by Guzmán) tell about prisoners and military mood. Acevedo interview. The material on Communists inspecting the BRAC files (which was not publicized at the time) comes from interviews with Denio Machado and Fernández Mell, substantiated by Senate testimony, Emtel 771 (via CIA agent) and the Bethel book. Other Communist activity is recorded by embassy dispatches and *Hoy* (available in Library of Congress). The U.S. recognition material comes from a series of dispatches. In *The Fourth Floor*, Smith decries the rush to recognition, but he does not mention his own businessmen's committee was urging it. Wollam, Rubottom, other State officials give their versions. Ferreiros, Lemuses, and Wollams describe Santiago mood. Bequer, Rego and others describe Moncada. Elmore tells about his own situation, as does Connie Wollam. Barroso interview details finding body. Llorente episode is from his interview and a lengthy *Bohemia* article. Domenech, Guayo Hernández described the firing squads. *Life* and *Bohemia* photos of executions are graphic.

CHAPTER 55—THE DOVES OF PEACE

On the trail with the caravan is described by participants in interviews: Castro, Trillo, Lussón, Guzmán, Castañeda (confirmed by the Dubois book), Blanco. The observation of barefooted, diseased peasants comes from Castañeda's *Bohemia* account. Several persons (including Franqui) have claimed that Castro really named the cabinet, engineering a false moderation, but Castro and Castañeda (now in exile) deny that: he knew few of the new ministers. Matthews's book discusses rebel hostility toward new converts. *Diario* dutifully reported Castro's views on Catholicism.

The arrival in Havana was covered by all news publications. *Bohemia* and Dubois book have especially descriptive accounts. *Cuban Insurrection* discusses the Castro trip to Directorio gravesite. Also interviews: Castro, Lussón, Blanco, Barroso, Urrutia, Ruby Hart Phillips (especially good on the surprising parting of the crowd), Castro's speech at palace comes from *Bohemia* version. *Revolución* has the most complete version of Camp Columbia speech, followed by *Diario de la Marina.* Varona and Duarte were both at Columbia that evening.

INDEX